Fodor's

FAMILY ADVENTURES

4th Edition

More than 700 GREAT TRIPS for You and Your Kids of All Ages

BY CHRISTINE LOOMIS

Fodor's Travel Publications • New York, Toronto, London, Sydney, Auckland
www.fodors.com

Fodor's Family Adventures

Editor: Holly S. Smith
Editorial Contributor: Mark Sullivan
Editorial Production: Linda K. Schmidt
Design: Fabrizio La Rocca, *creative director,* Guido Caroti, *art director*
Cover Illustration: Guido Caroti
Production/Manufacturing: Yexenia (Jessie) Markland

Copyright

Fourth Edition

ISBN 0-676-90159-X

ISSN 1528-3100

Important Tip

Although all prices, opening times, and other details in this book are based on information supplied to us at press time, changes occur all the time in the travel world, and Fodor's cannot accept responsibility for facts that become outdated or for inadvertent errors or omissions. So **always confirm information when it matters,** especially if you're making a detour to visit a specific place.

Special Sales

Fodor's Travel Publications are available at special discounts for bulk purchases for sales promotions or premiums. Special editions, including personalized covers, excerpts of existing guides, and corporate imprints, can be created in large quantities for special needs. For more information, contact your local bookseller or write to Special Markets, Fodor's Travel Publications, 280 Park Ave., New York, NY 10017. Inquiries from Canada should be directed to your local Canadian bookseller or sent to Random House of Canada, Ltd., Marketing Department, 2775 Matheson Boulevard East, Mississauga, Ontario L4W 4P7. Inquiries from the United Kingdom should be sent to Fodor's Travel Publications, 20 Vauxhall Bridge Road, London SW1V 2SA, England.

PRINTED IN THE UNITED STATES OF AMERICA

10 9 8 7 6 5 4 3 2 1

CONTENTS

A Note About This Book and the Author

Christine Loomis did not simply write *Family Adventures*—she has lived the book. A travel writer since 1984, she has long been an avid lover of the outdoors. After children, she knew she didn't want to give up the activities she enjoyed, from rafting and hiking to cross-country skiing. Not only were they too much fun, but she also wanted to share with her family her delight in the world around her. From the time her children were very young, Christine did research to find outfitters and ranches that would accept travelers of all ages. Since then, she and her family have also logged more than 25,000 miles exploring North America by RV.

As a travel writer and editor, Christine became increasingly aware she was not the only parent who wanted to continue adventuring with her family. At the same time, many outfitters, guide services, and schools noticed a growing interest in family adventure travel and began to expand their offerings. In writing this book, Christine selected her favorite sports and activities and chose the outfitters carefully. Many were people she and her family had taken trips with; others were recommended by traveling parents she knew and trusted. Still others were suggested by travelers like you. In every case, she conducted extensive interviews—asking many of the same questions listed in this book—and then decided whether to include the outfitters and schools.

Fodor's would love your feedback, positive and negative. If you have complaints, we'll look into them and revise our entries when the facts warrant it. If you've happened upon a special place we haven't included, we'll pass the information along to the writer. So please send a letter or postcard to the *Family Adventures* editor at Fodor's, 280 Park Ave., New York, New York 10017, or send e-mail to editors@fodors.com (specifying the name of the book in the header). We'll look forward to hearing from you. And in the meantime, have a wonderful trip!

Karen Cure
Editorial Director

GETTING STARTED ON THE ROAD TO ADVENTURE

The first thing you should know about adventure travel is that it's for everybody. Honest—everybody. You don't have to be a diehard daredevil or world-class athlete, you don't have to be young (though you can be), and you don't have to rough it unless you want to—even in the middle of the wilderness. In recent years travelers of every age—parents, children, and grandparents—have packed up comfortable clothing and headed into the great outdoors, where the possibilities for fun, learning, and excitement are as boundless and varied as the American landscape itself.

Outfitters, schools, and guide services have responded to the increased number of adventure-loving families by offering more family-oriented trips and activities, as well as departure dates just for families traveling with children. The choices for physical activities are many. Biking, boating, hiking, horseback riding, fishing, and snorkeling are only a few. Opportunities for learning and for expanding every family member's horizons abound as well. You and your children can work with scientists digging for dinosaur bones or aid an archaeologist uncovering ancient ruins. You can meet, live with, and learn about present-day Native American peoples and their culture in this country and in Canada.

Whatever your family chooses to do and wherever you choose to go, all the activities in this book provide opportunities to strengthen the bonds that connect family members to each other and to the greater world. I know this has been true for my family. With no TV and no phone to pull us apart, we seem to talk more, laugh more, and take the time to discover each other and the world around us.

Even the concept of what constitutes family entertainment is expanded in the world of nature vacations. Sometimes it's the array of stars in a vast, dark sky or the music of the river or stories told by guides around a campfire. On a rainy afternoon in the Adirondacks, my family—including my children Kira, Molly, and Hutch—played a spectacularly silly game of charades in a tent. On one ranch vacation we all paused from a fireside game of Uno to watch Hutch sleeping in his crib. He was about a year old then and hardly the focus of anyone else's good time. But for our family at that moment, he was the perfect entertainment to share and remember. It's not that such moments don't happen on other vacations or at home. It's simply that adventure vacations provide more time for such moments than any other type of travel I know.

I mentioned that Hutch was only a year old to make another point: there is no age at which you cannot enjoy adventure travel. To be sure, many trips and certain activities have age restrictions. Many don't, however, and today an increasing number of trips are available to younger children as outfitters and schools learn what families want and are capable of.

At the ripe old age of 4, Molly accompanied me on a four-night, five-day float and camping trip in the Tetons. She still remembers parts of that trip vividly: her terror during the thunder and lightning on the first two nights, her bravery during the storm on the third; her first fishing lesson; and that she got to spend special time with me, alone, while her siblings spent time with their dad. She remembers the two guides who taught her about wild huckleberries and told her stories about Jackson Hole. Molly also learned about our national parks and developed a budding love of the great outdoors. These things she will carry with her for a lifetime.

Adventure travel does have an element of risk that other vacations do not. This doesn't mean families should stay home; it means they should be prepared. Talk to your kids about safety. If you give them the responsibility of listening to guides' safety talks and then ensuring that your family does what's right, you are likely to find they will take this responsibility seriously. Parents need to listen to guides, too, and to be prepared in other ways, such as using appropriate safety equipment and carrying clothing for sudden changes in weather. When you book a vacation, don't exaggerate your family's abilities in order to be accepted on a particular trip. Not only will you put them at risk for injury, but your family—and the other participants—won't enjoy the trip.

On adventure vacations rules don't cut down on enjoyment; they increase it because they keep you safe even when risks are present. In addition, rules protect the environment and the wildlife you have paid to experience. Children who learn this at an early age have a world of exciting opportunities open to them.

All the outfitters, schools, and trip operators in this book are very good, but not every one of them is right for every family. The ranch that is perfect for a family with preteens may be less than ideal for a family with a 2-year-old. To help you connect with the right group, here's a list of questions you should consider before signing up, as well as some general trip-planning questions. In addition, you will find adventure-specific questions at the beginning of each chapter.

Questions to Ask

As you talk with each outfitter, you want to hear that your family will be wholeheartedly welcomed and that everything possible will be done to make this vacation work for all of you. By the same token, give the outfitter detailed information about the ages, abilities, and special needs of everyone in your family.

Will other children be on the same trip? If not, can you recommend an alternative date? Having peers on a trip can make a huge difference in how much fun your children have. It also lets you off the hook for entertaining them every minute. If your departure date is one for which only adults have signed up, consider traveling with another family you know or bringing along one of your child's friends. If you can be flexible about the date, you can probably find another trip on which families are already booked. Also, some adventure brokers and tour operators, as well as some outfitters, offer more than one kind of adventure, so even if there are no families on the July hiking trip, there might be kids on a canoe voyage around the same time.

Have the trip's guides worked with children before? If so, with what ages? Your guide should be comfortable with and knowledgeable about children the ages of yours. A guide who is used to working with children knows how to communicate information in an age-appropriate way, which both increases your kids' enjoyment and helps keep them safe.

Do you have child-size gear and clothing that will fit my child? Because technical and safety gear and clothing—whether it's bike helmets, Coast Guard–approved life vests, or extreme-weather clothing—are crucial for many activities, be sure to get accurate information ahead of time. Always check specific sizes of available gear and give outfitters your child's weight and height in addition to age, since the wet suit or cross-country ski boots that fit one seven-year-old may not fit another. Most outfitters send a pretrip list of required and suggested clothing and gear.

Do you include kid-favorite meals on your menus? Outfitters that work extensively with families know the kinds of food children like and make an effort to include some of those at all meals. However, if you have a picky eater, ask what's going to be on the menu and then see if special requests can be accommodated.

Are there any special activities for children on your trips? For example, do the guides tell stories to the kids about the area in which you'll be traveling? Does the naturalist line up activities that will interest children? Such activities are most common on designated family departures, so if this is important to you, book those trips.

What if I want to participate in an activity for which my child is too young? Some activities, such as hikes or trail rides, may be appropriate only for older kids. If that's the case, you need to know if your younger child can stay back at camp or the ranch with a responsible adult, or if your child can participate in an easier activity without a parent. Some outfitters offer daily options, including activities geared for kids only. The younger your children are, the more likely these situations will come up, so ask in advance to avoid disappointment.

How flexible is the trip itinerary? The hallmark of a good family guide is flexibility. When I took Molly on the Teton float, the itinerary included a long hike the first day and a change of campsites each of the four nights. With a 4- and a 5-year-old on the trip, the head guide changed the hike to a fishing lesson and kept us at the same campsite for two nights. It made a huge difference to the families.

What will the group size be? Although I believe group size is less important than the quality and attributes of an outfitter, it's still something to consider. Many outdoor enthusiasts think only in terms of small, intimate groups. Indeed, for some families that's optimal. Keep in mind, though, that larger groups are likely to have more companions for children as well as parents.

Will you supply references from others who have taken your trips? If possible, ask for a reference from both a parent and his or her children who were on the trip. Your child might enjoy hearing about the trip from a peer.

Where is the nearest medical facility? What emergency training and equipment does the guide have? When you're in the wilderness, the closest facility may be hundreds of miles away. Be prepared by bringing small amounts of normal childhood medications: acetaminophen (pain reliever), decongestant, cough medicine, and medication to prevent or cure upset stomach, diarrhea, and motion sickness. Ask your pediatrician for an antibiotic in powder form (you'll have to add water) or a type that doesn't require refrigeration—especially if you're traveling out of the country. Find out whether the guides know basic or wilderness first aid and CPR for adults and children and have wilderness training. If you'll be on the water, they should also know water safety and rescue. Also ask what medical supplies will be on hand (carry your own first-aid kit in any case) and whether there will be a radio with which to call for help if necessary.

Are passports or other official documents needed? If passports are required for adults, your child needs one, too; start this process well in advance of your trip. All children must have a social security number in order to get a passport. Children 13 and up must apply in person at a passport office or a designated post office; parents can apply for younger children. If only a birth certificate is required, it must be either the original or a notarized copy with a raised seal. Finally, some destinations require additional documentation. If you travel to Mexico with your child but without your child's other parent, you must bring a notarized letter from that parent stating you have permission to take your child to Mexico without him or her. Health documents proving any required inoculations are also necessary in some cases.

Will insects be a problem? Lots of wilderness areas have them, so be prepared. However, the most common insect-repellent ingredient, DEET, should be used with caution on children. Most health experts recommend applying DEET only on children's clothing, not directly on skin. There are some non-DEET repellents, too. Ask your pediatrician's advice.

What is done with diapers in the wilderness? Some outfitters accept infants on canoe voyages, but there is often no place to dispose of soiled diapers during a trip. Parents must store and carry out all diapers. Families that use cloth diapers must do the same thing because washing soiled diapers in or even near lakes and streams can contaminate the water.

How far in advance should we book our vacation? Adventure travel has become extremely popular, and trips—especially those designated just for families—often fill up quickly. The rule is this: book as far in advance as possible, but don't hesitate to call at the last minute if free time suddenly comes your way.

How much of a deposit is required, and when is the balance due? Most schools and outfitters require a deposit well in advance of a trip. You then pay the full amount just prior to departure.

What's the cancellation policy? You may or may not get a full or partial refund if you cancel your reservation early enough. Policies vary from full refunds up to 30 days before the trip to partial refunds up to seven days before departure to no refunds at all. If the outfitter offers cancellation insurance, take it, or look into getting insurance from other sources. That way you'll receive a refund if for any reason your family can't take the trip.

Are taxes and tips included in the cost? Generally, taxes and tips aren't part of the price, and these can add substantially to a trip's cost. Be sure to ask who customarily gets tipped and how much. Guides who are exceptionally good with children are invaluable, so if you're happy with a guide, tip generously; it could encourage other guides and outfitters to work on family-friendliness, too. If you're traveling to Canada, the GST (goods and services tax) is sometimes included in the cost, and it is sometimes refundable to non-Canadians; ask in advance.

How to Use This Book

Each chapter covers one sport or activity and profiles outfitters, companies, and schools that have great family trips. In most chapters the outfitters and schools are in alphabetical order; in a few the outfitters are given alphabetically within a region. Each profile has an age icon with the minimum age the outfitter or school accepts, but read the full description for specific requirements and occasional exceptions. The profiles have information about where the company operates and descriptions of the best trips for children of different ages. Each chapter ends with Resources, a section listing organizations, periodicals, books, and products of interest.

Families looking for adventure in a particular part of the country can use the section called Finding the Fun, which lists outfitters by the regions in which they operate. Here are the states in each region:

Northeast: Connecticut, Maine, Massachusetts, New Hampshire, New York, Rhode Island, Vermont

Mid-Atlantic: Delaware, Maryland, New Jersey, Pennsylvania, Virginia, Washington, D.C., West Virginia

South: Alabama, Arkansas, Florida, Georgia, Kentucky, Louisiana, Mississippi, North Carolina, South Carolina, Tennessee

Midwest: Illinois, Indiana, Iowa, Kansas, Michigan, Minnesota, Missouri, Nebraska, North Dakota, Ohio, Oklahoma, South Dakota, Wisconsin

Southwest: Arizona, Nevada, New Mexico, Texas, Utah

Rockies: Colorado, Idaho, Montana, Wyoming

West Coast: California, Oregon, Washington

The section has separate heads for trips in Alaska, Hawaii, and destinations farther afield. At the end of the book an appendix tells you the sports, activities, and outfitters in each state and country. There is also an index of outfitters.

Descriptions of outfitters and schools include a range of per-person trip prices for both adults and children, in most cases from the lowest price to the highest for each group. Sometimes adventure pricing is complex. It can depend on where you go, the number of people in your family, the accommodations you choose, and the season. It can also depend on the ages of your children. When an outfitter or school provided an age range for children's prices, this is included; when outfitters or schools did not provide this or felt different adventures would have different guidelines, no age range is mentioned. In listings where only one price range is given, there is no children's discount. Because there are so many variables, it's best to ask specific questions about trip prices. Most prices are in U.S. dollars, although we occasionally list Canadian prices only, with the designation "C$". The exchange rate at press time (spring 2002) was US$1 to C$1.60.

Finally, most information here concerns guided trips and tours, as well as courses in various outdoor activities. Why guides and instructors? Because for the vast majority of families, that is the safest way to take children into the wilderness or onto the water, or to introduce them to these kinds of adventures. There are, of course, excellent outfitters that will provide you with all of the equipment and maps you need to find your own way. Some of those are given, too, since they can be a good option for parents who are experienced wilderness travelers.

Guided trips have appeal even for parents proficient in a sport. Leading a trip requires many skills, including child CPR and lifesaving, basic and wilderness first aid, and water safety and rescue. Moreover, a parent can be an excellent hiker, cyclist, or kayaker, but if he or she isn't thoroughly familiar with the area or the particular river, guiding is better left to those who are. Besides, with everything that outfitters are offering families these days—storytelling, special children's counselors, and the company of lots of other kids—even the most resourceful parent is hard pressed to compete. Leaving the details to someone else has its rewards. You have more time to enjoy the area through which you're traveling, the insights of those who know it well, and most important of all, the company of your children. Happy adventuring!

ARCHAEOLOGY ADVENTURES

Digging in dirt comes naturally to most children, so it's not surprising that archaeology lends itself to family adventure. But it's not just the digging: children are often fascinated with ancient civilizations, with the ways people lived, worked, and played long ago. Add to that interest the opportunity to experience Native American cultures—such as those studied at archaeological sites throughout the American Southwest—and you have the stuff of an exciting family adventure vacation.

Uncovering ruins and pottery is a way for families to learn not only about ancient worlds but, by extension, about themselves. Archaeology is rewarding work; however, it *is* work. When you "vacation" by volunteering at a research site, you may not come home rested, and you probably won't have had time to read that novel you've been saving for months. On the other hand, you will return home with the satisfaction of knowing that by volunteering, your family has contributed to our understanding of the Earth's past, present, and future.

Questions to Ask

What kinds of objects have been uncovered at this site? Although archaeology is painstaking work, the rewards from uncovering something no one else has seen for hundreds or even thousands of years are great. But because you'll want your family to have reasonable expectations about the possibility of discovering such rewards, ask ahead of time what kinds of artifacts or other material might be found and how often volunteers like you find them.

How much time is spent digging? Generally, days are a mix of digging and other kinds of archaeological activities, but three to six hours of digging is typical. You might dig in the morning and work in a lab in the afternoon, or you might dig eight hours straight one day and not at all on other days. Some programs give you a few choices; at other sites the itinerary is more rigid. Be assured, however, that in most cases much of your time will be devoted to digging. If you don't want to spend many hours on your knees involved in fairly painstaking work, these trips are probably not for you.

Are there other activities? In some cases, other activities are available. There may be recreation areas nearby or places of interest related to the project. Some programs include hikes and day trips; on other projects the opportunity to pursue recreational activities may come only at night, if at all. If you feel your family will have a hard time focusing just on archaeology, choose a site with some alternatives.

Will I be with my children most of the time? Volunteers are often separated, working at different activities or in different areas of a site. If this concerns you, ask ahead of time.

What kind of housing is available? Travelers must often share facilities (kitchen, bathrooms), and males and females usually sleep in separate quarters. This may even include lodging a single parent separately from a child of the opposite sex. That's true for spouses, too. At the least you will probably share housing with part of the group. If this is a problem, see if other lodging arrangements can be made (utilizing tent sites instead of bunkhouses, for example). If there are no alternatives, you'll need to prepare your family for the possibility of separation.

What are the field conditions? These are scientific research sites, not vacation destinations. Field conditions are typically primitive—sites are hot, dusty, and dirty; and work often requires walking over uneven or rocky terrain. There may or may not be tarps or other kinds of shelter to shield you from hot sun or rain.

Are trip costs tax deductible? When you volunteer your time and labor on bona fide research projects, a portion of your fee is probably tax deductible, as are some of your out-of-pocket expenses and transportation costs to project sites. The tax code is complex, however, so check with your accountant or other tax expert.

Is it possible to get college credit for this volunteer work? In some cases, yes. However, if you are pursuing college credit, your trip may no longer be tax deductible.

Will there be opportunities to meet local residents? Whether you're traveling in this country or abroad, a research project can be an opportunity to meet people from another background or culture. At foreign sites, local residents often work at project sites or provide housing. Make cultural exchange part of your trip by reading about the area ahead of time. If another language is involved, try to use it as much as possible.

What's included in the cost? On multiday trips lodging and meals are included unless noted otherwise. Transportation to and from the sites is not usually part of the cost. If you'll be camping or staying in dorms or bunkhouses, you may need to bring your own camping gear and bedding. Tents are provided at some sites, but ask.

Instruction

You don't need any special skills or knowledge to participate in these trips because discussions about the project, lectures, and hands-on instruction in excavation and lab work are part of the experience. The excavation sites contain valuable and fragile materials, so you and your children will be taught the proper way to dig and to handle any finds. Advance information packets sometimes include reading lists of historical and cultural background material.

Finding the Fun

South: University of Alabama Museum of Natural History. **Midwest:** P.A.S.T. Foundation. **Southwest:** Denver Museum of Nature and Science, Earthwatch. **Rockies:** Crow Canyon Archaeological Center, P.A.S.T. Foundation. **Caribbean, Central America, Europe, Asia:** Earthwatch, Smithsonian Study Tours.

Favorite Digs

Crow Canyon Archaeological Center

12+

For more than 15 years Crow Canyon archaeologists have been working on a puzzle: Why did the ancient Pueblo people, who flourished in the Southwest until the late 13th century, suddenly abandon the area? Their mysterious disappearance is just one aspect of the research at this facility in southwestern Colorado, where an ancient village is being excavated with the help of interested students and other lay participants. Researchers hope work here will not only provide answers about prehistoric Pueblo communities but will also yield information that will benefit contemporary society, especially Native American cultures. Like those in Mesa Verde National Park, 10 mi (16 km) to the east, this important site is set among stunning, rugged cliffs and mesas. The nonprofit center is renowned for its preservation and educational efforts.

FOR FAMILIES. Family Excavation Week, usually scheduled once or twice each summer, is for parents, grandparents, and students in seventh grade or higher. Middle school students work about two half days in the field, with the rest of the time spent in the lab or in other activities and programs designed for this age group. High school students and adults alternate field work with time in the lab and experimental archaeology activities, such as learning how to use ancient tools or participating in an experiment on traditional farming techniques. Everyone begins the week by examining artifacts and reconstructing the cultures and chronologies they represent. At the end of the week the group joins a guided tour of Mesa Verde. There are evening lectures throughout the week.

Accommodations are in roomy log cabins built in the style of Navajo *hogans* (earth-covered dwellings). Families are housed together. You supply your own towels and bedding. There are no private baths or showers. Meals are served cafeteria style in the dining hall.

Crow Canyon Archaeological Center, 23390 Road K, Cortez, CO 81321, tel. 970/565–8975 or 800/422–8975, www.crowcanyon.org. Family Excavation Week: 7 days, $875 adults, $675 students under 18. Membership, which is required, costs $75 per family. Membership for other programs costs $20–$50, depending on age.

Denver Museum of Nature and Science

7+

The Denver Museum of Nature and Science, one of the finest facilities of its kind in the country, offers unusual and enlightening trips for families (see Canoeing *and* Rafting). One excursion is to Chaco Canyon, New Mexico. Although it's not a research-based dig in the same sense as other trips, this exploration of an ancient civilization is a learning vacation for those who love archaeology but don't necessarily want to spend days on their knees digging.

FOR FAMILIES. Chaco Canyon for Families, generally scheduled every other year, offers instruction in astronomy, anthropology, and archaeoastronomy (a discipline that focuses on the importance of the sky to various ancient human cultures), in addition to archaeology. The trip is led by teachers from Earth Knack, an expedition company specializing in the Stone Age. There are also guides from the Four Corners School of Outdoor Education, who help bring the history of the area to life. The setting, Chaco Canyon, is striking. This "Anasazi Capital," in a desolate area of northwestern New Mexico, was a thriving center of civilization from AD 900 to AD 1150. The Anasazi left behind a vast and complex network of roads, masonry walls, and stairways carved into cliffs, all connecting some 12 major pueblos and numerous smaller ones. Ruins of the road system and pueblos are now part of Chaco Culture National Historic Park, where the trip takes place.

Participants meet in Cortez, Colorado, then travel together to New Mexico. After settling into reserved campsites (bring your own tents and camping gear or RVs), the group tours the visitor center museum for background on Chaco Canyon. The itinerary varies from trip to trip, but typically there are lectures, discussions, and activities for different age groups, including making fire by friction, identifying plants, grinding corn for ash cakes, and gathering stones for axes. The group works on a simulated dig and learns about ruins, artifacts, and other aspects of archaeology. Evening programs are led by national park rangers. A highlight is the chance to experience one of Chaco Canyon's greatest archaeoastronomical phenomena, in the kiva Casa Rinconada. Researchers believe this kiva is part of an ancient astronomical observatory built so that light would enter a particular window only during the summer and winter solstices. This trip often coincides with the summer solstice.

Denver Museum of Nature and Science, 2001 Colorado Blvd., Denver, CO 80205, tel. 303/370–6304, www.dmns.org. June: 5 days, $700 adults, $600 children 7–12.

Earthwatch Institute

16+

Earthwatch Institute, a nonprofit organization, funds research projects of all types around the globe and brings lay participants together with researchers to work on these undertakings. The benefit to each group is clear: researchers have a pool of volunteers who provide not only labor but money to offset research costs, and volunteers can work beside great scientists from a wide variety of fields. Some 30 archaeological digs are described in the institute's catalog.

FOR FAMILIES. Earthwatch has many sites, so families usually make their choice based on location, historical period, and related activities. (Earthwatch leaders teach volunteers all they need to know to participate.) If Native American life interests you and your teenager, there are Hopi and Hopi-Zuni excavations in two sites in Arizona. Those who like Roman history can participate in excavations at a fort in northern England or a farm in Tuscany. A Bronze Age village in Spain, an island off the coast of Scotland, and a Belizean Maya village where civilization collapsed four centuries ago all have their own special appeal. You might also dig in Thailand, the Caribbean, and other parts of the United States.

In addition to excavating, volunteers are often called on to photograph or sketch artifacts and sites and to assist in lab work. Moreover, depending on the site, volunteers can experience other fields of interest. An anthropologist or archaeologist directs the team. If you work or stay with local people, you'll be exposed to another culture and language. Accommodations range from primitive campsites to modern hotels, and the group stays together unless it's being hosted by local families. The trips are very work-intensive—the team could be working 8 to 10 hours a day. New projects are announced monthly.

Earthwatch Institute, 3 Clocktower Place, Suite 100, Box 75, Maynard, MA 01754-0075, tel. 978/461–0081 or 800/776–0188, www.earthwatch.org. Year-round (all sites not available at all times): 7–14 days, $695–$1,995.

P.A.S.T. Foundation

12+

P.A.S.T. (Partnering Anthropology with Science and Technology) Foundation is a nonprofit organization devoted to the integration of archaeological projects into the K–12 curriculum. Much of its focus is on research that also has educational potential, and to that end P.A.S.T. is involved in projects across the U.S. and around the world.

FOR FAMILIES. The Kids Archaeological Program is designed to introduce kids to the science of archaeology and to get them involved with the people who practice it around the globe. Each summer P.A.S.T. runs kids digs that are open to families as well as to school groups and teachers. The projects change each summer, but typical are the excavation of an 1842 Red River steamboat in Oklahoma (in conjunction with the Oklahoma Historical Society). One of the more unusual projects is underwater archaeology in the shallows of the Firehole River in Wyoming's Yellowstone National Park, where scientists hope to piece together the history of one of the park's early hotels. The Firehole, runoff from Yellowstone's famous geysers, is warm, but currents can be stiff, making this project best for those comfortable in and around water. At most sites, children younger than 12 (accompanied by parents) might be considered, but talk to expedition leaders first. Accommodations are typically camping at the dig sites, and participants bring their own tent or camper and bedding.

P.A.S.T. Foundation, 9604 Cougar Drive, Bozeman, MT 59718, tel. 406/522–3779, www.pastfoundation.org. July or August, 5 days, about $100.

Smithsonian Study Tours

8+

Smithsonian Study Tours are programs of The Smithsonian Associates, the educational, cultural, and membership unit of the Smithsonian Institution. Tours, designed to reflect the interests and concerns of the Institution and its members, focus on history, science, and the arts.

FOR FAMILIES. Although tours change from season to season, several family adventures are always on the roster. Typical of the ambitious—and intriguing—trips for parents and their children is "China for Families," which includes assisting archaeologists in Xian, central China, dig for ancient relics at a working excavation site. The trip takes families from Beijing, where children can fly kites in Tiananmen Square, to The Great Wall at Mutianyu, and on to Xian and finally Shanghai. Working at a dig site in Xian is certainly among the highlights, but rivaling that is the climb up Xian's Wild Goose Pagoda and a visit to the tomb of China's first emperor. In Shanghai, the group cruises on the Huangpu River and rides a barge along the ancient Grand Canal. There's even a chance for your children to meet with Chinese middle-schoolers to learn what growing up in China is really like.

On family trips, Smithsonian study leaders gear talks to all ages so family members can

learn together about the people, history, and culture of the lands they visit. This particular trip may not run every year, so call for the latest information and full brochure.
Smithsonian Study Tours, Ripley Center, Suite 3077, 1100 Jefferson Dr. SW, Washington, DC 20560–0701, tel. 202/357–4700 or 877/338–8687, smithsonianstudytours.org. June: 14 days, $5,095–$5,835 adults (higher price includes round-trip air), $3,635–$4,375 children 8–15 (higher price includes round-trip air and a room with one adult or another child).

University of Alabama Museum of Natural History Expeditions

12+

The Alabama Museum of Natural History started its summer expeditions in 1979 to provide scientific field experience for students and teachers. The program has been an unqualified success. Known today as Summer Archaeology Camp, these seasonal expeditions have given more than 2,000 students, teachers, and families a chance to work side by side with archaeologists on real dig sites.

FOR FAMILIES. "For many young people, the Expedition has been the catalyst leading to a science major in college and a science career afterwards," says the museum's brochure. For families whose middle school or high school students have a real interest in science, this program is one of the finest of its kind. The weeklong camp generally runs just once each summer and is divided into four one-week sessions. Moundville Archaeological Park on the banks of Alabama's Black Warrior River is typical of the work sites. Occupied during the Mississippian Period (AD 1000 to AD 1500) and named for its 1,000-year-old earthen mounds on which temples, council houses, and homes once stood, Moundville was the capital city of one of North America's largest and most powerful Native American communities. As at all sites, campers and archaeologists work together to uncover the secrets of the people who once called this area home.

In addition to participating in digs, campers learn excavation techniques, lab procedures, and artifact identification. In the evenings, group members discuss the day's events and listen to staff presentations. The digs typically involve camping in the field.
University of Alabama Natural History Expedition, University of Alabama, Museum of Natural History, Sixth Avenue Smith Hall, Tuscaloosa, AL 35487, tel. 205/348–7550. June–Aug, 7 days, about $400.

Resources

Books

Children can get a general sense of archaeology and anthropology from *Adventures in Archaeology,* by Tom McGowen (Scientific American Sourcebooks); *Eyewitness: Archaeology,* by Jane McIntosh (Dorling Kindersley); *Archaeologists Dig for Clues,* by Kate Duke (part of the Let's Read and Find Out series, HarperCollins); *The Usborne Young Scientist Archaeology,* by Barbara Cork et al. (EDC Publications); *Young Oxford Book of Archaeology,* by Norah Moloney (Oxford University Press); and *Stones, Bones, and Petroglyphsogy,* by Susan E. Goodman & Michael J. Doolittle (an Ultimate Field Trip book, Aladdin Paperbacks). Although some of the following books on the American Southwest may be out of print, they're worth checking for in your local library: *The Ancient Cliff Dwellers of Mesa Verde,* by Caroline Arnold (Clarion); *The Anasazi,* by David Petersen (Children's Press); and *Cities in the Sand,* by Warren Scott (Chronicle Books).

For adults, Brian Fagan's *In the Beginning: An Introduction to Archaeology* (Pearson Education) is a general guide. Those digging in the Southwest will want to read *Ancient Land, Ancestral Places,* by Paul Logsdon (Museum of New Mexico Press); *In Search of the Old Ones: Exploring the Anasazi World of the Southwest,* by David Roberts (Touchstone Books); and *Chaco Canyon: A Center and Its World,* by S. H. Lekson, J. R. Stein, and S. J. Ortiz (Museum of New Mexico Press).

Also See

If digging vacations are for your family, see Digging for Dinosaur Bones and Other Fossils. If present-day native cultures are of interest, see Native American Experiences.

BIKING

Bicycle-loving parents no longer have to choose between their bikes and their tykes. Child-friendly inventions such as carts and tandems have made multiday cycling tours a feasible option for toddlers and preschoolers across the country. For families with older children, mountain biking is a popular vacation alternative. With all these choices, many families have begun choosing two-wheel road trips over four-wheel vacations.

The best option for families with very young children is a cart or trailer that attaches to the back of a bicycle. These contraptions, sort of like a baby carriage you pull behind you, work best on easy to moderate road tours. Among the trips that allow carts are road tours through Michigan's Amish country, nature-oriented treks in Washington's San Juan Islands, and scenic trips through Vermont.

A more recent invention is the child-size bike, minus the front wheel portion, that attaches to an adult's bicycle, turning the whole thing into a tandem. They're made especially for children ages 1–10. Some outfitters are starting to stock these neat bikes; if not, you can bring your own. There are even real tandem models, which allow one or two children to bike with you, as well as models with baby seats or support for special-needs children. The tandem device makes it possible for children to share the physical labor and also offers a safer, lighter, and more stable alternative to on-bike child seats and a less wind-resistant alternative to carts.

For families with preteens and teens, mountain biking can be a welcome physical challenge. However, since riding day in and day out strikes many in this age group as a monotonous proposition, outfitters have found great success with combination trips: biking and rafting, biking and horseback riding, biking and climbing. These trips are also good for families that enjoy bike rides but are not necessarily dedicated cyclists.

Whether you're road biking or mountain biking, it's best to search out those trips designated specifically for families. Cycling, like hiking, has a high appeal among empty-nesters and hard-core outdoor adventurers who challenge themselves by racking up the daily miles; some may feel hampered by a family's slower pace and need for more frequent stops. Moreover, some adults have little tolerance for even the best-behaved children. If your heart is set on a romantic New England inn-to-inn tour, do it when you and your spouse can get away as a couple. The good news is you won't be forced to settle for a less-than-appropriate trip. Every year there are more and more wonderful biking trips for families.

Questions to Ask

What are the target ages for your trips? Most outfitters have an excellent understanding of how well a child of a given age can meet the physical and mental requirements of the trip. Listen to the outfitter and go with the recommendations given.

How experienced or physically fit should my family be for this trip? This is an important question to ask up front. The outfitter will be able to recommend the best trips for families of all different levels, from those who cycle once or twice a year to those who bike regularly. Moreover, outfitters can also give you information about exercises to help you get in shape in the weeks before the trip.

How many miles a day do the trips average? Bike trips can cover as few as 8 mi (13 km) a day or as many as 50 mi (80½ km). Many children can handle 25 mi (40 km) a day, and those with some experience might ride as many as 35 mi (56 km). Ask very specific questions about the distance, the type of terrain, and whether there are options for shorter routes or van pickup. Make sure you choose a beginner trip if that's what you are. If hiking is included on a combination adventure, ask how many miles a day you will walk. Most children (depending on age and experience) can handle 3 to 8 mi (5 to 13 km), with the exception of toddlers or preschoolers, who can be carried in a backpack, provided you can handle the extra weight.

Do you rent children's bikes and helmets? Some outfitters allow children but do not provide bikes or other equipment for them. Others have rental equipment but only for children of a certain age or height. If you aren't planning to bring your own bikes and helmets, this is important. If you bring your own helmets, keep in mind that they should be of high quality and not the flimsy ones available at some toy stores. When in doubt about your equipment, ask the outfitter.

Do you allow carts or trailers? Some outfitters may rent them; others may not even permit them on tours.

Is there van support on the trip? Van support allows beginners to go on tours that have some intermediate terrain, and it gives a break to any cyclist who gets tired during the day. It's a crucial option for families with young cyclists since most routes aren't chosen with only the 8-year-old in mind.

Are guides qualified to fix bikes in case of a breakdown? Unless you know how to fix your bike, you'll want someone along who knows what to do.

What kind of food can we expect on our trip? Many bike trips include overnights at fine inns and resorts where exceptional food is part of the package. If your child is a picky eater, talk to outfitters in advance to find out whether they accommodate special requests. You may want to bring some of your child's favorite foods with you—but consider that you may have to carry the load.

Do you have children's rates? Many bicycle tour operators have discounts for children under a certain age and for children sharing a room with parents. Rates may vary according to how many children you bring; in addition, your discount may be smaller if there is only one parent on the trip. Some special family departures give parents an even bigger break off the regular cost of the trip.

What's included in the cost of the trip? Generally, all accommodations and meals are included, but van transfers and travel to and from the start of the trip are not. Guides, maps, and energy-producing snacks are part of the package. Bike rentals may be included, although that's more the exception than the rule. Helmets are often but not always provided; they are usually available for rent. Rates quoted in brochures are typically per person and based on double occupancy.

Instruction

In general, road touring companies don't offer much in the way of instruction, though some give minimal information about bike care and easy repair. Some companies have day or weekend courses devoted entirely to repair; these are especially useful for families that are considering becoming serious road cyclists (you might also find such courses at your local community college or health club). Mountain-biking tour operators are more likely to provide instruction on techniques that are helpful in off-road cycling.

Finding the Fun

Northeast: Backroads, Bike Vermont, VBT Bicycling Vacations. **Mid-Atlantic:** VBT Bicycling Vacations. **South:** Nantahala Outdoor Center. **Midwest:** Michigan Bicycle Touring. **Southwest:** Backroads, Escape Adventures. **Rockies:** Backroads, Wilderness River Outfitters. **West Coast:** Backroads. **Hawaii:** Backroads. **Canada:** Backroads. **Central America:** Backroads, Butterfield & Robinson. **Caribbean:** Iguana Mama. **South America:** Backroads. **Europe:** Backroads, Brooks Country Cycling Tours, Butterfield & Robinson, Ciclismo Classico. **New Zealand:** Butterfield & Robinson. **Africa:** Butterfield & Robinson.

Favorite Outfitters

Backroads

2+

Backroads, founded in 1979, is known for its ability to handle the details of a family trip with finesse and humor. Families can choose a bicycling-only vacation or a multisport adventure (see Hiking and Backpacking for more Backroads itineraries). Trips are relatively slow paced, giving youngsters time to explore tidal pools or wildflower fields. Family departures are scheduled in spring, summer and early fall, with a choice of destinations in the U.S., Europe, and beyond. Participants stay at inns or camp. On family trips, bikes for kids, teens, and adults are available; equipment rentals—including Burley carts for children up to 85 lbs (39 kg)—are extra.

FOR FAMILIES. Among the American trips are four tours in the San Juan Islands of Washington state, where the hills and killer whales delight many families. There are two biking tours; the other two are multisport trips. Family mountain-biking tours also run in the Sedona area of Arizona and in Idaho's Sawtooth Mountains and Sun Valley. Other bike tours travel around Banff and Jasper in the Canadian Rockies and in Nova Scotia. The multisport adventures go even farther afield, with trips to Glacier, Yellowstone, Grand Teton, and Hawaii Volcanoes national parks. Other regions on the itinerary include Maine, the Canadian Rockies, Belize, and the Galapagos Islands. Minimum ages for the trips vary from 2 to 10.

Backroads has a solid list of European family adventures, too, though most trips have a minimum age of either 6 or 10. All packages feature activities and sites that will appeal to children and parents alike, however. The six-day family bike trip through the Czech Republic includes Prague and southern Bohemia. Traditional cycling terrain is covered on three family trips to France, where you can explore the medieval villages and châteaux of the Loire Valley. Or, you can wind through Brittany and Normandy on France's northwest coast, taking in villages, D-Day beaches, and Mont St-Michel, the awe-inspiring island monastery and cathedral. The third adventure combines biking, hiking, and kayaking in the Loire Valley.

Other family biking tours are held in Denmark, Hungary, Tuscany, and the Netherlands, while the trip to the Swiss Alps combines biking and hiking. Remember, though, to take the high altitude into account when preparing for trips to the mountains. You'll generally need a day to adjust to altitudes over 6,560 ft.

Backroads, 801 Cedar St., Berkeley, CA 94710, tel. 510/527–1555 or 800/462–2848, www.backroads.com. Mar.–Aug.: 6–9 days, $998–$4,598 adults, 10%–75% discount for children, depending on age.

Bike Vermont

10+

The heart of Bike Vermont's business is inn-to-inn cycling tours in Vermont and the Connecticut River valley. The majority of Bike Vermont's lodgings have interesting histories and antique furnishings; some offer fairly sophisticated menus. Many are family-friendly, although not geared for very young children. Of particular interest to families may be the shorter tours on which riders are based in just one inn, cycling out each day to the neighboring villages and surrounding countryside. The company also offers bike tours in Ireland and Scotland, as well hiking and kayaking explorations in Vermont. Both children's and adult bikes are available for rent.

FOR FAMILIES. The best trips are the weekend Inn at Saxtons River tour, the three-day Moose Mountain Lodge tour, and the six-day trip to Proctorsville, each of which can be tailored for riders of all skill levels. The Inn at Saxtons River tour features easy riding, colorful New England villages en route, an old-fashioned swimming hole, and a friendly, low-key village inn. The Moose Mountain Lodge tour near Hanover, New Hampshire, is a bit more challenging than the other two. The trip to Proctorsville, in southeastern Vermont not far from Woodstock, takes you through a region nestled by lakes and threaded with rivers, where accommodations are definitely kid-friendly—the Golden Stage inn, for example, has an endless cookie jar to keep children happy.
Bike Vermont, Box 207, Woodstock, VT 05091, tel. 802/457–3553 or 800/257–2226, www.bikevt.com. May–Oct.: 2–7 days, $295–$1,160, adults, 10% discount for children who share a parent's room.

Brooks Country Cycling & Hiking Tours

ALL

Brooks has no age guidelines for families, but children of all ages have been on its tours. The company, based in New York City, offers day trips in the mid-Atlantic region as well as longer European tours. Note that seats and carts are not available for rental, however.

FOR FAMILIES. Children are welcome on all tours, but the best family option is the one-week Barging and Biking trip to Holland. This tour combines ancient cities, small villages, and spectacular cycling terrain that takes you over blue canals, through flower-filled fields, and beneath stately windmills. An exceptional network of bike paths crisscross Holland's level landscape, and much of the trip is along dikes above the canals. The comfortable barge accommodations feature spacious cabins, some private showers, and a sundeck for relaxed sightseeing. Professional, bilingual tour guides and 21-speed hybrid bicycles are included in the cost. Children's bikes, Slipstreamers (like Adams Trail-A-Bike, see Resources, *below*), and child seats are available.

Brooks Country Cycling Tours, Box 20792, New York, NY 10025, tel. 212/874–5151, www.brookscountrycycling.com. Apr.–Oct.: 8 days, $725–$845 adults, depending on season and cabin; 50% discount for children 4–11 sharing cabin with parents; 66% discount for ages 3 and under.

Butterfield & Robinson

3+

The well-known international luxury cycling company Butterfield & Robinson recently introduced family trips for parents with children as young as 3 years old. As with their adult tours, the family packages are superbly planned in terms of destination, itinerary, and accommodations.

FOR FAMILIES. B&R's journey to Ireland features separate departure dates for families with children ages 3 and up, 8 and up, and 12 and up. The group meets in Galway and takes the ferry to Inismor, the largest of the Aran Islands, where Gaelic is still the main language. Here you'll bike and hike to a 1,500-year-old fortress, then you'll head back to the mainland for three days of exploring Connemara in County Galway. Local villages, a castle, a musical instrument workshop, and turf bogs give you a real sense of life in this part of Ireland. While young children can sail, fish, or canoe, older kids and adults can horseback ride or play golf. The final two days are spent in Cong, County Mayo, where biking routes parallel the coast of Lough Comb and the Maumturk mountains. Here you'll stay in the 13th-century Ballynahinch Castle, where you can ride a horse and cart, take a boat on the lake, or play golf or tennis. Daily bike rides for this trip average about 25 mi (40 km), but there's always a van to give you a lift. Supervised activities are planned for children in the afternoons and evenings.

Other family biking trips venture into mainland Europe. For families with children as young as 3, there are biking tours in Holland and France's Breton Coast. Kids at least 8 years old can also tour with their parents in Normandy, the Loire Valley, and the Dordogne. Those 12 and older can venture into Tuscany, take a Prague-to-Vienna ride, take a biking and walking tour of the Sahara and Atlas Mountains in Morocco, or explore New Zealand's South Island. The Switzerland Family Bike & Walk has departures for families with kids 3 and up or 8 and up, but note that the Holland and Breton Coast trips don't have special departures for families with kids older than age 3. However, families with older children are still welcome to join the trip departures geared for younger kids.

Several different types of bikes are available for adults, and children's equipment includes special tandems, bike seats, and children's bikes.

Butterfield & Robinson, 70 Bond St., Toronto, Ontario, Canada M5B 1X3, tel. 416/864–1354 or 800/678–1147, www.butterfield.com. Mar.–Dec. (not all trips available all months): 5–10 days, $2,895–$4,995 adults, 10%–35% discount for children depending on age and lodging.

Ciclismo Classico

ALL

Ciclismo Classico is wholly dedicated to providing biking and hiking tours throughout Italy; in fact, it's the only bike touring company specializing in this country. The owner and staff all have Italian roots and speak Italian, and tours are put together and led by staff members (not subcontracted to outside companies or guides). Lauren Hefferon, who founded the company more than a decade ago, has personally logged more than 15,000 mi (24,150 km) bike racing and touring throughout Italy. She brings her own children with her, so she knows just what families want, need, and are capable of on a multiday tour. There's a strong mix of children's and adult activities, and the guides and hotel employees are extremely child-friendly. Ciclismo Classico takes exceptional care to provide something for everyone on its family trips.

FOR FAMILIES. One of the company's cycling vacations is especially geared for families with children of all ages. Tuscan Fantasy, which begins in Florence, is an eight-day, villa-based adventure in Tuscany, where the scenery is awash with terraced slopes, vineyard-covered hillsides, rolling farmland, and thick olive groves. The villa, Frattoria degli Usignoli (Farm of the Nightingale), has a restored 15th-century farmhouse with a pool. Each morning you can choose from three set bike routes of varying distances, which take you past medieval villages and castles, among other picturesque local sights. In the afternoon or early evening, you can try your hand at cooking, art, or speaking Italian; history lessons are also offered. Informative day trips take you to churches, a gelato factory, or a bike shop owned by an Italian cycling champion. The villa also has tennis and horseback riding facilities. Children are often invited to join local kids for a soccer game and the following victory celebration.

Ciclismo Classico has several other tours appropriate for families, including The Best of Southern Italy, Villas & Gardens of Veneto, and Venice to Bologna. Ask about children's discounts for these trips. Child care is available on all family getaways. Bikes cost extra, and note that size 14 (for a child about age 10) is the smallest rental. Burley carts and mini-tandem attachments can also be rented.

Ciclismo Classico, 13 Marathon St., Arlington, MA 02474, tel. 781/646–3377 or 800/866–7314, www.ciclismoclassico.com. May–Oct.: 6–9 days, $2,595–$3,195 adults, $400 ages 3 and under, $1,350 ages 4–7, $1,600 ages 8–16 (children must share a room with two adults).

Escape Adventures

7+

This mountain-biking outfitter's brochure immediately tells you that the company has a sense of adventure—and humor to match. "Hey, teenagers," it says, "we love your eclectic energy." Escape Adventures believes in playing hard, but its guides also understand limits. Forty-four support vehicles accompany every trip, and meals are planned to satisfy even demanding gourmets. You can rent camping gear and bikes for all ages. Most trips are in Utah and the surrounding states.

FOR FAMILIES. There are four multiday family tours in July and September, in addition to daily family hikes throughout the year. Children must have mountain-biking experience, and everyone should be in good physical condition. The 80-mi (129-km) Brian Head–to–Bryce mini-tour, three days of riding and camping, starts at Brian Head Ski Resort in south-central Utah and winds through aspen groves and lava beds on the way to Bryce Canyon National Park. There's a 2,000-ft ascent, but support vehicles are always nearby. On the four-day, 120-mi (193-km) Grand Canyon Family Tour, you cycle and camp in Arizona's Kaibab National Forest—notably the remote North Rim. The five-day, 170-mi (274-km) tour of Zion and Bryce national parks departs in July (camping) and September (inn and lodge stays). Utah's Color Country has it all: mountains, lakes, rivers, multihue canyons, and the region's natural rock sculptures. If your family has only a day to spare, you can sign up at any time of year for the Redrock Canyon Family Bike Tour, near Las Vegas.

Family tours meet in St. George, Utah; shuttles to the trailhead are free. There's also shuttle service from Las Vegas for an extra fee (free on Redrock Canyon tours).

Ages 12 and up can join all other tours. Combination trips pair biking with hiking, riding, rafting, canoeing, rock climbing, or cross-country skiing, among other sports. *Escape Adventures, 8221 W. Charleston, Suite101, Las Vegas, NV 89117, tel. 702/596–2953, www.escapeadv.com. Year-round: 1–5 days (family tours), $45–$819 adults, 50% discount for children 7–15 accompanied by an adult.*

Iguana Mama

ALL

"The Dominican Republic is a living classroom!" says the company's online brochure, so it's not surprising that in addition to great mountain biking, Iguana Mama gives its guests a taste of island history and culture.

FOR FAMILIES. Most of the multiday mountain biking tours are best for families with teens. The company is well-known for its five-day Dominican Alps tour, a ride that goes from sea level to 5,500 ft through the Dominican Republic's scenic, unspoiled mountains. A 10-day Coast-to-Coast tour takes riders from the Atlantic to the Caribbean via four mountain passes. Iguana Mama rates both tours as suitable for intermediate through advanced bikers, but the terrain can be quite difficult. If you're looking for challenging teen trips that explore the island's interior, these tours are perfect.

You can also combine mountain biking with one of the company's sailing, kayaking, hiking, rafting, kitesurfing, or snorkeling trips (*see* Snorkeling and Diving), opting to bike one day and choose another adventure the next. There are daily rides for all levels and ages. A great one for families is the full-day 3,000 Feet Downhill, which begins at the summit of the Cordillera Septrional overlooking the lush Cibao Valley. You wind approximately 3,000 ft down mountain roads, sample local fruits, and learn about culture and vegetation from your guide. Hard biking deserves a jump in the river, after which the group heads to a secluded inn for a poolside lunch. Family members who don't want to ride can enjoy the scenery from the support vehicle. There's a half-day version of this trek as well (but no lunch at the inn).

Families with very young children (who can either ride or sit up in a trailer) could sign up for the Islabon Coast Cruise, a combination bike and boat trip. Even beginner bikers will enjoy the bird watching and easy ride along the coast, learning about the flora and fauna as well as the daily lives of the island's fishermen. Families with experienced mountain bikers (minimum ages 12 to 14) can choose from several day trips, including one through one of the island's national parks. *Iguana Mama, U.S. Payment office: 38 Lake Lacoma Dr., Pittsford, NY 14534; Local address: Plaza Criolla, Cabarete, Dominican Republic, tel.809/571–0734 or 800/849–4720, www.escapeadv.com. Year-round: ½–10* *days, $40–$1,850 adults, $20—$68 ages 17 and under on day trips; ask about discounts for children on multiday tours.*

Michigan Bicycle Touring

ALL

A small family-run business, Michigan Bicycle Touring (MBT) has been guiding families through the valleys and hills of its home state since 1978. Michigan is geographically and culturally diverse: dunes and islands, orchards, farmland, meandering rivers, quaint towns, an Amish community, and an international center for performing arts are among its attractions.

FOR FAMILIES. Children are welcome on most MBT tours, but some are especially family-friendly. The two-day Sleeping Bear Bike & Kayak combines biking through peaceful countryside to the shores of Lake Michigan with an afternoon kayak trip on the easy-flowing Crystal River. Sleeping Bear Dunes itself is a mammoth sand dune spanning 7 mi (11 km) of lake shoreline, and also one of the state's great family playgrounds. Lodging is at cozy inns in the village of Glen Arbor. The two-day Amish Amble takes cyclists through Amish country to the Mendon Country Inn and to Colon, "Magic Capital of the World." Here, magician Harry Blackstone perfected his craft and helped form Abbott's Magic Manufacturing, the world's largest producer of magic paraphernalia. Magic shows are performed in Colon throughout the summer. For those who enjoy the performing arts, the five-day Interlochen Sightseer includes a chance to attend rehearsals and performances of music, theater, and dance.

MBT also has a two-day tour of Mackinac Island, with highlights of ferry rides, historic forts, awesome views of Lakes Huron and Michigan, and delicious local fudge. It's also the site of the 5-mi (8-km) Mackinac Bridge, the world's longest total suspension bridge, which connects Michigan's upper and lower peninsulas. No cars are allowed on the island, so road biking with children is a near-carefree experience. Instead of automobiles, there are lots of horse-drawn carriages, which is another attraction for families. The tour lets you choose from 8 to 25 mi (13 to 40 km) of biking per day, so even very young children can ride. Accommodations are at the Hamilton or Harbor View inns, which offer special family rates.

Michigan Bicycle Touring, 3512 Red School Rd., Kingsley, MI 49649, tel. 231/263–5885, www.escapeadv.com. May–Oct.: 2–5 days, $319–$1,199 adults, 15%–75% discount for children, depending on trip and age.

Nantahala Outdoor Center

ALL

Western North Carolina has great mountain-biking terrain, and Nantahala Outdoor Center (NOC) is as adept at teaching fat-tire cycling skills as it is at teaching paddling (see Canoeing *and* Kayaking).

FOR FAMILIES. Families with children age 13 and older can opt for a one-day sampler course that begins with a morning of instruction and ends with an afternoon trail ride at the popular U.S. Forest Service Tsali Recreation Area near the school. The course includes a guide, bikes, helmets, lunch, and even a water bottle. This is ideal for families that have been leery of purchasing expensive mountain bikes. With Nantahala's sampler, you invest a minimum of money and time to find out if the sport is up your family's alley.

If it is, NOC has other choices, too. Private instruction is the way to go if families want to stay together all day every day and have bike enthusiasts younger than 13. You can opt for an intensive day of instruction, a push-the-envelope ride, or a guided bike trip. The price for this includes everything the sampler does, and NOC has rentals from kid-size bikes to cutting-edge test models. If you opt for a few days of instruction, you can book lodging (motels, bunkhouses, private cabins) for an extra charge.

If you're looking for a weekend adventure, NOC has fall mountain-biking getaways for families with children 16 and older. Ride through western North Carolina's blaze of colors and get some solid mountain-biking experience under your belts at the same time. Themed weekends run throughout the year, many of which are suitable for families.
Nantahala Outdoor Center, 13077 U.S. 19W, Bryson City, NC 28713, tel. 800/232–7238, ext. 600, www.noc.com. Year-round: 1–3 days, 1-day sampler, $95; private instruction, $250–$350 per family per day, depending on number of people; fall weekend trips, $350.

VBT Bicycling Vacations

13+

In 1972 this company began offering inn-to-inn bicycle tours in Vermont. Today cyclists can choose from 6- to 17-day expeditions throughout the world. Although VBT doesn't have any families-only departure dates, children 13 and up can join all tours. Most trips are geared for families with some biking experience. All tours include bikes and helmets.

FOR FAMILIES. One of the best trips for parents and teens is VBT's Prince Edward Island, the North Atlantic Canadian province of classic fishing villages, dunes, white-sand beaches, and green rolling hills. PEI, as it's known, is also the setting for the classic turn-of-the-last-century novel Anne of Green Gables. Author Lucy Maud Montgomery lived on the island for a time and was inspired by the setting around her. You can visit the house where she stayed with her aunt and uncle, and where she was married. The tour takes in the green interior of the island and its rugged coastline, farmland, and beaches. Much of the riding is on a converted rail line that runs the length of the island, which makes for easy cycling through areas not accessible from the highway. Also of interest to families is a stop at the Basin Head Fisheries Museum, which features boats, maps, and gear from the local fishing community. At the Rodd Brudenell River Resort families can take an afternoon to swim, play tennis, or just enjoy the surroundings.

Two other six-day tours are great for families. The Martha's Vineyard & Nantucket trip offers easy riding and a chance to learn about the whaling and maritime history of the islands. You'll also have the chance to watch artisans creating such traditional New England crafts as baskets and scrimshaw. The Taste of Vermont tour includes visits to a maple syrup farm, a cheese-making factory, the President Calvin Coolidge Historic Site, and a glassblowing studio.
VBT, Box 711, Bristol, VT 05443, tel. 802/453–4811 or 800/245–3868, www.vbt.com. Mid-Apr.–Nov.: 6 days, $1,025–$2,495 per person.

Wilderness River Outfitters

12+

As its name implies, Wilderness River began as a rafting outfitter, but it now includes some of the most interesting biking and hiking trips around. Owners Joe and Fran Tonsmeire have been guiding wilderness expeditions since the '60s, and their knowledge and love of nature are evident.

FOR FAMILIES. Adults and children older than 12 can follow the trail used by the Nez Perce Indians to get to their buffalo-hunting grounds east of the Bitterroot Mountains. The Nez Perce Trail trip starts and ends in Missoula, Montana; travel is on a combination of paved and dirt roads through such exotic-sounding backcountry as the River of No Return Wilderness. You'll camp under the stars in forested meadows along the way. If you have time, this trip can also be combined with a Salmon River rafting expedition (see Rafting). The tour is suitable for beginners in good physical condition with some mountain-biking experience, as well as for more advanced riders. Bikes are included in the cost of the trip.

Wilderness River Outfitters, Box 72, Lemhi, ID 83465, tel. 208/756–3959 or 800/252–6581, www.wildernessriver.com. July–Aug., 6–9 days, $1,200–$1,600 adults, 30% discount for children under 13.

Resources

Books

Globe Pequot Press publishes several books on bicycling in various areas of the country; one series focuses on short bike rides, another on their favorite rides. *25 Bicycle Tours in Vermont, third edition,* by John Freidin (Countryman Press), written by the founder of VBT Bicycling Vacations, describes routes, lodging, and camping facilities and includes good maps and photos as well as advice on safe and successful touring.

Products

Adams Trail-A-Bike (1465 Kebet Way, Port Coquitlam, British Columbia, Canada V3C 6L3, tel. 604/552–2930 or 800/663–8916) makes a child's bike that attaches to an adult's bike, creating a sort of tandem. A number of outfitters have these for rent. If you're going with an outfitter who doesn't, contact customer service for a brochure; they can also tell you where you can buy or rent one in your area.

A number of companies make helmets for both children and adults. **Bell Sports** (1924 County Rd. 3000 N, Rantoul, IL 61866-9512, tel. 217/893–9300 or 800/456–2355) will send consumers a pamphlet on helmet use and safety, a catalog, and dealer information. **Giro Sport Design** (380 Encinal St., Santa Cruz, CA 95060, tel. 831/420–4000 or 800/294–6098) will send a catalog or give you the name of the nearest dealer, as will **Specialized Bicycle Components** (15130 Concord Circle, Morgan Hill, CA 95037, tel. 408/779–6229).

Also See

For trips on which you can bring bikes, *see* RV Adventures *and* Houseboating.

CANOEING

Serenity, although elusive in everyday life, is the very essence of a flat-water canoe trip, especially one that takes your family gliding through the still backwaters and meandering rivers of North America's great wilderness areas. Sounds are few—the rhythmic dip of your paddle, rustling leaves, the occasional cry of a bird startled into flight—so even normally boisterous children often quiet down to watch and listen intently.

There's a feeling of historical continuity in canoeing, too. Many of America's early European explorers—and those native to this land before them—traveled by canoe, using the pathways nature provided. Today canoeing is an excellent way to explore protected areas without negatively affecting fragile environments.

All this said, parents should know that children from ages about 6 to 10 can have a hard time sitting for long stretches of quiet paddling. Savvy outfitters frequently suggest combination trips that pair canoeing with hiking, snorkeling, studying nature, swimming, or fishing. Base-camp trips, which make day voyages from and return to a single site, are alternatives to long hours of paddling from camp to camp. The better multiday trips are those during which outfitters make frequent stops en route and set up camp early enough in the day for children to have time to run around. Before committing to an adventure, carefully assess your family's abilities, personalities, and needs.

Canoeing isn't only about quiet forays on mellow streams, however. White-water canoeing is fast-paced and exhilarating, and you can discover its challenges on some of the great rivers. Schools throughout the country offer courses for all kinds of families. Teens, especially, may welcome a family vacation if it entails exciting work with skilled instructors on rushing rivers. And parents may come away from such an experience seeing themselves and their teens in a whole new light. The bottom line is this: canoeing is for everyone—from utter beginner to skillful paddler, from quiet nature lover to wild white-water enthusiast, from rambunctious toddler to adventure-addicted teen.

Questions to Ask

Are child-size life vests provided? Any time you're in a boat, you need a Coast Guard–approved safety vest that fits properly. If the company you choose doesn't have the sizes you need, purchase them before your trip.

Are helmets needed? On a lake or pond you probably won't need a helmet, but on any river with even a minimum of white-water, a helmet is a good idea. Ask about white-water helmets for yourself and your children. If the right sizes aren't available from the outfitter, check at an outdoor store that sells equipment for white-water enthusiasts.

Is the guide/instructor trained in CPR, lifesaving, and first aid? What type of emergency equipment does the outfitter carry? When it comes to water and wilderness, accidents can happen—especially with children along. If you are going into the wilderness or will be a long way from a hospital or medical help, someone should be familiar with procedures for reviving and rescuing children and adults. These days many parents themselves take classes in child cardiopulmonary resuscitation and first aid, but you should also ask about an outfitter's training and emergency supplies. Is there, for example, a radio for emergency contact with a home base or local medical personnel?

Are instructors certified by a reputable organization, such as the American Canoe Association or the British Canoe Union? Certification is one important point for comparison among schools and instructors. Most guides are not certified; many, however, are members of state guiding associations, another indicator of commitment to safety and of the attainment of certain quality standards. You should also always ask about experience and the number of years a guide has worked.

What kind of canoes are provided? Different canoes provide different experiences. Some outfitters set their rate based on the number of canoes your family needs. A family of five might all fit in one canoe, depending on the type, or they might require two canoes if only smaller varieties are available. Do you want to learn solo paddling? Do you want to put children in the middle or give them a chance to paddle, too? Do you have lots of gear? There are many options, so ask questions to avoid surprises.

How many miles or hours does the group paddle each day? Multiday trips average anywhere from 5 to 12 mi (8 to 19 km) a day, with participants spending from two to six hours each day on the water. Courses generally require five or six hours a day of paddling, but some have longer days. Base-camp trips are usually more flexible, with options for families to stay closer to camp and do less paddling if they wish.

How many portages/carries are there and how long are they? Portages (or carries, in the Adirondacks) are those places where you must cross land to get from one body of water to another or to go around an obstacle on a river such as a waterfall. When you portage, you carry the canoes and equipment by hand. Although portages are sometimes a necessity, many can be avoided by changing routes. Talk to guides about your family's abilities. Although small children can manage some portages and even help carry equipment, big people take on most of the burden. With portages ranging from a few yards to more than a mile, the route is an important consideration when you're choosing a trip.

What's the group size likely to be? Scheduled trips may take only from 6 to 12 people, especially in wilderness areas where permits are limited. Base-camp trips in state parks often allow for 25 or even 30 in a group. In courses, students are usually divided into groups averaging from three to six people per instructor.

Is fishing a possible activity on the trip? If so, and if you'd like to do a little angling, ask the outfitter for the minimum age for a fishing license in the state where you'll be vacationing and where you can pick one up before the trip starts.

What's included in the course or trip? Course prices listed here cover instruction, equipment, and lunch, unless otherwise noted. For a few your fee pays for lodging, too. Trips include canoes, camping gear (sleeping bags and pads often aren't included), meals, guides, and some instruction, unless otherwise noted. Transportation to and from the put-in and takeout site may be extra.

Instruction

All outfitters in this chapter provide instruction in basic canoeing and general water and wilderness safety. Some teach paddling and maneuvering techniques as a matter of course, others only if asked. Schools are geared for instruction at all levels. Canoeing is appealing because you can begin to do it with almost no instruction, although there are many skills to master if you want to enjoy the sport to the fullest.

Finding the Fun

Northeast: Adventure Quest, Bear Cub Adventure Tours, L.L. Bean, Sunrise County Canoe Expeditions, Wilderness Inquiry. **Mid-Atlantic:** Outward Bound. **South:** Nantahala Outdoor Center, Wolf River Canoes. **Midwest:** Boundary Country Trekking, Gunflint Northwoods Outfitter/Gunflint Lodge, Kayak & Canoe Institute, Outward Bound, Wilderness Inquiry. **Southwest:** Kayak & Canoe Institute. **Rockies:** Boulder Outdoor Center, Denver Museum of Nature & Science. **Canada:** Kayak & Canoe Institute, Sunrise County Canoe Expeditions, Wells Gray Chalets & Wilderness Adventures, Wilderness Inquiry.

Favorite Schools and Guides

Adventure Quest

7+

A little more than 8 mi (13 km) south of Woodstock in east-central Vermont, a 40-acre preserve of green woodlands and rolling hills makes an ideal classroom setting for students at Adventure Quest, one of the country's top paddling and outdoor schools. Although Adventure Quest focuses on teaching children and teens—and excels at doing just that in summer camp programs for kids 7 to 17—its family workshops are every bit as good. Because the workshops are customized, you can schedule them at your family's convenience.

FOR FAMILIES. If you want to learn white-water paddling, sign up for Adventure Quest's open canoeing workshop. An open canoe has special equipment for white-water use; like a kayak, the craft can be rolled, a maneuver in which the boat turns 360° with the paddler still sitting in it. Either one or two people can paddle, using single-blade paddles, but the canoers kneel for stability and better visibility. Like all of Adventure Quest's family workshops, this one gives parents and children the knowledge and skills they need for safe outings on their own, and it's geared to the group's abilities and interests. On average, a group with some canoeing skills but no white-water experience starts on flat water and moves to white-water in one to two days. Participants spend about six hours each day on one of several local rivers—the White, the Ottauquechee, or the Connecticut.

You can book a workshop for one day, but multiday sessions provide a continuity that will get you out on your own faster. Woodstock has plenty of lodging and Adventure Quest has both camping sites and reasonably priced rooms.

Adventure Quest, Box 374, Brownsville, VT 05037, tel. 802/484–3639, www.adventurequest.org. Apr.–Oct.: 1 or more days, $275 per day for up to 4 people, $50 more for each additional family member.

Bear Cub Adventure Tours

5+

In the 6 million acres of northern New York's Adirondack Park, you'll find outstanding canoeing opportunities and a wilderness of surprisingly rugged terrain. More than 30,000 mi (483,000 km) of brooks and streams meander through these ancient mountains, feeding into 1,000 mi (1,610 km) of rivers. If that's not enough, there are 2,300 ponds and lakes. Besides being enthusiastic about taking families into the wilderness, owner Gary Marchuk is certified in canoe instruction, water safety and outdoor emergency care, and CPR. He has studied environmental conservation and also happily shares historical anecdotes—all of which make him a terrific choice for families.

FOR FAMILIES. Bear Cub, based in the two-time Olympic village of Lake Placid, offers customized family canoe trips each summer. These multiday trips mix canoeing with Adirondack history, nature studies, geology, swimming, hiking, fishing, exploring, and camping. These are usually base-camp experiences unless participants would rather organize an overnight trip. Bear Cub also offers scheduled half-day and one-day wilderness trips that families can join.

Adirondack Park abounds in terrific canoe routes, but Gary favors three areas for family trips. The St. Regis Canoe Area, the state's only designated canoe area, has no motorboats or crowds—just beautiful lakes and ponds in an 18,000-acre wilderness area. Remote but easy to access, and requiring only one short carry, the trip from Bog River Flow to Low's Lake makes another great family route. The 14-mi (23-km) Low's provides exceptional lake paddling. Those who prefer rivers can opt for the Raquette, with its rushing falls, splashing otters, and soaring ospreys. Gary has some colorful stories about people who guided and visited here more than 150 years ago.

Canoe clinics for all levels are offered by request. A two-day class on calm and scenic waters teaches basic paddling skills, canoe maneuvers, self-rescue techniques, and all about safety, equipment, and outfitting. A two-day white-water training program for canoers with basic skills takes students from moving water to rapids. Paddling strokes, eddy turns, upstream ferries, wave surfing, river reading, and rescue skills are covered. The number of white-water canoes for rent is limited, so book this program well in advance. A note of caution: biting black flies are present from mid-May to mid-June—bring repellent and netting.

Bear Cub Adventure Tours, Box 1334, Lake Placid, NY 12946, tel. 518/523–4339. May–Oct.: ½–5 days, $55–$145 per adult per day, $45–$90 children 11 and under. The bigger your group, the less cost per person. Ask about clinic prices. Canoe rentals, $35 per day.

Boulder Outdoor Center

12+

The Boulder Outdoor Center (BOC) concentrates primarily on kayaking courses and trips (see Kayaking), but it offers canoe classes as well. The Boulder–Denver area is an excellent beginning point for a variety of adventures, so families can combine canoe instruction with other activities for a multisport vacation. BOC has many years of experience teaching river skills to both adults and children.

FOR FAMILIES. Private instruction for both lake and river canoeing is offered. Your family can learn together at the Boulder Reservoir, on Boulder Creek, or on other local rivers. You can rent what you need, including a canoe, from BOC. Choose either a half- or full day of instruction, and bring along the whole family; with four people, the price goes down.

Boulder Outdoor Center, 2510 N. 47th St., Boulder, CO 80301, tel. 303/444–8420 or 800/364–9376, www.boc123.com. May–Sept.: ½–1 day, $95–$275 per person, depending on the day and number of people.

Boundary Country Trekking

ALL

Minnesota's Boundary Waters Canoe Area (BWCA) is the premier canoeing destination in the United States. Thousands of clear blue lakes mirror the towering pines and granite cliffs of this northern wilderness that stretches across the Canadian border. Linking the lakes are well-worn trails first walked by Native Americans, then by French fur traders and other European explorers. Today families follow these same paths, carrying canoes from one pristine lake to the next on backcountry paddling adventures. Ted Young, Boundary Country Trekking's owner, has guided groups through the BWCA for more than 40 years.

FOR FAMILIES. The Introductory BWCA Canoe Adventure, designed for both novice canoers and families, is a three-day guided trip with two nights of camping in the BWCA. Ted shares his knowledge of local history and lore, and he's ready and willing to teach canoeing and camping skills. Routes vary but generally require five or six portages, the longest of which is about ¼ mi (½ km). You paddle from 5 to 10 mi (8 to 16 km) each day and stand a good chance of seeing moose, loons, ospreys, eagles, or even the ferocious fisher, a relative of the mink. The trip fee covers lodging the nights before and after the trip, either at the company's cabin or in a local inn along the Gunflint Trail.

Ted and his company also run longer canoe adventures for those with boating and wilderness experience, as well as one-day paddles to several lakes. And there are trips that combine paddling with mountain biking for families with older children who want to do a little of each.

Boundary Country Trekking, 7925 Gunflint Trail, Grand Marais, MN 55604, tel. 218/388–4487 or 800/322–8327, www.boundarycountry.com. May–Sept.: 1–5 days, $85–$895; children's discounts vary for each trip.

Denver Museum of Nature and Science

8+

The Denver Museum of Nature and Science, one of the country's best museums of its kind, welcomes families on a variety of outings (see Archaeology Adventures), including canoe trips in Colorado. Museum associates lead the trips with experienced canoe guides, sharing their knowledge of wildlife, astronomy, ancient civilizations, and more. One note: do try to visit the museum itself, as the exhibits are superb.

FOR FAMILIES. The adventures geared to families are the museum's three-day trips down the Yampa, Gunnison, or Colorado River. The Yampa flows through the towns of Steamboat Springs and Craig in Northern Colorado before emptying into the Green River near the Utah border. Families paddle a remote 38-mi (61-km) stretch of it between Craig and Juniper Hot Springs, most of it inaccessible by any other means. High canyon walls, Indian pictographs, eagles and antelope, and lush open meadows make up the scenery in this area of rich geologic and human history. With few rocks or other obstructions, the Yampa is an ideal river on which to practice canoeing technique. The Gunnison is a 41-mi (66-km) trip that begins just below Delta, Colorado, and passes through the Escalante State Wildlife Area and Escalante and Dominguez canyons. Although the upper Gunnison through Black Canyon is a white-water thrill-seeker's dream, this trip follows the lower Gunnison, which is a calmer route for beginning canoeists. You'll paddle past towering walls of red sandstone and hike into canyons with deep swimming holes and waterfalls. Along the way you'll see blue herons, hawks, and eagles above you, as well as ancient petroglyphs etched into canyon walls. Bring a pole (and license) if you'd like to fish.

The Colorado River through Ruby and Horsethief canyons is slightly slower and wider than the Gunnison. The 26-mi (42-km) journey starts south of Fruita, Colorado, in the heart of dinosaur country (see Digging for Dinosaur Bones and Other Fossils). Like the Gunnison, the Colorado flows between massive walls of red sandstone and shale. There are side canyons to explore, petroglyphs to decipher, and wild creatures to spot. Plus, you'll still have plenty of time for swimming and lazing on the riverbanks.

Although you don't need extensive canoeing experience, these journeys have a pre-trip canoe practice session at Denver's Cherry Creek Reservoir a couple of days before the trip begins. There's more advanced instruction on the rivers. Trip cost includes canoes and canoe equipment, life jackets, meals, cooking necessities, and drinking water; participants must bring their own tents, sleeping bags, and pads. Participants must also get to Cherry Creek and the put-in site on their own, though car-pooling is possible.

Denver Museum of Nature and Science, 2001 Colorado Blvd., Denver, CO 80205, tel. 303/370–6304, www.dmns.org. June–Aug.: 3 days, $305 adults, $215 children 8–12.

Gunflint Northwoods Outfitters/Gunflint Lodge

ALL

The Kerfoots excel at introducing families to the joys of the wilderness. They've been in the business for almost 70 years guiding, outfitting, and running Gunflint Lodge in Minnesota's Boundary Waters Canoe Area. If your family already has some experience with wilderness canoeing and camping, the Kerfoots will custom-design and outfit a self-guided paddling adventure for you.

FOR FAMILIES. In summer, canoe trips for families begin and end with an overnight at Gunflint Lodge. One of the best tours is the Guided Whispering Waters Trip, which explores the waterways and old forest wilderness of the BWCA. Here you can watch beavers feeding, listen to stories and the sounds of the forest, and help set up camp. You paddle from three to five hours per day. The Rustic & Plush Combo Package features several days of wilderness canoeing mixed with several days in a modern lakeside cabin at the lodge. While at Gunflint, families can take guided nature walks, boat on the lake, and take a one-hour horseback ride (for kids over age 7).

Gunflint's specialty, though, is personalized guided family adventures of any length and difficulty (or lack thereof). Ask about the number and length of portages (when you have to carry your canoe around waters that can't be paddled) when working out your itinerary. Even if you're not experienced but you'd like to strike out on your own, the Gunflint staff can provide a family orientation course on paddling and camping—and show you a variety of easy routes.

Gunflint Northwoods Outfitters/Gunflint Lodge, 143 S. Gunflint Lake, Grand Marais, MN 55604, tel. 218/388–2296 or 800/362–5251, www.gunflintoutfitters.com. June–Sept.: 8 days, $849–$1,195 adults, $495–$595 children 4–12 for scheduled trips. Rates vary according to length and requirements for custom- and self-guided trips; 25% discount for children 4–12, children under 4 free.

Kayak & Canoe Institute

7+

The Kayak & Canoe Institute, part of the Outdoor Program at the University of Minnesota at Duluth, sponsors some trips but really focuses on instruction. Classes range from the most basic clinic for beginners to certification courses for canoe instructors.

FOR FAMILIES. Two-day fundamentals courses, many over weekends, teach the basics of solo and tandem white-water canoeing. These classes, for ages 15 and up, utilize several high-performance tandem and solo designs. White-water boats are outfitted with thigh straps, knee pads, and floatation devices for maximum control and safety. Most classes are based near Duluth (bring your own bag lunches), but a Fundamentals II course takes place on the Vermilion River, near the Canadian border, and includes camping and meals. Courses teach canoeing basics: equipment design, stroke technique, rescue, river reading, and safety. The main function, though, is to prepare you to outfit your own trip, so instruction is provided on trip planning, route finding, and packing. Families with children ages 7 and up can take private classes in both flat water and white-water canoeing.

In terms of trips, the Institute generally offers one or two canoe outings each year. Past trips include 10-day adventure on Utah's San Juan River, combining moderate white-water canoeing and canyon hiking; a 14-day trip to Manitoba on the Bloodvein River, winding through provincial parks, quiet lakes, and rapids with portages around several waterfalls; and a 14-day northern adventure on the Seal River and into the western side of Hudson Bay where seals, polar bears, and Beluga whales were all in close proximity. Most wilderness trips require at least an intermediate level of paddling.

Kayak & Canoe Institute, Outdoor Program, University of Minnesota at Duluth, 121 Sports & Health Center, 10 University Dr., Duluth, MN 55812, tel. 218/726–6533, www.umdoutdoorprogram.org. Feb.–Aug.: ½–14 days, $170–$1,400 per person, $160 for 2 people taking 4-hr private instruction.

L.L. Bean

8+

L.L. Bean, the outdoor store and catalog company based in Freeport, Maine, has conducted canoeing workshops for many years. The store sells canoes and gear, and classes introduce families to canoeing skills and equipment; there's no pressure on students to buy anything, however.

FOR FAMILIES. The Parent and Child Canoe Camping Trip, offered several times a summer, is one of the best options for families. The three-day getaway gives adults and kids a chance to learn how to plan and pack for an overnight canoe trip, as well as basic paddling techniques. "Leave no trace" camping skills are taught at your campsite on a Maine lake shoreline, and everyone pitches in to put up tents, cook, and clean up. There's plenty of time after chores to tell stories by the campfire.

Families with children age 14 and older can also join four- and seven-day paddling trips on Maine's Moose and Allagash rivers. Abundant wildlife and fine scenery make these excellent canoeing adventures. Trips include all camping equipment but you have to provide your own lodging the first and last nights.. On the shorter side are the 3½-hour Quick Start Your Canoe courses offered near Freeport throughout summer. Participants focus on solo and tandem paddling, refining strokes, and what to do if the canoe capsizes. Instructors also provide tips on loading a canoe and knots to keep it securely tied in place.

L.L. Bean, Freeport, ME 04033, tel. 207/865–4761 or 888/552–3261, www.llbean.com. May–Sept.: 3½ hrs–7 days, $50–$895 per person, $750 for one parent and one child in the Parent and Child course; $375 each additional participant.

Nantahala Outdoor Center

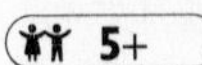

In addition to lakes, rivers, and mountain scenery that entice canoers of every level, western North Carolina can also claim a superb paddling school. If your family is serious about learning paddling or improving its skills, Nantahala Outdoor Center (NOC) stands second to none in terms of quality and variety of courses; you can develop your skills on a number of the area's rivers. Before or after your canoeing adventure, you might visit the nearby Great Smoky Mountains, which draw families from all over the country to hike, trek with llamas, or explore Great Smoky Mountain National Park, among many other outdoor pursuits.

FOR FAMILIES. The one-day Family Paddling Sampler, for parents with kids at least 8 years old, is designed to give families a chance to "taste test a new adventure sport either for a one-day thrill, or as an introduction to a lifetime recreational pursuit." You have your choice of vessels, including canoes. Participants in regular courses—including two- to six-day sessions for novice, intermediate, and advanced paddlers—must be 16. Despite some differences based on group dynamics and the instructor's style, all classes emphasize a mix of effective paddling techniques, safety, and fun. NOC's catalog gives information on assessing your skills; look at it before deciding on a class. There are also multiday adventures that mix camping with paddling white-water rivers in the Chattahoochee National Forest of northern Georgia and the free-flowing Chattooga River, on the border of South Carolina and Georgia. Advanced paddlers who want to check out the white-water river used in the 1996 Olympic games can sign up for paddling the Ocoee, in eastern Tennessee. If you don't want to commit to longer courses, try one of NOC's samplers; the minimum age for these one-day clinics is 13. Meals and lodging, either at NOC in shared facilities or in local motels, are included in multiday course prices.

Another alternative for families is private instruction. Children can take private canoeing classes with parents; a family with a very young child would probably stick to the lakes in the area. Families opting for private instruction pay extra for staying at NOC (about $50–$70 per room per night, if available) or nearby lodging arranged by NOC.

Nantahala Outdoor Center, 13077 U.S. 19W, Bryson City, NC 28713, tel. 828/488–2175 or 800/232–7238 Ext. 600, www.noc.com. Mar.–Oct.: 1–7 days, $95–$1,150 per person; for each adult in the Family Sampler, one child gets a 50% discount.

Outward Bound

14+

Parents and children can choose from two locations to challenge themselves and one another. In Maryland, canoe the upper Potomac as it winds through a series of bends, its left bank rising from several hundred to thousands of feet up into the Green Ridge State Forest. The other location is the Boundary Waters Canoe Area in Minnesota, a land of thousands of lakes and old growth forests. Like all Outward Bound programs, these are not just about learning sports skills; they're about learning life skills, too.

FOR FAMILIES. Weeklong parent–child canoe courses often involve eight-hour days on the water. Maryland courses begin and end in Baltimore; if water levels are low, the course may change to a river other than the Potomac. Typically students learn how to "read" a river as well as safety and rescue techniques. Portaging is one of the challenges faced by students in Minnesota, but by week's end they'll be old hands at this and other canoeing skills. The course, which meets in Duluth, also includes rock climbing and rappelling. As with all Outward Bound classes, canoeing is only part of the focus. The goal is also to improve communication and to foster mutual respect and trust between parent and child.

Outward Bound, 100 Mystery Point Rd., Garrison, NY 10524, tel. 914/424–4000 or 800/243–8520, www.outwardbound.org. June–Aug. 8 days, $995 per person.

River Odysseys West

5+

Known as one of the top family rafting companies (see Rafting), ROW has also ventured into the world of canoeing, and brings the same high-quality experience and exceptional staff to its Missouri River adventure as it does to all of its rafting trips. Co-owner Peter Grubb has taken his own two children on this journey and feels that it not only offers an excellent canoeing adventure but that it also gives kids (and parents) a very special perspective on one of the great chapters in American history.

FOR FAMILIES. There are special family departures on ROW's Journeys of Discovery on the Missouri River; trips set aside for families who want to canoe, play, and learn together. The route follows the Lewis & Clark National Historic Trail on Montana's Wild & Scenic designated Upper Missouri River, and family departures include a historian who likes to work with kids. A recent trip featured Cort Conley, a father and author of nine books on western river lore and history. An expert on western boatmen, river running, and homesteading, Cort shared many stories of the Missouri and the people who ran it or crossed it. Another family departure featured Peter Roop, a Wisconsin State Teacher of the Year who has authored or co-authored 60 children's books, including one about Lewis and Clark and another about Sacagawea, the Indian woman who helped guide them. These trips bring U.S. history to life in a remarkable way, and they give families a chance to relax together while paddling, floating, and hiking through towering bluffs, covered with juniper, cottonwoods, cactus, and wildflowers. ROW's five-day itinerary also takes you 12 mi (19 km) farther than most trips on this river, into the stunning Missouri River Breaks (also known as the Badlands).

As with all ROW journeys, this one includes stellar guides who know how to make a river trip fun. Each day they trek ahead of the group to set up a luxury camp, so that everything is ready when you arrive. They cook gourmet meals and afterward tell stories under the evening stars, tales of the men and women who shaped this country. ROW was the first outfitter on the Missouri to travel by Voyageur canoes, which replicate the experience of the early fur traders. Experienced paddlers, however, can opt for smaller modern canoes instead. Trips begin and end in Great Falls, Montana.

River Odysseys West, Box 579FB, Coeur d'Alene, ID 83816, tel. 208/765–0841 or 800/451–6034, www.rowinc.com. June–Sept.: 5 days, $1,165–$1,265 adults, $995–$1,075 children 10–17, $795–$895 children 5–9.

Sunrise County Canoe Expeditions

5+

Sunrise County is the nickname for Maine's Washington County, in the easternmost section of the state along the Canadian border. Sunrise has been organizing family trips since its inception and prides itself on providing white-water instruction for even young children. A number of its guides are raising their own families "on river."

FOR FAMILIES. Sunrise frequently recommends its "home" river, the St. Croix, for families. The St.Croix flows along the Maine–Canada border and is a short drive from the company's base camp. Designated a Canadian Heritage River, it meanders through a chain of lakes, woodlands, and meadows, providing easy to moderate paddling ideal for families with young children. It's also a principle nesting area for bald eagles. Parents with adolescents and teens might choose to head west instead, joining Sunrise on either the Rio Grande or San Juan River in Texas and Colorado, respectively. Families can explore box canyons and natural hot springs on the Rio Grande and hike to ancient ruins near the San Juan.

Sunrise doesn't offer families-only departure dates, but it does try to group families together. Customized trips are always another option; ask about prices, which vary depending on family size and requirements. Minimum ages are usually determined on a case-by-case basis.

Sunrise County Canoe Expeditions, Cathance Lake, Grove Post, ME 04657, tel. 800/748–3730, www.sunrise-exp.com. Apr.–Oct. (not all rivers all months): 4–6 days, $695–$1,295 per person with discounts for two adults signing up together on some trips; 33%–50% discount for children (age limit varies).

Wells Gray Chalets & Wilderness Adventures

ALL

Based just outside British Columbia's Wells Gray Park, this outfitter specializes in trips to the park's rugged interior. In more than a million acres of backcountry, multihue flower meadows ring still lakes, and snow remains almost perpetually on the surrounding peaks. Lava canyons and ash cones—created by the long-ago volcanic activity that formed much of the area—add geologic texture and contrast. Wells Gray is a destination of extraordinary beauty that draws canoers because of the exceptional lake paddling.

FOR FAMILIES. You can choose between a six-day wilderness canoe trip paddling two magnificent lakes—Clearwater and Azure—or an adventure that combines three days of hiking and three days of canoeing, with one night at a bed-and-breakfast in between. Clearwater and Azure lakes are each 17 mi (27 km) long, with numerous inviting campsites. None, however, is more beautiful than Azure's Rainbow Falls, a wide, white, crescent-shape beach at the spot where Angus Horn Creek tumbles into the lake. Guides try to schedule a two-night layover here to give families a respite from the normal four to five hours of paddling each day. This trip has one short portage.

On the combination trip hikers stay at either Fight or Trophy chalet (both owned by the company), heading out for three- to six-hour hikes each day. There's no need to pack much; the chalets have kitchens, baths, bedding, books, games, and even sandals. For the canoeing portion, the group goes out paddling several hours each day from a lakeside base camp.

There are also three-day canoe adventures, and families are welcome on all of Wells Gray's trips. Owners Ian and Tay Briggs offer parents a wonderful opportunity to introduce children not only to Canada but to Canadian and European families, who are the majority of trip participants.

Wells Gray Chalets & Wilderness Adventures, Box 188, Clearwater, British Columbia, Canada V0E 1N0, tel. 250/587–6444 or 888/754–8735, www.skihike.com. June–Sept.: 3–6 days, $260–$570, 25% discount for children under 14.

Wilderness Inquiry

2+

Wilderness Inquiry (WI), a nonprofit organization, strives to bring all kinds of people, including those with disabilities, into the wilderness. "Our trips are shared cooperative adventures that combine the strength and positive energy of all the members in the group," executive director Greg Lais says. Whether or not disabilities are involved, this goal is exactly what many parents hope to achieve in traveling with their children. Based in Minnesota, Wilderness Inquiry offers canoeing adventures all over the country. Once you book a trip, sit with your kids at the computer and visit the Web site (www.wildernessinquiry.com), which features trip details and facts on local history, geology, and folklore.

FOR FAMILIES. Of interest to parents and children are the family canoeing and camping trips. The base-camp adventures are ideal for younger paddlers—there's no daily packing and unpacking, and routines are easy to maintain. However, camp-to-camp trips allow you to experience even more of the spectacular countryside.

At 32,000-acre Itasca State Park, the state's largest, you can explore prehistoric archaeological sites and 500-year-old native burial areas during a four-day base-camp adventure. The highlight of any visit, though, may be a small stream just 15 steps across—the headwaters of the mighty Mississippi. When you're not jumping back and forth across America's most famous river or relaxing at base camp, paddle on beautiful Lake Itasca or take a hike through the pines. Two other base-camp adventures are the Yellowstone National Park Family Canoe (minimum age 5), with paddling on Yellowstone Lake and hikes to Old Faithful and other park must-sees, and the Superior National Forest Family Canoe (minimum age 8), which takes families to several lakes and offers swimming, fishing, and camping beneath towering red and white pines.

Families with children age 5 and up can join the three-day St. Croix River family canoe trip, which departs just a two-hour drive from Minneapolis. Designated a National Scenic Riverway, the St. Croix flows through remarkably pristine wilderness areas; a portion of the trip takes place in St. Croix State Park. Wilderness Inquiry uses 24-ft cedar-strip voyageur canoes on this trip. Each of these exceptionally stable boats holds from 7 to 10 people and has enough space for a kind of play area for children in the middle. Sandstone cliffs and stands of pine and balsam line a river that was once a loggers' highway and an important gateway for adventurers of the last century, who settled towns such as Stillwater, Taylors Falls, and Lindstrom. There are numerous small islands and sandy beaches to stop at and creek mouths to explore—but no portages. Guides teach basic canoeing techniques throughout the trip.

What better place to paddle WI's handmade voyageur canoes than on a five-day adventure in Voyageurs National Park? Travel as the fur traders did while you explore the Kabetogama Peninsula. From your campsites at Wolf Pack Islands you can paddle Rainy Lake or even cross over the border into Canada to see Sixdeer Island. Listen carefully and you might hear the unmistakable cry of the loon, or the high-pitched howls of wolves in the distance. The park also has one of the highest concentrations of river otters in the United States.

For families who'd like to explore the easternmost country, Maine's Junior Lakes Family Canoe is ideal for families with kids at least 8 years old. Paddle two- to three-person, 17-ft canoes through a series of wilderness lakes on the border of Maine and New Brunswick. These lakes form the headwaters of Maine's St. Croix River and provide the ideal setting for a family introduction to backcountry canoeing. There's a good chance of spotting osprey and eagles as you glide in and out of bays and inlets, and campsites are set in waterside spruce forests.
Wilderness Inquiry, 808 14th Ave. SE, Minneapolis, MN 55414-1516, tel. 612/676–9400 or 800/728–0719, www.wildernessinquiry.com. June–Sept.: 3–5 days, $120–$595 adults, 50% discount for 16 and under.

Wolf River Canoes

ALL

In 1982 Joe Feil opened Wolf River Canoes on what the company considers to be one of the world's greatest canoeing rivers. What makes the Wolf so great? World-class beaches of powdery white sand—and lots of them. If this sounds intriguing, head to the Mississippi coast, about halfway between Mobile and New Orleans. Clean and uncrowded, the Wolf winds peacefully past magnolias and cypresses, wild azaleas and cottonwoods. It is a river that any family, even beginners, can handle without a guide.

FOR FAMILIES. You can plan everything from a paddle of a couple of hours to a camping trip of several days, and Joe will set you up with all the equipment, information, and directions you'll need. The Wolf's sandbars are ideal for picnicking and camping, and there are swimming holes galore. Most trips float you back to your car so you can travel at your own pace. This is a river for all kids; Joe imposes no age limit as long as parents are responsible for their children. Teens can even paddle alone if their parents say it's okay. Joe's canoes are 16 ft long, with two seats, so a child can sit comfortably in the middle. A family paddling with two small children might be able to use one canoe, but talk to Joe first. If you're on a multiday trip, you may want to add a solo kayak for older children or travel in two canoes. As for camping, just pick your sandbar and pitch your tents (Joe will give you tips on what to bring). Then sit back, relax, swim, and enjoy what life on the Wolf has to offer. Although human sightings are rare, you may see great blue herons, ducks, wild turkeys, and otters.

This is an excellent river to tackle on your own, but if you have a group and want a guide, Joe will be happy to make arrangements with you—though you'll still have to help with the camp chores and cooking.
Wolf River Canoes, 21652 Tucker Rd., Long Beach, MS, tel. 228/452–7666, www.wolfrivercanoes.com. Year-round by reservation: 1–4 days, $35–$75 per canoe or kayak, $150 per day extra for a guide.

Resources

Organizations

Several organizations set standards and guidelines for outfitters and guides. **America Outdoors** (Box 10847, Knoxville, TN 37939, tel. 865/558–3595 or 800/524–4814, www.americaoutdoors.org) is the national association for river guides. Ask for its magazine listing outfitters and guides.

The **American Canoe Association** (7432 Alban Station Blvd., Suite B226, Springfield, VA 22150, tel. 703/451–0141, www.acanet.org) publishes a newsletter, *The American Canoeist.* The **Professional Paddlesports Association** (7432 Alban Station Blvd., Suite A-111, Springfield, VA 22150, tel. 703/451–3864, www.propaddle.com) will send information on U.S. guides and outfitters, or you can go to www.propaddle.com.

Periodicals

Canoe & Kayak (Box 3146, Kirkland, WA 98033, tel. 800/692–2663, www.canoekayak.com) prints an extensive list of schools and outfitters in the back of the magazine and has several stories each year about family paddling.

Books

Globe Pequot Press has a veritable library of books on canoeing, among them *Basic Essentials: Canoeing, Basic Essentials: Canoe Paddling, Canoeists Q & A,* and *The Complete Book of Canoeing,* as well as guides to specific areas and rivers. *Paddle America,* by Nick Shears (American Canoe Association, $17.95), represents one man's effort to provide a central place for paddlers to get all the information they need about waterways and outfitters in various regions of the country.

Also See

If your family loves paddling rivers, lakes, and coastal waterways, *see* Kayaking *and* Rafting. Some trips in Wildlife Encounters combine boating and animal watching.

CATTLE DRIVES

My friend David has traveled throughout this country and much of the world. Of all his adventures, the cattle drive he went on tops his list of great vacations. Why? Because, he says, his abilities and endurance were tested, and he was able to meet the challenges head-on. He discovered, in fact, that he was capable of more than he ever thought possible—and it was fun.

That, in a nutshell, is what a cattle drive is about for modern-day families. You work hard, play hard, and fall into your sleeping bag exhausted at night—but you feel great about yourself and your day. What better gift to give children than positive reinforcement about their abilities and accomplishments? And that's not the end of it, for you get to nurture this self-esteem in places of awesome beauty. You also have the opportunity to learn about American history, modern-day ranching, and wilderness ecology.

There's another important aspect to cattle drives, too. Many third-, fourth-, and fifth-generation ranchers have entered the tourism business because they believe it's a way to preserve both their ranches and a unique way of life that's fast disappearing. When your family goes on a cattle drive with an honest-to-goodness rancher, you will hear a heartfelt account of a way of life that shaped America's history and economy for years. City Slickers notwithstanding, cattle drives are an excellent mix of adventure, education, hard work, and old-fashioned fun.

Questions to Ask

How experienced do we have to be? In most cases, not very. Some drives take folks who have never ridden horses; others require riding experience. Generally it depends on the terrain or sometimes on the livestock. Always ask first, so that you?ll choose the right drive for your family.

Is the drive walking only? Can experienced riders go faster? Ranchers tend to put inexperienced riders in the back or on the sides of the drive. If you want to work hard, stay up front. There's usually a place for riders of any ability, but some drives are more suited to very good riders.

How many hours a day are spent in the saddle? Six or seven hours is the average for the drives listed here, with some as few as four or as many as 10. Whatever the length, the bottom line is it's plenty long enough to make you sore if you aren't used to it. Bring acetaminophen or another pain reliever for aches, as well as adhesive bandages and antibiotic cream for saddle sores. A little discomfort is part of the adventure.

If someone gets tired of riding, are there options? On ranch-based drives or on those with a base camp, you may be able to quit early. On drives accompanied by a wagon, you can probably trade your horse for a wagon seat. On trail drives, though, there are few options. Anyone considering a cattle drive should think carefully about whether the family can handle a single-activity vacation for between four and seven long, hard days in a row. Kids, in particular, may get bored on drives that offer no breaks or other activities.

Is this a real drive—that is, one moving cattle for a purpose—or is it simulated? There are outfitters that move cattle solely to entertain tourists, but they are not among those listed here. A ranch with real needs will provide you with a real experience.

How many guests go on the drive? From 10 to 20 is average, plus wranglers and a whole lot of cattle.

Are cowboy boots necessary? What about gloves? Most drovers recommend boots—and not brand-new ones. Get everyone in the family a pair, and break them in well before the drive. Why? Cowboy boots are designed to keep your feet from slipping through the stirrups. If that happened and you fell, you'd probably be dragged by the horse. As for gloves, a pair of decent leather ones will protect your hands from sores and allow you to handle a rope better. Everyone should have a pair.

Do you have helmets? When we asked this question, the answers ranged from "Yep, but no one wears them" to utter amusement. No one will require you or your child to wear a riding helmet, so you have to decide on your own. The bottom line: a helmet is the safe way to go. You can purchase riding helmets at a store that sells riding apparel and equipment.

Where will we sleep? On ranch-based drives guests generally stay in cabins or lodge rooms. Drives that use a permanent or semipermanent cow camp might have wall tents or cowboy teepees. On trail drives a campsite is set up each night, and guests sleep either in tents or cowboy style—under the stars.

Are there showers? Some drives do offer this amenity. I wouldn't pick a cattle drive based on the presence or absence of showers, but if you care about this, ask.

What kind of food is served? Hearty and delicious chow is typical. Besides all the steaks and barbecue and Dutch-oven desserts, most drives also have salads and fruit. Some outfitters can even accommodate vegetarians if asked ahead of time.

Will there be women and girls? Every rancher in this chapter said at least half the participants in its drives are female. In some cases, there are many more women than men. One outfitter speculated that this is because women are often better riders. Whatever the reason, cattle drives are not just a man's world, although men still outnumber women among the wranglers and drovers.

What's included in the cost? Drives include everything from the first day of the adventure to the last, meaning tents or cabins, meals, a horse, some instruction, and stock to move, unless otherwise noted. Some also include lodging the night before the drive starts and transportation to and from the nearest airport. You have to bring your own sleeping bag on some drives but not on others. Airfare to the ranch or meeting site is not included.

Instruction

All ranchers provide riding instruction to anyone who wants or needs it. Children as well as adults have their riding ability checked before the drive starts, and there's discussion of basic safety issues and how to handle life on the trail. If you're a good rider, you'll be taught more advanced techniques of herding, trailing, and rounding up cows. On some ranches you learn to brand, provide health care for livestock, check fence lines, or even help castrate calves. Roping is taught on every drive. Beyond that, most ranchers want to teach participants about the complexities of modern-day ranching and about the cultural and natural history of the land.

Finding the Fun

Southwest: Cottonwood Ranch, Hunewill Circle H Guest Ranch, Rockin' R Ranch. **Rockies:** Double Rafter Cattle Drives, GORP Travel, Hargrave Cattle & Guest Ranch, High Island Ranch and Cattle Company, Laredo Enterprises, Montana High Country Cattle Drive, Off the Beaten Path. **West Coast:** Hunewill Circle H Guest Ranch.

Favorite Cattle Drives

Cottonwood Ranch

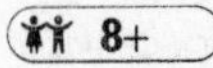

For five generations the Smith family has raised cattle in Elko County, Nevada, on a ranch 6,200 ft up in the high desert. Twelve hundred head of cattle and 100 horses roam some 40,000 acres of ranch property and thousands of additional leased acres. Although many guests come just for the ranch experience, one of Cottonwood's biggest draws is its famous six-day horse drive in June, as well as cattle work throughout the summer.

FOR FAMILIES. If you've never experienced the staggering beauty of a herd of horses on the run over wild and rugged land, sign up for Cottonwood's spring drive. After meeting at the ranch, the group of no more than 16 travels by van to the Jackpot or Elko area, where 100 horses are corralled and ready to move. You'll drive the horses 40 mi (64 km) on the trail along rimrock canyons, over the North Fork of the Little Salmon River, and on to the ranch. Horses move a lot faster than cattle, so the drive requires some riding experience and a minimum age of 12.

In order for your family to try cattle work—gathering, rounding up, and moving the herd to new pastures—your children only have to be 8 years or older, and you don't need a lot of experience. You work mostly at the ranch (on some summer days cattle work is based at a high camp), though you can be out all day working hard if you choose. Accommodations are in a seven-bedroom lodge, with both private and shared baths. There are hayrides, cookouts, and occasional singalongs, but the scenery and wildlife make up most of the trip's entertainment.

Cottonwood Ranch, HC 62, Box 1300, O'Neil Rte., Wells, NV 89835, tel. 775/752–3604 or 775/755–2231, www.guestranches.com/cottonwood. June: 6 days (horse drive), $1,400. May–Sept. (ranch stay only): $200 per day, 20% discount for children under 16.

Double Rafter Cattle Drives

8+

Double Rafter has been operating cattle drives in the Big Horn Mountains on the Wyoming–Montana border for more than 100 years. The ranch was homesteaded in 1887, and the same family has been working it ever since. Today, you can experience the same country, the same 48 mi (77 km), the same canyons as cowboys on this ranch have for over a century. Little has changed as cattle are herded up and down the Big Horn Mountains, from ranch to high country camp and back. You can expect 10 to 12 family crew and 15 to 20 guests. This is work with a purpose: to move the cows to different grazing areas. You aren't just moving them for the sake of giving paying guests an idea of what an old-fashioned cattle drive was like—this is the real thing, just as it's done every year. There are two very different experiences offered.

FOR FAMILIES. The first is a true drive and although you don't need riding experience (the ranch will match you to an appropriate horse), you should be in good physical condition. The minimum age on drives is 12, but talk to rancher Krayton Kerns first; if your child is younger, can ride, and is really enthusiastic about the work, he'll consider it. Over six days and nights you'll help move cows and calves from the ranch to high country (June and July) or the reverse (September). Depending on which drive you're on, you'll move anywhere from 150 to 500 cows with calves from 6 to 16 mi (10 to 26 km) each day, rising early and arriving back at your camp at about noon. There should be time for fishing, hiking, swimming, learning to rope, playing cards, or just resting your weary bones. Lodging is in canvas wall tents, tepee tents, or chuck wagons, and your gear will move either by chuck wagon or pack mule. In June the herd generally goes up to about 4,000 ft, right at timberline. In July, it's on up to 9,000 ft. Along the way you'll pass through narrow, steep-sided canyons and other dramatic landscapes. As Krayton Kerns notes, few people have the words to describe it, and "others, harboring acrophobic tendencies, can't describe it either because they spend a good part of the trip with their eyes closed." At the end of the drives you'll all gather at the historic Mint Bar on Main Street in Sheridan, Wyoming, to take in a last bit of cowboy authenticity before heading back to civilization.

Double Rafter's second adventure, the five-day Summer Cow Camp, fills the bill for families with younger children as well as anyone who wants an authentic cattle experience but one that's somewhat flexible. Once the herds are in the mountains, families can join wranglers on the range as they cut out strays, rope and doctor sick cattle, and perform all the normal chores of wrangling in high pastureland. A good part of the time is spent making sure that the cows stay where they're supposed to. According to Kerns, "Cattle don't really care for USDA Forest Service grazing plans. The task becomes one of convincing 500 mother cows that of 63,000 total acres, they need to spend the next five days grazing only one specific 600-acre canyon. See the problem?" You can also fish and play cards, listen to stories about the history of the area (Custer made his infamous last stand near here), and be as much of a cowpoke as you want.

Fly into Sheridan, Wyoming, 30 mi (48 km) from the ranch, or Billings, Montana, 125 mi (201 km) away, for either adventure. Ranch hands will meet you at the airport or at your hotel by noon, and you'll be in the saddle by 6 PM the first day.

Double Rafter Cattle Drives, ranch headquarters: 521 Passcreek Rd., Parkman, WY 82838; office: 419 E. Main St., Laurel, MT 59044, tel. 406/628–2320 or 800/704–9268, www.doublerafter.com. June–Sept.: 5–6 days, drives, $1,785 per person; camp, $995 adults, $495 children 18 and under.

GORP Travel

10+

In addition to its extensive international trips, GORP Travel offers many Western U.S. adventures. Working with a variety of outfitters and ranchers, GORP has come up with a list that includes some of the best family adventures for experienced and novice cowpokes alike. Among them is an authentic cattle drive.

FOR FAMILIES. Set on a 50,000-acre Montana ranch, The Big Sky Cattle Drive is an adventure that goes beyond just moving cattle (although that's a big part of the work, too). Parents and kids with solid riding experience can walk and ride a few miles in the worn boots of today's real ranch hands, helping to gather, brand, vaccinate, tag, and trail cattle as necessary. Typically guests help move the cows to summer pastures in spring, and round them up for the return to the ranch in fall. There are approximately 4,000 head of cattle, so there's always something to do, but you can take time out to fish, relax at the ranch, or explore nearby Glacier National Park.

Guests generally stay in the ranch's five-bedroom guesthouse, heading out each morning to work the cattle. Accommodations are plain, simple, and homey, and you'll need to bring your own sleeping bags. During scheduled drive weeks, there's often some form of old-fashioned cowboy entertainment at the ranch in the evenings.

GORP Travel, 10055 Westmoor Dr., Suite 215, Westminster, CO 80021, tel. 877/532–4677, gorptravel.gorp.com. May–Oct.: 7 days, $1,329 adults, $999 children 10–12.

Hargrave Cattle & Guest Ranch

10+

Forty miles (64 km) west of Kalispell, Montana, the Thompson River creates a valley of broad green meadows and cool pine forests. Native Americans trapped and fished in the area, and homesteaders made a living growing hay. The Hargrave Cattle & Guest Ranch, with its main buildings tucked at the head of the valley, spreads out over 88,000 acres of mostly leased land. There are only from 15 to 19 guests at a time even in the busy summer season, and Ellen Hargrave makes every one of them feel at home. Visit nearby Glacier National Park while you're here; if you don't have a car, the Hargraves will lend you one.

FOR FAMILIES. This adventure is not a cattle drive or roundup in the traditional sense; you won't be camping out on the trail. During the day, it's an honest-to-goodness cattle experience—but you'll have hot showers and a down comforter on your bed at night. If you want to test your mettle as a cowhand, this is an excellent place.

In calving season (April and May), guests help with a variety of chores. Mothers-to-be need to be checked every three hours throughout the day and night before they give birth, and you can get up with the wranglers to do it. There's also branding, ear tagging, riding herd, or even giving the calves their first vitamin shots.

In May and June the cattle are driven to pastureland about 10 mi (16 km) from the main ranch. The pastured cattle are then rounded up and brought back during September and October. On those drives guests might stay on the trail as long as eight hours a day. Lunch is usually a picnic out of the saddlebag, beside a stream or up on the mountain. Sometimes you're moving moms and calves, other times it's bulls. The opportunities for experiencing real ranch life are endless here; the more you do, the more you'll learn. Families can opt for all the traditional ranch-stay activities, too, like swinging off a rope over the lake, singing cowboy songs, canoeing, fishing, and getting up close and personal with the ranch animals.

Hargrave Cattle & Guest Ranch, 300 Thompson River Rd., Marion, MT 59925, tel. 406/858–2284 or 800/933–0696, www.hargraveranch.com. Year-round (Apr.–Oct. for most cattle work): 6 days, $1,255–$1,840 per person, depending on lodging.

High Island Ranch and Cattle Company

12+, 16+

High Island in Wyoming is not anywhere near water. However, when you stand and look around at the high peaks, you almost feel as if you're on an island—hence the name. Your family can come here to help brand and care for cattle, join a traditional trail drive, or be a part of an authentic re-creation of an 1800s cattle drive.

FOR FAMILIES. The 130,000-acre ranch has several drives and one spring branding week. The drives, which cover about 15 mi (24 km) per day over rough sage and prairie high country, are for ages 16 and up only. Ages 12 and up can participate in branding week at the ranch, where accommodations are in rustic cabins. Fly into Cody, and someone from the ranch will pick you up.

On drives, plan on spending the better part of the day in the saddle chasing and pushing cattle from winter pasture to summer pasture on the vast ranch land. Depending on the season, the drive moves cattle from a lower lodge at about 6,000 ft to an upper lodge at 9,000 ft, or the reverse. The group camps on a different part of the trail each night; although tents are available, almost everyone sleeps in the open unless the weather is really bad. You stay in rooms in the very simple lodges at both ends of the drive. There is sometimes entertainment—a cowboy poet and singer or someone to teach you clog dancing—but most wranglers are happy just to crawl into their sleeping bags for the deep and peaceful sleep of someone who's done a hard day's work and done it well. If you want to learn roping, buy a rope from the ranch, and one of the wranglers will be glad to teach you.

Once each summer High Island re-creates an 1800s drive, in which period clothing is worn and all cooking and sleeping arrangements are as they would have been before the turn of the 20th century. The ranch provides shirts, armbands, dusters, and silk "wild rags" (a bandanna). Don't wear watches or newfangled gear—everyone tries to be as authentic as possible. The biscuits are legendary, and the traditional sweet-and-sour cider vinegar drink is popular. They do use coolers to keep the food safe, but they're covered in canvas, and, yes, outhouses are still available. This is an experience of a lifetime for history buffs; 16 is the minimum age.

High Island Ranch and Cattle Company, 346 Amoretti, Suite 10, Thermopolis, WY 82443, tel. 307/867–2374. June–Sept.: 7 days, $1,300, $1,600 for 1800s–style drive.

Hunewill Circle H Guest Ranch

9+

One of California's top guest and cattle ranches, the Hunewill Circle H is in the eastern Sierra Nevada, near the northeastern border of Yosemite National Park. It's often booked far in advance for the popular summer months, but one of the great experiences here is working the cattle in the fall.

FOR FAMILIES. The big drive takes place the second week of November, when the herd travels from the Hunewill's summer ranch to the winter ranch 50 mi (81 km) away in Nevada's Great Basin area. It's a good choice for families who don't want to sleep out every night. You move the herd over five days, spending anywhere from five to nine hours a day in the saddle. Your route goes through sage and piñon desert, up into the Sweetwater Mountains, and down into the wide, high desert of Nevada; ask about the Paiute cemetery that you pass on the way. Each night vehicles drive you back to the ranch and your comfortable cabin. There's a maximum of 25 participants, who must be intermediate to advanced riders and at least 12 years of age.

In September regular ranch guests can help round up the herd of about 300 and move it from high pastures down to the ranch. You'll be out one full day, returning to the ranch that night. Adult beginning riders and experienced children as young as nine can go on this one. There are other activities, such as roping lessons and Border collie and sheep demonstrations, but riding is the main focus, with horsemanship instruction, swim rides, cavalry maneuvers, and the like. Children six and up can ride the trails at the ranch. It's very much a family operation, run by several generations of Hunewills, including kids. Welcoming and relaxing, it's a terrific experience. Many guests fly into Reno, 120 mi (193 km) away, and drive a rental car to the ranch.

Hunewill also offers special focus weeks at the ranch during the year. Cattle Work Week, typically in May or June, is for intermediate and better riders ages 12 and older. You ride with a Hunewill family member and help with branding, cutting, and moving the cows. In addition to the big fall drives, guests can participate in cattle moves during the regular summer ranch season.

Hunewill Circle H Guest Ranch, in summer: Box 368, Bridgeport, CA 93517, tel. 760/932–7710; in winter: 200 Hunewill La., Wellington, NV 89444, tel. 775/465–2201, www.guestranches.com/hunewill. Sept. (ranch stay, including roundup): 5–7 days, $760–$1,178, depending on cabin; Nov. (drive): 7 days, $1,050; 25% discount for children 10–12; 50% discount for children under 10.

Laredo Enterprises

10+

Lifelong ranchers Bob and Judy Sivertsen own and operate Laredo Enterprises. Although their own Montana ranch isn't conducive to an authentic drive because of farming and development in the area, the Sivertsens wanted to give families an understanding of today's cattle business. To do this, they teamed with the owners of a ranch on the North Fork of the Milk River, less than 30 mi (48 km) from the east gate to Glacier National Park. The ranch is also on the Blackfeet Indian Reservation, and guests have an opportunity to work along with people from the Blackfeet Nation and to learn a little about their heritage. Laredo offers five cattle drives each year.

FOR FAMILIES. At the Rumney Ranch, both children and adults must be experienced riders. This terrain is challenging—50,000 acres of ranch right up against the Rockies. Fly in and out of Great Falls for these five drives in May, June, September, and October (some packages include transportation to and from the airport). Rumney runs more than 4,000 head of cattle, and you participate in all forms of ranch work. Guests stay in the bunkhouse as a rule. Plan on covering from 10 to 25 mi (16 to 40 km) a day, although despite the long hours moving cattle to different pastures, you do return to the ranch each night. During drive weeks there's cowboy entertainment on one or two evenings, and there's always good fishing. The most spectacular evening entertainment at Rumney, though, is viewing the abundance of stars.

Although cattle drives are scheduled on specific dates, the Rumney Ranch will take guests on other weeks as well, and there's a guesthouse in which families can stay. Because this is a working ranch and not a traditional guest ranch, there's no entertainment—in fact, families will probably need to entertain themselves at times during their stay. But there are also opportunities for families to join in with the real work of the ranch, including riding with cowboys and cattle. Families who want to skip ranch work one day can explore Glacier National Park, just 25 mi (40 km) away.
Laredo Enterprises, Box 2226, Havre, MT 59501, tel. 406/357–3748 or 800/535–3802, www.laredoenterprises.com. May–Sept.: 7 days, $1,249–$1,330; parents with 2 or more children get 12% discount off adult rate; also ask about day rates.

Montana High Country Cattle Drive

12+

This organization of five Montana ranchers and outfitters is trying to diversify in order to keep their ranches as they've been for generations. John Flynn, whose family came into the area in the 1860s as miners and horse traders, is the group's point man. Soft-spoken but passionate about ranching and what that life has to offer, he believes those who have participated in a working cattle drive go home with a new perspective on life. There are generally two drives in June and one in August.

FOR FAMILIES. This is about as authentic as it gets. When you sign up to move cattle with this company you'll spend six days out on the trail between Bozeman and Helena, 30 mi (48 km) from the source of the Missouri River. Each of the 40 participants is assigned to a wrangler (four guests to each wrangler) who will assist you throughout your stay. There's also a safety and riding clinic the first morning. Whether you're beginning or experienced, there's a place for you—five or six can even just ride in the wagon.

Depending on the drive, cattle travel from a 4,000-ft valley up to 7,000 ft, through sagebrush, juniper, yucca, and alpine meadows to lodgepole pine and spruce forests, or back down to the ranch. Views of Old Baldy rising nearly 10,000 ft in the Big Belt Range remind you that this is Rocky Mountain country. Plan on four to six hours a day on the trail, which is about how long it takes to move between 400 and 1,200 head of cattle approximately 8 mi (13 km). This is a big drive; the herd is 1½ to 2 mi (2½ to 3 km) long. If you've never seen real cow dogs—usually Border collies and Australian shepherds—hard at work, here's your chance. They're remarkable animals.

In addition to a regular cook, the procession usually includes an authentic restored chuck wagon, from which cobblers, cinnamon rolls, and homemade ice cream are served. The outfitter can accommodate vegetarians with advance notice; otherwise it's mainly barbecue. You sleep in tent camps along the trail. Entertainment might be a singer–poet or the "rattlesnake guy," who brings his snakes out for everyone to see and touch. John Flynn's brother, who has a master's degree in range management, shares his knowledge and demonstrates which high-mountain plants are edible.
Montana High Country Cattle Drive, 674 Flynn La., Townsend, MT 59644, tel. 406/266–3534 or 800/345–9423, www.montanacattledrive.com. June, Aug.: 7 days, $1,550.

Off the Beaten Path

ALL

Bill and Pam Bryan work with many of the West's best outfitters. Because their company specializes in customized vacations and small-group departures, they've had the opportunity to find out from both guests and outfitters exactly what makes a successful western vacation.

FOR FAMILIES. Off The Beaten Path no longer works with specific ranchers just for cattle drives, but if you tell them the type of experience you have in mind and your goals for your family vacation, they'll find a good match. Customizing is one of this company's greatest strengths, and the fact that they've spent many years working with both families and outfitters makes them well-qualified to come up with a trip to meet your vacation needs and dreams. If you've looked through this chapter and haven't found anything that excites you, give Pam and Bill a call. If they can't find what you want, chances are it simply doesn't exist.

Off the Beaten Path, 27 E. Main St., Bozeman, MT 59715, tel. 406/586–1311 or 800/445–2995, www.offthebeatenpath.com. Mar.–Oct.: Days vary. Custom consulting fees: $300–$1,000 per trip depending on length and complexity of itinerary.

Rockin' R Ranch

12+

About 37 mi (60 km) north of Bryce Canyon National Park, the 1,000-acre Rockin' R is in a stunning area of Utah where red-rock canyons open onto wide green valleys. The ranch lodge has 41 rooms, but even with a large number of guests you still experience the land in a very personal way. People tend to be in different areas doing different things. The cattle drives take a maximum of 20 guests at a time.

FOR FAMILIES. The ranch leases 50,000 acres from the forest service; drives take place within the borders of Dixie National Forest. The group stays at one of the ranch's two permanent cow camps. Sweetwater, at 7,000 ft, is set in the foothills of the Boulder Range among the pines. The Griffin Springs camp edges a meadow at 10,000 ft; if you can brave cold water, you can take a swim in the nearby lake and spring. The camps have wall tents and mattresses.

Cowhands stay in the saddle about seven hours a day, moving the cattle, helping doctor any sick stock, and checking miles of fence. Even when the 1,000 head of cattle split into two drives, the herd can still be as much as 2 mi (3 km) long. Everyone is pretty tired at night, but there's singing around the campfire and entertainment by a cowboy poet and a cowboy singer–guitarist. Deer, antelope, and elk are often seen on the trail. The Rockin' R also offers horse-packing trips (see Horse Packing).

Rockin' R Ranch, Reservation Office, 10274 S. Eastdell Dr., Sandy, UT 84092, tel. 801/733–9538, www.rocknrranch.com. June–Oct.: 4–6 days, $625–$1,250 (includes 1 night at ranch before drive begins).

Resources

Organizations

The **Dude Ranchers' Association** (Box 471, LaPorte, CO 80535, tel. 970/223–8440, www.duderanch.org) has information on more than 100 guest ranches in 12 western states and two Canadian provinces. Not all are working cattle ranches, but the association can identify these and help your family choose an appropriate one. The organization's Web site includes links to western gear and wear, travel planning, and answers to frequently asked questions.

Books

The Arbuckle Cafe: Classic Cowboy Stories, by V. S. FitzPatrick (Yellow Cat Publishing), is a fascinating collection of turn-of-the-20th-century cowboy tales, transcribed by a cowpuncher. *Montana Pursuit* (Aegina Press, tel. 304/429–7204), by J. T. Flynn, is Montana cattleman John Flynn's novel. He calls it "an adventure hunting mystery," with lots of local geography and color. If you're driving cattle with him, pick up a copy first.

Also See

If you want a western riding experience that is generally a bit slower and more relaxed than a cattle drive, see Horse Packing. The chapter on Ranches lists other places where you may work with cattle.

COVERED WAGON ADVENTURES

Few experiences give families a feel for the Old West and pioneer life in the way a wagon train can. Some "modernization" to wagons (rubber tires and padded seats) means you'll be more comfortable than pioneers were, yet wagon masters today take care to preserve the authenticity of the experience by following wagon train traditions and historic routes. Education is mixed with fun as guides spin stories about the men, women, and children who persevered in the face of tremendous difficulties to reach the West and about the mountain men, Native Americans, and Pony Express riders who sometimes appeared on the trail.

Because wagon trains are easygoing adventures, they can accommodate a variety of ages in a way many western experiences cannot. In most cases members of your family can ride saddle horses in addition to traveling in the wagons, but you certainly don't have to, so no special skills are necessary. All you need is a willingness to suspend disbelief and for a few days to imagine you are traveling across the United States 150 years ago.

Questions to Ask

Can guests help? Guests are often encouraged to help with camp chores and to learn traditional skills such as cooking over an open fire and driving the wagons. In some cases you are responsible for taking care of the horses and helping set up camp each night. Find out what's expected of your family and especially what the children are allowed to do. Pitching in helps you re-create the real experience.

Are there horses to ride? Typically guests take turns riding a few saddle horses brought along for that purpose. On one particular wagon train all guests have the option to ride for half of each day, but it's not a requirement. Some guests choose to walk part of the way, too, which is in keeping with what pioneer wagon trains were really like. The minimum age for riding horses may be higher than that for riding in the wagons.

What are the sleeping arrangements? Guests on most wagon train adventures sleep in tents provided by the outfitter, though on some trips you may sleep in the wagons. On still others, guests opt to sleep under the stars, the way cowboys and pioneers did. If your children have never slept in sleeping bags or tents before, borrow equipment in order to try this experience or let them test sleeping bags and tents at an outdoor store.

What kind of food is served? Hearty meals are the norm on these trips, with most offering standard chuck-wagon fare—beef, beans, and biscuits are typical.

Some outfitters go farther, with near-gourmet meals, including fresh salads and fruit, as well as fresh-baked desserts.

What kinds of bathroom facilities are provided? Several wagon trains pull a separate wagon with a chemical toilet or other toilet facility. Those that camp on forest service land have access to regular toilets or outhouses. Young children going into the wilderness for the first time may be reluctant to use unfamiliar kinds of toilets. Ask ahead of time so you can prepare your youngsters if necessary. Showers on the trail are rare, but a minimal amount of water for washing up is generally available.

How many miles are covered each day? Traveling between 6 and 12 mi (10 and 19 km) is typical. Wagons are not a speedy means of transportation; instead, they let you settle into a slower mode and take in the country and history in a relaxed way.

Will there be other recreational activities on the trip? Some trips do allow for hiking, swimming, or other activities at the campsites. On many trips, though, it takes an hour or two to set up camp once you arrive; then it's time for dinner and evening activities such as campfire programs and other western-style entertainment. This is why some outfitters think a child should be at least six for this experience. If you don't ride horses and if you get bored sitting, this may not be the trip for your family.

Are the guides knowledgeable about wagon train history and local lore and about the area's plant and animal life? History—both human and natural—is a big part of a wagon train experience, so make sure guides are going to provide that.

Will there be surprise "attacks" during the trip? Although this is fun entertainment for most, young children may be scared by these re-creations of wagon train experiences. Even though outfitters don't like to ruin the surprise, explain that you need to prepare your child ahead of time.

What's included in the cost? Wagons, food, tents, and use of horses for at least part of the time are included on the trips, unless otherwise noted. In some cases you must bring your own sleeping bags. Some outfitters will pick up guests at a local airport or other location; others require you to get to the trailhead on your own. Because wagon trains generally start first thing in the morning and return in the afternoon, you'll probably have to arrange local lodging the night before the trip starts and possibly at the end of the trip, too.

Instruction

A covered wagon adventure requires no prior experience or ability: If you don't know how to set up a tent, the crew will teach and help you. If you or your children don't know how to ride, you'll get some pointers. You'll only be traveling at a walk on the horses, so even the inexperienced should be just fine. On some wagon trains young children may not ride or may have to be led by parents. Take the opportunity to learn a new skill out on the trail, whether it's cooking over a fire or taking care of the horses—the majority of wagon masters and guides really want to share their knowledge with you.

Finding the Fun

Midwest: Grandtravel, Oregon Trail Wagon Train. **Rockies:** GORP Travel, Grandtravel, Myers Ranch Wagon Trains, Teton Wagon Train and Horse Adventure, Wagons West.

Favorite Wagon Trains

GORP Travel

5+

Old logging roads through Bridger-Teton National Forest, just outside Jackson, Wyoming, provide ideal trails on which to relive a piece of American history. The Grand Tetons, the Gros Ventre, and Wind River ranges form an inspiring backdrop. Your wagon train crew will meet your family in Jackson and drive you to the trailhead, which is north of town toward Grand Teton and Yellowstone national parks.

FOR FAMILIES. Pioneers never had it so good. These wagons are cushioned with rubber tires and foam-padded seats that convert into deluxe bunks at night. You can expect four or five wagons on this train and a maximum of 25 people. One benefit of traveling with this group is that they're happy to let guests help drive the wagons. Each guest also rides horseback for half of each day. Children as young as 7 or 8 can ride, but they must have some experience; those 10 and up don't need previous experience. Most days there's time for fishing and hiking, and guests visit a historic homestead, too. At night plan on singing cowboy songs around the campfire.

GORP Travel, 10055 Westmoor Dr., Suite 215, Westminster, CO 80021, tel. 720/887–8500 or 877/440–4677, gorptravel.gorp.com. June–Aug.: 4–6 days, $675–$875 adults, $565–$775 children under 14.

Grandtravel

7–17

Grandtravel's Western Parks, Western Space trip attempts to bring the romance and adventure of the West alive for grandparents and grandchildren. This itinerary, like all of Grandtravel's trips, is specifically designed to meet the needs of both senior citizens and children; travel is primarily by motor coach. But that doesn't mean coddling: Grandtravel is for active people who love new experiences. There's a lot to take in on this journey from Rapid City, South Dakota, to Jackson, Wyoming, including a ride in a covered wagon.

FOR FAMILIES. Two trips—one for grandparents with grandkids ages 7 through 11, one for grandparents with grandchildren from 12 to 17—are offered each summer. The amount of time spent in the bus each day varies quite a bit. The groups visit important landmarks, natural wonders, and national monuments and parks, and participants have a chance to meet Native Americans and cowboys who share their perspective on the West, past and present.

In Rapid City members of the Lakota tribe give a presentation. In Cody, Wyoming, the groups visit the impressive Buffalo Bill Historical Center, which includes the Buffalo Bill Museum, the Whitney Museum of Western Art, the Museum of the American Indian, and the Winchester Arms Museum. You also stop at Mt. Rushmore, in South Dakota, and Devil's Tower, in eastern Wyoming. There's lunch at Old Faithful in Yellowstone, and in Sheridan, Wyoming, you make a visit to a historic ranch to see what life was really like during the early 1900s. On the day of a float trip on the Snake River, the group climbs into covered wagons, accompanied by cowboys and mountain men, for a dinner trip in Cache Canyon outside Jackson.

There is no camping on this adventure (lodging is in hotels with private baths), but you can still appreciate the heart of this experience: the rugged beauty of the West and the strength and courage of its people.
Grandtravel, 6900 Wisconsin Ave., Suite 706, Chevy Chase, MD 20815, tel. 301/986–0790 or 800/247–7651, www.grandtrvl.com. July–Aug.: 10 days, $3,490–$3,690, depending on number of family members.

Oregon Trail Wagon Train

5+

The 2,000-mi (3,220-km) Oregon Trail was the pioneer wagon route from Independence, Missouri, on the Missouri River, to the Columbia River region of the Pacific Northwest. In the 1840s alone at least 10,000 pioneers made the arduous trek through northeastern Kansas, up along Nebraska's Platte River, and on to Fort Laramie in Wyoming. From there they crossed the Rockies at South Pass, journeyed through Snake River country, and if they made it all the way, stopped finally in the Willamette Valley in Oregon. Today, as people rush across I–80 in minivans and RVs, it's hard to imagine what this journey was really like.

FOR FAMILIES. Starting from a base camp in Bayard, just north of the Platte River in western Nebraska, the wagon train makes a circular tour through rolling hills and prairie along portions of the original Oregon Trail. Five wagons for 40 people is typical. Some wagons carry 16 passengers; some hold only four. All of the guides—current or former cowboys or retired farmers—are well versed in the history of the Oregon Trail and the area.

Participants can ride in a different wagon each day to get a different perspective, and many choose to walk much of the route, as the original pioneers did. The group takes turns riding the saddle horses, too. (Children must be at least 6 and have previous riding experience.) At night, before turning in to your tent and sleeping bag (both supplied), you might be surprised by a Pony Express "delivery" or an "Indian attack," after which the visitors will share stories and historical information. Guests are encouraged to participate in camp chores and to lend a hand with cooking.

A noon-to-noon mini-version of this trek, called 24 Hours of 1850, doesn't include as many experiences but still gives you lots of trail history and adventure. Before or after your trip, visit nearby Chimney Rock National Historic Site, the famous landmark on the Oregon Trail that marked the end of the prairie.
Oregon Trail Wagon Train, Rte. 2, Box 502, Bayard, NE 69334, tel. 308/586–1850, www.oregontrailwagontrain.com. June–Sept.: 1 and 4 days, $200 and $550, respectively, for adults; $175 and $450, respectively, for children under 12.

Teton Wagon Train and Horse Adventure

4+

When the wagon master shouts, "Roll the wagons!" the train rumbles onto the back roads of Targhee National Forest, between Grand Teton and Yellowstone national parks in Wyoming. These modern-day prairie schooners, as they were originally named because of their resemblance to "sails on a sea of grass," have rubber tires and padded seats but are otherwise authentic. Gentle riding horses are also available for adventurers who would like to ride from camp to camp, or trail ride farther into the backcountry. Riders have access to waterfalls and viewpoints inaccessible to the wagons.

FOR FAMILIES. Three wagons and up to 40 guests travel to a different area each day, forming a circle once camp has been reached. Two camps are on the shores of alpine lakes, where loons, trumpeter swans, moose, elk, and deer are likely to be seen. The wagon train arrives early enough that guests have time to hike, swim, canoe, or just relax. This range of recreational activities makes the trip perfect for younger children, who may need a change of pace.

Cowboys from the Double H Bar Ranches run the train and provide western-style amenities and entertainment. Meals are cooked in Dutch ovens over an open fire, and evenings are spent around the campfire, singing and listening to cowboy yarns. Mountain men, "Indians," and Pony Express riders pay surprise visits during the trip.

There are U.S. Forest Service outdoor toilets at all campsites. All camping gear, including tents and comfortable sleeping bags, is provided. And remember: this is high country. You need lots of sunscreen during the day and warm clothes at night.
Teton Wagon Train and Horse Adventure, Box 10307, Jackson Hole, WY 83002-0307, tel. 307/734–6101 or 888/734–6101, www.tetonwagontrain.com. June–Aug.: 4 days, $745 adults, $695 children 9–14, $645 children 4–8.

Wagons West

ALL

Wagons West takes willing adventurers through the Bridger-Teton National Forest and into the Mount Leidy Highlands on the northeastern edge of Jackson Hole, Wyoming. This is definitely wagon country, and wagon masters and hands alike are proud of their Western heritage. You can expect about 50 guests on wagon trains with this outfitter.

FOR FAMILIES. All ages are welcome to join the covered wagons as they head into northwestern Wyoming wilderness. You can ride in the wagons—and even help drive them—or ride horses alongside them. There are lots of stops, and you'll usually get to camp early enough in the afternoon to hike, fish, or relax. It's prime wildlife country, too, where you might spot moose, coyote, bear, and raptors. This area is also the calving grounds and summer range for the large Gros Ventre elk herd.

Plan on hearty meals that include filling portions of ham, bacon, sourdough flapjacks, chicken, steak, stews, and salads. Everything is cooked in Dutch ovens over an open flame and served family style from the chuckwagon. At night you can sleep in your wagon, in a two-person tent, or under the stars. However, it gets chilly after sundown even in summer, so bring warm clothes.
Wagons West, Box 1156, Afton, WY 83110, tel. 307/886–9693 or 800/447–4711, www.wagonswest.com. June–Aug.: 2, 4, or 6 days, $340–$865 adults, $300–$765, 14 and under. Four or more booking a 4- or 6-day trek receive a 10% discount.

Resources

Books

To spark children's interest in wagon trains, look up a copy of Ellen Levine's *If You Traveled West in a Covered Wagon* (Scholastic Trade). Another good choice is Kristiana Gregory's *Across the Wide and Lonesome Prairie: The Oregon Trail Diary of Hattie*

Campbell (Scholastic Trade), a detailed, diary-style book describing a young girl's wagon train journey in the mid-1800s.

Organizations

You can get information about the history of the Oregon Trail, as well as a reading list and other materials for families, from the **Oregon-California Trails Association** (524 S. Osage, Independence, MO 64050, tel. 816/252–2276) and **Jefferson National Expansion Memorial** (11 N. 4th St., St. Louis, MO 63102, tel. 314/655–1700).

Also See

For more adventures that can take your family back to the days of the Old West, *see* Cattle Drives, Horse Packing, *and* Ranches.

CROSS-COUNTRY SKIING AND SNOWSHOEING

Cross-country skiing is gaining in popularity in the U.S.—and for good reason. The sport, also known as Nordic skiing, gives families a wonderful workout in the wintry outdoors, often at a lower cost than a downhill-skiing vacation. Although this slower, more easygoing sport may not hold the thrill of downhill skiing, you don't have to contend with the crowds or the noise, and there's less chance for injuries. Cross-country skiers stride and glide through silent, snowy forests into the heart of nature, to backcountry wilderness areas where you're more likely to encounter deer than other humans.

Snowshoeing is also gaining popularity, and equipment can now be found at almost every major ski area. If you can walk, you can snowshoe, which makes this sport an excellent way for families to experience the winter wilderness. Telemarking combines the thrill of downhill skiing with the serenity of cross-country routes, though in spirit it's closer to cross-country skiing. The sport is included in this chapter because a few well-known North American ski resorts are now starting to teach telemarking to children, a sign that it's an up-and-coming trend.

Although most cross-country ski lodges and day-use areas don't feature the extensive children's programs found at downhill resorts, many now carry child-size equipment. Some even have special sleds that parents can use to tow their youngest children behind them as they ski. Lessons and other children's activities are most available during holidays, though some family activities are offered throughout the ski season. Besides ski lodges, multiday tours with outfitters and even single-day ski classes are opportunities for cross-country ski adventures. Most lodges and outfitters have both groomed and ungroomed terrain, which is an advantage if your family has skiers of differing abilities.

The listings in this chapter are an eclectic mix of backcountry wilderness possibilities, courses, ranches, and inns and lodges with either new or innovative family programs. This selection—which focuses on less-publicized establishments rather than well-known cross-country resorts—is by no means exhaustive, as there are hundreds of day-use lodges and ski centers throughout North America where cross-country skiing is available. If you're comfortable skiing without a guide, you can also set out on countless trail systems in national forests and parks. Once your family has some experience, you'll find thousands of trails on which to hone your skills and enjoy winter's beauty far from the madding crowds.

Questions to Ask

What kinds of skiing do you teach? Instruction in the traditional diagonal cross-country stride is commonly available and the most appropriate for families, because even fairly young children can master it. Skating, a style used by more experienced skiers, and telemark, a cross between downhill and cross-country techniques, may also be taught.

Are instructors certified by the Professional Ski Instructors Association? Some terrific skiers may not necessarily be great teachers of skiing. PSIA-certified instructors not only know how to ski, they've been taught how to teach. This can be especially important when it comes to children. Ask the lodge, school, or outfitter if instructors are certified, and particularly if they are trained to work with children. You want an instructor who will use age-appropriate language and have expectations that are on a par with young students' skill and stamina levels.

What kind of clothing and equipment are needed? You work hard and get warm when you cross-country ski, so wearing layers of clothing is important. It's not generally necessary to invest in the expensive outerwear downhill skiers require. Fleece and wool garments and wind-resistant shells are good choices; all clothing should be breathable. Beyond this, the weather will dictate specific clothing needs. Skis, cross-country boots, and poles are pretty much all the equipment you'll need. Many skiers like to take backpacks with them to carry extra clothing, water, and snacks. One tip for parents: If you ski with your children and they're slower than you are, wear extra clothes; you'll get cold going at their pace.

Is equipment available for rent? For children, too? Lodges and ranches usually rent skis, poles, and cross-country boots, but outfitters may not. If gear isn't available, ask for the name of a reputable rental shop in the area. In either case, be sure their children's equipment will fit a child the size of yours—ask specific questions about what you need. Supplies of child-size items are often limited, so try to make reservations for equipment when you make your trip arrangements.

Are trails groomed or ungroomed? Groomed trails (those on which machines have packed down the snow and sometimes even preset tracks) are easier to ski. Families with beginner or intermediate skiers should look for a high ratio of groomed to ungroomed trails. In most cases you'll find a mix of trails, a plus if your family has skiers of different skill levels.

Is there terrain for all abilities? Look for ski territory with a combination of flat, open land—such as meadows—along with steeper, more challenging terrain. It's typical for areas to cover a variety of landscapes.

How long are the trails? Do they connect to other systems? Most trail systems have a number of shorter loops and longer routes, so you can get away from the main area without committing to an all-day venture. Lodges and ranches often border national or state forests or recreation areas, and their trails may connect to a larger network of trails, usually ungroomed, where you can ski for long distances and have the wilderness practically to yourself.

What other activities are available? You will sometimes find sledding, hiking, wildlife viewing, horseback riding, sleigh riding, and other outdoor winter activities in cross-country ski areas. Families who don't want to spend all of their time skiing will probably do best at a ranch or lodge.

What's included in the cost? Accommodations, meals, trail passes (if required), and activities are included in the fee for ranches and lodges, unless otherwise noted. Equipment is occasionally part of a package, as is instruction, but more often they cost extra. There may or may not be an extra charge for tours. Outfitters usually include lodging and meals on multiday trips, guide service, and permits (if necessary); equipment is generally extra. The price for schools covers instruction only, unless otherwise noted.

Instruction

Most guides and tour leaders will teach the basics of cross-country skiing, but if you want to develop more than a passing knowledge of the sport, choose a lodge, ranch, or school where instruction is the focus. That doesn't mean you have to spend a lot of time in classes before you can explore the great outdoors. Unlike beginning downhill skiers, who usually require a considerable amount of instruction before they can venture to most areas of the mountain, cross-country novices can ski many trails while they're still learning. Know your limits, though. Don't tackle long routes unless you have the stamina to finish—there may be no shortcuts back.

Finding the Fun

Northeast: Appalachian Mountain Club, L.L. Bean, Telemark Inn. **Midwest:** Gunflint Northwoods Outfitters/Gunflint Lodge. **Rockies:** Beaver Creek Resort, C Lazy U, Izaak Walton Inn, Lone Mountain Ranch, Off the Beaten Path. **Canada:** Off the Beaten Path, Wells Gray Chalets & Wilderness Adventures.

Favorite Outfitters and Lodges

Appalachian Mountain Club

5+

The Appalachian Mountain Club (AMC) is perhaps best known for its hiking programs and other summer activities (*see* Fishing; Hiking; Backpacking; *and* Trekking with Llamas and Burros), but it does offer a few winter courses. AMC's Catskill campus—near Phoenicia, New York, in the heart of the Catskill Mountains—is just 8 mi (13 km) from Frost Valley Ski Center, an excellent cross-country area. You can bring your own skis or rent equipment at Frost Valley; lodging and meals for families are in the Full Moon Lodge, AMC's Catskill center.

FOR FAMILIES. AMC generally holds its Cross-country Skiing for Families courses each February. Typically there are two instructors for the class of about 20 students, made up of parents or grandparents with children ages 6 to 12. Whether your family includes inexperienced or accomplished skiers, this course is for you. Families are taught together; learning games keep children interested, but the instruction meets the needs of all ages. Instructors cover techniques for negotiating both uphill and downhill terrain, as well as skiing flat terrain using the traditional diagonal stride. Another option is AMC's Winter Family Fun weekend, also in February. Besides cross-country skiing, parents or grandparents with children ages 5 to 10 go tubing, sledding, skating, and animal tracking; there are also winter nature studies. When the sun goes down the group gets together around a campfire and explores trails on a night hike. *Appalachian Mountain Club, Box 366, Longlake, NY 12847, tel. 518/624–2056 for Catskill campus, www.outdoors.org. Feb.: 2 days, $225, 50% discount for children under 10, 10% discount for AMC members. Price does not include nominal day-use fee for Frost Valley.*

Beaver Creek Resort

6+

Beaver Creek is one of the premier ski resorts in the country, part of the extensive Vail family, and about 10 mi (16 km) west of Vail itself. Beaver Creek is a bit smaller and quainter, however, with a stunning central mountain village, ice skating rink, and superb ski school. Best known for its downhill acreage, Beaver Creek also has extensive cross-country trails and a Cross-Country and Snowshoe Center with many terrific family programs—among them, telemark workshops for all levels. Telemarking, a hybrid of downhill and cross-country skiing, opens up a world of new possibilities for venturing into backcountry or onto a variety of trails away from traditional ski areas. Of course, it's a great sport for ski areas, too.

FOR FAMILIES. In addition to general telemark workshops, the center has started offering full-day Women's Telemark Workshops on Saturdays during the ski season. Sundays are Kids' Tele Day for ages 6 through 16. Although parents and kids don't learn together during these workshops, they can at least learn the same techniques over the same weekend. Moms, aunts, or grandmothers who had their lesson the previous day can support and encourage young children who are trying this sport for the first time.

The coolest thing about Kids' Tele Days is instructor Ned Ryerson, better-known as "Tele Ned." A top U.S. telemark racer and the National Chairman of the Tele Ski Association, he's been teaching since 1985 and he's particularly good with kids. His sense of humor, simple language, and vivid imagery help children understand telemark moves, and he's endlessly patient and encouraging. Ned also helped design Garmont's children's tele boot, and he brings children's equipment with him to the workshops.

The center also offers snowshoe outings, classes, and tours for all ages, some including information about the winter flora and fauna of the Rockies.

Beaver Creek Cross-Country and Snowshoe Center, Beaver Creek Resort, Beaver Creek, CO 81620, tel. 970/845–5313 or 800/427–8308, beavercreek.snow.com. Dec.–Apr. (not all months): 1 day, $57 per person, $87 including lift ticket. Children's rentals included in course price; adult rentals, $22.

C Lazy U

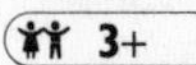

This ranch, tucked high in the Colorado Rockies in a valley carved by Willow Creek, has been open since 1925. Its summer family programs are excellent, but C Lazy U is also a winter wonderland, a paradise for cross-country skiers looking for daylight backcountry adventure and serious nighttime pampering. You can wander over 15 mi (24 km) of groomed trails and 8,500 acres of unspoiled wilderness, of which 850 belong to the ranch. Instructors and guides will help you make the most of your skiing, whether you prefer diagonal style, skating, or telemark. Downhill skiers are not forgotten, though—the ranch provides shuttle service to nearby Winter Park and Silver Creek.

FOR FAMILIES. The ranch's comprehensive children's program is divided into three age groups (3–5, 6–12, and teens) and runs for two weeks around Christmas and New Year's, as well as over Presidents' Day weekend in February. Group sizes vary depending on the number of guests with youngsters. While adults are on the trails, children receive daily ski instruction and participate in other winter activities. Ski games, snow tubing, sledding, and being pulled on an inner tube behind a snowmobile are favorite snow sports. The ranch offers indoor crafts as well, and a skating pond is lighted at night (skates of all sizes are available).

Families can also head out together to ski the groomed trails or the backcountry. At the ranch's Nordic center, cross-country ski gear (included in the price) comes in many sizes—there are even strap-on skis for very small children.

For horse lovers, C Lazy U has a winter riding program. You can use the 10,000-square-ft indoor arena or wander through the valley and mountains on silent, snowy trails for a riding experience that's unique to the season. The ranch's Belgian draft horses can also take you for a whirl in an old-fashioned sleigh.

C Lazy U, Box 379, Granby, CO 80446, tel. 970/887–3344, www.clazyu.com. Dec.–Mar.: 2 days (minimum stay), $150–$240 per night per adult, 40% discount for children under 18. Weekly rates during holidays, $1,700 per adult, 20% discount for children under 18.

Gunflint Northwoods Outfitters/Gunflint Lodge

ALL

At this four-season resort on Gunflint Lake in northern Minnesota, families can take guided and self-guided ski adventures along more than 70 mi (112 km) of groomed and tracked trails through Superior National Forest, which borders the Boundary Waters Canoe Area. Trails range from a flat, easy 3-mi (5-km) loop to longer routes over more challenging terrain. This is one place where you don't need to worry about having enough powder; the average winter snowfall is over 10 ft.

FOR FAMILIES. Families booking the Wild Winter package can take advantage of guided ski trips, snowshoeing, and a half-day each of dog sledding and *skijoring* (dog sledding on cross-country skis). The lodge doesn't have formal ski lessons, but if you need instruction a staff member can fill you in on the basics, and rental skis and snowshoes are included in the package price. The Kerfoots, owners of Gunflint Lodge, recommend a minimum age of 8 for accompanying parents on the trails; experienced adult skiers can carry babies in backpacks. You can stop at any of the four Gunflint resorts to call for a pickup if you're too tired to make it back on skis to your lodge. On the trails, three warming huts with radiant propane heaters make convenient rest stops; the heaters are on timers, so you don't even have to remember to turn them off when you leave.

Although the wilderness skiing is superb, not everyone in your family has to be a cross-country skier to enjoy the lodge. You can relax in a sauna or hot tub or accompany your children on a stroll to search for wildlife. Be sure to head to the main lodge every day at 3:30, when the Kerfoots put 50 lbs (23 kg) of corn out in the yard, and dozens of wild deer arrive for an afternoon snack. At night you can bundle the family up and walk out on the lake for some amazing stargazing.

Gunflint Northwoods Outfitters/Gunflint Lodge, 143 S. Gunflint Lake, Grand Marais, MN 55604, tel. 800/362–5251, www.gunflintoutfitters.com. Dec.–Mar.: Wild Winter: 4 days, $625 adults, 50% discount for children 4–12, children under 4 free. Daily rates: $199–$349 per night for the first two people depending on lodging and meal plan, additional person $40–$72 per night; on weeklong stays the 7th night is free.

Izaak Walton Inn

3+

One of the great cross-country ski inns, Izaak Walton is about 60 mi (97 km) from Kalispell, just outside Glacier National Park in Montana. Now listed in the National Register of Historic Places, the inn was built in 1939 by the Great Northern Railroad to house snow-removal crews. Memorabilia and authentic furnishings carry you back to the romantic era of early train travel, and four renovated cabooses have been converted into guest quarters. Amtrak still stops practically at the door.

FOR FAMILIES. The inn has long been recognized for its superb lessons and tours for adults and experienced skiers, but its innovative children's program is equally deserving of merit. Games and fun activities help build skills and get children used to the winter outdoors. Depending on how many children are present, lessons may be on an individual or group basis. The inn has trails and areas for young children just learning to ski and rents equipment for ages 3 or 4 and up (depending on the child's size); snowshoes are also available.

Package trips are the best way to go here. Families staying on the inn's five- or seven-day plan are entitled to a guided ski tour of Glacier National Park. This all-day tour is best for teens and adults, but groups that include younger children can take half-day tours over Glacier's easier trails. Kick sledding, another activity for families, uses Scandinavian sleds that work something like those used for mushing—but with no dogs. You balance on the runner with one foot and push with the other; since the action is similar to skiing, it's an easy way to get a feel for the sport while having fun.

Izaak Walton Inn, Box 653, Essex, MT 59916, tel. 406/888–5700, www.izaakwaltoninn.com. Nov.–Mar.: 3–7 days, $370– $755 per person for family of 3; children's rates available on packages.

L.L. Bean

6+

L.L. Bean, the famous outdoor and catalog store in Freeport, Maine, has long stocked winter gear and clothing for families, so it's not surprising that its education department—well known for canoeing and fly-fishing courses—also provides instruction in cross-country skiing and snowshoeing.

FOR FAMILIES. All of Bean's traditional beginner courses have a minimum age of 14 and a strong focus on technique. Lessons are conducted on groomed terrain (often on a golf course in Freeport that has groomed tracks) with a mix of easy, moderate, and challenging trails. You'll be taught both diagonal skiing and skating techniques. Instructors stress learning balance, sliding, and feeling confident on skis; they also discuss proper clothing and ways to stay warm while skiing. You must arrange your own lodging, but the school supplies a list of local accommodations. The courses are just 1½ hours long, but instructors may take an additional 15 minutes at the end of class to answer students' questions about specific problems. For intermediate and advanced skiers, the Level II and Level III courses are about two hours long. Courses are scheduled most Saturdays throughout the ski season. Although equipment isn't provided, you can rent or buy it at the L.L. Bean store.

Bean also has some overnight programs, including a wilderness winter getaway, scheduled each winter. Families stay at the renowned Balsams in New Hampshire, skiing or snowshoeing with guides on the resort's extensive and well-maintained trails. Meals, lodging, instruction, and equipment are included in the price. Whether or not your whole family signs up for LL Bean's weekend course, the Balsams is a terrific resort for parents and children.

Bean also occasionally offers parent-and-child cross-country skiing courses for parents with kids between the ages of 6 and 13. The emphasis is on fun, with games like pizza tag, hand soccer, and dodge ball, which help families learn the basics of gliding, turning, and stopping. If this format appeals to you, check the current catalog or call for more information.

Finally, Bean also runs snowshoeing workshops in the same area of Maine as its half-day skiing courses. The emphasis is on technique: using poles, negotiating hills, and making repairs on the trail. Equipment is included in the price.

L.L. Bean, Freeport, ME 04033, tel. 888/552–3261, www.llbean.com. Jan.–Feb.: 1½ hrs–3 days, $30 per parent/child pair, $10 each additional family member in parent-and-child courses, $20–$60 per person for regular courses; $485–$622 per person for 3-day Winter Wilderness program, depending on dates and accommodations.

Lone Mountain Ranch

3+

Lone Mountain is a year-round family guest ranch near Montana's Gallatin Canyon, down the road from Big Sky Resort and a short drive from the northernmost border of Yellowstone National Park. The ranch's renowned naturalists don't stop working in winter; instead, they lead cross-country ski tours, including treks into the Spanish Peaks region and Yellowstone's backcountry, that meld excellent skiing with education about the winter environment and the area's natural history. The 23 roomy one- and two-bedroom log cabins at the ranch have rock fireplaces or Franklin stoves in addition to electric heat, and the outdoor hot tub is popular with all ages. Lunch on the trail is an impressive gourmet affair—and no one skips the fantastic meals in the tremendous log-and-stone dining lodge.

FOR FAMILIES. There's no formal children's program at Lone Mountain in winter, but youngsters are always welcome. Group lessons are an option if enough kids are at the ranch; otherwise, individual instruction can be arranged. Rental equipment fits ages 3 and older. Lone Mountain has nearly 50 mi (81 km) of tracked and groomed trails that wind through meadows, up along ridges, down into mountain valleys, and through portions of the Gallatin National Forest. Miles of ungroomed trails give you access to exceptional backcountry skiing.

A particular favorite with families is the groomed Ranch Loop, a 3½-mi (6-km) trail across rolling terrain that takes you through aspen groves and open meadows. Ermines, moose, coyotes, and a variety of winter birds may be seen along the trail. Because the path goes into wilderness areas but also passes near ranch buildings, you feel both miles away and close to home, which can be comforting for children and beginners.

Among the backcountry tours with naturalists (all at an extra charge), Spanish Peaks is appropriate for teens and adults with skiing experience. Yellowstone is less technical, and older children with good skiing skills are welcome on the shorter (four- to five-hour) tour over moderate terrain. Before joining a tour, every guest must take one lesson or be otherwise evaluated by the staff.

Families also have the option to snowshoe, go sledding, or head for the downhill slopes at Big Sky, 7 mi (11 km) away. Horse-drawn sleighs can carry guests to a lantern-lighted log cabin for dinner.
Lone Mountain Ranch, Box 160069, Big Sky, MT 59716, tel. 800/514–4644, www.lmranch.com. Dec.–Apr.: 7 days, $1,525–$2,250 adults, $950 children 4–12, $425 children 2–3. Price does not include rentals and lessons.

Off the Beaten Path

12+

Although Pam and Bill Bryan of Off the Beaten Path are known primarily for their customized summer vacations in the Rockies, Southwest, and Alaska, their organization also offers a variety of winter escapes, including cross-country ski adventures in Yellowstone National Park, at the B Bar Ranch, and in the Canadian Rockies.

FOR FAMILIES. In addition to skiing, most of these trips feature other activities that make wintertime totally fun for children and parents. Among them: snowshoeing, wildlife viewing (especially in Yellowstone), tobogganing, sleigh rides, skijoring, and soaking in hot springs. Although the scheduled cross-country ski trips are not geared toward children, the company works with many families on a custom basis, so you can adapt one of the trips with regard to timing, destination, and the amount and level of activity. Custom trips are definitely pricey, but every detail—accommodations, food, guide services, and daily skiing—is taken care of. Your guide can take you on a variety of trails, from groomed to pure untracked backcountry powder, and instruct you on skiing techniques. You'll also learn about the diverse ecosystems through which you venture.

Access to Yellowstone is limited, so you must book a custom trip there at least nine months in advance. The other destinations are more flexible, and even last-minute arrangements may be possible. The company can also arrange all travel and ski rentals (at an extra charge) if you wish.
Off the Beaten Path, 27 E. Main St., Bozeman, MT 59715, tel. 406/586–1311 or 800/445–2995, www.offthebeatenpath.com. Dec.–Mar.: 6–8 days, $2,000 and up; custom nonguided trips available for less.

Telemark Inn

ALL

A range of adjectives fits the turn-of-the-20th-century Telemark Inn, 10 mi (16 km) from Bethel in southwestern Maine: Rustic, elegant, intimate, remote, and historic all accurately describe the wood-paneled retreat, which has hand-built cabinetry and a huge stone fireplace. Well known for its llama treks in summer (see Trekking with Llamas and Burros), the inn becomes a winter mecca for families that like to cross-country ski. Six rooms sleep two to four guests each, and everybody likes the wood-fired sauna. Many lodging packages are available, some with breakfast only, some with three meals. You can also get hearty home-cooked meals packed for the trail.

FOR FAMILIES. Twenty miles (32 km) of groomed skiing trails surround the inn; most are wide and tracked for both diagonal and skating styles. Families with ski experience may want to head into the maintained trails beyond the inn, which are part of the backcountry system of the White Mountain National Forest. At night there's skating on a pond lighted by kerosene lanterns and gatherings in the lighted tepee out on the meadow. Parents can choose a romantic ride in a horse-drawn sleigh built for two or a family outing in the six-seater.

Instruction in both traditional skiing and telemark is available for an extra charge. Families have the option to rent equipment even for very young children; request this when you make your reservation. Parents can strap on a *pulk* (a ski sled used to pull toddlers) if their stamina and skiing ability allow. Small children get the feel of ski movements by holding on to a nylon rope with a handle, like those used for waterskiing, while being pulled by parents or instructors.

Families that want to try something really cool should ask about skijoring, a sport that originated in Norway. Also known as dog skiing, skijoring resembles dogsledding on cross-country skis. One or more dogs pull you with a specially designed nylon rope and harness. There's no minimum age (6- and 7-year-olds have skijored successfully at Telemark) but you do need to be at least an intermediate Nordic skier and have a good rapport with animals. Young skiers can practice on the close-in flat areas; more experienced skiers can tackle the extensive trail system. Telemark Inn has a kennel full of dogs trained in skijoring, and guests are welcome to bring their family dog—which should weigh at least 35 lbs (16 kg) to learn the sport. However, families considering the latter option should be serious about the sport and check first with the inn; note that dogs stay in a kennel, not in your room. Skijoring is included in the Sunday–Friday five-day ski package.

The inn is beginning a program for handicapped skiers, so ask about it if someone in your family is physically challenged. This is also a great place for snowshoeing, and equipment and guides are available.

Telemark Inn, RFD 2, Box 800, Bethel, ME 04217, tel. 207/836–2703, www.telemarkinn.com. Dec.–Mar.: 2–5 days, $240–$599 adults, $170–$499 children under 15. Weekends and holidays, $120 per day per adult, $85 for children, which includes lodging, meals, and activities. Ski lessons run $15 per person per hr for group, $25 for private ski or skijoring instruction.

Wells Gray Chalets & Wilderness Adventures

1–2+

Of the three chalets owned and operated by this group, only Fight Meadow Chalet is really suitable for family cross-country skiing. If you're up to the challenge of a helicopter flight to get there and several days of skiing in wilderness areas inaccessible to the less adventurous, this Canadian company, based eight hours from Seattle, Edmonton, and Calgary, will provide a memorable guided experience for your family. Once you have plenty of experience and knowledge of backcountry safety and survival skills, you can book the chalets on your own, including the two that require heavy ski-touring and ski-mountaineering equipment.

FOR FAMILIES. All guides are certified instructors and will teach families about skiing, wilderness travel, ski mountaineering, and avalanche safety. Fight Meadow Chalet is surrounded by a large alpine meadow system that is ideal for novice skiers in spite of its remoteness. More advanced slopes are also easily accessible, so there's something for everyone. Families take a helicopter to the chalet; the inbound flight is part of the trip cost. Unless they're up for a four- to eight-hour trek (depending on skiing ability), most are also flown out (an extra C$110). The road out is the only marked trail; the rest of your skiing is on unmarked, ungroomed, untracked backcountry snow. Scheduled trips to the chalet are limited, but groups of 6 to 12 can arrange their own trip on the dates of their choice.

Wells Gray Chalets & Wilderness Adventures, Box 188, Clearwater, British Columbia, Canada V0E 1N0, tel. 250/587–6444, www.skihike.com. Dec.–Apr.: 5 days, C$770, 25% discount for children under 13.

Wilderness Inquiry

1+

One of the great things about this company is that it welcomes every kind of adventurer, from young to old, from unskilled to advanced, and from athletic to physically or mentally challenged. Whatever the makeup of your group, Wilderness Inquiry will accommodate you.

FOR FAMILIES. The Winter Family Weekend, at a cabin lodge on the St. Croix riverway along the Wisconsin–Minnesota border, is the quintessential cold-weather adventure for all ages and includes a little bit of everything. In addition to cross-country skiing you can try dog sledding, snowshoeing, family games, and nature programs. Although the temperature can range from -40°F to +40°F (-40°C to 5°C), you won't be roughing it. Accommodations are in cozy, rustic cabins set amid pines and rolling hills. The modern lodge facilities include heated showers (a short distance from cabins), and trails have warming huts to rest in while you're exploring. Adventures here are easy and for everyone, as they bring out the very best that winter has to offer.

Wilderness Inquiry, 1313 5th St. SE, Box 84, Minneapolis, MN 55414-1546, tel. and TTY 612/379–3858 or 800/728–0719, www.wildernessinquiry.org. Jan.–Mar.: 3 days, $495 adults, $245 children under 17.

Resources

Books

The Hut Handbook, by Leigh Girvin Yule and Scott Toepfer (Westcliffe Publishers, tel. 303/935–0900), is an excellent guide for any family considering a backcountry hut experience. Whether you ski or snowshoe in, or stay for a night or longer, there's a ton of information here, including a chapter just for parents and children.

Organizations

The **Cross Country Ski Areas Association** (259 Bolton Rd., Winchester, NH 03470, tel. 603/239–4341) has information on the importance of lessons, how to dress properly, how to get started in the sport, and great places to do it. The organization's Web site, www.xcski.org, lists available publications, travel and tour information, and links to other cross-country ski sites—it even provides details on skiing with your dog. It also includes a state-by-state listing of the more than 200 members of the association, with information about trails, ski schools, available rental equipment, day care, general facilities, and more.

Periodicals

Cross-Country Skier (MD 60, 1107 Hazeltine Blvd., Chaska, MN 55318, tel. 612/361–6760 or 800/827–0607), published October–February, is an excellent publication for beginning skiers and those interested in the latest gear, cross-country getaways, or even racing. Among the many articles of interest to parents are some on children's gear and cross-country ski vacations for families.

Also See

For more winter adventures, see Dogsledding. Many of the adventures also include some cross-country skiing.

DIGGING FOR FOSSILS

Dinosaurs may be extinct in the real world, but they're alive and well in the hearts and minds of children everywhere. Long before a certain purple dinosaur commandeered the airwaves, dinosaurs were a formidable presence in children's books, games, TV shows, movies, and imaginations. Ask your average 5-year-old how to pronounce *hadrosaur,* and she'll tell you without stumbling over a syllable. When my own daughter, Kira, was 5, she would quiz her father and me about dinosaurs endlessly, but we never reached her level of expertise. If Dinamation International Society's Family Dino Camp had existed then, I would have taken her in a flash.

Today families can choose among places all over the world where they can dig for bones and help in paleontology labs. Most of these digs are dinosaur related; however, whale fossils, mammoth and saber-toothed tiger bones, as well as plant fossils, are found at working digs, and you or someone in your family might be the first to uncover them for all the world to see.

Paleontology is mostly painstaking, slow, hot, and tedious work. Consider in advance whether your child has a real interest in and the personality to enjoy this type of multiday vacation. Even Dino Camp, which offers a variety of child-friendly activities, is best for youngsters who already appreciate the subject. Of course, some children do discover a love of paleontology once they get involved, but it could just as easily turn out the other way. Teens and parents as well should fully discuss the itinerary, accommodations, hours, and location of a particular trip before committing. These experiences are definitely work. They're also great fun—if you're into it—and always an incredible learning experience. Because multiday digs can be too much for some families, I've included one-day dig opportunities as well. These can also be a good way of trying out the experience before signing up for a longer trip. Whichever type of adventure you choose, you just might find that at the end of the trip, you'll be able to match your offspring's knowledge, if not their all-embracing love, of these prehistoric wonders.

Questions to Ask

Is it possible to talk directly to the expedition coordinator or leader? In many cases this is a prerequisite. The trip leader wants to make sure that you are right for the trip and that you're aware of what the expedition entails. For parents it's especially important to discuss a child's ability, experience, and interest with someone who's been out in the field.

What are the typical conditions? Some work sites are extremely primitive; others are in towns with modern conveniences and amenities. You might be in the desert or by the ocean. Knowing the conditions can help you find the expedition that meets your family's needs.

What accommodations are available? Tents, dorms, hotel rooms, condos, government or university housing—all these are possibilities. What can your family handle? How well will you fit into community housing? This is an important consideration for any trip.

Has an expedition uncovered an important fossil lately? Dreams of a big find are part of the draw for this kind of vacation. Ask in advance how many bones or fossils have been uncovered at that particular site and how many have been uncovered by trip participants like you. Neither you nor your children should have unreasonable expectations, but dreams are definitely in order.

Is there lab work or other work related to digging? You might have a chance to assist in a real paleontology lab; to record, sketch, or keep notes out in the field; or to analyze soil samples or amber. Paleontology encompasses a variety of skills.

What kind of clothing is appropriate? Much digging work is hot and dirty. You may also hike long distances, and digs may or may not provide shade or shelter from the elements. Even in the desert the best clothing may be long-sleeve cotton shirts and long pants. Boots are probably preferable to sandals on many sites, and hats can be an important accessory. Review clothing lists carefully, paying particular attention to sun protection.

Will my child and I spend all our time together? Usually this is the case, but at places such as Dinamation International Society's Dino Camp, you do not.

Are other activities available? Is there anywhere to swim? Does the schedule allow time to hike or bike or eat out or shop? Does the area have museums or other local points of interest? Some trips provide opportunities for such activities; other digs, particularly those in remote areas, are strictly geared toward accomplishing work. If this matters to you, choose accordingly.

What does the expedition cost include? Accommodations, food during the trip (participants often help with cooking), and local transportation are included, unless otherwise noted. Transportation to and from the expedition site is usually extra. Expeditioners who will be camping out will probably need to bring their own sleeping bags and, perhaps, tents. Because accommodations vary greatly, be sure to find out what you're paying for. Day dig fees generally include lunch and sometimes snacks.

Instruction

It's assumed that most people do not know a great deal about the intricacies of digging for fossils, so lectures, talks, and hands-on lessons are very much part of the fun on this type of adventure. Reading lists of books and other materials about paleontology are often part of the pretrip information for expeditions. Any advance reading you do will definitely enhance your family's experience.

Finding the Fun

Midwest: Earthwatch Institute, The Mammoth Site. **Southwest:** Denver Museum of Nature and Science. **Rockies:** Denver Museum of Nature and Science, Museum of Western Colorado, The Wyoming Dinosaur Center. **Canada:** Royal Tyrrell Museum. **Mexico:** Earthwatch Institute. **South America:** Earthwatch Institute.

Favorite Expeditions

Denver Museum of Nature and Science

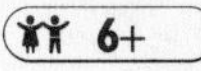

Put children, rafting, and dinosaurs together, and you have a perfect family adventure package. Among its many outdoor study programs, the museum generally schedules a family rafting trip in Utah each summer that touches on paleontology, geology, river ecology, and anthropology, in addition to plain old river-rafting fun. You do not need to be a museum member to join their trips.

FOR FAMILIES. Families in The Jurassic Journey/Green River Raft Trip meet the trip's study leader in Vernal, Utah at the Utah Field House of Natural History. After a tour of the museum, it's on to Dinosaur National Monument and Fossil Bone Quarry, where huge dinosaur fossils have been excavated. Outside the monument, families hunt and dig for their own fossils and visit Indian rock art sites. Days two through five, it's on to the Green River to raft through 2,000-ft Lodore Canyon. Off the water, guides lead hikes to ancient native sites and historic outlaw cabins, with excellent chances of seeing bald eagles, bighorn sheep, and river otters. In-camp games highlight the natural environment of this southwest river canyon. Scientists from various disciplines lead the trip, and all children between ages 6 and 12 receive a Dinosaur Discovery Kit with fun activities and games.

Denver Museum of Nature and Science, 2001 Colorado Blvd., Denver, CO 80205, tel. 303/370–6304, www.dmns.org. July: 4 days, $769 adults, $600 children 6–12.

Earthwatch Institute

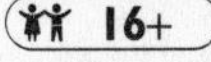

Earthwatch helps fund several fossil-finding programs, in addition to dozens of other scientific projects around the world. As part of that funding, Earthwatch arranges for adventurous participants to join scientists on site and work as assistants. Your fee partially defrays the cost of running the project. As scientists find it increasingly difficult to get funding from such traditional sources as the government and universities, organizations like Earthwatch become even more valuable.

FOR FAMILIES. In light of increased evidence of global warming and changes in the level of the world's oceans, it is all the more important to learn about the effects of protracted climate change on habitats and animals. In Tecolatlan, Mexico, a rugged volcanic landscape of the Sierra Madre, and Guanajuato, east of the Sierra Madre range, two paleontologists have been studying an animal migration that occurred when sea levels were lower and opened a land bridge between South and North America. Doctors Oscar Carranza Castaneda and Wade Miller have 56 years of field experience between them, and you can join them in surveying the desert hills for fossils, chiseling out bones, gluing found fragments, and screen-washing sediment for teeth, seeds, and bones that are the keys to past environments.

What makes this area so important is a mass migration north and south that began 3.5 million years ago. At this time, camels, giant ground sloths, mastodons, glyptodonts (Volkswagen-size armadillos), early horses, and carnivores—including the infamous saber-toothed cats—traveled through the isthmus of Central America, leaving an amazingly rich fossil record of their journey. Since 1990, Earthwatch teams have collected some 5,000 specimens at these sites, including the most complete fossil horse ever found in Mexico. Volunteers share rooms in hotels; the Parador del Cortijo Hotel in San Miguel de Allende, the base for the Guanajuato digs, even has a pool.

Perhaps no site in the world is as currently intriguing to paleontologists as the area dubbed Triassic Park, a desert valley of eroded formations and soaring cliffs in south central Argentina. Discoveries span the entire Triassic period, when dinosaurs first appeared and then dominated the world for the next 160 million years. Scientists and Earthwatch volunteers have already unearthed four new specimens of Eoraptor, as well as the first known infant rhynchosaurs. Participants are based in a camp without running water or electricity, so previous wilderness experience is suggested.

Closer to home is an Earthwatch dig near the town of Marmarth in southwestern North Dakota, where paleontologists are gathering evidence that supports the theory that a meteor did, in fact, crash into earth 65 million years ago and was the primary cause of the demise of dinosaurs. At this site volunteers stay in private rooms in a local historic house. Earthwatch volunteers also dig in Hot Springs, South Dakota, a site famous for mammoth remains. Here, in the southwest corner of the state, locals are justifiably proud of the relics of these woolly creatures. They've raised money to fund continued research and helped build a complex over the site that shades workers from the sun and allows tourists to watch the digging. Expedition participants stay in local homes and can expect a warm welcome from Hot Springs residents. *See also* The Mammoth Site, *below.*

Scientists ask Earthwatch for funding throughout the year, so sites do change. Ask for the latest information when you call.
Earthwatch Institute, 680 Mt. Auburn St., Box 9104, Watertown, MA 02471-9104, tel. 617/926–8200 or 800/776–0188, www.earthwatch.org. Year-round (not all digs at all times): 7–15 days, $995–$1,795.

The Mammoth Site

7+

In 1999 The Mammoth Site celebrated the 25th anniversary of its discovery during excavation for a housing project. Happily, the housing project was forgotten when the first mammoth bones and tooth were inadvertently unearthed, and The Mammoth Site in Hot Springs, South Dakota, became one of the nation's most important paleontological digs and one of the world's largest exhibitions of excavated Ice Age mammal remains in situ. While only day digs are offered here, Hot Springs is the southern gateway to the Black Hills, an area where family adventures and learning experiences abound (*see* Covered Wagon Adventures, Rock Climbing, *and* RV Adventures).

FOR FAMILIES. A visitor center covers the sinkhole where mammoths were trapped and died 26,000 years ago. Because it's covered, the site is open year-round and in poor weather. Walkways allow you a close-up view of scientists and volunteers working at the site (including Earthwatch volunteers here in June and July, *see above*), making it a particularly child-friendly excavation. Parents and children can watch paleontologists and marvel at the huge size of "Sinbad," a life-size replica of a Columbian mammoth, or check out the area where "Napoleon Bone-A-Part," the most completely articulated skeleton uncovered here, was found lying on his back. While going from the parking lot to the main building you'll get a sidewalk geology lesson, which outlines the geologic formation of the Black Hills area. There's also a touch-screen exhibit in the visitor center explaining the geology of the Black Hills, the Ice Age, and plate tectonics. There are guided tours of the site leaving every 15 minutes in summer up until 45 minutes before closing time, which is 8 in the evening from mid-May through most of August. Tours are given less frequently off-season and not at all between November and February.

Each summer the site runs a Junior Paleontologist Excavation program. Interested children from age 7 to 15 can practice excavation techniques using real tools, learn to identify fiberglass replicas of mammoth bones, take field notes, and map areas. The program runs every afternoon at 3.

The Mammoth Site, Box 692, 1800 Hwy. 18 Truck Rte., Hot Springs, South Dakota, tel. 605/745–6017, www.mammothsite.com. Museum: daily year-round, $5.13–$5.40 adults, $3.51 children 6–12, free children 5 and under. Junior Paleontologist Excavation program: mid-June–mid-Aug. daily, $6.48.

Museum of Western Colorado

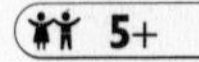

The Museum of Western Colorado runs several museums in and around Grand Junction and Fruita, Colorado. Among them is Dinosaur Journey, with its fantastic lifelike robotic dinosaurs, real fossils, and a working paleontology laboratory where many of the fossils found in the area are prepared. It's from Dinosaur Journey that the working digs originate.

FOR FAMILIES. One-day adventures run most Tuesdays and Thursdays throughout summer. These are full-day programs in which families spend the mornings working side-by-side with paleontologists uncovering 100- to 150-million-year-old bones from the bottom of prehistoric lakebeds in the area around Fruita and Grand Junction, Colorado. Typical bones of this region are those of the Upper Jurassic meat-eater Allosaurus and the giant plant-eaters Apatosaurus and Camarasaurus. More recently, bones of the armored dinosaur Mymoorapelta have been found. After lunch, families tour Dinosaur Journey and go behind the scenes at the lab to learn the art of preparing bones for display and study.

On three-day digs the group visits three different dinosaur excavation sites in the area: Rabbit Valley, Split Rock, and a site near Douglas Pass. Families also tour the museum and then cast and prepare their finds in the working lab. The adventure starts and ends with a group barbecue. Lodging for both day and multiday digs is on your own.

Museum of Western Colorado Dinosaur Expeditions, Box 20000, Grand Junction, CO 81502-5020, tel. 970/242–0971 or 888/488–DINO, www.wcmuseum.org. June–Aug.: 1–3 days, $95–$695.

Royal Tyrrell Museum

7+

Alberta's Royal Tyrrell Museum, the first Canadian institution devoted entirely to paleontology, is in Drumheller, about 90 mi (145 km) northeast of Calgary and 180 mi (290 km) south of Edmonton. The museum is named for Joseph Burr Tyrrell, who found the first dinosaur skeleton in the Drumheller area in 1884. The area is rich with fossils, a fact reflected by the museum's expansive collection. Here you'll find displays of more than 200 dinosaur relics, most of which were found in the Drumheller vicinity and in Dinosaur Provincial Park, 120 mi (193 km) to the southeast. The dinosaur specimen collection is the largest under one roof anywhere, but the museum also has family and children's dig programs that vividly bring to life the dinosaur era and the advancements of paleontology.

FOR FAMILIES. Day Digs are for adults and for children ages 10 and older accompanied by parents. Available weekends in June, daily in July and August, the one-day digs give families the opportunity to work with museum staff excavating real bones and recording scientific data at a site in the Red Deer River Valley, only minutes from the museum. Advance reservations are required. The day starts at 8:30 AM with a behind-the-scenes tour of the museum's fossil collection. After a short van ride and an easy, 10-minute hike to the site, participants (limited to 12) dig most of the day. You're back at the museum by about 4, and as the dig fee includes museum admission, you'll probably want to spend the remaining hours of the afternoon exploring the museum and viewing the many fossils that were mapped and collected just as you did it on your dig.

Children too young for Day Digs or who would rather spend time with peers can opt for Vacation Day Camps, designed for ages 7 through 12. The camps, which run in the afternoon from about 1 to 4:30, offer a mix of activities. Campers hike in the surrounding badlands, dig in the fossil beds, create a cast of a fossil to take home, and play a dinosaur survival game (apparently the dinos who met their demise in this area 65 million years ago were unaware of how to play). Families can get back together at day's end to see the museum or to explore Drumheller. For family members of all ages who'd rather not dig, there's the two-hour Dig Watch—a guided tour of the quarry, with lots of information about the dinosaurs who lived in Alberta and a chance to talk to the museum's working paleontologists.

Summer in Alberta's badlands can be hot (typically 86°F–100°F), but with clouds and wind the area can be cool, too. So be prepared for a range of temperatures. As for lodging, Drumheller has everything from campsites and hostels to hotels and bed-and-breakfasts. And when you've seen all the dinosaurs Drumheller has to offer, head to Dinosaur Provincial Park for more.

Royal Tyrrell Museum, Box 7500, Drumheller, Alberta, Canada T0J 0Y0, tel. 403/823–7707 or 888/440–4240, www.tyrrellmuseum.com. May–Aug.: Day Dig, C$85 adults, C$55 children 10–15; Vacation Day Camp, C$25 children 7–12; Dig Watch, C$30 for a family of 4.

Wyoming Dinosaur Center

ALL

The Wyoming Dinosaur Center dig site in Thermopolis has unearthed one of the largest dinosaur finds in recent history. What makes it particularly unusual is the number of species uncovered in this one area. For instance, they discovered one of the most complete camarasaur skeletons ever found, along with the remains of apatosaurs, allosaurs, stegosaurs, diplodocus, and others. Lots of human types come to Thermopolis, too: some to see the mineral hot springs and surrounding park, some to enjoy the Wyoming Dinosaur Center's excellent museum, some to participate in real paleontology work—and some come for it all!

FOR FAMILIES. There's no minimum age for Dig-for-a-Day, where families work beside paleo-technicians. It's demanding work, though, and children and adults should be prepared both physically and mentally. This is not a re-created site but one in which scientists are still making important discoveries. Typically diggers are on site from about 8:30 to 4; however, buses come and go throughout the day, so it's possible to leave earlier.

If you want to split up for part of your stay, there are several options. Kids' Dig is for children from 8 to 12, while Teens' Dig is for those from 13 to 15. Although younger groups are involved in activities of their own, parents and older teens can try Dig-for-a-Day. Kids' Dig is typically offered once each month in summer. The two-day program includes digging for bones at the working site, taking dino art classes, going on geology walks in Hot Springs State Park, and learning answers to such questions as "How many Big Macs could a T. rex eat?" (The answer, in case you can't wait, is several thousand, assuming the meat-loving rexes spit out buns and lettuce.) Teens' Dig runs once in August. It's a 1½-day program giving teens a chance to dig for dinosaurs, prepare bones in the lab, and cast dinosaur bones. Families get back together at about 4.

Nondiggers can explore the center's excellent museum, with its life-size dinosaur skeletons, displays, and dioramas. The museum has a prep lab, too, where visitors can watch paleo-technicians working on bones found at the dig site. Family members who don't want to dig but do want to see where the bones are can take a bus from the center for a site tour. There's a combination ticket that includes the museum and dig site tour. At day's end families can regroup and head to the park to soak their own bones in the hot springs.

For multiday trips, families make their own lodging arrangements in town at one of the many motels, hotels, bed and breakfasts, campgrounds, or RV parks.

The Wyoming Dinosaur Center, Box 868, Thermopolis, WY 82443, tel. 307/864–2997 or 800/455–3466, www.wyodino.org. Year-round (weather-permitting for digs): Dig-for-a-Day, $250 per day for a family of 4; discounts for multiday digs; Kids' and Teens' Digs, $50; museum and site tour ticket combination, $36 for a family of 4.

Resources

Books

Many children's book publishers have dinosaur books, but Dorling Kindersley offers one-stop shopping for dinosaur lovers. Titles for younger children include *The Big Book of Dinosaurs, Walking With Dinosaurs: 3-D*, and the *Ultimate Dinosaur Sticker Book*. Older children and adults can check out *Dinosaurs and How They Lived, Prehistoric Life, DK Pockets: Dinosaurs*, and *The Ultimate Dinosaur Book*. Clarion Books also has an interesting take on these prehistoric giants, *Dinosaur Parents, Dinosaur Young*, by Kathleen Weidner Zoehfeld. Using evidence from the most recent fossil finds, Zoehfeld shows that many dinosaurs were actually caring parents.

Dino-Trekking: The Ultimate Dinosaur Lover's Travel Guide, by Kelly Milner Halls (John Wiley & Sons) lists just about every place across North America where you can see a dinosaur indoors or in its natural habitat, including many of the places listed in this chapter. The author also provides sources for hard-to-find, must-have dinosaur items, such as dinosaur soap (particularly useful after you've been out in the field digging).

Dinosaur Safari Guide, by Vincenzo Costa (Voyageur Press, tel. 651/430–2210 or 800/888–9653), lists more than 160 dinosaur quarries, museums, parks, and trails throughout the United States and Canada. Costa also provides an excellent pronunciation guide and solid introductory material about dinosaurs, as well as a discussion of current extinction theories. The book is now out of print; try on-line booksellers and libraries.

Products

Coop's Maps (Lone Mountain Designs, tel. 800/259–3139, www.coopsmaps.com) publishes a series of four regional map guides to North American dinosaur sites and museums. They can be found in bookstores.

Also See

If digging is what you love to do, look into family camps at ancient Native American ruins and other types of digs described in Archaeology Adventures.

DOGSLEDDING

Dogsledding may well be on the farthest edge of "soft" adventure. This is not a sport for timid spirits; it's for the adventurer who wants excitement that pushes the limits. Working with the dogs is physically demanding and involves spending a lot of time in the cold—bone-chilling cold. Temperatures as low as -40°F (-40°C) are common, and if you are miles out in the wilderness, you can't suddenly change your mind about the trip. You must be prepared, and you must really want to go. That goes for your children, too. They need to be ready for cold, hard work, including caring for the dogs, and real wilderness.

But if the thrill and romance of dogsledding appeal to your family, you'll find it to be one of the all-time great adventures. Dogs run at a fairly fast pace—it's not uncommon to travel between 30 and 40 mi (48 and 64 km) a day—so you can cover a good amount of wintry territory. By the end of your trip you'll feel a closeness to your dogs, to your guides (some of whom may be natives whose people have traveled this way for generations), and to the raw and wild land through which you'll dash. Ask anyone who's ever done it; they'll tell you how the experience changed them and that they are the better for it.

Questions to Ask

Will we mush our own sled and dogs? Some trips give every participant a sled to work; on other trips you share sleds with a family or staff member and spend time snowshoeing and cross-country skiing in addition to mushing (as traveling by dogsled is called). Decide what activity your family wants most and go with the outfitter that provides it.

How many miles are covered each day? Typically, anywhere from 15 to 35 mi (24 to 56 km) traveled over a four- to eight-hour period make up a day of mushing, though there are variations. Ask before you sign up, and consider how strenuous the itinerary is and how strong your family's abilities are before making a final decision.

What is the temperature going to be on the trip? The temperature in northern Canada will likely be well below zero in March but a relatively balmy 15°F to 20°F (-9°C to -7°C) in May. If you have a 12-year-old, you might choose the warmer May trip. A cold child is definitely a miserable child, and if your children are unhappy, in truth, you will be, too.

What outerwear or gear is provided? Some outfitters supply nothing; others offer traditional caribou clothing, parkas, special boots, and gloves, in addition to sleeping bags and tents. Check and recheck the clothing lists outfitters send you and ask questions about gear. If you're depending on the outfitter to provide severe-weather outer clothing, make sure it's available in your child's size as well as yours. If you bring your own, do not skimp and do not deviate from the outfitter's suggestions. The winter wilderness is a deadly place without proper clothing and equipment.

How much camp and dog work is expected? On some trips clients and guides work equally, setting up camp, harnessing and unharnessing the dogs, feeding and caring for the dogs, and helping prepare meals. Other outfitters offer a more catered experience. If you are real doers, go with an outfitter that will depend on you to be a working member of the expedition.

How long have you been running dogs in this area? Knowledgeable guides are especially important when you're dealing with severe conditions and extreme temperatures. You want a company with several years' experience not only in the area but also with the particular itinerary. Before you plunk down a considerable chunk of change, you want to be sure that all possible kinks have been worked out. You're also looking for a crew that will know how to deal with emergencies small and large quickly and in a professional way.

What kind of accommodations and meals are available? Cabins, tents, igloos, and even hotel rooms are possibilities. Winter camping can be surprisingly cozy and comfortable, but if it's not for you, or if you have younger children who might not be up to this challenge, choose an outfitter with more permanent lodging. As for meals, some outfitters offer a selection, and much of the food is incredibly good. Even if it isn't, it tastes great in the frozen wilderness. Food is fuel out in the cold, so most meals are the real stick-to-your-ribs type: stews, chili, spaghetti, and lasagna, and snacks such as gorp and brownies. Alcohol is generally not part of the menu.

What's included in the cost of the trip? Most dogsledding adventures start and end in remote wilderness areas, so you'll probably pay extra for transportation there. In addition, because of the location and limited transportation, you may have to overnight at your own expense before and/or after a trip. The per-person prices for all trips listed here include lodging or camping, meals, guides, instruction, sleds, and dogs, unless otherwise noted. You may be lent some expedition clothing and supplies; however, you will have to buy, borrow, or rent quality cold-weather gear of your own, including, in some cases, sleeping bags. Local transportation or pickup at airports might be available at no cost or for a nominal fee, so ask.

Instruction

The time spent on instruction depends in part on how involved you are in driving and caring for the dogs; much of it will take place during the trip. But no matter how many times you watched *Sergeant Preston of the Yukon* as a child, your family will need instruction in driving a sled. Good dog teams are valuable, and no musher will turn his or her team over to someone who can't drive a sled properly. Moreover, dogsledding can be dangerous; by listening to your guide and learning the proper commands, safety procedures, and techniques, you ensure your family's safety as well as that of the dogs and anyone else on the trail.

Finding the Fun

Northeast: Adventure Guides of Vermont. **Midwest:** Boundary Country Trekking, Gunflint Northwoods Outfitters/Gunflint Lodge, Outward Bound, Trek & Trail, Wilderness Inquiry. **Rocky Mountains:** GORP Travel. **Alaska:** GORP Travel. **Canada:** Arctic Odysseys, Boundary Country Trekking, Kanata Wilderness Adventures/Wells Gray Ranch, Snowy Owl Sled-Dog Tours.

Favorite Outfitters

Adventure Guides of Vermont

8+

Adventure Guides of Vermont (AGVT) is the customer service branch of the Vermont Outdoor Guide Association, a professional guide association and adventure travel network. Its members offer more than 70 outdoor activities throughout Vermont and New England, many with family programs. Although Vermont has no guidelines or standards for outfitters, Adventure Guides requires that its members meet any existing national standards for each specialty and that all guides be certified in CPR, first aid, and wilderness first aid. Among AGVT's members are several dogsledding guides, some perfect for families. Among them is Ed Blechner, who owns and operates Konari Outfitters. He's a former teacher who still visits schools in the Northeast and educates children about winter outdoor skills and about dogs and dogsledding. He loves to work with families and knows just how to present the necessary information.

Most of the trips are in and around Goshen and the Green Mountain National Forest, both in central Vermont, or around Lake Champlain. Goshen, once called Moosalamoo (meaning "Moose here") by the native population, doesn't have all that many moose these days, but it does have rolling hills, forests, and historic Native American sites and trails. Snowmobiles like the area, too, and they pack down the trails perfectly for the sleds. You may run into some snowmobilers, and you'll certainly see cross-country skiers. Still, winter travel in Vermont forests is light in comparison to summer months. Lake Champlain stretches 120 mi (193 km) and touches Vermont, New York, and Canada. Two-thirds of it lies in northwestern Vermont, and you can travel with your dogs around these shores if the snow is right.

FOR FAMILIES. Ed will take children as young as 8 only if they can ski moderately well. There's no riding on these trips, which range from single-day to five-day outings. You either mush (all members of the group take turns) or cross-country ski. Occasionally there's snowshoeing, too. That doesn't mean you have to be an expert, however. The guides take one family out at a time, and the trip is organized at the pace you can handle. February has the best conditions for dogsledding in either area. Don't forget to ask about skijoring, which amounts to being pulled on skis by a single dog. You might fall a lot, but the youngsters will love it. Outfitters supply tents on overnights; bring your own sleeping bags or ask Adventure Guides about renting locally.

Adventure Guides of Vermont, Box 3, North Ferrisburgh, VT 05473, tel. 802/425–6211 or 800/425–8747, www.adventureguidesvt.com. Dec.–Mar.: 1–5 days, $150–$565 per person for a family of 3 or more.

Arctic Odysseys

12+

Arctic Odysseys pioneered consumer-oriented group travel in the High Arctic, and though the company changed ownership in 1994 there isn't a better outfitter with which to explore the almost unimaginable treasures of the seemingly infinite Arctic wilderness. Customized trips and small groups (between one and three people per guide) are the trademark of the company.

FOR FAMILIES. You and your Inuit guide will plan your family's personal dogsled odyssey; the five-day and nine-day itineraries start and end in Ottawa, Ontario. Children and adults must be in excellent health and good physical condition. Although trips are available mid-March through May, for families with children owner Robin Duberow recommends May, when the temperature warms up to 15°F to 20°F (-9°C to -7°C).

On this trip through Nunavut in northern Canada (formerly the Northwest Territories), you spend the first and last nights in a hotel in one of several Inuit communities on Baffin Island. Tents or traditional snow houses (igloos) provide shelter on the other nights of your journey. Itineraries vary according to weather conditions and what you and your guide decide, but you'll typically travel to an inland lake as well as to the open sea and the very edges of the ice floes. You may encounter polar bears, seals, or ptarmigans, and (conditions permitting) you'll ice-fish for arctic char. The most rewarding part of the experience, however, may well be the chance to experience a world unknown to most through the eyes of a people whose ties to the land remain strong and deep. If three or six nights out in the Arctic seem too much for your family, you can opt to add extra nights in the hotel ($140 per person per night) and travel by dogsled on day trips only.

During the very cold season traditional Inuit caribou clothing is available for rent; children's sizes are available. The outfitter will send you a list of clothing and gear and give you the names of catalogs and regional chains from which you can purchase it. The trip's cost includes two nights in the hotel and the flight between Ottawa and Nunavut.

Arctic Odysseys, 2000 McGilvra Blvd. E, Seattle, WA 98112, tel. 206/325–1977 or 800/574–3021, www.arcticodysseys.com. Mid-Mar.–May: 5–9 days, $3,275–$4,000.

Boundary Country Trekking

9+

These folks started offering dogsled trips in 1978, and they've been giving ordinary adventurers extraordinary thrills ever since. Most trips take place in northern Minnesota's winter wonderlands—the Boundary Waters Canoe Area, the wild and scenic Brule River valley, and Superior National Forest. The company headquarters is near Grand Marais on the Gunflint Trail (Route 12), about 130 mi (209 km) north of Duluth. It's here, on the rugged coast of Lake Superior, that many of the sledding journeys begin. Trips are limited to six participants. Accommodations vary with the particular trip but may include yurts (dome-shape tents or huts) along the trail, rustic cabins, a homey lodge, or Arctic Oven tents (which can hold a heater).

FOR FAMILIES. Best for families, especially those with children in the 9- to 12-year-old range, is a three-day mushing excursion through the Boundary Waters Canoe Area and Superior National Forest. BCT doesn't allow passengers in the sled baskets, but will allow children as young as nine to drive a sled, usually one with just two dogs so that it's manageable. And, of course, guides will teach everyone all they need to know to mush safely and have fun doing it. Parents should know that on family trips, mushing time may be shorter than usual because children will probably want to head back to the cabin sooner than adults might.

Although family adventures vary greatly, the average mushing distance on most trips is between 20 and 25 mi (32 and 40 km) per day; on some of the longer trips you may travel farther, but you won't do it on an empty stomach. Meals include such treats as grilled rainbow trout and a Mongolian fire-pot dinner for those overnighting in a yurt. Two nights are spent in a cabin, the third in a yurt. While there are no specific family departures, the BCT Web site posts dates families have scheduled so others can join those trips if there's room. There are two- to five-day scheduled trips in Minnesota, or you can set up your own customized camping trip for any dates between November and March as long as dogs are available. Sleeping bags and pads are provided on all camping trips. This company also offers eight-day treks through the Canadian Arctic. *Boundary Country Trekking, 7925 Gunflint Trail, Grand Marais, MN 55604, tel. 218/388–4487 or 800/322–8327, www.boundarycountry.com. Nov.–Apr.: 2–8 days, $695–$1,895 per person.*

GORP Travel

You can experience the power and majesty of the Brooks Range as generations of Alaskan natives have—on a traditional mushing sled, with only the sounds of your dog team racing and the swoosh of the runners over pure north-country snow. Yet dogsledding through the Arctic wilderness requires no previous experience; you need only a sense of adventure and good physical condition because you'll be traveling 15 to 30 mi (24 to 49 km) in four to eight hours each day. Depending on the trip, accommodations are in lodge rooms, tents, or communal cabins, and everyone helps with chores.

GORP Travel, which contracts with top outfitters, puts you in the capable hands of the Mackey family, well known in the dogsledding world since several family members have won the Iditarod (also known as the Yukon Quest), the 1,049-mi (1,689-km) race from Anchorage to Nome in which exhaustion and rampaging moose are just two of the difficulties racers encounter.

FOR FAMILIES. Families with kids 12 and up can try two- and three-day lodge adventures, which begin with a one-hour flight from Fairbanks to Bettles in the Alaskan Arctic—with views of the Brooks Range and Gates of the Arctic National Park. The historic Bettles Lodge, with its family-style meals and Jacuzzi, is your base. You'll learn the art of mushing on the first day, then spend the next few days exploring the numerous surrounding trails before returning to the lodge each evening. If you wish to tour the village and meet local Eskimos, that can be arranged. Lodge trips run from December 1 through April 15.

Everyone works together on the eight-day trips, which run during February and March. These trips start from Bettles and take you along the Koyukuk River and through the boreal forest, where wolves and caribou roam the high, rugged peaks. The first and last nights are spent at the Bettles Lodge; on the other nights you stay in heated wall tents along the trail. Late-spring trips have warmer temperatures (lows below zero at night but in the teens and 20s during the day) and as much as 15 hours of daylight. On clear nights you will have a chance to experience nature's pyrotechnics with the aurora borealis. Airfare between Fairbanks and Bettles is $225 per person; trip prices do include transportation to and from the airport in Bettles.

Closer to home are the three- to four-day Wind River Range Trips where you travel at the speed of dog exploring the headwaters of the Wind River and the mountain peaks of Wyoming. The Wind River Range offers dramatic and changing topography. You might run through snow-laden forests or dash across the frozen flats high up on the Continental Divide. Under the careful guidance of veteran musher Scott Smith, you'll be taught basic techniques and traditional mushing commands, and learn firm control of your rocketing sled. Yet as with any dogsledding adventure, it's the relationship with the dogs themselves over the course of the trip that your family will remember most. Wilderness yurts and a variety of secluded backcountry lodges provide warmth and comfort come night, when it's time to come in from the trails. These trips are for families with teens 16 and older. On all of these trips, participants must mush their own teams and sleds. With prior notice, riding passengers can often be accommodated.

GORP Travel, 1055 Westmoor Dr., Suite 215, Westminster, CO 80021-9962, tel. 877/532–4677, gorptravel.gorp.com. Dec.–Apr.: $675–$2,270 per person.

Gunflint Northwoods Outfitters/Gunflint Lodge

4+

The Boundary Waters Canoe Area wilderness (BWCA) encompasses more than a million pristine acres of forests and lakes in northeastern Minnesota. Ideal for dogsledding, the area receives an average snowfall of more than 10 ft each winter. Here you can find the kind of solitude that few modern-day families ever experience. Gunflint Lodge, on Route 12, the famous Gunflint Trail, serves as base camp. The lodge has 24 winterized cabins with kitchens, in addition to the main lodge, which houses the reception area and dining hall. The lodge sits on the shores of Gunflint Lake, which is divided almost in half by the border between Minnesota and Canada. In winter, as in every season, families are warmly welcomed.

FOR FAMILIES. Get an introduction to dogsledding in the Wild Winter package, which is really an introduction to winter activities of all kinds. You and the kids can try cross-country skiing, snowshoeing, and a half-day of dogsledding during the four-night stay. The package includes all activities, plus lodging, meals, and rental equipment. And if the days rev you up and give you a feeling of accomplishment, the nights—spent in a first-class cabin with fireplace, hot tub, and sauna—are all about cozy togetherness.

Throughout winter Gunflint offers daily dogsled rides on which mushers take two guests out with a team of 10 to 12 huskies. Capacity is limited, so the lodge suggests making reservations for dogsledding when you book your accommodations.

Gunflint Northwoods Outfitters/Gunflint Lodge, 143 S. Gunflint Lake, Grand Marais, MN 55604, tel. 800/362–5251, www.gunflintoutfitters.com. Jan.–Mar.: 1 hr–4 days. Rides $30–$158 per person, package $625 per person.

Kanata Adventure Specialists/Wells Gray Ranch

6+

Western Canada remains a rugged land of wild, untamed beauty, with mountain ranges that rise from deep blue lakes into piercing blue skies. You can experience the region's vast winter landscape with the help of Kanata Adventure Specialists, which makes all the bookings for Wells Gray Ranch. Popular with Europeans and Canadians but less well known to Americans, this year-round guest ranch sits at the entrance to Wells Gray Park, one of British Columbia's largest provincial parks. Riding is the main summer activity, but in winter the Kanata dogs and guides are busy giving ranch guests and nonguests the thrill of sledding.

FOR FAMILIES. Sign up to mush or ride (a sled can hold one musher and one child riding) on five- or eight-day adventures. For the most part adults will do the mushing; however, a strong preteen or teen with an interest in learning can probably do so. Owner Mike Mueller says parents should talk to him about their child before deciding on a trip. If Mike thinks it will work out, he'll bring a lighter sled and run it with fewer dogs for a young musher.

The five-day Musher Package takes you from the ranch to Grizzly Mountain Plateau, where you'll spend two nights in a rustic log cabin at a base camp. Each day you'll mush over abandoned logging roads, along lakeshores, and over mountain ridges. Those who choose the eight-day trip spend the first few nights at the ranch. After a training day, you head out for day trips and then follow the itinerary of the five-day adventure. You have to bring your own cold-weather clothing and sleeping bag or rent from Kanata (no children's sizes are available for rent, though).
Kanata Adventure Specialists/Wells Gray Ranch, Box 1766, R.R. 1, Clearwater, British Columbia, Canada VOE 1NO, tel. 250/674–2774, www.canadian-adventures.com. Dec.–Mar.: 5–8 days, C$850–C$1,850 per person, 25% discount for children under 12.

Outward Bound

14+

Outward Bound's dogsledding and cross-country skiing courses, held in Minnesota, are among its most challenging. That doesn't mean your family must already be expert in or even familiar with winter skills, but you must all be physically and mentally prepared for the challenges you will face. Your reward for such hard work is the self-empowering knowledge that you can succeed in ways you never believed possible.

FOR FAMILIES. In December and March parents and teens can take the combination dogsledding and cross-country skiing course together. You'll spend eight days in the Boundary Waters Canoe Area, traveling the silent, snowy forests and lakes by skis and by dog team. Up to six participants mush and ski from four to six hours, covering 2 to 10 mi (3 to 16 km) a day. You don't need to be an expert skier—beginner level is fine. In addition, you'll learn how to care for the dogs and run them, how to construct a winter shelter, and how to remain safe and comfortable during winter camping. There's a chance to try snowshoeing, too. As with all Outward Bound courses, everyone helps set up camp and prepare food each evening. And although winter sleeping bags, gear, and parkas are provided, you'll need to bring your own clothing, including boot inserts.
Outward Bound, 100 Mystery Point Rd., Garrison, NY 10524, tel. 914/424–4000 or 888/882–6863, www.outwardbound.org. Dec., Mar.: 8 days, $995.

Snowy Owl Sled-Dog Tours

3+

If you find yourself experiencing the delights of winter in the Banff or Lake Louise region of Alberta, try a day, evening, or overnight dogsledding adventure with Snowy Owl. Created by Charles and Connie Arsenault in 1983, Snowy Owl features activities that draw on Connie's youth in Canada's wilderness parks, where her father was a ranger. Charles, too, spent much of his youth with a father who loved and appreciated the backcountry and who enjoyed sharing it with his children. As a result, both of the Arsenaults were taught to be independent, creative, and resourceful, and to appreciate the fact that children can learn early about the wilderness and what it has to offer. They, in turn, love sharing their homeland and backcountry with families of all kinds.

FOR FAMILIES. Few winter landscapes offer more pristine beauty than this region of the Canadian Rockies, and now you can experience its wonders from the unique perspective of a handcrafted oak sled. Trips in the Canmore and Kananaskis areas include the 2½-hour Goat Creek Passage, which takes families around Spray Lake and Goat Pond and features a lesson in navigating a team over bridges. Sunfeather Winterlude is the company's half-day tour on a trail system that winds through towering black spruce forests and along Goat Creek. The full-day Spirit of the Dog Society tour lets you live a day in the life of a Canadian musher, beginning at sunrise with all 150 Snowy Owl huskies in their kennel and continuing until dusk with such activities as snowshoeing, sledding, and tracking. The two-hour Moonlight Rendezvous and two-day Ghosts of Fortune Mountain tours feature an introduction to Native lore and beliefs; the highlight of the latter is an overnight in a heated Sioux tepee. Note that tour reservations should be made at least 48 hours in advance, as the winter season around Banff and Lake Louise is extremely busy.

Snowy Owl Sled-Dog Tours, Box 8039, Canmore, Alberta, Canada, tel. 403/678–4369 or 888/311–MUSH (6874), www.snowyowltours.com. 2½ hours–2 days, Dec.–Apr.: $115–$920 (Canadian) adults, $55–$255 8 and under.

Trek & Trail

10+

The winter woods of northwestern Wisconsin and Lake Superior prove a dramatic backdrop for adventuring. Trek & Trail has been running dogsled trips in this area since 1989. The well-qualified instructors capably teach their winter survival skills and mushing expertise to others, and their enthusiasm for the majesty and solitude of the wilderness in winter is contagious.

FOR FAMILIES. One-, two-, and three-day trips are available. For families who want to try working with dogs but don't know if they want to invest two or three days in it, a Mushing Day Trip is the answer. The program runs from about 9 to 4 and provides a great introduction to the sport. Your base is the company's cabin, where you'll spend a half-day learning about mushing and the rest learning such winter skills as animal tracking, fire starting, plant identification, and finding food and water in the winter wilderness. If you want to immerse yourself in learning for a couple of days, try the two-day Dogsledding and Cabin Base Camp Adventure, the only overnight sledding trip on which children under age 16 are allowed. Your eight-person cabin is rustic but cozy; accommodations for longer trips are tents, tepees, and snow shelters.

After a three-hour winter safety course, including information about ice rescue, nutrition, hypothermia, and winter camping, you'll be ready to use the cabin as a base from which to take day-long trail runs. This traditional sugaring cabin was built by the Newago family, members of the Red Cliff Tribe, which uses it at maple-sugar time, when the family is harvesting and cooking down the syrup. Family members come out to spend the evening with you Friday night, telling stories of present-day and historical "sugar bushing" and other facets of Native American life. Saturday and Sunday you'll learn a variety of winter skills and graduate from running four- or five-dog teams to 10-dog teams, if you wish. You can even try a night run. If your children are enthusiastic and comfortable with the dog teams, they can learn to mush, too; otherwise, they can ride with guides. No winter adventuring experience is necessary, but you must be in good physical condition, and you must bring appropriate clothing.

Families with children at least 16 years old can join the three-day trek in Lake Superior's Apostle Islands. No winter camping experience is required—you'll learn it all on the trip. Besides camping skills, you'll pick up cross-country skiing and snowshoeing, in addition to learning how to work with a team of sled dogs. You'll stay in log cabins, snow shelters, or tepees.

Trek & Trail, Box 906, Bayfield, WI 54814, tel. 800/354–8735, www.trek-trail.com. Jan.–Mar.: 1–3 days, $99–$495 for adults; 30% discount for children under 13.

Wilderness Inquiry

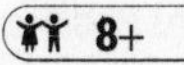

Since 1978 this nonprofit organization has brought together people from diverse backgrounds—including people with disabilities. Teaching, learning, and sharing are the foundations on which every course is built. The wintertime courses are all about embracing the chilly beauty of the wilderness under cover of deep snow. You and your kids may be surprised at how much outdoor adventure northern Minnesota has to offer, even when the mercury dips well below freezing.

FOR FAMILIES. The Family Ski & Dogsled is a five-day trip into the Boundary Waters Canoe Area, where you'll follow ancient Native American trails through deep snow and pine forests and across the many frozen lakes. The outfitter will consider younger children, but call to discuss it; 2-year-olds have taken this trip.

You pick your routes and then ski, snowshoe, dogsled, and take on the challenge of winter wilderness survival. If you or your child has a disability, ask Wilderness Inquiry about its facilities for accommodating your needs. Most daily outings are 3 to 8 mi (5 to 13 km). You can also choose to relax with a cup of hot chocolate in the remote but comfortable YMCA Camp Menogyn lodge (with sauna), where you spend your nights. There's an optional overnight camp-out in tents, snow shelters, and double sleeping bags under the dark, starry skies. One of the mushers who regularly works this trip taught his own children to run dogs at age 4, so a child's ability isn't prejudged. If your 8-year-old is ready and willing, he or she can stand on the runners with a musher and get the feel of driving a sled.

Wilderness Inquiry, 1313 5th St. SE, Box 84, Minneapolis, MN 55414-1546, tel. and TTY 612/379–3858 or 800/728–0719, www.wildernessinquiry.org. Dec.–Mar.: 5–6 days, $595–$945; children under 17 generally receive 50% discount. Round-trip van transportation from Minneapolis (6 hrs each way) is $60.

Resources

Organizations

The **International Sled Dog Racing Association** (HC 86, Box 3380, Merrifield, MN 56465, tel. 218/765–4297, www.isdra.org; membership $35) will send information on the sport (an introductory brochure is available for $2), and a sample copy of its magazine, *Info,* published 10 times each year.

Books

Gary Paulsen, whose passion for years was dogsledding in the Minnesota wilderness, writes in *Woodsong* (Penguin, ages 8 and up) about his dogs, his home, and his participation in the 1,049-mi (1,699-km) Iditarod dogsled race. *Dogteam* (Dell), also by Paulsen, is a picture book about the beauty of a nighttime dogsled run.

Also See

For more winter adventures, look at the trips in Cross-Country Skiing. For more adventures with animal companions, see Horse Packing *and* Trekking with Llamas and Burros.

FISHING

City kids, country kids, small- and big-town kids—they all love to fish. Whether it's the connection with water or the lazy, Huckleberry Finn feel of floating along with no place in particular to go, I don't know. Maybe it's the challenge, or maybe it's the simplicity of the endeavor. In a high-tech, high-speed world, fishing takes you back to a simpler era when families made their own fun. Fishing requires almost nothing except patience and a little time.

Of course, there is an art to it. In particular, fly-fishing, which involves almost continuous casting with an artificial fly, is a learned skill. It has complexities (avoiding people, trees, and reeds while casting, for example) and intricacies (knowing where fish lurk and what they eat) beyond what most of us associate with fishing. There is a right and wrong way to cast—and you can bet those wily trout in streams across the country know that by now.

Today families can discover, or rediscover, the joys of fishing in a number of ways. There are schools and clinics that teach specialized skills, usually fly-fishing, and outfitters that will take you out and teach you while you vacation. You can find lodges that focus on fishing and provide instruction as well as good old-fashioned fishing fun. Children of almost any age can fish, though most outfitters agree that fly-fishing takes a level of coordination and understanding most children under 12 don't possess. For this reason lodge-based fishing and lake fishing are often best for families with young children. But the bottom line is really this: Fishing, in one form or another, is for everyone.

Questions to Ask

What method is taught? Most schools concentrate on fly-fishing, but instruction in spin casting (casting a line with a worm or lure or other bait and slowly reeling it in), trolling (dragging a line behind a moving boat), and other techniques is also available. Fly-fishing is harder for young children than trolling, so consider your youngsters' ages and abilities, as well as their levels of tolerance for sitting or standing for long periods, before booking.

Do you have equipment for kids? Experts disagree on whether a shorter rod is necessarily better for children, but be sure there's a rod your child can use comfortably. Children older than 12 and those large for their age don't usually have a problem with the adult equipment generally available either as part of the package or for rent. Children who are younger and smaller may have problems with available rods, so buy or borrow your child's equipment before you leave home. Get detailed information from the guide or school about what kind is best, though. *Fly-Fishing* *with Children*, by Philip Brunquell (see Resources, *below*), has an excellent section on buying rods for kids.

What kind of fish can be caught? Trout is the primary focus at most schools and on many wilderness trips, but there are other possibilities. Bluefish, bonitos, salmon, walleyes, and northern pike also provide a challenge for anglers of all ages. Even within species there can be differences in ease of catch. Because children may have less patience than adults, try to choose a fish or an area likely to bring success.

Where does casting instruction take place? You'll be taught how to throw a line out in such a way that a fish will take whatever lure or bait you're offering. Most schools have casting ponds stocked with trout; in some cases instruction takes place on a river or even in the surf. On a guided trip you put skills to work in real situations rather than the artificial environs of a stocked pond. However, guided trips can be expensive, and since children like the ponds, a school's simulated environment isn't necessarily a drawback. Schools also give families a chance to try the sport to see if they like it and to test equipment before investing in it. Before booking either alternative, make sure the scenario is what you want.

How much time is spent in the classroom? Many schools use about half the course time to give lectures on equipment and environmental concerns, present slide shows, lead fly-tying demonstrations, and discuss pretty much anything that's not directly related to casting. Be certain your children understand that the entire class will not take place near water. In some cases no time is spent by the water, so read descriptions carefully.

Are licenses needed? In most states adults need a fishing license, but children under a certain age do not. Sixteen is a common cutoff, but in some states 12-year-olds must have one. Check with the school or your guide. Find out if you can purchase your license from them, or if you have to stop somewhere before your class or trip begins. The cost may be anywhere from $4 to $40 or so. In a very few courses a temporary license is part of the course fee.

Can we keep the fish? In most cases, no. The sport lies in outsmarting the fish, and the primary goal of most schools and guided trips is to teach you to catch fish, not to keep them. "Catch and release" is the phrase you'll hear; it means once you catch your fish, you must quickly unhook it and place it back in the water. Many places recommend barbless hooks for that reason. Ask if you need to bring them.

Are there activities for nonfishing family members? You'll probably find more to do besides fish at lodges rather than at schools or with wilderness guides. Some guided trips, however, are perfect for photographers or wildlife artists or for anyone who simply likes relaxing in a boat. A number of schools are in towns or areas that are popular family destinations. Even if one of you isn't fishing, you can still have a family experience.

How far in advance should we book? For parent-child courses, which are very limited in number, booking several months in advance is a good idea. On the other hand, last-minute cancellations are always possible, so don't hesitate to call.

What's included in the cost? Guided trips include boats, guides, all meals, most camping equipment (you usually have to bring or rent a sleeping bag), life vests, instruction, and transportation to and from the river, unless otherwise noted. Fishing equipment is occasionally available, but check. The cost of lodge-based trips generally covers lodging, meals, and the use of a boat; private guiding is extra. School prices include equipment but reflect course costs only, without lodging or meals, unless otherwise noted. Transportation to and from schools, lodges, or guided trips is never part of the price given.

Instruction

Instruction is the focus of a school course, but a good guide on a trip will always provide instruction, too. If you have specific interests—fly tying, casting techniques, learning about equipment—let your guide know ahead of time so he or she can prepare materials and equipment as necessary. Ask in advance whether there are charts of local fish or written materials or directions on fly tying or using equipment. Some children (and some adults, for that matter) learn better by visual clues.

Finding the Fun

Northeast: Appalachian Mountain Club, L.L. Bean, Orvis Fly Fishing School. **Midwest:** Gunflint Northwoods Outfitters/Gunflint Lodge. **Mid-Atlantic:** Orvis Fly Fishing School. **South:** Orvis Fly Fishing School. **Rockies:** L.L. Bean, Montana River Outfitters, Orvis Fly Fishing School, Telluride Outside. **West Coast:** Canyon Fly Fishing Workshops, Fly-Fishing Outfitters Clinics. **Canada:** Babine Norlakes Lodge.

Favorite Schools and Outfitters

Appalachian Mountain Club

The Catskills campus of this venerable organization sponsors a fly-fishing clinic based at Full Moon Lodge, not far from Phoenicia, New York. Although the course is strictly a landlubber affair—you don't actually go out on the water or even near a stream—your family does get to enjoy a spring weekend in the Catskills while learning the techniques and skills necessary to fish for trout on your own.

FOR FAMILIES. Instructors, all members of the Upper Susquehanna Chapter of Trout Unlimited, have plenty of fishing experience; some are New York State–certified guides. This organization's members focus on enjoying fishing themselves and promoting fly-fishing across the country. The class is limited to 20 people and includes lodging

Friday and Saturday nights, as well as all meals from Saturday breakfast to Sunday lunch.

Participants spend some time in a classroom setting, learning how to select tackle, tie flies, and read the waters (recognize the kinds of places fish like to lurk and feed); instructors also teach a bit about entomology as it relates to fly-fishing. Saturday's class runs from about 9 to 5, while Sunday's ends around noon. Casting instruction takes place in a big field, with no hooks on the rods. Equipment is available for free if you don't yet have your own.

Appalachian Mountain Club, Box 366, Long Lake, NY 12847, tel. 518/624–2056 for Catskills campus; tel. 603/466–2721 for general information, www.outdoors.org. Apr.: 2 days, $215 for adults, 50% discount for children under 10. Family membership is $65, and members receive 10% discount on classes.

Babine Norlakes Lodge

ALL

Pierce and Anita Clegg, owners and managers of the Babine Norlakes Lodge, have four children of their own. They love having families as guests, and their guides enjoy teaching kids about fishing. There aren't many activities if you don't want to fish—maybe a little volleyball or badminton. And, of course, the Cleggs' children are around for play companions.

The lodge itself, in a remote area of northern British Columbia, is accessible only by boat or floatplane. Eight hand-hewn cabins sleep two to four, and generators supply electricity; two of the cabins are larger and have kitchens, if you prefer to cook. This woodsy, isolated living does not lack nice touches. In the morning Pierce personally visits each cabin, serving coffee, tea, or hot chocolate to guests and starting up each cabin's woodstove or stove oil heating. Guests gather for a big breakfast in the main lodge and make their lunch from a buffet; then most head out onto Nilkitkwa Lake and the Babine River for some of the best trout fishing in North America.

FOR FAMILIES. Accommodations include a boat, with no limit on fuel, so you are free to fish as much as you like. The lodge encourages catch-and-release only (and requires all steelhead to be released) in order to preserve the population. The fish here are all wild; there's no stocking, no hatchery. Most guests bring their own equipment, though a few rods are available for guests' use, and the Clegg children generously loan their life jackets.

First-time guests receive one day of complimentary guiding; you can hire guides other days for an additional charge. With enough notice, Anita can arrange to have a mother's helper on the property (at an extra charge) so you and your spouse can spend some time fishing on your own.

In keeping with the informal atmosphere, minimum ages and pricing structures are flexible. Anita says, "Preschoolers and youngsters are free until they really start fishing." At that point they receive a 50% discount. Large families, she adds, "can usually make a deal."

Babine Norlakes Lodge, Box 1060, Smithers, British Columbia, Canada V0J 2N0, tel. 250/847–6160, www.babinenorlakes.com. May–Aug.: 4–8 days, C$1,200–C$2,500 for adults.

Canyon Fly Fishing Workshops

10+

Trinity Canyon's Joe Mercier is an avid angler and committed environmentalist. What he offers are complete ecosystem orientations of northern California's Shasta/Trinity National Forest, Trinity Alps Wilderness, and the basin of the Trinity River, all within the context of fly-fishing. "What I combine," he says, "is service and education." By his own reckoning he knows every rock within a hundred miles of Weaverville, and he likes nothing better than introducing visitors to the beauty and diversity of this area.

FOR FAMILIES. Workshops are for anglers and outdoor enthusiasts of all skill levels. If you have a child younger than 10, or if someone in your family has a disability, talk to Joe ahead of time and he'll accommodate them. Half- or full-day instruction is tailored to the needs, interests, and ages of participants, and even nonanglers will find much to learn. The initial portion of the program includes a presentation on the region's human and natural history, along with demonstrations of fly-fishing techniques and equipment. After that, participants wade into the lakes, rivers, and streams of the Trinity watershed. Joe emphasizes that what he offers is instruction, not a guide service, and catch-and-release is a condition of his workshops. Joe specializes in instructing students about gear, and he'll let you try different types of equipment before you make a major buying decision. He also provides all tackle and equipment for the workshops.

If you're planning to overnight in the area, ask Joe about activities in addition to fishing, as well as for lodging suggestions.
Canyon Fly Fishing Workshops, Box 2820, Weaverville, CA 96093, tel. 530/623–3306, www.shasta.com/trinityfly. Year-round: ½–1 day, $180–$275 for 1–2 people; others in your group can attend with you for a small additional charge.

Fly-Fishing Outfitters Clinics

12+

This group has run clinics since 1985, both in San Francisco and on streams and rivers in various parts of northern California. Because Fly-Fishing Outfitters (FFO) also owns well-regarded equipment shops, it will provide rods and reels for clinics, but you'll have to bring or rent tackle.

FOR FAMILIES. FFO stores offer clinics on casting, rigging, and fishing, and trips are held on a variety of Bay Area waters and California rivers, including the Sacramento, Truckee, Trinity, and Feather. FFO's Peter Woolley says families are welcome participants in any of the company's clinics or trips as long as the children have a real interest in angling and the attention span necessary to handle the information. And although he says 12 is generally a realistic minimum age, he'll consider younger children—but only after talking with parents. The lessons have a fairly structured itinerary and adult orientation, but if you're flexible with your travel dates you can join an outing with other families. While land-based clinics are great for learning the basic skills, these trips let parents and children try out their talents on scenic rivers that capture the sport's romance and heart. Also advantageous is the chance to spend a night camping with guides who will happily talk fishing and fish stories, even after clinic hours. Bring your own camping gear. You'll fish for rainbow and brown trout, but it's strictly catch-and-release.
Fly-Fishing Outfitters Clinics, 3533 Mt. Diablo Blvd., Lafayette, CA 94549, tel. 925/284–3474. July: 1–2 days, $150–$300.

Gunflint Northwoods Outfitters/Gunflint Lodge

ALL

Members of the Kerfoot family, who own the outfitting-guide service and the lodge, have been welcoming adventurers of all ages to this Minnesota wilderness retreat since 1928. The lodge itself, about 150 mi (242 km) north of Duluth, sits on the 9-mi (14-km) shore of Gunflint Lake. Many families visit the lodge for a week, taking canoeing and fishing trips into the vast Boundary Waters Canoe Area (BWCA). Others stay at the lodge only before or after a guided or self-guided adventure. Both the lodge and the guiding service will take children of any age, though different activities have specific age requirements.

Whatever your choice, a talk with Bruce Kerfoot will convince you that Gunflint and families are made for each other.

FOR FAMILIES. Children age 6 and up staying at the lodge at least seven days will be taken out on a children-only half-day guided fishing trip twice during the week. They'll learn spin casting with some live bait and some artificial lures as they try their luck on walleyes and smallmouth bass. A family with children of any age also has the option of hiring one of Gunflint's excellent guides for a full-day trip (at an extra charge) on one of the many lakes in the vast BWCA. Guests may decide whether to keep or free their catch, as long as it's within the legal catch-and-release guidelines. Lodge-based guests can use Gunflint's canoes and kayaks free of charge; there are child-size kayaks, too. Families on the all-inclusive package also have use of a motorboat; other guests pay extra for this. The Gunflint nature program runs from June to September, with about 30 free activities a week, including hikes, bird-watching, moose searches, and boating to interesting sites—even evening beaver watches.

The 24 cabins at Gunflint Lodge give families various options. Sixteen rustic "canoer" cabins sleep from four to six in one big room; a bathhouse with hot showers, toilets, sinks, and a sauna is nearby. The more luxurious cabins have one to four bedrooms, bathrooms, and carpeting, and each has a sauna; the most deluxe have outside hot tubs. Among the family package options are a housekeeping plan, for those who wish to cook their own meals, and a modified plan that includes dinner daily.

You can also book camping trips of two or more days with Gunflint's regular guiding service. Smallmouth bass are easier to catch than other local fish, so they're a good choice for children to try for on these adventures. An ideal family trip takes you to Rose Lake, in the eastern portion of the BWCA along the Canadian border. It requires about a five-hour paddle the first day, and there are two portages on the trip. There's no minimum age, but the trip is a lot easier once children are out of diapers. Bruce recommends a four-night trip. "The kids come back wishing it had been a little longer, not complaining that it was a couple of days too long," he says, and that gives them the best possible introduction to the wilderness.

Gunflint Northwoods Outfitters/Gunflint Lodge, 143 S. Gunflint Lake, Grand Marais, MN 55604, tel. 218/388–2294 or 800/362–5251, www.gunflintoutfitters.com. May–Sept.: 7 days, $295–$3,200 for family of 4, depending on cabin choice and meal package; less if children are under 4, more if more than 4 in your family. Guiding costs $125 per person per day, with 50% discount for ages 4–12.

L.L. Bean

12+

The stated mission of this renowned outdoor store and catalog company is to help people enjoy the outdoors through its products, services, and education. L.L. Bean opened a fly-fishing school in 1980 and inaugurated a parent-child introductory course at the company's Freeport, Maine, headquarters in 1993. It's been going strong ever since.

FOR FAMILIES. Once or twice each summer L.L. Bean schedules a two-day parent-child course that runs from 8:30 to 5 both days and includes lunch. Instruction takes place outside Freeport, often at Fogg Farm, which has both a natural and a stocked pond. Participants remove their shoes and wade in, picking up rocks and studying reeds in order to get to know a fish's environment—and what it eats. Once you know what the fish like to eat, you try to match it in your lure box. The dozen parent–child pairs in the course also learn fly-casting and fly-tying techniques, how to read the water, and how weather can affect fishing conditions. The minimum age is 12, but the school is flexible if you have a younger child who is really interested. Lodging isn't part of the deal, but participants receive a list of area accommodations ranging from campgrounds to a luxury hotel. Be sure to check out L.L. Bean's store, which has quality outdoor clothing and gear for all ages, while you're in the area.

Families with fishing aficionados 12 and up can join any of Bean's other fishing schools. These include introductory and intermediate schools, as well as such specialized courses as saltwater, Atlantic salmon, and western trout fly-fishing schools. Introductory courses are held in Freeport. The intermediate and specialty courses are all in popular fishing areas in Maine and western Virginia, and the costs cover lodging.

One good choice for families is the three-day Fly Fishing at The Balsams adventure, which takes place at one of the great old family resorts in Dixville Notch, New Hampshire. The fly-fishing course has a relaxed atmosphere and is taught by one of Bean's highly regarded instructors, using top-of-the-line equipment. Students learn casting, feeding habits of trout, essential knots, and more. Because resort guests aren't required to take the course, this is a particularly good option for families with different interests. Evenings are free for families to spend as they wish, and the location makes it great for avid fishers, outdoor enthusiasts, and kids alike.

The school follows the catch-and-release policy. All graduates receive a copy of the *L.L. Bean Fly Fishing Handbook* in addition to a diploma and pin.

L.L. Bean, Freeport, ME 04033, tel. 207/865–4761 or 888/552–3261, www.llbean.com. June–July (parent–child school): 2 days, $600 for parent and child; additional participants $300 each. Apr.–Oct. (all other courses): 1–5 days, $200–$1,195 per person.

Montana River Outfitters

Craig Madsen of Montana River Outfitters believes that the best class in the world puts you out on a river catching wild fish with guides who love what they're doing—and that's just what this organization offers. Guides take only two anglers in a boat (two to eight guests in all on a trip) in order to personalize instruction and service. The "classrooms" are the Missouri, Smith, and Flathead rivers. Most people bring their own rods and waders, but you can rent them if necessary. The company follows the catch-and-release policy.

FOR FAMILIES. Craig recommends a five- to seven-day trip on the Smith, along 60 mi (97 km) of river with no public access. Limestone canyons, cliffs, and meadows cradle a river so narrow here you can often cast to either side. The rainbow and brown trout are plentiful, but they're strong and smart, so patience is necessary. Instruction is informal but, thanks to the guide-to-guest ratio, quite personalized. Although the season is short (May to July is the optimum time), the Smith is one of the most reliable trout streams in Montana, which makes it a good choice for anglers of all ages. But it's a river for nonanglers and for families with mixed interests, too, because of its excellent side hikes, caves, Native American pictographs, and spectacular scenery.

Another great five- to seven-day family trip is the South Fork of the Flathead. Getting there adds to the adventure—it's two days in by horse, with all equipment and food packed along (although you don't need to be an experienced rider). The resident cutthroat trout are easy to catch, which can be very satisfying to children (and adults). The South Fork of the Flathead flows through the heart of the Bob Marshall Wilderness in northwestern Montana, offering excellent fishing set against the beauty and drama of a backcountry landscape in one of the most remote areas in the lower 48 states.

There are also several trips on the wild and scenic Missouri River. Rich in the history of pioneers, steamboats, and Lewis and Clark, the Missouri can be floated by raft, kayak, or canoe as part of a partially or fully guided trip. This is generally a warm-water habitat with a wide variety of resident species, but few trout. The Missouri between Great Falls and Helena, however, is known as one of the most productive trout areas in the world. Trout populations here are measured in the thousands per mile, making this one of the best stretches for dry fly-fishing in the west. Also, because of the controlled water flow, fishing is excellent on this portion of the river year-round. You can take half- or whole-day trips, or choose a complete, guided two- to seven-day package. You can fly-fish or spin cast, so it's ideal for all ages and abilities. Three- to five-day float trips with an emphasis on history (much of it related to Lewis and Clark) and geological formations are available, too. You can see historical buildings and sites, hike, swim, and, of course, fish.

To join most of Montana River Outfitters' trips, you generally fly into and out of Great Falls. Representatives of the outfit will pick you up at the airport and take you to your pretrip lodging (not included in the price, but they can arrange it), then transport you to the start of the trip. After your adventure they'll drop you off at the airport. At the end of the Flathead trip you fly out of Kalispell. To avoid the drive to the airport—which includes 80 mi (130 km) of dirt road—you can have a small plane pick your family up close to the river (at an extra charge) and fly you to Kalispell.

Montana River Outfitters, 923 10th Ave. N, Great Falls, MT 59401, tel. 406/761–1677, 406/235–4350, or 800/800–8218, www.mt-river-outfitters.com. Mar.–Oct.: 1–7 days, $245–$3,495 adults; children's pricing on some trips.

Orvis Fly Fishing School

12+

Orvis, the long-established fishing-tackle manufacturer, opened the first fly-fishing school in the country in 1967 at its Manchester, Vermont, corporate headquarters. It has since added corporate center campuses in Colorado, Idaho, Massachusetts, Georgia, Wisconsin, California, Maryland, and New York. Hundreds of Orvis retail outlets (where you can buy fishing gear and outdoor clothing) also run courses, but the individual stores choose their offerings. The clinics at the corporate centers generally remain the same from year to year.

FOR FAMILIES. Orvis's parent–child school is a two-day event, usually scheduled twice a year in July at the Vermont campus. The course accommodates up to 10 pairs, which split into smaller groups (parent and child stay together). You spend half the time in the classroom, the other half at the casting ponds. They follow the catch-and-release policy.

The course meets from about 9 to 4:30 both days and emphasizes basics: rigging a fly rod, tying essential knots, trying various fly-casting techniques, and learning what fish eat and which lures to use. You also learn how to "mend" your line by adjusting its placement in the water based on currents. Not surprisingly, Orvis schools also emphasize proper equipment and clothing, and the gear provided is strictly Orvis.

The school recommends that you sign up for parent-child courses several months in advance—January is not too early for the July school. Children 12 and up can also participate in Orvis's regular courses, but adults should note that the parent–child course has less structure and more emphasis on fun.

The popular women-only schools in Colorado are another option for mother–daughter pairs. These are run like regular courses: The class of 36 or so divides up, and lecture time is lengthier and more detailed than in parent–child courses. As with all Orvis courses, the price does not cover lodging, but reservationists give detailed information on local accommodations. One popular choice in Vermont is the Equinox Hotel.

Orvis Fly Fishing School, Rte. 7A, Manchester, VT 05254, tel. 802/362–8513 or 800/235–9763. Apr.–Oct. (all courses not available all months): 2–3 days, $370–$430.

Telluride Outside

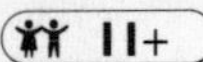

The rivers of southwestern Colorado teem with trout, and the mountain town of Telluride, with the Uncompahgre National Forest to the north and the San Juan National Forest to the south, makes an enviable base from which to pursue them. Telluride Outside has been guiding and teaching fly-fishing for more than 15 years, and the outfitter welcomes parents and children who want to fish and learn together. The company is somewhat flexible on ages; call and consult with the staff before booking any family clinic or trip.

FOR FAMILIES. Telluride Outside lets you choose between "walk and wades" (where you fish standing on the bank or in the water) and "floats" (fishing by boat). The company concentrates on local rivers, streams, and lakes, including the San Miguel and the Dolores Rivers. The San Miguel probably suits families best. Although its fish aren't as big, there are lots of them, so you don't have to be as exact on your cast or your drift as you do on a river with just a few big fish spread out between pools. A one-day trip with instruction covers such topics as approach (trout behavior and reading the water), presentation (equipment and fly casting), and fly selection. You're on your own for lodging each night in Telluride.

To get in shape, consider taking Telluride Outside's half-day casting clinic before a trip. Guides review various casts in detail, and the outfitter provides all equipment. All trips and courses are catch-and-release.

Telluride Outside, Box 685, Telluride, CO 81435, tel. 970/728–3895, www.tellurideoutside.com. June–Sept.: ½–1 day, $185 for one person with a guide for a half day; $395 for three guests with a guide for a full day.

Resources

Books

John Bailey's *Superguides: Fishing* (Dorling Kindersley) is a large-format book with lots of information and pictures for anglers age 8 and up. It covers everything from history of fishing and casting to lures, gear, and accessories.

Kids Gone Fishing, by David Maas (Creative Publishing International, Minnetonka, MN, www.howtobookstore.com), features descriptions of common fish, with lots of photos of happy kids fishing and catching. The author, who spent five seasons as an instructor and guide at a fishing camp for kids, provides all the basics on gear and how to use it.

Fly-Fishing with Children, by Philip Brunquell, M.D. (Countryman Press), is an excellent guide, with sections on buying equipment and diagrams on casting and fly tying.

Also See

For more river and lake adventures in which fishing is possible, *see* Canoeing, Kayaking, *and* Rafting. The Horse Packing chapter also lists trips during which families can fish at lake and river campsites.

HIKING AND BACKPACKING

Hiking is one of the most popular adventure vacations, in part because of accessibility. A family can hike just about anywhere, anytime. There are treks for all ages and all abilities and for campers and noncampers alike. Some families enjoy carrying major backpacks into remote wilderness areas; others prefer the comfort of a cozy inn or lodge each evening. Hiking itself doesn't require lots of expensive equipment (although campers need gear), nor does it involve a large investment of time. Even day hikes with young children can be fun—and educational—family adventures.

So why sign up with a group or outfitter when hiking is something you can so easily do on your own? To begin with, outfitters work in the same areas year after year and really know the country—a benefit for your family's trip planning and safety. Whether you're heading into the wilderness or hiking inn to inn, there are myriad details to take care of: mapping a great route, arranging for backcountry permits, finding a campsite, booking accommodations, and so forth. Guides do all this in advance. They also provide a wellspring of facts and memorable stories, as well as a level of safety individuals usually can't match. Moreover, they can get you into some areas that might be inaccessible to you on your own—unless you have backcountry experience and are well equipped with appropriate safety and camping gear.

Outfitters also contribute to the educational aspect of your family's experience. The naturalists and outdoor educators who accompany you on many trips can share the wonders of nature with your children—and answer their many questions—in a way you probably can't. In addition, if your family has hikers of differing abilities, you may need to compromise on the route when you're on your own. Guided trips generally have two to three hiking options each day. Experienced hikers can be challenged by steep trails and long distances while beginners take shorter routes at a slower pace as they build their stamina and skills.

Traveling with an outfitter can make financial sense, too. They have up-to-date gear, which means you don't have to go out and buy it. Tents, pads, tarps, cooking equipment, fire starters, topographical maps, backcountry first-aid kits, compasses, and radios are necessary in the wilderness. Unless you're certain that camping and hiking are long-term family interests, why invest in so much equipment?

Finally, when you travel with a hiking company, especially on a trip geared for families, you're guaranteed companions, not just for yourself but for your children. You'll meet families from all over the world that share your love of the outdoors. Most important, perhaps, children help motivate each other. This can make a big difference when you're still several from camp, and your 5-year-old doesn't want to walk any farther.

Of course, you can hike on your own; there are city and state parks and recreation areas with marked and maintained trails within a short drive of most communities—even large cities. These are good trails on which to introduce children to hiking and to build your family's skills. But try a guided trip for that multiday exploration of backcountry or unfamiliar locales, or for a special adventure that integrates hiking with history, ecology, botany, marine biology, or sociology. You'll be amazed at what you see and what you can learn.

Questions to Ask

How far will we hike each day? The trips listed here average from 3 to 8 mi (5 to 13 km) per day for the easy options; some hikes are as short as 1.8 mi (3 km) and others as long as 12 mi (19 km). Challenging options generally range between 6 and 12 mi (10 and 19 km) per day. Although size and experience are factors, in general you can expect a preschooler to walk from 1 to 3 mi (1½ to 5 km) a day, and 5- to 8-year-olds to handle between 5 and 8 mi (8 and 13 km), depending on the terrain and their experience.

How difficult is the trip? Most hiking companies designate trips as easy, moderate, strenuous, or difficult. All the trips in this chapter are easy or moderate, unless otherwise noted. Difficulty is determined by the distance you hike, the ascent or descent, and the trail surface. One company puts it this way: an easy trip is the equivalent of a half hour of walking three times per week. Moderate and challenging routes are the equivalent of a half hour of aerobic exercise two or three times per week. These guidelines may help you decide your family's ability level, but you should also ask lots of questions and be candid about the fitness and normal activity level of everyone in your family.

How often can we rest? Outdoor experts know that children need to stop more often than adults, but everyone needs to rest on the trail. Taking a couple of breaks in the morning and afternoon, in addition to stopping for lunch, is good for the group. Along the trail you'll pause frequently to look at everything you're out there to see: views, bugs, interesting plants, wildlife. To rush down the trail is to miss the point. If your guide tries to hurry you or your children, ask him or her to slow down.

Who carries the gear? Sometimes you do; sometimes support vehicles lug the heavy stuff while you hike. In general, if the trip is a backcountry trek with a different campsite each night, everyone in the group will probably be expected to carry a backpack of at least 30 pounds. If this isn't for you, check out inn-to-inn hiking; support vehicles usually take all but what you need in your day pack. On lodge-based treks, you leave almost everything in your room while you hike each day.

Are there any special safety precautions for kids on the trail? Although you're with a group and guides, there's a remote chance someone might get separated from the group for a while. Carrying a whistle is a good idea. If your children can read, write safety instructions and place them in their day pack or backpack. Children should know when to blow the whistle, how to use three sticks or stones to mark the direction they've gone, and to stay in one place if it gets dark.

What if my child is too tired to finish a hike? A good trail strategy is to encourage children along the way, whether they are tired or not. Praise all their accomplishments—making it up hills, making it until break time, making it to the next bend in the trail. You and they will be surprised at their natural abilities. For those times children really can't go on, you should know your options. Some trips include van support; others have shorter loops you can take. Once you've committed to a trail in the wilderness, though, your choices may be limited.

Will an experienced hiker be bored on easy or moderate hikes? On family trips the key is to look at the experience in a new way. You won't cover the same distances you're used to, and you won't be on terrain that's as challenging. On the other hand, you will have opportunities to see the world through your children's eyes, to slow down, and to share your knowledge of the trail with them. If you feel the need for a challenge or two, take a trip that has several hiking options every day. You and your spouse can take turns between walking with the children and going on more difficult hikes.

How many people will be in the group? Camping trips usually accommodate from 10 to 20 people, inn-to-inn trips typically have between 15 and 25, and lodge-based trips as many as 30 or 40. Individual listings for outfitters note any exceptions to these averages. Remember, however, that the group is divided every day into two or three smaller hiking groups based on ability and preference. You will rarely hike with more than 10 or 11 people at one time.

Do my kids need hiking boots? In some cases and on some terrain, boots may be better than sneakers because they provide more support. Some good national outlets sell children's outdoor wear (see Resources, *below*), and hiking boots come in a range of prices. After the trip boots are useful at camp and around town.

Are day packs needed? Most outfitters ask each hiker to carry his or her own day pack; that goes for children, too. Even preschoolers can carry a small pack with the essentials: safety instructions, water, trail snacks, and rain gear.

Are snacks available? Outfitters usually provide trail snacks each day, but they may not hand them out as often as your children need them. They also may not have what your youngsters like, so pack easy-to-carry energy-producing trail snacks in your family's day packs. Good choices include dried fruit, nuts, hard salami, and trail mix. If you have hard cheese or bagels at breakfast, take leftovers on the trail. A word of caution: in wilderness areas, especially bear country, it's not safe to keep food in your tent. At night give snacks to your guides to put in safe containers.

What's included in the cost? On a camping trip the outfitter supplies guides, meals, tents, and sleeping pads unless otherwise noted. Inn-to-inn trips or expeditions that use lodges and hotels typically include guides, lodging, and most, but not necessarily all meals. Participants must sometimes get to the trailhead on their own or meet at a designated spot for group transfer to the trailhead. The cost may cover airport pickup and delivery. Airfare and lodging before or after the trip dates are not part of the price, although most outfitters can help you book these.

Instruction

Those companies or organizations that sponsor courses, such as the Appalachian Mountain Club, provide instruction as well as fun. Efficient hiking techniques, orienteering, nature studies, and lessons in packing a backpack and setting up reliable camps are typical of what your family can learn from a course. Although vacation-oriented trips aren't geared to teaching, you learn a tremendous amount anyway. Good guides and naturalists are sources of wilderness wisdom who will share their knowledge of everything from animal prints to edible berries.

Finding the Fun

Northeast: Appalachian Mountain Club, Backroads, Outward Bound, Sierra Club. **Mid-Atlantic:** National Wildlife Federation. **South:** Backroads, National Wildlife Federation, Wilderness Inquiry. **Southwest:** National Geographic Expeditions, Smithsonian Study Tours, Southwest Trekking. **Rockies:** Austin-Lehman Adventures, Backroads, National Geographic Expeditions, National Wildlife Federation, Outward Bound, Sierra Club. **West Coast:** Backroads, Sierra Club. **Alaska:** Alaska Wildland Adventures, Camp Denali, Mountain Travel Sobek, Sierra Club. **Hawaii:** Backroads, Butterfield & Robinson, GORP Travel, National Wildlife Federation, Sierra Club. **Canada:** Austin-Lehman Adventures, Backroads, Butterfield & Robinson, Canadian Mountain Holidays, GORP Travel, Mountain Travel Sobek, Sila Sojourns, Wells Gray Chalets & Wilderness Adventures. **Mexico:** Southwest Trekking. **Central America:** Backroads, Butterfield & Robinson. **South America:** Mountain Travel Sobek. **Europe:** Backroads, Butterfield & Robinson, Ciclismo Classico, Cross Country International, Mountain Hiking Program Innsbruck, Swiss Federal Railways. **Africa, Asia, New Zealand:** Butterfield & Robinson, Synago.

Favorite Outfitters

Alaska Wildland Adventures

12+

Alaska Wildland Adventures has made an effort to design trips that meet the needs of all kinds of travelers—families, seniors, those looking for a challenging trip, those looking to mix lots of activities into one vacation. What all of the company's adventures have in common, however, is that each one showcases this great northern state in all its elemental beauty and power.

FOR FAMILIES. The Alaska Explorer Safari is an excellent choice for families. It includes two nights of camping in Kenai National Wildlife Refuge and two nights in Denali National Park, interspersed with stays in cozy cabins (with hot showers). From the Kenai Riverside Lodge, you'll have two days to hike and explore the wildlife refuge and Chugach National Forest. After driving north to Talkeetna and on to Denali National Park, you'll set up tents within sight of the awesome mountain from which the park takes its name and join ranger-led hikes. In addition to hiking and camping, the safari will take you rafting on the Kenai River and provide lots of opportunities for observing Alaska's famous wildlife, especially in Denali National Park and on the Kenai Fjords National Park Cruise.

Alaska Wildland Adventures, Box 389, Girdwood, AK 99587, tel. 907/783–2928 or 800/334–8730; 800/478–4100 in AK, www.alaskawildland.com. June–Sept.: 10 days, $2,695–$3,295.

Appalachian Mountain Club

ALL

The Appalachian Mountain Club (AMC) sponsors too many hiking, backpacking, and camping courses to list all here. Three campuses in three mountain ranges—New Hampshire's White Mountains, New York's Catskills, and the Poconos in eastern Pennsylvania—allow AMC to develop classes that are both extensive and varied. The club's family workshops, available at all campuses except the Poconos, are particularly worthwhile. In AMC parents and children find teachers and outdoor professionals who give them the skills to go out and enjoy the wilderness on their own.

FOR FAMILIES. At the White Mountain campus, families have lots of activity choices, depending on their experience, skill levels, and preferences. "Introduction to Family Hiking" and "Basic Hiking & Camping for Families" are perfect for novices who want to learn how to enjoy and be safe in the great outdoors. "Using Maps to Improve Your Hike" is great for those who already love to hike but want to improve their outdoor skills. A range of subjects and activities are covered, including forest ecology, map and compass reading, low-impact camping, and nature crafts. You camp overnight. The "Curious Explorers at Zealand" hike follows a 2½-mi (4-km) trail to AMC's Zealand Falls hut, where preschoolers (ages 3 to 5) spend the night with their parents and guides. The general "Curious Explorers" hike is for ages 4 through 8 and their parents; the overnight on that trip is at AMC's main lodge at Pinkham Notch Visitor Center. AMC also has two family hut adventures, one at Lonesome Lake and one at Zealand Falls, which combine hiking with overnight stays in the club's wilderness huts. There's also an Elderhostel intergenerational adventure in the White Mountains for grandparents and grandchildren.

In the Catskills a Grandparent–Grandchild Nature Weekend for ages 5 and up brings different generations together for a night hike and hands-on discovery of the natural environment. The group stays at Full Moon Lodge in the High Peaks region of the Catskills. A workshop for all ages, Introduc-

tion to Family Backpacking and Camping, incorporates moderate hikes and overnight camping. At this campus tents and backpacks are available for rent.
Appalachian Mountain Club, Box 298, Gorham, NH 03581, tel. 603/466–2721 for White Mountains and AMC headquarters; 518/624–2056 for Catskills; www.outdoors.org. Apr.–Oct. (all courses not available all months): 1–6 days, $39–$295; 50% discount for children under 10. AMC family membership $65; members receive 10% discount on all workshops.

Austin-Lehman Adventures

7+

The best tour operators—and Austin-Lehman is one of the very best—are able to create trips that meld all the elements of a great family adventure: fun and learning, family time and time with peers, challenges and moderate workouts, group activities and free time, going for it and relaxing. In other words, this type of trip combines the best of all possible worlds to make both kids and adults feel satisfied and successful. It's a tall order, and, frankly, many tour operators succeed in parts of this mission but not in others. ALA, however, succeeds 100%—and then goes above and beyond with little extras that make guests feel like part of a very special family.

This, in a nutshell, is what sets ALA apart from other family hiking specialists. Dan Austin and Paul Lehman totally understand what families are about, and their understanding is reflected in every aspect of the trips they offer. They also bring decades of experience in management and travel to ALA (Dan Austin was co-owner and operator of the well-respected adventure travel company Backcountry), which means that much attention is paid to the small details. My family and I give Austin-Lehman, and the truly exceptional guides with whom we traveled, an enthusiastic eight thumbs up, our highest honor (those are all of the thumbs we have).

FOR FAMILIES. There are four family adventures to choose from, all of which are multisport and include hiking. The Canadian Rockies adventure will take you from Calgary to Kananaskis, then on to Banff and Lake Louise, for hiking, biking, rafting the Kananaskis River, riding horses through wildflower meadows, and munching on snacks at a teahouse high above the startling blue of Lake Louise. And although the guides themselves are exceptional, they also call on incredible experts for the walk on Athabasca Glacier—where, even in August, you bundle up in hats, gloves, and jackets.

Two trips in Wyoming are based in Jackson Hole and Yellowstone. Guests on the Grand Teton trip get to hike, bike, paddle, and horseback ride in this dramatic national park. The Yellowstone adventure takes in a bit of Montana (Bozeman and Chico), but the heart of the trip is exploring and coming to understand the geological wonders of the park. There's plenty of wildlife, waterfalls, and hot springs, and lodging includes the famous Old Faithful Inn and Mammoth Hotel. Family Montana covers some of the same territory—Bozeman, Chico, and a day at Yellowstone—but adds Paradise Valley and the passes, lakes, and valleys of Gallatin National Forest.
Autin-Lehman Adventures, Box 81025, Billings, MT 59108-1025, tel. 406/655–4591 or 800/575–1540, www.austinlehman.com. July–Aug., 6 days, $1,995–$2,195 per person. Children sharing accommodations with parents receive a $300 discount.

Backroads

ALL

Backroads, with one of the largest selections of family trips of any adventure-travel company, seems to add more family departures every year. By the time you try all the hiking

Backroads currently offers, new destinations will be beckoning families to the trails of North America and beyond. Whichever you choose, you'll never really be roughing it; the company uses only top-notch properties for its inn trips, and the group leaders and guides provide uniformly excellent service.

FOR FAMILIES. In total, Backroads offers 23 different family walking, biking, or multisport vacations to points in North America, Latin America, and Europe. Two of these—one in Costa Rica, the other in the Czech Republic—are strictly focused on walking. All of the others that include hiking are multisport adventures. Among these are trips in France, Canada, Switzerland, Belize, Washington, Hawaii, Montana, Wyoming, North Carolina, and Maine. Some of these are inn trips, some are camping.

The family walking adventure in Costa Rica is an inn trip for families with kids age 6 and older. Using several inns as bases, you'll discover the country's incredibly diverse landscape. You'll venture to majestic Arenal, one of the world's most active volcanoes, soak in a hot springs, explore the Monteverde Cloud Forest (and search for the elusive quetzal), and sway in hammocks on the beach at Tango Mar. Also for ages 6 and up is the Czech Republic Walking trip, where families stroll through fields and shady lanes in the Southern Bohemia region, past castles reminiscent of those in classic fairy tales. An expert local guide provides an insider's view of the life and history of the region. Although Prague isn't included in the itinerary, families may want to make the capital a pre- or post-trip stopover. If you want to camp, try the Kananaskis adventure in the southeastern corner of the Canadian Rockies, where you hike, raft, and mountain bike through the rugged, alpine terrain.

The family multisport trip to Montana's Glacier National Park is an inn tour that includes stays at the historic Many Glacier Hotel, on the shores of Swiftcurrent Lake, and at Glacier Park Lodge, an impressive timber hotel at the foot of Squaw Peak Mountain. Families hike and horseback ride in the high country, raft the Flathead River, and bike across the mountains. The trip also includes kayaking (minimum age 6). Hawaii Multisport, for ages 10 and older, is an exploration of the Big Island that has you hiking to the craters of Kilauea with a volcanologist and kayaking the Kohala Coast. Lodging ranges from the renowned Volcano House in Hawaii Volcanoes National Park to the elegant Orchid at Mauna Lani resort. Also tropical is the Belize Multisport, where your family will meet Mayan natives, hike to hidden falls, bike and canoe, tube down the Mopan River to Clarissa Falls, and snorkel the world-famous aqua waters off Placencia.

And among the old favorites in the Backroads list are hiking, biking, and kayaking trips in and around Puget Sound and Washington's wildlife-rich islands. There are also hiking, biking, and rafting adventure in Yellowstone and Grand Teton national parks. Both of the latter trips have inn and camping options.

Backroads, 801 Cedar St., Berkeley, CA 94710, tel. 510/527–1555 or 800/462–2848, www.backroads.com. July–Aug., 6–7 days, $998–$2,798; 10%–75% discount for children, depending on age and accommodations.

Butterfield & Robinson

3+

Butterfield & Robinson (B&R) believes a walking trip "should move along at a leisurely pace, like a well-told story." This analogy works well for family hikes, too. Although the number of B&R hiking trips designated specifically for families may be few, the destinations are exceptional. This is a luxury operation, and prices reflect the high quality of the tours, staffing, and accommodations.

FOR FAMILIES. B&R has recently expanded its specialty family trips, which is good news for adventurous families with kids of all ages. The majority of these are for parents with kids at least 12 years old, but there are also several trips open for children as young as 3. All trips have the signature B&R combination of awesome scenery by day, first-class amenities by night.

B&R's first walking trip for families with children as young as 3 was the Switzerland Bike & Walk from Lausanne to Gstaad, a multisport combination trip that now has one departure for ages 3 and up and another for ages 8 and up. This is an ideal itinerary for family members who aren't up to the demanding work usually necessary on mountainous cycling excursions, as here you hike the mountains and bike the valleys. The Family Dolomites trip, for ages 8 and older, is a five-day excursion beginning in Bolzano in northwestern Italy and ending in Venice. Some alpine routes are challenging; however, parents with very young children can utilize trams and chairlifts to give youngsters a boost up to higher elevations, where they can then easily hike through the hills and valleys of this impressive range. This region, the Alta Badia (high Abbey), is culturally diverse as well. In Covara, where you spend the first two days, three cultures and languages come together. It is as much influenced by nearby Austria as by Italy, and most people speak Italian, German, and Ladino (a mix of Latin, Italian, and German heard today only in this part of Italy and in the Swiss Engadine Valley). The hotels B&R chooses for this trip—from Covara to San Cassiano—are particularly family-friendly. One hotelier invites the group to the home that has been in his family for generations, where he proudly demonstrates his yodeling.

Families with children at least 8 years old can also sign up for Bears and Whales: Walking and Kayaking in British Columbia, as well as the Hawaii Adventure, which includes hiking the rim of Haleakala. Families with kids at least 12 years old can opt for a multisport combo in Belize that mixes hiking with kayaking and snorkeling. Two excellent hiking and biking trips also take place in Morocco and New Zealand (see Biking). Although destinations may change from year to year, you can be certain that wherever the company decides to take families, it will be a trip of a lifetime, as memorable for B&R's attention to detail as for the destination itself.

Butterfield & Robinson, 70 Bond St., Toronto, Ontario, Canada M5B 1X3, tel. 416/864–1354 or 800/678–1147, www.butterfield.com. July–Aug.: 5–7 days, $3,650–$4,995 adults, 10%–35% discount for children depending on age and lodging.

Camp Denali

8+

Camp Denali (the native name for Mt. McKinley) is one of Alaska's great destinations for family vacations, especially for families that want to get away from it all. Its location in the geographic center of the 5.7 million acres of Denali National Park puts it seven hours from the nearest town. Camp Denali's commitment to the preservation of the park's unique ecosystem guides all the activities it offers. And the lodge's wilderness setting is remarkable—it's one of only two park lodges with views of Mt. McKinley. Freshly baked goods, jams, and syrups made from the tundra's bountiful supply of wild berries, and fresh greens from the lodge's innovative greenhouse (heat is made from recycled waste) mean excellent food. The camp consists of central public buildings and 17 cabins.

FOR FAMILIES. There are no separate activities for children; walking and hiking take center stage for everyone. Although Camp Denali has no hard-and-fast rule about the minimum age, it's felt that children 8 and older will have the best experience. You can hike the few maintained trails or head for the backcountry. Naturalists lead hikes of varying lengths; your family can also map out a route with the help of lodge employees.

Hikes can take you to see beavers at work, grizzlies digging for food, or moose and caribou silhouetted against Denali itself. You can also try canoeing in Wonder Lake or biking the park road.

Families have a number of other ways to learn more about Denali. Evening activities—slides and naturalist talks—attract all ages. Camp Denali's Natural History Resource Center has interactive exhibits in addition to a herbarium and extensive resource library. Throughout the season, too, experts lead multiday special-interest sessions on topics from the aurora borealis to nature photography. There are no additional charges for these programs.

Camp Denali, Box 67, Denali National Park, AK 99755, tel. 907/683–2290, www.campdenali.com. June–mid-Sept.: 4–8 days, $1,035–$2,415 adults, $780–$1,820 children under 12. Price includes all meals, activities, and round-trip transportation from Denali Park rail station.

Canadian Mountain Holidays

ALL

The Cariboo, Purcell, Bugaboo, and Selkirk wilderness areas of southern British Columbia may be too challenging for many families to hike into on their own. With a helicopter lift from one of its lodges each day and treks for every ability, Canadian Mountain Holidays (CMH) helps hikers of all ages discover mountain landscapes that are as breathtaking as they are remote.

FOR FAMILIES. At the company's five lodges, groups of about 11 are divided by ability and taste, so you can hike with your family or go your separate ways and meet back at the lodge. Hikes from Cariboo Lodge, about 80 mi (129 km) southwest of Jasper in the Cariboo Mountains, lead to massive glaciers and heather-filled alpine valleys. The Bobbie Burns Lodge is about 195 mi (314 km) west of Calgary, deep in the Purcell Range. Trails high on Grizzly Ridge have unparalleled views of the vast Conrad Icefield and the Bugaboo and Vowell peaks. Bugaboo Lodge, across Grizzly Ridge from the Bobbie Burns, sits at the base of the Bugaboo Glacier. The terrain here encompasses sunny meadows and blue alpine lakes, forests, glaciers, waterfalls, and rushing mountain streams. Valemount, the company's newest lodge, accommodates only 20 guests and sits just outside the town of Valemount in the Cariboo Mountains, about 80 mi (129 km) southwest of Jasper. In summer Valemount runs a multi-adventure trip, which is especially good for families; it includes horseback riding, rafting, fly-fishing, and heli-hiking.

CMH offers a four-night family adventure once each summer at Adamant Lodge, in the Selkirk Mountains. In addition to daily heli-hiking, there are activities for children that focus on learning and playing in this magnificent wilderness area. Families may hike together, or they may spend a day hiking separately with their own age group. At night in the lodge, parents and children come back together to swap stories of their adventures over a gourmet dinner. There are evening activities for the whole group, and Adamant has a climbing wall that draws all ages. Children's programs on this trip are geared for ages 5 to 14.

Children of about age 6 and older are welcome on any trip. Because CMH doesn't have a strict age minimum, families with young children can enjoy these remote areas. The company requests, however, that parents with children under 6 call and discuss details before booking a stay.

The lodges have from 10 to 29 rooms each, all with private baths. Local transportation is included in the price but differs for each lodge. For Bugaboo, Bobbie Burns, Valemount, and Adamant, transportation from Banff is included; guests at the Cariboo Lodge meet in Jasper or Valemount.

Canadian Mountain Holidays, Box 1660, Banff, Alberta, Canada TOL 0C0, tel. 403/762–7100 or 800/661–0252, www.cmhski.com. July–Sept.: 3–7 days, C$1,382–C$3,055 adults: children 14 and under receive a 25% discount.

Ciclismo Classico

ALL

There are but a few companies I can recommend as highly as this one. Perhaps more important, my children feel exactly the same way: they would travel again with Ciclismo Classico (CC) in a heartbeat, which says a lot about CC's ability to create a trip that all ages can love. From start to finish CC guides go out of their way for parents and for kids, providing just the right mix of challenges and easy days, education and laughter. There wasn't a situation that came up—and some always do when traveling with kids—that the guides didn't handle brilliantly. But what we all remember best is their warmth and generosity of spirit.

Known primarily for its stellar biking adventures, Ciclismo Classico also mixes a good deal of hiking and other activities into its family-oriented trips in the Dolomite range of northwestern Italy. Director (and mother of two) Lauren Hefferon has been leading trips there for more than a decade. All of the staff, including Lauren's husband, are Italian or of Italian descent, and the company has a vast network of guides and hoteliers in Italy. In short, when you go to Italy with Ciclismo Classico, you're going with people who share their passion for the country and an insider's depth of experience.

FOR FAMILIES. Fly into Milan, then catch a train to Bolzano, where group members are met and shuttled to the four-star Alpenroyal Inn in Selva Gardena, base for the eight-day trip. In the heart of the intensely beautiful Dolomites, the family-run Alpenroyal has a wholly relaxed atmosphere and plenty of amenities, including indoor and outdoor pools and a spa, wine cellar, and fitness course. The friendly, personable owners make kids feel incredibly welcome, as does the entire staff (one of the waiters was near tears when he said good-bye to my son, and the feeling was definitely mutual). Part of the adventure for children ages 2 to 12 is Camp Ciclismo, where they'll get to know farm animals, meet local children, and play on a playground. Don't miss mini-golf in town, either!

Mornings are dedicated to guided hikes for all levels. You can expect to hike between 5 and 15 mi (8 and 24 km) each day along easy paths, through fields where the ringing of cowbells echos through the valley, and even up to the ruins of an ancient castle. The best part of the day may be reaching the *rifugios*, the mountain huts where simple but memorably delicious lunches are served. There are also optional bike rides for experienced cyclists along some of the world's most spectacular roads and passes—including Passo Sella, Passo Pordoi, and Passo Falzarego—which cover 30 to 50 mi (48 to 80 km) a day. In the afternoon you can expand your mind with natural history talks, cooking lessons, craft demonstrations, photography clinics, and excursions to nearby villages. Or you can just laze by the pool, play tennis or golf on the hotel's grounds, have a chess game on the garden board, or take up bocce. A trip highlights is a visit to the Sud-Tirol Museum of Archaeology in Bolzano, the resting place of Otzi, the 3,000-year-old man found in the Alps by hikers a few years ago.

A new trip for 2002 is the Mediterranean Multi Sport, which mixes hiking, cycling, swimming, and learning adventures on the island of Sardinia. The second largest of the Mediterranean's islands, with 3,200 miles of coastline, Sardinia is truly a world unto itself. Indigenous Sards have preserved their traditional language, folklore, and ethnicity, making the island a sort of living history museum. In the midst of high cliffs, white sand beaches sloping into the turquoise sea, and dramatic forests, mountains, and canyons, this trip to Sardinia offers a view of rural Mediterranean life. The group spends three nights on the coast and four nights in the interior so that you cover the highlights of the island's culture and landscapes.

Ciclismo Classico, 30 Marathon St., Arlington, MA 02724, tel. 781/646–3377 or 800/866–7314, www.ciclismoclassico.com. June–Oct.: 8–9 days, $2,595 adults, 40% discount for children 3–16 sharing accommodations with parents, $200 for children 2 and under sharing with parents. Bike rental is $150.

Cross Country International

8+

Cross Country International (CCI) offers walking vacations across Europe. One look at CCI's catalog of trips will show you that owners Karen and Roy Lancaster choose destinations that are rich in history as well as natural beauty—wonderful, memorable classrooms without walls.

FOR FAMILIES. While most of CCI's vacations are suitable for families, several stand out. Scotland is a land of pastoral landscapes and rugged coastlines. Its history, populated by wizards, queens, and brave warriors, can't help but fascinate children and adults alike. And then there's the warmth of the Scottish people, which of all the reasons to visit this land may be the most compelling. The Scottish Castles Walk takes place in the Borders region, not far from England. Folk tales about this land abound, and parents may want to read with their children about Sir Walter Scott, wizard Michael Scott, King Arthur, Mary Queen of Scots, and Robert the Bruce before arriving, as the itinerary includes places associated with all of them. You'll visit a 12th-century abbey, walk through heather-covered hills, stop at castles and lochs, and stroll along the River Tweed, walking about 6 to 10 mi (10 to 16 km) each day.

Provence Walk, covering about the same number of daily miles, takes in the land where Julius Caesar, Cezanne, Monet, and Van Gogh all made their mark. Here in this small area of southeastern France, famous for its herbs and cooking, walkers have views of both the magnificent Alps and the blue Mediterranean Sea. For another view of the Mediterranean, families might choose the Crete Walk. On this island, which claims Europe's oldest civilization (the Minoan era, 3000–1400 BC), you will walk gorges and villages, swim in the sea, and perhaps see the lammergeier, one of Europe's largest birds of prey. Families should plan on being out four to six hours each day, with some ascents and treks along rugged footpaths.

Cross Country International, Box 1170, Millbrook, NY 12545, tel. 800/828–8768, www.equestrianvacations.com. June–Aug.: 6–7 days, $1,050–$1,890 adults, 25% discount for children age 11 and under sharing a room with parents.

GORP Travel

6+

GORP Travel works with a variety of outfitters, primarily in the American West but also around the world. Although there are many hiking vacations in its catalog, two in Hawaii and Canada stand out as especially good family trips.

FOR FAMILIES. The 10-day, four-island Hawaiian Hiking Odyssey for families with children ages 12 and up takes in Kauai, Maui, Lanai, and the Big Island, combining hiking with kayaking and snorkeling in Hawaii's alluring waters. The group stays in inns and bed-and-breakfasts along the way. You hike the dramatic sea cliffs of Kauai's Na Pali Coast, visit a wildlife refuge, and swim in both the ocean and the island's serene lagoons. On Maui you trek into the jungle and swim under the waterfalls of the West Maui Mountains. No trip here is complete without a hike into Haleakala, a dormant volcano with a spectacularly massive crater at its center. This is the longest hike of the trip—9 mi (14 km) down into the crater and back out. Mid-week the group sets sail on a 50-ft catamaran to snorkel the pristine reefs around the island of Lanai. The Big Island of Hawaii is the most rugged. You explore Kilauea and the rest of Volcanoes National Park, with its still-active volcanoes, as well as snorkel along the Kona Coast and participate in a traditional luau before heading to the Kona airport (transfers are included in the cost).

For heli-hiking in the Canadian Rockies, your family can join lodge-based trips that include helicopter transportation to the remote wilderness areas where you hike each day. This adventure, for ages 8 and up, lets you choose from a number of trip lengths and itineraries. Depending on the lodge you select, the trip begins either in Banff, in Alberta, or in Kelowna, in southern British Columbia. Relaxing in whirlpools and saunas at the lodges makes a perfect end to perfect days—as long as your idea of perfection is trekking high wilderness trails with not another soul around. Up to 48 guests can stay at the lodges, but hiking groups aren't bigger than 10 or 11.

GORP Travel, 10055 Westmoor Dr., Suite 215, Westminster, CO 80021, tel. 720/887–8500 or 877/440–4677, gorptravel.gorp.com. Year-round (all trips not available all months): 4–10 days, $975–$2,750 adults, $690–$1,890 children (age 14 and under on the Canadian trip).

Mountain Hiking Program Innsbruck

8+

No city is as committed to bringing tourists into the high country as Innsbruck, which is probably best known as the two-time host of the Winter Olympic Games and for its world-class skiing. Yet this Austrian city in the heart of the Alps also offers world-class hiking and walking in summer and fall—and it couldn't be easier for visitors to experience.

FOR FAMILIES. Mountain Hiking Program Innsbruck has an extensive agenda for families staying in town and at resorts in the surrounding villages. Although the program doesn't cost a cent, participants must have an Innsbruck Card, which provides tourists with either free or reduced admission to a variety of local attractions and public transportation, including cable cars. Each morning guides from the Alpine School Innsbruck meet hikers at Congress Innsbruck in town and then lead them on one of 40 possible routes in the surrounding hills and mountains. Hikes are generally three to five hours in length, and though participants should be in good physical condition, mountain-climbing know-how isn't necessary. If you didn't pack your hiking boots or day packs, no problem—the program includes free loaner boots, rucksacks, and a tour book. Weather is changeable, especially in fall, so you should be prepared with appropriate outdoor clothing, rainwear, sunscreen, and layers. It's a good idea to take snacks, too. You can go every day if you wish. Guides will award your family with badges: bronze for one hike, silver for three, and gold for 10.

Once a week there are also free Lantern Hikes, on which hikers carrying lanterns walk up to Gasthof Heiligwasser above Igls to spend a "rustic" evening at the hut. For the truly adventurous, there are free glacier hikes in July and August that take you over a path of ice and snow at 10,496 ft—with views well worth the effort. You can also arrange a two-day hut trek with the Alpine School (extra charge). Those who want to really explore the area should try the Hiking Pass Innsbruck, available at any lift ticket window, which gives you repeated access to the lifts and cable cars that take you up to the best hiking trails. You can pick up a comprehensive hiking and touring map and get information on all of the hiking in and around Innsbruck at the tourism office in town.

Innsbruck Tourist Office, A-6021, Innsbruck, Burggraben 3, Austria, tel. 43/512/59850, www.tiscover.com/innsbruck. June–Oct.: daily, free.

Mountain Travel Sobek

8+

The company combines two of the most well-known names in adventure travel, Mountain Travel and Sobek Expeditions. The two came together as one company in 1991, thereby combining several decades of experience, expertise, and the best adventure contacts in the world. Although it's better known for its challenging adventures into remote and untracked regions, Mountain Travel Sobek also has a softer side—its extensive trip list includes 17 journeys designated "fun for all ages." While there aren't specific departures just for families, the trips are guaranteed to meet the desires and expectations of all kinds of adventurous travelers, even those without lots of wilderness or trekking experience.

FOR FAMILIES. Four of the "fun for all ages" trips are mostly about hiking. Families with kids as young as 8 can sign on for Wild Alaska, an 11-day adventure with four days of easy to moderate hikes. The trip starts and ends in Anchorage, and in between you'll explore Alaska's southeastern coast and mountains, including Kenai Fjords National Park, Resurrection Bay, Prince William Sound, Matanuska Valley, and the rugged vistas of Wrangell-St. Elias National Park. Families with kids 10 and older might like the seven-day Canadian Rockies Sampler, which combines three days of easy to moderate hikes with rafting and horseback riding. Base camp is rustic Goat Mountain Lodge in British Columbia, near the Alberta border. Don't let the setting fool you, though—the lodge is known for its gourmet meals.

If going south is more your style, head to Peru or Ecuador, where the journeys are as much about culture as adventure. On the 10-day Andean Explorer you'll hike at 11,000 ft through a land of mountains, rivers, and pre-Hispanic and colonial history; stroll the streets of Cuzco, former capital of the Inca Empire; and raft the Urubamba River through the Sacred Valley of the Incas. There are stops at the ruins at Pisac and Ollantaytambo, plus you'll hike the final leg of the traditional Inca Trail from Chachabamba to Machu Pichu.

Six days of the nine-day Hikng the Haciendas of Ecuador trip are devoted to easy to moderate hiking at about 12,000 ft. Hidden away in Ecuador's verdant highlands are ancient haciendas, most dating to the 16th century. Once part of a network of farming estates (some are still working farms), many have been converted into gracious country inns. The diverse ecological regions of the Andes mountains include grasslands, cloud forests, and volcanoes, and you'll hike through areas known for abundant and resplendent birdlife. You'll also have a chance to visit local artisans and Ecuador's famous craft market at Otavalo. Don't be surprised if your kids like bargaining for goods at the markets as much as they like meeting giant birds up close and personal at a condor reintroduction project, or visiting an impressive ecological reserve.

Mountain Travel Sobek, 6420 Fairmount Ave., El Cerrito, CA 94530, tel. 888/687-6235, www.mtsobek.com. Year-round (all trips not available all months): 7–11 days, $1,650–$3,360 per person (no children's rates on hiking trips).

National Geographic Expeditions

8+

It's hard to think of a company more suitable for taking families—or anyone else, for that matter—out to discover the world. National Geographic Expeditions are led by the National Geographic Society's renowned experts: writers, photographers, explorers, researchers, and scientists. Many of the trip leaders are the same people whose stories and photographs are found in the magazine. And though some explorers rough it, these trips are created in the tradition of the society's early explorers, who apparently had a penchant for living in luxury while on their expeditions. The society believes that "voyages of discovery and adventure are well complemented by amenities and comfort," so they select first class accommodations and restaurants where available, and the staff is specially selected to work with children on family trips.

FOR FAMILIES. Four Corners Family Adventure explores the rich history and geology of the Four Corners region of the United States, including Mesa Verde National Park, Canyon de Chelly, and Monument Valley. It's perfect for families who want to combine hiking with cultural learning. Each year one of the departures is led by Mark Varien, Director of Research at Crow Canyon Archaeological Center (see Archaeology Adventures), who is an expert at helping families better understand the science of archaeology and the culture and history of the ancient people who once populated the American southwest. The trip starts and ends in Cortez or Durango, Colorado. Over the course of nine days you'll hike to cliff dwellings in Mesa Verde National Park, Utah, near the San Juan River, and in Canyon de Chelly. You'll see rock art and raft the San Juan River, and you'll spend time with Native guides and families of both the Navajo and Hopi tribes. One of the highlights is always the horseback ride through the shadows of the magnificent buttes and spires of Monument Valley.

National Geographic has other family trips available, but the list can change, so call for the latest information.

National Geographic Expeditions, Box 65265, Washington, DC 20035-5265, tel. 888/966–8687, www.nationalgeographic.com/ngexpeditions. July–Aug.: 8 days, $2,095 adults, $1,895 ages 8–17.

National Wildlife Federation Family Summit

ALL

Each year the National Wildlife Federation (NWF) offers at least one Family Summit, and the location varies from year to year. In 2001 the Summit was at Canaan Valley, West Virginia; the 2002 Summit was in Big Sky, Montana. Other settings have included the YMCA of the Rockies in Colorado, North Carolina, California, and Hawaii. Typical of other NWF programs, this one has a focus on conservation and enlightened care for and use of the planet. "A week-long environmental discovery program in spectacular natural settings for people of all ages and backgrounds" is how the Federation describes it. These programs are extremely popular—many families attend year after year—so it's necessary to sign up very early. Information about the following year's Summit is on the Federation's Web site (www.nwf.org) in the fall and early registration ends January 1, which gives you some indication of just how early families commit to this excellent program.

FOR FAMILIES. Each Summit has programs for all family members, starting with preschoolers. The groups are broken down by age: 3–4, 5–12, 13–17, 18–25, and 26+. Childcare during daily class time is provided for infants and toddlers, with a staff ratio of 1 caregiver to 5 children. Preschoolers take part in the Your Big Backyard Preschool Program, based on the NWF magazine of the same name. Micro-hikes, touch-and-feel expeditions, and nature crafts round out the program. Ages 5–12 are Junior Naturalists, ready to study streams, go on nature hikes, partake in wildlife investigations, and try outdoor games. The goal? To encourage kids' natural curiosity and help them make discoveries about the world. Teens might be gone all day on hikes or participating in team-building and outdoor skill sessions, while the program for young adults is all about action: water sports, hikes, natural history excursions, and more. General activities always include hiking; there are usually hikes each day geared for various abilities, some all-day adventures. Each Summit's programs are specific to that location. For the 2002 Summit in Big Sky, for example, activities included field trips to Yellowstone National Park; classes on elk, bison, wolves, and grizzly bears; geology; regional dinosaur studies; Native American studies; photography; birdwatching; and astronomy.

National Wildlife Federation Family Summits, 11100 Wildlife Center Dr., Reston, VA 20190-5362, tel. 703/438–6000 (NWF headquarters), or 800/606–9563 (Summits Information). June–July: 7 days, program fees $500 adults, $250–$425 ages 3–17, depending on age, $3–$5 per hour childcare charge for ages 2 and under. Housing and meal costs vary at each location. For Big Sky rates for studios to 3-bedroom condos plus all meals and taxes range from $485–$2,148 per adult for the week, depending on the room and number of people. Children 12 and under are free, but have to purchase a $175 meal plan.

Outward Bound

13+

Outward Bound seeks to equip students of all ages with skills to last a lifetime. Although the wilderness is the venue for the learning, the skills are meant to serve students well in every arena of life, including work, school, play, and, perhaps most important, relationships. The Parent–Child courses in particular are at least partially about strengthening the bond between parents and their children. The self-confidence, self-esteem, determination, and knowledge about self and others that are by-products of every Outward Bound course, however, will serve teens well in every relationship. After all, these are the same things that parents try to instill in their kids on a daily basis, so taking an Outward Bound course is a way to reinforce what you've already been doing.

FOR FAMILIES. Outward Bound has two backpacking courses for parents and teens to take together, one in the Mahoosuc Mountains of Maine, the other among the 10,000-ft peaks of Montana's Pioneer Mountains. In Maine, participants hike through dense forests, up some of the highest peaks in the northeast, and along some of the most challenging parts of the Appalachian Trail. The jagged, imposing peaks of the Pioneers, southwest of Butte in Montana, offer the vast, impressive vistas for which the west is known. The courses involve carrying heavy packs—40 to 60 lbs (18 to 27 kg)—and learning a variety of important wilderness skills, from map and compass navigation to expedition planning. Naturally, these courses involve participants setting up and breaking down camp, and challenging themselves on different trails each day.

Outward Bound, 100 Mystery Point Rd., Garrison, NY 10524, tel. 914/424–4000 or 800/243–8520, www.outwardbound.corg. July–Aug.: 8 days, $945–$1,095 per person, plus $75 application fee. Financial aid available for some courses.

Sierra Club

ALL

Of the Sierra Club's 30 family trips, 19 focus primarily on hiking. The majority of these explore western states, but you'll find several eastern destinations each year, too. Sierra Club leaders are highly experienced in guiding families. All trips, family and otherwise, emphasize respect for and preservation of America's wilderness areas. This is one of the few organizations of its kind to welcome children on some service trips as well—expeditions that involve clearing and maintaining trails or doing other projects to assist the park service.

FOR FAMILIES. There are family trips for all ages, but not all trips are suitable for every age. Families with preschoolers (ages 3 and 4) have a choice of two trips at Clair Tappaan Lodge in the Sierra Nevada high country. Family Camp at the Lodge gives participants a taste of the wilderness with the comfort of a lodge at night. After spending the days hiking and swimming in the area around Donner Pass, families can join in campfires and language lessons. The other Tappaan Lodge trip is for grandparents and grandchildren. Together, these two generations can hike, swim, ride the tram to the top of Squaw Valley, visit the Donner State Museum, and learn about the natural world of the Sierra Nevada. Families help with cooking and chores on these trips. A Spring Break in the Rockies is for those who yearn to explore the high country of Rocky Mountain National Park., outside of Estes Park, Colorado.

The club's outings for all ages—including babies in backpacks—explore the Cape Cod National Seashore of Massachusetts and Rocky Mountain National Park in Colorado. On the Cape Cod itinerary families camp in Wellfleet and hike, bike, swim, whale-watch, and visit the Massachusetts Audubon Sanctuary salt marshes, among other adventures. The Rocky Mountain Ramble in Colorado focuses on daily hikes of varied difficulty in alpine meadows, around high-country lakes, and to waterfalls, glaciers, and Longs Peak. You stay in a comfortable lodge, with programs for children ages 2½ through 17, fishing, and a swimming pool.

Children as young as 5 are welcome on an easy hiking trip in the Stehekin Valley of North Cascades National Park in Washington or on the Acadia Family Trip in Acadia National Park, which is geared for families with children between the ages of 5 and 10. The Washington trip is based in tent cabins at a rustic ranch, the Acadia trip is for those who want to camp out. Both adventures offer trails easy enough for 5-year-olds. In Washington the group will travel by ranch van to a different trailhead each day. The Stehekin Valley is only accessible by foot, boat, or float plane (you'll arrive by boat), so its natural beauty has not been altered by development. Acadia is all about tidepools and shorelines, shorebirds and curious sea creatures such as sea cucumbers and sea stars. The focus of the trip is the national park, which is on Mt. Desert Island off Maine's rocky coast. Families have the options of canoeing, kayaking, and whale-watching.

Families with kids age 9 and older might consider the Mitre Basin Family Backpack, in the Golden Trout Wilderness, and Sequoia National Park. This is a trip best for experienced backpackers—those who would relish the optional challenge of climbing a 13,000-ft peak. Over five days, you'll cover a 24-mi (39-km) route, with a total elevation gain of about 4,000 ft. There's a nonhiking layover day at Mitre Basin. The club feels this trip is best for ages 9 to 12 (most teens would find the pace too slow).

For families that want to combine their vacation with outdoor work, The Sierra Club has a multigenerational trail service trip in the San Juan range of southern Colorado. The goal is to help eradicate invasive non-native weeds from high meadows, as well as to work on trail maintenance, but the club also seeks to teach participants, regardless of age, about wilderness conservation. In addition to working, there's plenty of time off for exploration of this spectacular terrain. With work and base camps at 10,000 to 11,000 ft, you'll rarely be without a view to remember.

Among other possibilities are the grandparent–grandchild trips in Hawaii and the Alaska family lodge trip. Sierra Club's outings change annually, and the ones listed here are typical of its family trips but may not be offered every year. However, you can choose from a roster of fun, challenging, and educational trips, whether your children are

toddlers or teens, and whether you are parents or grandparents. Participants bring their own tents and gear on camping trips.
Sierra Club, 85 2nd St., San Francisco, CA 94105, tel. 415/977–5522, www.sierraclub.org. Apr.–Sept.: 4–8 days, $295–$1,295 adults, $295–$995 children 16 and under. All participants 18 and up must be Sierra Club members; application and fees ($39 per person, $47 per couple) can be sent in with the trip reservation form.

Sila Sojourns Wilderness & Creative Journeys

10+

Sila is an Inuit word for nature and free-spiritedness. To the people of the Arctic, it signifies a mysterious power in the universe. A walk through Canada's Yukon wilderness will help you understand why Joyce Majiski and Jill Pangman gave their company this name. Nature's scale here is immense, giving a sense of an undefinable force. Joyce and Jill, longtime Yukon residents, have considerable wilderness experience as guides. They bring another dimension to their company as well: both are biologists, naturalists, and fine artists. Their trips challenge adventurers to stretch their physical and creative limits.

FOR FAMILIES. Although Sila has some scheduled hiking, rafting, and kayaking sojourns, the company specializes in custom-designed trips. All journeys start and end in Whitehorse; any wilderness flights are included in the trip cost. Joyce recommends two areas for custom family treks. In either, a hiking trip can be combined with a four- to six-day rafting adventure down the Alsek River to Lowell Lake, where the calving Lowell Glacier provides a visual and auditory feast.

For ages 10 and up, Primrose Lake, a half-hour flight from Whitehorse in the southern section of the Yukon, offers moderate hikes that follow game trails across rolling hills and past clear lakes and streams. The land changes from alpine meadows to northern boreal forests of spruce, poplar, and lodgepole pine. With some of the hiking above tree line, there are uninterrupted views of the landscape and opportunities to see Dall sheep, grizzlies, black bears, and moose. You spend two nights of the trip in a wilderness lodge; on the rest you camp out.

Bordering Alaska in the southwest corner of the Yukon, Kluane National Park encompasses 8,500 square mi, with glaciers, river valleys, and mountains that are dramatic and untamed. Challenging hiking terrain makes this trip best for ages 16 and up; the park contains both Mt. Logan and Mt. St. Elias, the second- and third-highest peaks in North America. An astonishing variety of wildlife inhabits the park: moose, wolves, foxes, lynx, wolverines, otters, and black bears, as well as a large grizzly population. You camp in alpine areas or by rivers and glaciers.

Some multi-activity trips for women focus on the creative process. Mothers and teenage daughters who want to experience the wilderness and explore perspectives on creative writing, journal keeping, and other means of artistic expression should ask about these camping or lodge-based trips. Depending on the location, participants hike from a lodge, kayak on Atlin Lake in northern British Columbia, or even canoe or raft.
Sila Sojourns, Box 31258, Whitehorse, Yukon, Canada Y1A 5P7, tel. 867/633–8453, www.silasojourns.com. June–Sept.: 3–12 days, C$100–C$250 per day, 10%–20% discount for children under 18.

Smithsonian Study Tours

8+

One reason to choose Smithsonian Study Tours is for the quality of its study leaders, men and women who are experts in the region through which you travel and on the cultures found there. The study leaders are with the group for the entire tour, and they're chosen for their ability to share their enthusiasm and knowledge with you. While they offer insights and insider's views you simply wouldn't get on your own, the tour manager also makes certain that your travel details are taken care of—so you don't have to think about anything but enjoying the experience and learning with your children.

FOR FAMILIES. Hike in and around the Grand Canyon and learn about the geology and wildlife of the region from Smithsonian study leader and naturalist Jennifer Beltz. Grand Canyon Family Adventure is an inn- and lodge-based journey, which includes such highlights as a jeep tour of Sedona's backcountry, with its sculpted red rocks, and rafting on the mighty Colorado River through Glen Canyon. The group will hike Sunset Crater, among other places, and have a chance to explore Native lands. The trip includes special programs for young people and for adults, with activities that are as much fun as they are educational.
Smithsonian Study Tours, Ripley Center Suite 3077, 1100 Jefferson Dr. SW, Washington, DC 20560-0701, tel. 202/357–4700 or 877/338–8687, smithsonianstudytours.org. June: 7 days, $2,095 adults, $1,275 children 8–15.

Southwest Trekking

ALL

John Heiman Jr. founded Southwest Trekking because he wanted to be outdoors and to share the natural world with anyone who wanted to come along with him. A father himself, he especially likes to help families experience what nature has to offer. "I respect the children's place in the outing," he says, meaning every individual in his groups, adult or child, counts. John's tours are highly customized—no big-group departures with this company. Treks can be all-inclusive (he'll provide everything you need, including camping gear) or on an as-needed basis (if you have your own tents and sleeping bags, why pay for his?). A native of Tucson, John specializes in treks in pristine areas of Arizona and Mexico.

FOR FAMILIES. Families can explore one of John's favorite destinations, the Dragoon Mountains, and an area known as Cochise Stronghold, east of Tucson. In the mid-19th century Cochise, a Chiricahua Apache chief, held off the U.S. cavalry for six years, in part because of the remoteness and ruggedness of this land. It's fully accessible for car camping, though, making it an ideal family destination. Beauty, history, legend, challenge, accessibility—what could be better?

Committed to ecotourism, Southwest Trekking has been working with the local people of the Colorado River delta and upper Gulf of California region in Mexico to establish a program for visitors that would benefit the area's farmers. The result, Spatial Journeys, opens a sensitive, remote, and fragile environment to visitors and gives you a unique opportunity to learn about the culture, social history, and flora and fauna of the region, as well as the environmental concerns its residents face. You visit the homes of local families and have a chance to meet farmers, fishers, schoolteachers, biologists, and children. The trip's educational aspect makes it appropriate for families with older children. You also hike through volcanic formations, snorkel and swim on beaches to the south of the Gulf of Santa Clara, and canoe through the Cienega de Santa Clara—49,400 acres of wetlands.

Southwest Trekking works on a custom basis, and you can talk to the company about your family, how much time you have, where you want to go, and what you want to do. John and his staff will put together a trek that suits everyone in your family.
Southwest Trekking, Box 57714, Tucson, AZ 85732, tel. 520/296–9661, www.swtrekking.com. Year-round: ½–multiple days,

$60–$150 per day adults, $30–$75 per day children under 12. Outfitter's expenses are additional on multiday treks.

Swiss Federal Railways

ALL

There are many reasons to take your kids to Switzerland. The country is beautiful, friendly, and clean; there are four languages to introduce them to (German, French, Italian, and the ancient Romansch language of the Engadine Valley); children under 16 ride free on Swiss public transportation (including trains); and Swiss parents are everywhere hiking, dining, and traveling with their children. It's a family-friendly country in every respect, and it offers some of the most spectacularly scenic hiking in the world—thanks in large part to the extensive, well-planned, and efficient Swiss Travel System, of which Swiss Federal Railways (SBB) is a part. Here is a chance for those families who want to plan a trip on their own to do so, but with the expert help of SBB and RailEurope. You can create your own itinerary, pick your own hotels, and treat yourselves and your children to a country and culture that offers in abundance what every family hiking vacation should—extraordinary natural beauty and endless opportunities for family bonding, learning, and renewal. Add to that fabulous food and surprising ease of travel, and it's hard to come up with a more perfect walking or hiking destination for North American families.

FOR FAMILIES. All of Switzerland lends itself to family hiking, but there are some highlights that shouldn't be missed. Parc Naziunal Svizzer is Switzerland's only national park and the largest nature reserve in the country, with an area of 169 square km rising from 420 to 9,519 ft. Because the park was founded in 1914 by a group of scientists, it remains a virtually wild and intact natural landscape, and there are strict rules for its use. Nothing can be touched or disturbed. The park's 50 mi (80 km) of marked trails are well maintained, and the signs are in five languages (including English), so you won't miss any important information about the area's natural history or the wildlife—including ibex, chamois, marmots, deer, and golden eagles. One of the park's best features is the nature trail, with signs especially for children that encourage active observe and understanding of park life (try to remember the hand signs for various birds and trees, then test yourselves at the end of your visit). The park is easily reached by train to Zernez, but your first stop should be the information center at the Chasa dal Parc right near the station, where you can pick up English-language guidebooks and brochures, including a written guide to the family-perfect nature trail.

Switzerland has an excess of stunning rail routes, but the Bernina Express is surely one of the most spectacular. All along its way between Chur, Switzerland and Tirano, Italy (via St. Moritz, Pontresina, and the Engadine Valley), it offers not only what is arguably the best alpine scenery in the world, but access to hiking for all abilities and ages. You might stay in the friendly resort town of Pontresina (far less "haute" than neighboring St. Moritz), then hop on the Bernina Express for a day of hiking, getting on and off as you choose (using one of the Swiss Rail Passes or Swiss Card). Ride the train to Alp Gruem, where you can hike an easy path overlooking the Alps, valley, and winding rail tracks down to Morteratsch. There, join dozens of Swiss families walking the mile trail to the glacier. Along the way signs explain how global warming and the start of the Industrial Revolution have contributed the glacier's retreat—more than 480 ft since 1900. If it's lunchtime, indulge in hearty gnocci and pumpkin soup at the trackside restaurant. Although the hiking is superb, what your kids might like best is the train itself, and the miles of steep, curving track and tunnels it winds through as it climbs the Alps.

Parts of Switzerland are known for the exquisite painted decorations on village buildings (*sgraffito*), and no place offers better examples than the tiny village of Guarda, northeast of Zernez. Stay at the Hotel Meisser, with its spacious family-size suites, then hike around the countryside to your heart's content. Further north is Appenzell, heart of the Canton of Appenzell Inner Rhodes, famous for those huge Swiss alpenhorns and for cheese. Hotels are within walking distance from the station, and from here you can use both trains and cable cars to explore easy trails with views of Switzerland, Austria, and Lichtenstein in one panoramic sweep.

These are just a few of the possibilities. SBB can give you ideas on planning your hiking routes using the trains (which, by the way, go directly to and from the airport in Zurich), and you get all the information you need about passes from RailEurope here in the United States. You can also contact a Swiss tourism office. You must buy a pass or Swiss Card, which conveniently includes all of Switzerland's public transportation—trains, buses, and boats—in order for kids to ride free.

Swiss Federal Railways, booked through RailEurope in North America, tel. 888/382–7245 in the U.S.; 800/361–7245 in Canada. Swiss Pass $132–$525 for adults, depending on class of travel and number of days purchased.

Synago

12+

Synago is an ancient Greek word meaning "to lead together," and that's exactly the spirit of this small company run by two young adventurers who have wisdom, experience, and ability far beyond their years. Buzz Henczel and Jasmine Cross have guided in destinations around the world, and they specialize in team building, experiential leadership, and outdoors skill-building for children and adults. I can tell you firsthand that they are both extremely gifted at connecting with children, and know how to make a trip work for both children and adults. They have a passion for exploring the world and for sharing it with others, and they both possess the one indispensable attribute essential for guiding and travel: a terrific sense of humor. Kids love them, and I can think of no better people with whom to travel to such exotic destinations as Nepal, their signature trip. I would trust my family with them without reservation.

This said, these *are* exotic destinations, and Synago is about experiencing them as they really are. As Buzz and Jasmine note on their Web site (www.synago.com), "In our destinations you will almost certainly have to contend with . . . relative inefficiencies, a more relaxed attitude to time, cancellations and closures without explanation, outdated facilities, suspect plumbing, and apparently mindless bureaucracy." If your family can cope with such things and has a desire to experience life as it really is in ancient, distant lands, Synago is for you.

FOR FAMILIES. Synago has a strong connection to Nepal and frequently leads trips there. Unlike many tour operators, though, they are more than willing to include families on these treks. They will customize any trip to your family's specifications—in fact, that's what they most frequently do—but they also have some scheduled trips, including the twice yearly Everest Base Camp Trek in April and October. The trip begins and ends in Kathmandu, where you can explore ancient temples and surrounding valleys. The mountain adventure starts with a flight over the singular, awe-inspiring landscape of the Himalayas to the village of Lukla in the northeast Khumbu region. This isn't a camping trip; instead, you hike from teahouse to teahouse, remote village to remote village, immersed in the Sherpa and Nepalese cultures. In addition to Everest Base Camp, which you reach on day 13, you visit Buddhist monasteries and Hindu shrines, and have an opportunity for a once-in-a-lifetime view of Mt. Everest from 18,200-ft Kala Pattar, the highest point on the trek. The itinerary is flexible, the pace determined by the group. And while 12 is probably a good age to consider as minimum, if you have a younger child who is an experienced hiker and can adjust to foreign cultures and heady heights, Synago will consider your request.

Synago, Box 61008 Kensington PO, Calgary, Alberta, Canada T2N 4S6, tel. 403/605–2490 or 866/479–6246 (in the U.S. and Canada). Apr. and Oct. (Nepal): 22 days, C$4,250, including international airfare from Vancouver. Custom trips vary greatly, depending on destination, length, and itinerary.

Wells Gray Chalets & Wilderness Adventures

8+

The Cariboo Mountains reign over the 1.3 million acres of Wells Gray Provincial Park in southeastern British Columbia, a pristine land of alpine meadows and mountain lakes. Wells Gray Chalets & Wilderness Adventures, a family business, operates two high wilderness chalets and a secluded valley cabin here; a separate guest ranch (not owned by this company) is near the entrance to the park. The chalets can be rented individually without guides or used as part of a guided hiking trek. Although there's no stated age limit, the hut-to-hut hike is very challenging—perfect for families with teens. Families with children under age 8 should talk to staff members before booking a vacation. Because of increased interest, the company now designates a hiking trip in August just for families.

FOR FAMILIES. If you have preteens and younger or just can't decide whether you prefer land or water, ask about the Canoe and Trek Combo. Families camp along the shore of Clearwater Lake for three days of canoeing, then spend a night at Wells Gray Guest Ranch before beginning three days of trekking based at a secluded mountain hut.

Parents with teens or children with solid backcountry experience might opt for the company's premier trip, the seven-day hut-to-hut trek. Although it's just a little more than 1½ mi (2½ km) to Trophy Mountain Chalet, the ascent is about 1,700 ft. This area presents the most rugged terrain of the trip; you can reward yourself with a swim and glorious views. Table Mountain Cabin, the next stop, is reached by crossing the Trophy Mountains and descending into isolated Moul Valley. Fight Meadow Chalet, the third and last hut, is 6,500 ft up at the head of an expansive alpine meadow. There are no trails between huts; this is true wilderness hiking for those who want to challenge themselves and each other. Parents should be sure of their own and their children's abilities before undertaking this trek.

Wells Gray Chalets & Wilderness Adventures, Box 188, Clearwater, British Columbia, Canada V0E 1N0, tel. 250/587–6444 or 888/SKI–TREK, www.skihike.com. June–Sept.: 7 days, $430–$565 adults, 25% discount for children under 13.

Wilderness Inquiry

ALL

Wilderness Inquiry has traditionally run lots of canoeing trips for families, as well as dogsledding and ski adventures (see Canoeing *and* Dogsledding). It has a hiking trip on its roster as well, and like all Wilderness Inquiry programs, this trip is open to all people of all abilities and physical challenges.

FOR FAMILIES. Cumberland Island Family Hiking takes place on a Georgia island three to four hours north of Orlando. Cumberland Island is a National Seashore with pristine sandy ocean beaches perfect for family camping. The group will catch the ferry at St. Mary's, just over the Georgia border from Florida, for the boat ride across Cumberland Sound. As you hike on paths through dense oak forests or along the ocean's edge, you're likely to see wild horses, loggerhead turtles, fiddler crabs, and that peculiar southern resident, the armadillo. (Note that the paths are wheelchair accessible.) Families can also play games, swim, and create fantastic sandcastles, which may not last but will provide memories. Kids may participate in some of the island's ranger-led programs as well. Plan on hiking about ½ to 2 mi (1 to 3 km) each day. The campsite, between the forest and the ocean, has bathrooms and showers, but there's cold water only.

Wilderness Inquiry, 808 14th Ave. SE, Minneapolis, MN 55414-1516, tel. 612/676–9400 or 800/728–0719, www.wildernessinquiry.org. Mar.–Apr.: 3 days, $295 adults, $150 ages 16 and under.

Resources

Books

For solid information on taking children into the wilderness, check out *Kids Outdoors: Skills and Knowledge for Outdoor Adventures*, by Frank Logue (McGraw-Hill), *The Sierra Club Family Outdoors Guide*, by Marlyn Doan (Sierra Club Books), and *Kids in the Wild*, by Cindy Ross and Todd Gladfelter (Mountaineers Books, tel. 800/553–4453). Michael Elsohn Ross's *The Happy Camper Handbook* (Yosemite Association, tel. 209/379–2648) comes with a flashlight and rescue whistle and is full of essential camping information for school-age children; parents can read it aloud to younger children, too. Families serious about backpacking will find good practical advice in *Basic Essentials Backpacking*, by Harry Robers, revised by Adrienne Hall (Globe Pequot Press). Talk about basics—it even tells you how best to walk with a heavy pack. You don't have to be going with Outward Bound to find *The Outward Bound Backpacker's Handbook*, by Glenn Randall (Lyon's Press), one of the best outdoor guides around. With humor and insight, Randall offers a wealth of information, including such things as how warm a sleeping bag, you need and the pros and cons of internal frame backpacks. Randall is also the author of *The Outward Bound Map & Compass Handbook* (Lyons Press). Finally, *Using GPS*, by Bruce Grubbs (Falcon), *Route Finding*, by Gregory Crouch (Falcon), and *Hiking with Dogs*, by Linda B. Mullally (Falcon), will prove useful to outdoors families with those specific interests.

Products

The following companies sell clothing or footwear for wilderness-loving families. **Patagonia** (8550 White Fir St., Box 32050, Reno, NV 89533, tel. 800/638–6464, www.patagonia.com) is an excellent mail-order source for clothing and outerwear. You can also buy the company's products in most stores that sell outdoor and camping clothing and accessories. **REI outdoor stores** (Sumner, WA 98352-0001, tel. 800/426–4840, www.rei.com) are found nationwide; items can be ordered from their catalog, too. REI's own brand is excellent. **Nike** (1 Bowerman Dr., Beavertown, OR 97005, tel. 503/671–6453 or 800/344–6453, www.nike.com) has hiking boots, water sandals, and aqua socks for all ages, as well as some children's sports clothing and outerwear. **Hi-Tec Sports USA** (4801 Stoddard Rd., Modesto, CA 95356, tel. 209/545–1111 or 800/521–1698, www.hi-tec.com) makes hiking boots and "adventure racing shoes" for children and adults. **L.L. Bean** (Freeport, ME 04033, tel. 800/441–5713, www.llbean.com) has a camping catalog that includes a section on family camping gear and equipment. There's also a children's catalog with outdoor clothing and more.

The following companies make camping gear for children and adults. **Tough Traveler** (1012 State St., Schenectady, NY 12307, tel. 518/377–8526, www.toughtraveler.com), a parent-owned and -operated company, produces quality outdoor gear and luggage for children. Call or write for a catalog. **Mountainsmith, Inc.** (18301 W. Colfax Ave., Building P, Golden, CO 80401, tel. 303/279–5930 or 800/426–4075, www.mountainsmith.com) manufactures day packs suitable for most ages and inner-frame backpacks for older children and adults. **Crazy Creek Products** (Box 1050, Red Lodge, MT 59068, tel. 406/446–3446 or 800/331–0304, www.crazycreek.com) makes camping comfortable with 12 models of take-anywhere fold-up soft chairs.

HORSE PACKING

Like hiking adventures, horse-packing trips take your family into some of the world's most incredible backcountry wilderness areas. But because these are on horseback, you don't have to walk on your own two feet to get there, and you don't have to carry a heavy backpack. Often it's not even necessary to be an expert rider. Adults and teens need no riding experience on many horse-packing trips, although for everyone's safety and enjoyment outfitters often require that children under the age of 11 or 12 ride moderately well and be comfortable around horses. For this reason, horse packing (with a couple of exceptions) is not usually appropriate for families with very young children. Anyone else who wants to experience glorious land and a mode of travel that has been around for centuries should give it a try.

There's another nice benefit to horse-packing trips. Because horses and mules are capable of carrying a lot more than a human, you can escape the spartan atmosphere of long backpacking adventures: food and supplies are first-rate and plentiful.

Questions to Ask

How much time is spent riding each day? On average, outfitters keep you in the saddle from four to six hours per day, but on some trips you may ride as long as eight hours. Depending on the group's size and whether the camp destination is specific or flexible, riding time can also change from day to day. Keep in mind that layover days are usually figured into multiday trips, too. Also, remember that even if you have some riding experience under your belt, a day in the saddle can leave you aching and dealing with saddle sores. The discomfort doesn't usually last that long, but do bring acetaminophen or another pain reliever, antibiotic cream, and a bunch of adhesive bandages.

Will the horses travel a faster gait than a walk? Most horse-packing trips are primarily walking because they often take place in hilly or otherwise challenging terrain. Although horses are very surefooted, walking is the safest way to negotiate these trails, both for horse and rider. Sometimes wranglers allow good riders to go a bit faster under controlled circumstances. If your family cares about this, speak up when you're booking. If you can't work something out, consider a cattle drive (see Cattle Drives), which often allows a faster pace.

Are there activities other than riding? Packers generally return to camp early enough in the afternoon to give your family time for hiking, swimming, and maybe even fishing. You usually need to bring your own fishing gear, however.

Is there a weight limit to what we can bring? Often, yes. A 30-pound limit per person is typical, and you should pack in duffel bags, not hard-sided suitcases.

Are riding boots necessary? Some packers require boots; even if they don't, everyone in the family should have them for safety and comfort. Shoes without adequate heels may allow your foot to slip through the stirrup. If that happened and you fell off as a result, you'd be dragged. Be sure to break new boots in well before the trip.

Is a cowboy hat or a riding helmet needed? A cowboy hat will keep the sun off your face and your hair out of your eyes, and that can be important. It won't, however, protect your head if you fall. Some outfitters provide helmets; most don't require them. To keep yourself and your children safe, you should wear them. You can buy helmets at stores that sell riding apparel and equipment.

Should we bring a camera? You bet. Keep it in a case for protection against dust and dirt, and talk to packers about stopping occasionally for a good shot (most, actually, will tell you when a great photo op is coming up). Don't leave the group to get a good picture without telling someone first; you could get lost. If you're not comfortable carrying a camera when you ride, it can usually go in a saddle bag with your stuff.

What kind of food is served? If your family likes outdoor cooking—hearty egg-and-pancake breakfasts, Dutch oven meals, barbecue, steaks, salads, fruit, and desserts—you'll like the meals just fine. Special requests can usually be accommodated, so ask.

What kind of lodging is provided? These are backcountry trips. Sleeping is almost always in tents—or cowboy style, under the stars, if you prefer. A few packers use cabins or lodges.

What facilities are available for bathing and showering? Do you like the smell of horses? You should, because it will be the predominant odor on a horse-packing trip. At the end of the day, though, some outfitters do provide portable showers or shower trailers. If you're staying in lodges or cabins, you may have access to showers.

What's the typical group size? The average is from 8 to 12, though some outfitters take as few as four and others as many as 20. Between two and five wranglers and/or packers accompany the group. A large group isn't necessarily bad because it provides lots of companionship, and a small group isn't necessarily good if you don't want to be the only ones in the group.

What's included in the cost? Prices for the trips listed here include wranglers and/or packers, a horse, sleeping quarters, all meals from start to end of the actual pack trip, and local transportation to and from the trailhead, unless otherwise noted.

Instruction

Horsemanship is part and parcel of every horse-packing trip; the wranglers will give you pointers and informal instruction on the trail. Your family can also learn about such specifics as feeding horses, grooming animals, and saddling bags. While you're out in the wilderness, guides will teach you about the cultural and natural history of the land, as well as wildlife identification.

Finding the Fun

Midwest: Wilderness Pursuit. **Southwest:** Cottonwood Ranch, GORP Travel, Rockin' R Ranch. **Rockies:** Adventure Specialists, American Wilderness Experience/GORP Travel, Fantasy Ranch, Great Divide Guiding & Outfitters, Skinner Brothers, WTR Outfitters/White Tail Ranch. **West Coast:** Mammoth Lakes Pack Outfit. **Canada:** GORP Travel, Spatsizi Wilderness Vacations.

Favorite Packers

Adventure Specialists

10+

Based on a 5,000-acre ranch in southern Colorado, Adventure Specialists is set amid the rugged Sangre de Cristo Mountains, the gentler Wet Mountains, and the Arkansas River. In addition to riding and horse packing with the 70 animals in its stables, you can also hike, bike, climb, and raft, depending on the trip.

Owners Gary Ziegler and Amy Finger emphasize natural history and environmental awareness. Gary earned a doctorate in archaeology, discovered the ruins of an ancient city in Peru, and has made first ascents of several 20,000-ft South American peaks. Amy, a geologist, has studied languages, flora, and ecology extensively. She's worked with horses most of her life.

FOR FAMILIES. Three adventures are especially appropriate for families. The three-day pack trip into the Sangre de Cristo Mountains is best for spirited children 10 and up who are ready for a challenge. They should have some riding experience and be comfortable around horses. There's one base camp, and rides go through dense forests and up to shimmery alpine lakes. The Surf and Turf trip combines the three-day pack trip with two days of rafting on the Arkansas; because the river is Class III and IV white water, the minimum age is 13. In between riding and rafting, you return to civilization, where hot showers, sit-down dinners, and comfortable beds await.

For a completely different experience, Mountain Sports Week offers rock climbing, two days of riding the open range, a day of mountain biking, and a day of rafting. Participants are based at the ranch in a camp with a large dining and kitchen tent, showers, and individual tents for sleeping. Children under 10 might be considered on an individual basis, but this is a physically challenging week. You can also customize your own course, choosing any of the activities.

Transportation to and from Colorado Springs, 1½ hours away, is included in all packages. Ask about trips to Mexico, Peru, and Spain.

Adventure Specialists, Bear Basin Ranch, Westcliffe, CO 81252, tel. 719/783–2519 or

719/630–7687, www.gorp.com/adventur. May–Oct. (all trips not available at all times): 3–5 days, $525–$950.

Cottonwood Ranch

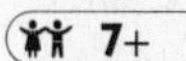 7+

A horse pack trip with the Smiths is a gem of an adventure, far off the beaten path in Nevada. Their family ranch, 75 mi (121 km) north of Wells in the northeast corner of the state, is near nothing—except clean, quiet high desert and the exquisite landscape of the Jarbridge Wilderness. Horace Smith will share with you his love of a land that few have a chance to experience.

FOR FAMILIES. Guests spend the first night at Cottonwood Ranch, then take off for five days in the wilderness. Deep canyons and high peaks make this terrain appropriate for riding at a walk only, and you'll hit the trail from about 9 to 4 each day. Camps with wall tents and cook tents are set up by the wranglers before you arrive. Photo stops are numerous, and you visit abandoned mining cabins that look, according to Horace, "like the old miner just went into town for a day and forgot to come back." There's plenty of wildlife on the trail and good fishing at Emerald Lake (some gear is available); you can also swim in the lake if you can stand the cold water. On the last night you reach the old mining town of Jarbridge and stay in a remodeled barn turned hotel.
Cottonwood Ranch, HC 62, Box 1300, O'Neil Rte., Wells, NV 89835, tel. 775/752–3604, 800/341–5951 (ranch), or 775/752–3135, 775/752–0817 (cell), www.guestranches.com/cottonwood. July–Sept.: 7 days, $1,500, 20% discount for children under 16.

Fantasy Ranch

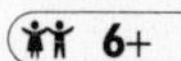 6+

You won't meet a harder-working outfitter than Jim Talbot of Colorado. He'll clear snow from the trails by hand if Mother Nature hasn't cooperated by the time the season's first horse-packing trip is scheduled. Jim's personality is effective with children, which makes him a good teacher, and he's enthusiastic and knowledgeable about the magnificent wilderness that is his backyard. He's also flexible—he won't bend safety rules, but he's willing to work with families to bring their pack-trip dreams to life.

Fantasy Ranch has a five-bedroom lodge, a base for horseback riding, hay-wagon rides, barbecues, and overnight stays. Families can also hike, fish, and bike in the area. When the weather turns cold, come to the ranch for a day of winter riding through the snowy landscape.

FOR FAMILIES. Ages 6 and up can try an overnight in the Oh-Be-Joyful Wilderness northwest of Crested Butte, Fantasy Ranch's hometown. These trails are gentle, but the views and scenery—rushing waterfalls and massive rock formations—are classic Colorado. Children ages 6 through 8 who have never ridden will be led by one of the wranglers. Children 8 and up can take a two- to five-day pack trip into the superb riding country of the West Elk Wilderness area, where the Rockies rise above the meadows and mountain lakes. You can camp or stay in a rustic cabin (extra charge) on the boundary of the wilderness area.

One of the all-time great pack trips for experienced riders age 13 and up is Jim's Crested Butte to Aspen adventure. The three-day ride between the two mountain towns starts at 9,000 ft, just east of Crested Butte, on trails through Maroon Bells Wilderness. You camp in the mountains, then ride four or so hours the following day before descending into alpine meadows and the trailhead outside Aspen. A van takes you into town for an overnight in this world-class resort. Lodging in Aspen is included, but you're on your own for meals. The next morning you begin one of the most spectacular rides anywhere—up and over 11,800-ft East Maroon Pass, then back into Crested Butte.

You need to bring your own sleeping bag and pad; add fishing gear if you want to fish. *Fantasy Ranch, Box 236, Crested Butte, CO 81224, tel. 970/349–5425 or 888/688–3488, www.fantasyranchoutfitters.com. July–Oct. (for pack trips): 2–7 days, $125–$1,400 per person.*

GORP Travel

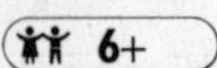

If you haven't picked the area in which you want to ride, check out the GORP Travel Web site (gorptravel.gorp.com), which lists more than 200 horseback adventures worldwide. The company has evaluated the outfitters, knows which ones work best with families, and can make recommendations based on experience and solid knowledge.

If the scheduled trips don't work for you, the company will also customize a family trip for ages 6 and older. Your imagination and willingness to meet adventure head-on and are the only limits to the horse-packing vacation of a lifetime.

FOR FAMILIES. One trip takes riders age 8 and older across the ridges, peaks, and alpine meadows of the Canadian Rockies of Alberta, to the deep wilderness habitat of elk and bighorn sheep. June is calving season for elk, so sightings are generally plentiful then; September is rutting season, and the distinctive bugle of mature bull elk can be heard day and night. This is an active holiday on which riders help with camp chores and horse care, and weather is unpredictable, so be prepared. You can choose from 5-, 7-, and 10-day treks.

In the Lower 48, children age 10 and up can explore Wyoming's Grand Teton Range, 18 mi (29 km) southwest of Jackson. The land is unspoiled, but guests aren't: the camp, up at 7,200 ft, has a dining tent and spacious wall tents with cots, rugs, and wood stoves. Day rides take you through old growth stands of aspen, fir, and spruce into wild-flower meadows and up to summer snow-fields. Two nights of the week are reserved for a trip to the Jackson rodeo. Farther south, families with children 8 and up can ride through the mesas, meadows, canyons, and rugged landscape of the Weminuche Wilderness, part of Colorado's magnificent San Juan Mountains, with chances of spotting eagles, bighorn sheep, mountain lions, and elk. Although you'll camp along the trail, motel lodging in the western-slope town of Durango can be arranged before and after this trip.

Families interested in the Southwest might choose to explore Monument Valley, a wild western landscape straddling the Arizona–Utah border. Towering mesas and sand- and wind-sculpted monoliths define the valley, which is within the Navajo Nation. At the base camp, near Thunderbird Mesa, expect spacious wall tents, sleeping cots, bedrolls, pads, sheets, pillows, a hot-shower trailer, and fine food each afternoon.
GORP Travel, 10055 Westmoor Dr., Suite 215, Westminster, CO 80021, tel. 720/887–8500 or 877/440–4677, gorptravel.com. Year round: 3–10 days, $395–$1,750 per person; custom trips average $160 per day. Children's discount available on some itineraries.

Great Divide Guiding & Outfitters

8+

Richard Jackson, who has nearly 20 years of guiding and outfitting experience, leads every group, with his son along as a wrangler. All Richard's trips take place in Montana's Lewis and Clark National Forest, which is surrounded by Glacier National Park, the Blackfoot Indian Reservation, the Bob Marshall Wilderness, and the Great

Bear Wilderness. The combination of the Jacksons' expertise and the countryside makes Great Divide's adventure and wilderness credentials impeccable.

FOR FAMILIES. A mixture of activities on two layover days makes one five-day trip a particularly good choice for families. On Monday morning the group is picked up in East Glacier Park for a 45-minute drive to the Jacksons' ranch, where gear is packed and guests meet their equine companions. A four-hour ride brings you to a broad mountain meadow and a clear stream, which will be your home for two nights. The next day your family can opt to spend time riding, fishing, hiking, or working with cattle pastured in the area. After breakfast Wednesday the group rides on to Two Medicine River and a campsite with views of Glacier National Park, where you have the same choices of activities.

Everyone helps set up and break down camp, and evenings center on cowboy cooking, cowboy poetry, and guitar music around the campfire. Bring your own fishing gear, or rent from Richard. You can rent sleeping bags as well.

Great Divide Guiding & Outfitters, Box 315, East Glacier Park, MT 59434, tel. 406/226–4487 or 800/421–9687. June–Sept.: 5 days, $795 adults, $695 ages 17 and under with an adult.

Mammoth Lakes Pack Outfit

7+

The old pioneer trails of the eastern Sierra Nevada and the John Muir Wilderness lead riders over high mountain passes and into hidden valleys where brilliant wildflowers dazzle the eyes and animals peer at you curiously from shaded glens and rocky outcrops. The area is well known to the folks at Mammoth Lakes Pack Outfit; in fact, you'd be hard-pressed to find an outfitter with a longer, richer local history than this one. Started in 1915 by the great-grandfather and grandfather of owner John Summers, Mammoth Lakes loves to share its "backyard" with families. You can book a variety of scheduled and custom guided trips that accommodate riders of all ages and abilities.

FOR FAMILIES. Mammoth Lakes sends out a brochure describing the various camping areas and the length of time it takes to get to each. Families with children ages 7 to 9 must book a custom guided trip; scheduled trips are for ages 10 and up (but this is flexible). Families with young children who'd rather spend less than three hours on the trail might choose Skelton and Woods lakes, which are available on custom trips only. You don't lose out on views by staying close to the trailhead, because this area is at an elevation of about 10,000 ft.

Families with kids 10 and up who can handle longer rides can trek three to four hours over 10,700-ft Duck Pass, camping along the timberline near Duck and Pika lakes. Also for over-10s is Purple Lake, 4½ hours away, which makes an excellent base camp for rides and hikes into the surrounding countryside. You can choose a full horse-packing trip, where the horse and a packer remain with you, or a spot trip, where you ride in, set up base camp, and then are left to enjoy your family and/or friends in solitude, with a pre-arranged pick-up time to return by horse to civilization.

Mammoth Lakes Pack Outfit, Box 61, Mammoth Lakes, CA 93546, tel. 888/475–8747, www.mammothpack.com. June–Sept.: 4–6 days, $695–$990 per person scheduled trips, $345–$525 per person spot trips; ask about custom and extended pack trips.

Rockin' R Ranch

8+

The southern half of Utah contains country so magnificent that it's divided into five national parks. Rockin' R Ranch, in Antimony, is 37 mi (60 km) north of Bryce Canyon National Park and not far from Zion, Capitol Reef, Canyonlands, and Arches. Adventurers could easily spend many days exploring the area any number of ways, but no one will be disappointed by a pack trip into the backcountry adjacent to the Rockin' R.

FOR FAMILIES. On a six-day trip you take the trail leading from the ranch up into canyons, over creeks, under quaking aspens, and onto the Aquarius Plateau, with views across the valley and down into Bryce Canyon National Park. Each night the wranglers set up camp and have dinner waiting when you come off the trail. There's time for fishing as well as a free afternoon for hiking, photography, or just plain loafing. On one of the days you take a break from trail riding to try your hand at real cowboy skills, rounding up some of the ranch's stray cattle or learning to rope.

On the last day out you can check your aim in skeet, pistol, or rifle shooting. Then you leave your horse on the plateau and head by van to Bryce Canyon National Park for an afternoon hike. Later, just outside the park, the group rides in a covered wagon and faces a staged attack on the wagon. After dinner and a local rodeo, you overnight in the ranch's comfortable quarters, which is included in the cost of the trip. Also included is lodging and dinner at the ranch the night before the trip begins.

If your family doesn't have six days, go for the four-day version, which doesn't include Bryce or some other activities. You can also join a cattle drive here (see Cattle Drives).

Rockin' R Ranch, Reservation Office, 10274 S. Eastdell Dr., Sandy, UT 84092, tel. 801/733–9538, www.rocknrranch.com. June–Oct.: 4–6 days, $700–$1,300.

Skinner Brothers

ALL

Robert, Monte, and Courtney like nothing better than to share their beloved Wind River Range with families. These Wyoming mountains are not as well known as the neighboring Grand Tetons, but they are impressive in their own right. The brothers' tremendous experience with children comes from running summer wilderness camps for youngsters age 10 and up, but they also customize horse-packing trips for groups as small as two. The Skinners have a few scheduled trips as well, a good choice if your family wants to ride with other families.

FOR FAMILIES. Customize your own trip, and the Skinners will provide everything except personal gear, sleeping pad and bag, and fishing license. You can spend as many days as you want on guided rides into the Bridger Wilderness and Wind River Range. Choose a base-camp experience (the Skinners refer to this as a stationary pack trip) or move camp each night (a moving pack trip).

The Participants Wilderness trip is a one-week scheduled group adventure. The age range for this has been from 6 months to 92 (though I don't advocate taking infants on horses). Guides help children take part in all activities and make it a terrific experience. You can spend time hiking, riding, and fishing, so these pack trips can meet almost anyone's needs. Bring your own fishing gear if you want to fish.

Families with children age 13 and up can also join the Peak Rangers Holiday, a one-week combination pack and mountain-climbing trip. You don't need experience in either riding or mountaineering, but you should be in good shape. Experienced climbers can ascend Gannett Peak, Wyoming's highest.

Skinner Brothers, Box 859, Pinedale, WY 82941, tel. 307/367–2270 or 800/237–9138, www.wyomingoutdoors.com. July–Sept.: 2–7 days, $150–$350 per day for scheduled and custom trips.

Spatsizi Wilderness Vacations

5+

For the past 30 years the Collingwood family has run the only guide and outfitting service permitted to operate in Spatsizi Plateau Wilderness Park, one of Canada's truly untouched wilderness areas. Spatsizi comes from the Tahltan word meaning "red goat," a name given to the mountain goats that roll in the iron-oxide-rich soil of the park. Goats aren't the only animals at home among the peaks, plateaus, and glaciers of Spatsizi. There are sheep, caribou, and moose, black bears and grizzlies, wolves, and hundreds of species of birds. About 200 mi (322 km) north of Smithers, this remote park in northern British Columbia has only about 200 human visitors each year.

FOR FAMILIES. The Collingwoods will help families choose among three pack trips into the Spatsizi wilderness. The first is a six- or eight-day, multi-activity base-camp trip in the Eaglenest Mountains. You travel past Cold Fish Lake and onto Bug Lake and the trip's base camp. The camp has a shower house and cozy log cabins, a welcoming place to return to after riding through the rugged valleys and up into the mountains each day. There are opportunities to canoe, hike through the Eaglenest Ecological Reserve, and test your fishing skills in some of the great trout streams of the north. Photographers will probably be able to capture most varieties of the park's wildlife.

Those who want to travel deep into the most isolated regions of the park should sign up for the nine-day expedition to Buckinghorse Lake and the Fireflats, the headwaters of the Spatsizi River. This trip is probably best for children with some riding and wilderness experience. In July the area is the nursing grounds of mountain caribou and home to a large moose population. If you like fishing, try for a rainbow trout on Buckinghorse Lake; these can weigh in at 6 lbs (2½ kg). Facilities here are restricted to very rustic tent sites.

The Saddle to Paddle trip lets you experience the Spatsizi wilderness both by horse and by canoe. Start the 10-day adventure at Hyland Post, a trading post built in the 1920s on the Spatsizi River. From this base camp the group begins its three-day horse trek into the heart of the park to Laslui Lake. You overnight at Laslui Lodge with its first-class accommodations and meals, then head onto the Stikine River for five days of paddling to the confluence of the Spatsizi and Stikine rivers. It's helpful to have some riding experience for this trip, though canoeing experience isn't necessary.
Spatsizi Wilderness Vacations, Box 3070, Smithers, British Columbia, Canada V0J 2N0, tel. 250/847–2909 or 866/847–9692, www.spatsizi.com. July–Aug.: 6–10 days, C$1,850–C$3,150, 15% discount for ages 18 and younger. Price includes bush-plane flights between Smithers and park.

Wilderness Pursuit

6+

Wilderness Pursuit runs both wilderness pack trips and youth horse camps in central Wisconsin, in the area of Eau Claire. Trails wind through the 133,000 acres of the Clark County Forest, a remote track of land with bluffs, wooded ridges, wetlands, and plenty of wildlife. Once logging territory, the land was deeded to the county back during the depression and has been well forested ever since. Wilderness Pursuit is a long-time family enterprise that now includes three generations taking part. What the folks at Wilderness Pursuit like best is the fact that many of their guests have become good friends. It's not hard to understand when the owners explain, "We all love to meet new guests—even our horses love it!"

FOR FAMILIES. The company's custom-made, "primitive" outings can be up to six days long. Most treks cover 10 to 15 mi (16 to 24 km) per day. It's about relaxing, though, and the group pace is set according to the least experienced rider. At night you'll sleep in tents, setting up camps at several different locations along the way. These are participatory trips, meaning you help with both camp and horse chores, so if your kids have always wanted to learn how to care for their very own horse, this is the outfitter for you. Guides teach adults and kids about riding and horse care, and the trips are as good for beginners as for experienced riders. When families book a trip, the company tries to schedule other families on the same trek. *Wilderness Pursuit, North 5773 Resewood Ave., Neillsville, WI 54456, tel. 715/743–4484, wpursuit.tripod.com/. May–Oct.: 2–6 days, $160–$600 per person.*

WTR Outfitters

8+

WTR Outfitters is based at a 950-acre ranch and outfitting operation in the Blackfoot Valley, about 65 mi (105 km) east of Missoula, Montana. The heart of the operation is horse-packing trips, both customized and scheduled, and riders can follow trails right from the ranch into the Bob Marshall Wilderness Complex, which covers about 2 million acres.

FOR FAMILIES. You don't need to have riding experience to take part in WTR's adventures. Karen Hooker, owner and outfitter, considers children younger than 8, but you must ask permission. What Karen cares most about is sharing with all kinds of people "a way of life worth preserving, a place of relaxation and meditation essential to American stability." If any place can have this kind of abiding effect, it's the Bob Marshall Wilderness Complex, which has a vista of incomparable beauty around every switchback. This is an area of cool streams, deep trout holes, flowering meadows, and emerald lakes. And even within this soul-stirring scenery, some places stand out—such as the world-famous 22-mi (35-km), 1,000-ft Chinese Wall.

State-of-the-art tents, excellent food, and a latrine with a real toilet seat secluded in its own tepee define the luxury campsites WTR provides. These are also progressive trips, which means a new campsite most nights. There are wildflower and bird guides to study on your trip if you wish, but much is learned—and laughed about—around the campfire each night, too. *WTR Outfitters, 520 Cooper Lake Rd., Ovando, MT 59854, tel. 406/793–5666 or 800/987–5666, www.wtroutfitters.com. June–Aug.: 3–11 days, $220 per day adults; 10% discount for children under 17; groups or families of 4 or more get 5% discount.*

Resources

Organizations

There is no national association specifically for horse-packing outfitters. However, most states have guide and/or outfitting associations and licensing agencies, which you can locate these through state tourism offices. **American Outdoors** (4607 N.E. Cedar Creek Rd., Woodland, WA 98674, tel. 360/225–5000, www.americaoutdoors.org) is the association for many different types of outdoor outfitters and operators, who pay for membership. The association won't recommend one member over another, but it can give you lists of members. Because many guest ranches run horse-packing trips, you can also contact the **Dude Ranchers' Association** (Box 471, LaPorte, CO 80535, tel. 970/223–8440, www.duderanche.org), which represents more than 100 ranches in states throughout the West and in Canada, and has information on ranch activities, including pack trips.

Also See

If multiday riding treks and ranch work appeal to you and if you want to ride a little faster, *see* Cattle Drives. Families with children too young for a horse-packing trip may find the chapter on Ranches helpful. At some ranches a parent and older child may have the opportunity to join a short pack trip while the rest of the family stays at the ranch.

HOUSEBOATING

When you step behind the wheel or in front of the tiller of a houseboat, your destiny is your own. You and your family can explore hidden coves, camp out on a deserted beach, or hike up from the water's edge when the mood strikes you. You can sail as much or as little as you choose in a day, skim the shoreline to watch for wildlife, or seek the deep places where the best sport fish are found. Much of the heart and history of our nation lies along the shores of waterways that have made exploration and economic growth possible, and you can discover that, too, if you wish. On the other hand, with your houseboat as a movable feast and private lodge, your family might choose not to leave it at all (except, perhaps, by water slide when you want to cool off). Floating, relaxing, watching the scenery drift by—these are also options. The bottom line: when you are your own captain and crew, the choices are all yours.

Houseboating is a remarkably safe and roomy way to travel. Top speed is only about 6 to 9 mi (10 to 14 km) per hour, so you take it easy whether you like it or not. And because activities such as swimming, biking, hiking, and fishing, are built into a houseboat vacation, it has appeal for families with children of all ages. Babies can watch the landscape go by and feel the breezes. They can ride in backpacks or bike seats, and they sleep soundly to the rhythmic rocking of the boat. Preschoolers and school-age children love the variety of daily activities and the constantly changing scenery. Teens love the waterskiing opportunities and freedom to explore on their own. Everyone loves the water slides, on which the young—and the young at heart—can zip and splash into the water.

Check to see if your boat has a running logbook. Children like to read and add to these journals, in which previous renters have jotted down the secrets and wonderful discoveries they made on their journey: the best coves and beaches, the best restaurants, the short trail that wasn't mentioned in the area brochure. Who knows, your family might even be inspired to keep a journal of its own as your trip goes on—something you can all look back on in years to come.

Questions to Ask

Do I need any previous boating experience to captain a houseboat? Most companies do not require boating expertise, but some do.

What are the other requirements? Most companies ask that the renter and those who will be steering the boat be above a certain age and hold a valid driver's license.

Do you have life jackets that fit my child, or will I have to bring my own? Some companies have vests for infants; others do not. Be prepared to give your child's weight and chest measurement so you will know for sure if there is a Coast Guard–approved safety vest that will fit. Boating and sporting goods stores sell life jackets if you need to buy one.

What are the rules regarding the use of life vests when the boat is in motion? Some companies require that all children under a certain age wear a life vest whenever you're moving. Whether or not this is mandatory, it's a good idea. Talk to your children ahead of time about the importance of wearing a life vest. If necessary, borrow one so your child can wear it around a while and get used to it. You don't want your children to spend the vacation complaining. If you prepare them well ahead of time, it shouldn't be an issue.

What security deposit and/or insurance is required? All companies ask that you send a sizable deposit well in advance of your sailing date. That deposit is usually not counted toward your rental fee, and it will not be given back until you return the boat in the same condition in which you took it out. Check to see how many days prior to your trip you can cancel without forfeiting all or most of your deposit. In addition to a deposit, some companies require you to purchase damage insurance; others offer it as an option. Some have their own insurance, with deductibles that range from $250 to $1,500. Renters may be able to lower the deductible by adding a few dollars a day to the rental fee. Because you are generally responsible for paying the deductible in the event of damage to the boat, or for the damage itself if there is no accident insurance, you'll have to decide whether purchasing optional insurance is worth the extra money up front.

How early can I arrive for my rental? Some companies let you sleep on the boat the night before you depart; others have a very specific timetable for your arrival. If you need to be on Lake Powell, for example, at 9, you will have to arrive the previous night and make arrangements for camping or staying in a lodge.

What are the cabin arrangements? Houseboats differ, and depending on the makeup of your family or group, one boat may be better for you than another. Some boats come with double beds; others have a mix of queen beds, doubles, and bunk beds. Some are more luxurious but sleep fewer people. Some beds offer more privacy than others. Asking for brochures that show the various boat layouts will help you avoid disappointment with your accommodations.

What extras do you provide? Water slides, small power boats you can tow and use for waterskiing, dinghies, fishing gear, tubes, and other water toys are available through some rental companies, especially those operating in the western United States. These will add expense, but they can make your experience even more fun.

Do you have maps, information about regional sights and attractions, and suggestions for where to stop? If you are unfamiliar with the part of the country through which you'll be traveling, this is important. Almost all rental agents have navigational charts and maps on board, but you also want information and directions for the sights you shouldn't miss. There are many places to walk or bike along the popular houseboating rivers and canals, and many lakes have excellent hiking trails near their shores. You can also check out a guidebook and buy regional maps if you need to, but remember that part of the joy of this type of travel is being completely spontaneous. You don't have to be locked into a rigid itinerary.

What's the cost of fuel and docking? Most, but not all, houseboat rental companies work like car rental companies. They give you the boat with a full tank, and you must return it with a full tank or pay to have it filled on your return. Marine fuel prices are about 30% higher than car fuel prices. Docking charges vary greatly depending on whether you opt for a private marina or a state park. Charges for private marinas are generally by the foot and can range from 65 cents to $2 per ft per night. State parks typically charge $10–$12 per boat per night. Of course, what's great about houseboats is that in most places you don't need to tie up at established docks, so these charges will often be minimal.

Is there some place to buy food when we arrive? If you're arriving by car, buy your food supplies at a regular grocery store before boarding. Stores in resort towns and at marinas tend to be very expensive. If you're arriving by plane, you'll probably have to shop at the marina, but you'll save some money by bringing what you can with you and purchasing only perishables at the last minute.

What is the rental fee and what's included? Rental rates are affected by many factors, including the size of the boat, the season, and the number of days you wish to rent. Many houseboating companies operate for three or even four seasons, and rates change dramatically during the year. Moreover, some of the things that cost extra in summer may be part of the package in off-seasons. Amenities may also affect price or at least alter how much you get for your money. Some boats come with linens; some don't. Some have grills for cooking out on deck, but others have only galley stoves. Microwaves, generators, stereo cassette players, TVs, and VCRs all may be included, or they may be extra. There's a huge variation in what you pay and what you get, so ask lots of questions. All boats in this chapter have sleeping accommodations, a galley to cook in, a refrigerator, a bathroom, safety equipment, life vests for adults and older children, plates and pots and pans, and drinking water. Also included in the cost is parking for your car while you're houseboating. The range of rates given goes from the least expensive boat in low season to the most expensive boat in high season.

Instruction

All houseboat rental companies give a short course—generally one to three hours—before you can take the boat out. Houseboats are so easy to steer that most, though not all, rental companies do not require previous boating experience. In addition, all rental units have extensive information and instructions posted on board for reference. Although houseboating is not difficult, it's still important to pay attention to the initial lesson and to take notes as you go through the information with the company. Docking, for example, can be tricky, especially in more congested waterways. Make certain older children listen, too, because some information given will be about safety and the use of equipment. If you're traveling with very young children, arrange in advance for a spouse or an older child to take charge of little ones so you can concentrate on crucial information during the pretrip session.

Finding the Fun

Northeast: Mallory Line–Collar City Charters, Mid-Lakes Navigation Company, Remar Rentals. **South:** Forever Resorts. **Midwest:** Forever Resorts. **Southwest:** Forever Resorts, Lake Powell Resorts & Marinas, Seven Crown Resorts. **West Coast:** Forever Resorts, Seven Crown Resorts. **Canada:** Remar Rentals, Waterway Houseboat Vacations. **Mexico:** Forever Resorts. **Europe:** Crown Blue Line.

Favorite Houseboat Companies

Crown Blue Line

ALL

Crown Blue Line has boats in six European countries. In Holland you can cruise the heart of Friesland, navigating the lakes and canals surrounding Amsterdam all the way north to Leeuwarden, Sneek, and beyond. Villages and islands mark the canals of the Venetian Lagoon in Italy, where you might begin at Chioggia and cruise up the Sile River, or the Brenta Canal with its painted facades. Many of the lagoons and canals are separated from the Mediterranean by only a sandbar, so you can choose to spend a day at the beach of Lido or Bibione, if you wish, before continuing on your journey. The Caledonian Canal passes through the famous Loch Ness in Scotland, and though your children may want to spend the entire week searching for the elusive monster, it would be a pity to miss the country's other mountains, lochs, and glens. Ireland's restored, 19th-century Shannon-Erne Canal offers excellent cruising, as does the River Shannon. The lakes and rivers around Brandenbourg and Mecklenbour, in Germany, are all about nature and wildlife, though you'll find plenty of good restaurants along the way. The company's base at Marina Wolsfbruch features swimming, water sports, and other activities (as well as a sauna and a Jacuzzi), so you'll have plenty to do before and after your trip.

By far, though, the most extensive offerings are in France, where ancient canals wind through every part of the country. Boaters navigate through myriad locks tended by keepers whose homes and gardens might have been plucked from the canvas of an Impressionist painting. One of the gems of the waterways is the less-traveled Canal du Rhone a Sete, which follows the Mediterranean in the southernmost countryside. This route also meanders through the Camargue wildlife refuge and nature reserve in the southwestern corner of Provence, which is famous for its white horses, black bulls, green salt marshes, pink flamingos, and vibrant blue skies.

Few Americans venture here, perhaps because the area doesn't entice with the country's usual heady mixture of history and wine. Yet, there are stunning ancient cathedrals and quaint medieval towns, such as Aigues-Mortes, that can satisfy anyone's desire to be steeped in history. True, it's a quiet voyage, but traveling in a sleek Clasiques through this remarkable region is a way for children in particular to discover many local delights: small fishing villages, medieval fortresses, sun-drenched Mediterranean beaches, tidal canals, new foods, and diverse lands where ancient landscapes and modern ways effortlessly coexist. Most of all, there's the pleasure of spending days gliding through an ever-changing landscape and living, if even for a short time, on a floating home.

FOR FAMILIES. Crown Blue Line has 34 different types and lengths of boats in three classes: Crown, Canal, and Princess. The Crown-class Classique is a modern cabin cruiser that sleeps eight in four cabins. There are two toilet/showers (one fore and one aft), a large galley with apartment-style cooking facilities, and lounge that can accommodate all aboard, as well as an upper deck with an umbrella table, chairs, and built-in seating. You can steer the houseboat from inside or out, though the only reason to steer from below is inclement weather. There's a bike rack on back, as many of the canals have dirt roads or paths perfect for biking alongside them. If you need a larger boat, ask for the Grand Classique; the rest of the line's boats are smaller. Most boats sleep three to ten people.

What kids love about houseboating is simply being on the water. This is an ideal family vacation because it's relaxed and you're all together on board, yet you can take side trips off the boat as you wish. Crown Blue Line's modern boats are amazingly stable and comfortable—even kids can drive them easily in the stretches between locks. Negotiating the locks, however, can be a challenge: going up, water pours into the lock, creating a force that makes holding the ropes hard work, and the boat must be kept close to the side walls. And although the company maintains that anyone can drive these boats, it's not quite as easy as they suggest. It takes a little getting used to if you haven't done it before, and the locks are more difficult than anyone lets on.

Beware, too, that not all of Crown Blue Line's base personnel are equally informative. When we took one boat out of Castelnaudary on the Canal du Midi, we were given almost no information about the challenges of negotiating the locks—and no one suggested getting lock gloves (an absolute necessity if you don't want blisters). The instructor, who gave us a brief driving lesson, never mentioned that you must keep the boat away from the side wall when the water is going down because the lip of the boat can get caught on the wall otherwise. At Port Cassafieres, however, the staff provided much information and helpful advice about the boats, towns, and what to expect on the waterway.

To be fair, all the information you need is in the literature you receive either ahead of time or when you pick up your boat. Still, get to the base a little early so you can read everything before you depart. Once you get the boat and the brief instructions, everything goes quickly and you won't have time to read the fine print.

Crown Blue Line, 510 Sylvan Ave., Suite 204, Englewood Cliffs, NY 07632, tel. 201/569–9588 or 888/355–9491, www.crownblueline.com. Mar.–Nov. (not all countries available all months): 7 days, $780–$4,370, depending on country, boat, and season.

Forever Resorts

ALL

With Forever Resorts, families have a choice of houseboat rentals on 10 lakes across the country. Lake Mead, spanning the Arizona–Nevada border, and Lake Mohave, just below Hoover Dam and south of Lake Mead, offer the starkly beautiful, dramatic landscapes unique to those places where water and desert meet. The Lake Mead National Recreation Area comprises more than 3,000 square mi (7,770 square km) of desert terrain, as well as Lakes Mead and Mohave, which were both formed by the damming of the Colorado River. Hiking, rock climbing, fishing, windsurfing, and sailing bring millions of visitors to the area each year. In central California is Lake Don Pedro, 2½ hours from San Francisco and 40 mi (64 km) from Yosemite National Park, in the foothills of the Sierra Nevada. Covering more than 13,000 acres with over 160 mi (258 km) of shoreline, the lake was created in 1971 when the Don Pedro dam was built on the Tuolumne River. California's Delta region, near Stockton, offers 1,000 mi (1,610 km) of waterway to explore and yet another view of the West from your deck: rich farmland, towns, and riverside restaurants. About an hour west of Redding in northern California, tranquil Trinity lake is backed by the snow-capped peaks of the Trinity Alps and features shady, tree-lined coves perfect for exploring and swimming. Anglers can try their luck against landlocked Kokanee salmon.

Missouri's Lake of the Ozarks and Table Rock Lake are more lush and greener still. Both are in populated areas that draw visitors for a variety of sights and experiences. With more than 1,300 mi (2,093 km) of shoreline, Lake of the Ozarks is huge and well developed, although there are hidden coves and wooded areas in which you can still find privacy. The Lake of the Ozarks Marina, where you pick up your houseboat, is near Camdenton, about 1½ hours north of Springfield, Missouri. Table Rock Lake, created in 1958 when the Table Rock Dam was completed, is 15 minutes from popular Branson, Missouri, and is surprisingly peaceful considering the town's well-known nightlife. The lake was a destination for families looking to get away from it all long before country music stars began to call the area home, and it's still one reason many families come to the area.

Pine trees line the shore of Georgia's Lake Lanier, which is more than 63 mi (101 km) long and about an hour's drive northeast of Atlanta. Here you'll find excellent swimming, fishing, and waterskiing, plus hundreds of islands that are ideal for exploring by houseboat. With mild spring and fall temperatures, Lake Lanier is an excellent choice for families looking for affordable off-season getaways.

If you want to travel to foreign shores, try Lake Amistad (Spanish for "friendship") in the Amistad National Recreation Area bordering Texas and Mexico, about 150 mi (242 km) west of San Antonio. A joint project between the two countries, the lake was created by damming the Rio Grande just below its confluence with Devil's River. The recreation area has more than 400 archaeological sites, including caves and mounds you can view along the lake. Native American pictographs dating to more than 10,000 years ago can be seen by boat at Panther Cave in beautiful Seminole Canyon. The lake is clear and blue; southwestern scuba enthusiasts call it paradise.

Farther north, way up on the Texas Panhandle, is Lake Meredith National Recreation Area and Lake Meredith itself, one of the best-kept secrets of the area. Although the surrounding landscape is desolate and windblown, the lake and the Canadian River that feeds it have canyons, sheltering cottonwoods, and some of the best walleye fishing in the state.

FOR FAMILIES. All boats sleep 10 people. Standard features include linens, two refrigerators, a microwave, 1½ baths, central air and heat, and a gas grill. There's excellent fishing on these lakes, and licenses are available at all marinas. The company has life jackets for all ages.

What will the children like best? *Every* boat has the all-important—and monumentally fun—water slide. And children and teens are always delighted to learn that each boat comes with a cassette player and a TV with VCR. (Parents may be less enthusiastic about this.)

Forever Resorts, Box 52038, Phoenix, AZ 85072, tel. 800/255–5561, www.foreverresorts.com. Year-round (all lakes not open all months): 3–7 days, $995–$6,295.

Lake Powell Resorts & Marinas

ALL

Nearly 2,000 mi (3,220 km) of shoreline defined by massive, red sandstone formations and piercing blue skies make Lake Powell on the Arizona–Utah border one of the great houseboating lakes in North America. The lake is 186 mi (301 km) from end to end, but you can take forever to cruise its length if you choose. There are 96 major canyons to explore, ancient pictographs and ancestral Puebloan ruins to ponder, and hiking trails, fishing coves, and beaches of shifting sands on which no footprints will be found. Nonne-Zoshi (Rainbow Turned to Stone) is the Navajo name for Rainbow Bridge, the tallest natural stone arch in the world. You can easily hike to it from the shore. The busiest season on Lake Powell is summer; if you're looking for days of solitude, book in spring or fall—when the weather is still fine, the rates are lower, and the water is still warm enough for swimming. You get your houseboat from one of the four lake marinas operated by Lake Powell Resorts & Marinas.

FOR FAMILIES. You can choose from six lengths and four classes of vessels: standard, captain, sport, and admiral. Boats sleep from 6 to 12 people, and amenities vary based on vessel class, but all include life jackets for infants through adults. Depending on the boat, you'll have a queen or double bed; some have bunk beds for the children. Linens are included in the admiral category, water slides in the captain and admiral categories.

Separate small power boats are available for an extra charge at the marinas, as are fishing boats. Tow one behind your houseboat, and use it to explore small inlets or to go onshore for an overnight camp-out. Waterskiing equipment and tubes can also be rented. Carp, a mixed-review fish for most adults, are a child favorite because they're so easy to catch throughout the lake. Fishing licenses can be purchased at the marinas, but bring your own poles.

Lake Powell Resorts & Marinas, Box 56909, Phoenix, AZ 85079, tel. 602/331–5200 or 800/528–6154, www.visitlakepowell.com. Year-round: 3–7 days, $1,059–$5,995.

Mallory Line–Collar City Charters

ALL

Once a thoroughfare of commerce but now a path for pleasure boats, the 363-mi (584-km) Erie Canal opened in 1825. Linking Albany to Buffalo, and thus the Atlantic Ocean (via the Hudson River) to the Great Lakes, the Erie was the longest, grandest, and most ambitious canal in New York State. It was, in fact, one of the great engineering feats of its time. Today the Erie has been rediscovered and revitalized, and you can trace the history of the state and several of its canals as you travel through the picturesque New York State Canal System. There is more to see and do than a family could cover in a one-week cruise. The Canalway Trail, for example, currently encompasses 150 mi (242 km) of trail segments adjoining the canal on which families can hike, bike, and view wildlife.

There are hundreds of towns at which to tie up on the canal system, and you can shape your adventure as you go. You don't have to stick to the Erie, either. From Troy, where Mallory Line–Collar City Charters is based, boaters can travel north on the Champlain Canal all the way to Whitehall and the southernmost entry to Lake Champlain. Those who motor south on the Hudson will find natural wetlands and woods, graceful herons, villages, and sandy beaches.

FOR FAMILIES. Boats sleep up to six people, with two private staterooms and a fold-out double bed in the saloon. All linens are included, as are two bathrooms (or heads, in nautical terminology), a hot-water shower, a cabin heater for cool nights, and a marine band radio. The galley has a double sink, gas stove and oven, refrigerator with freezer, and lots of room. Mallory Line–Collar City Charters also offers a family-friendly attitude. A call requesting information on life jackets for infants elicited this response: "If we don't have the right-size life jacket for your child, we'll find one." This is also one of the few rental companies to allow pets (at an additional charge of $50 each).

What your children will care about most, though, are locks, locks, and more locks. There are 57 throughout the New York State Canal System, and they never fail to amaze. Traveling through the Waterford Flight, the first series of locks—five in all—on the Erie, your boat will be raised a whopping 169 ft in less than 2 mi (or, for Canadians and Europeans, a dizzying 52 m in less than 3 km). That's cool enough to intrigue children of all ages, including your normally blasé teenager.

Before or after your boating adventure on the Erie, stop in Chittenango, just east of Syracuse, to visit the birthplace of L. Frank Baum, beloved author of *The Wonderful Wizard of Oz*. There's a yellow-brick road in town. Whether it will get you to the Emerald City is uncertain, but if you visit the area in May, you won't want to leave anyway—that's the time of the annual Ozfest, with parades, games, and activities for modern-day Munchkins.

The company also offers one-way cruising between Troy and Westport on Lake Champlain. The boat comes with two bikes and a dingy, and the staff will move your car to your endpoint for an additional $300.

Mallory Line–Collar City Charters, Troy Town Dock and Marina, 427 River St., Troy, NY 12180, tel. 518/272–5341 or 800/830–5341, www.canalboat.com. May–Oct.: 7 days, $1,800–$2,900.

Mid-Lakes Navigation Company

ALL

For the uninitiated who think New York State begins and ends in New York City, a canal cruise will be an eye-opener. Upstate New York is a land of rolling hills, farms, and historic villages. You can start your houseboating adventure either in Cold Springs Harbour Marina, just a few minutes from downtown Syracuse, or at Midlakes Erie Macedon Basin, about 20 minutes from Rochester. From either, you can travel east or west on the famous Erie Canal. You might also choose to travel the Cayuga–Seneca Canal to Seneca Falls, or head east to Oneida Lake and north on the Oswego Canal. Your family can access state parks, including the eastern border of the 6-million-acre Adirondack Park (the largest American park outside Alaska), Finger Lakes National Forest, and two wildlife refuges from the New York State Canal System.

FOR FAMILIES. The houseboats sleep two, four, or six passengers. Families with small children might be able to fit one or two more on board, but talk to the company about your needs ahead of time. All boats come with a gas range and gas grill, bedding, and a VHF radio. Nonskid surfaces are perfect for families with younger children or grandparents, and all windows have safety glass. There's a built-in swim ladder on every boat; you'll find two bicycles, too. You can also bring along your own bikes and strap them on the roof. Ride your bike on the Erie Canal Heritage Trail Access at Palmyra, just southeast of Rochester.

If you boat on the Erie as far as North Tonawanda, near Buffalo, stop at the Allan Herschell Carousel Factory Museum (Herschell is a well-known American carousel maker). In Seneca Falls you'll find the Women's Rights National Historical Park and National Women's Hall of Fame. The biggest adventure of all in New York are the locks that raise and lower boats almost 50 ft in some places.

Mid-Lakes Navigation Company, Box 61, 11 Jordan St., Skaneateles, NY 13152, tel. 315/685–8500 or 800/545–4318, www.midlakesnav.com. May–Oct.: 7 days, $1,800–$2,300.

Remar Rentals

ALL

Long before there were people or boundaries, long before time even existed, flower petals fell from the heavens onto the St. Lawrence River, creating the Thousand Islands. The native people who told this legend called the islands Manitouana (Garden of the Great Spirit), and even today the name fits. A rich and remarkable diversity of plant and animal life thrives on these islands strung along a 50-mi (81-km) stretch of the mighty St. Lawrence between New York state and Ontario, Canada. There are more than 1,800 of them—plenty to keep a houseboating family exploring for days. Some islands belong to the United States; some are Canadian. Twenty-one are part of the St. Lawrence Islands National Park, Canada's smallest national park but no less impressive because of this. Clayton, New York, juts out into the river, giving Remar Rentals the perfect starting point for cruising the Thousand Islands, the St. Lawrence Seaway, and Canada's Rideau Canal System. Remar's steel-frame boats are similar to those used on Great Britain's canals. This is one of the few rental companies that require previous boating experience, due to the rocky shoals around the islands and the large seagoing vessels that travel parts of the river.

FOR FAMILIES. Boats range from 38 to 55 ft and sleep from 6 to 10 people. Guides to the islands and waterways are provided on board so you can plan the route that best meets your family's interests. Remar supplies linens, and a TV is standard. A small dinghy comes with every houseboat, making island exploration fun and fishing in small coves a must.

Remar Rentals, 510 Theresa St., Box 159, Clayton, NY 13624, tel. 315/686–3579. June–Sept.: 2–7 days, $550–$1,875.

Seven Crown Resorts

ALL

On a houseboat vacation, location is as important as it is in real estate. What do you want to see every day when you're sitting on deck or piloting your floating hotel? Seven Crown rents houseboats in four different areas. For summer peaks still laden with snow, towering evergreens, and wildflower meadows, you can head to Lake Shasta in northern California. Its 370 mi (596 km) of shoreline offer more exploring than there's time for on one trip. Should you want to sightsee away from your boat for a few hours, Shasta Caverns, Shasta Dam, Mt. Lassen's volcano, or local fossil beds make good excursions.

Near Stockton, 80 mi (129 km) west of San Francisco, is California's Delta region. Here, more than 1,000 mi (1,610 km) of rivers, tributaries, and channels create a meandering network of waterways with lush, uninhabited islands and historic towns to explore. The fishing is good and blackberries are plentiful in summer, but you can also dine at one of the riverfront restaurants you pass. Plenty of coves and inlets provide solitude, but in the Delta you'll share the waters with oceangoing vessels heading in and out of the port at Stockton, as well as sailboats and an occasional Chinese junk.

Seven Crown also has boats on Lakes Mead and Mohave, on the Arizona–Nevada border. Mead's 550 mi (886 km) of shoreline are ringed by beaches, cliffs, and dramatic rock formations; when the lake is high enough, you can see the west end of the Grand Canyon from your deck. The glassy blue waters of Mohave have long appealed to houseboaters. You can take a challenging hike to see ancient petroglyphs carved into sheer cliffs along the shore, while sandy beaches entice you to enjoy Mohave's softer side.

FOR FAMILIES. Boats sleep 6, 8, or 10 at all locations; the Grand Sierra style of boat, available on the lakes but not the Delta, sleeps 14. Boats are equipped with everything you need except bedding, food, drinks, and personal items; they even have a microwave and barbecue. Most boats have both a shower and tub in the bathroom, an important convenience for families with young children. The Grand Sierra, however, has two bathrooms but no tub. Pets are welcome on boats and at all marina motels used by families before or after houseboating. There's no extra charge on boats, but there is a $25 refundable deposit for pets in motel rooms, plus an additional room charge of $5 per day per pet.

Seven Crown operates seven marinas or marina-resorts; two on Lake Shasta, three on Lake Mead, and one each at the Delta and Lake Mohave. You can rent your houseboat at five of them and small take-along boats at all seven. Groceries, ice, tackle, and fishing licenses are available, too. Marina lodging varies with location; there are hotel and motel rooms and RV sites.

Seven Crown Resorts, Box 16247, Irvine, CA 92623, tel. 800/752–9669, www.sevencrown.com. Year-round: 3–7 days, $650–$2,950.

Waterway Houseboat Vacations

ALL

Green forests, blue water, sandy beaches, quiet coves, and hundreds of miles of undeveloped wilderness are what you'll find at Shuswap Lake in southeastern British Columbia, one of Canada's best houseboating lakes. Hiking, diving, and climbing rocks are popular. You can also jet-ski and fish, and there's golfing nearby. There are plenty of secluded spots for picnicking, barbecuing, and overnight camping as well.

FOR FAMILIES. Waterway's houseboats sleep 10 to 18 and have fully equipped kitchens, maps, and child-resistant railings. These houseboats come with water slides and AM/FM cassette stereos. Voyager and Mirage models have hot tubs on the upper deck; Mirage 54s even have a fireplace in the living room. Waterway also has a wheelchair-friendly boat with a wheelchair elevator to the upper deck, two medi-beds, and a special-needs bath. It's also equipped with a lift so that all passengers can use the hot tub.

Waterway Houseboat Vacations, Box 69, Sicamous, British Columbia, Canada V0E 2V0, tel. 250/836–2505 or 800/663–4022, www.waterwayhouseboats.com. Apr.–early Sept.: 3–10 days, $579–$5,399.

Resources

Periodicals

Every spring *Houseboat* (520 Park Ave., Idaho Falls, ID 83402, tel. 800/638–0135) publishes a special vacation guide with extensive rental and destination information, including specifics about the marinas from which you'll be renting (such as whether they have a motel or RV campground), places to leave your car or RV while you're houseboating, advice about local fishing, and more.

Books

The Amazing Impossible Erie Canal (Simon & Schuster), by Cheryl Harness, a critically acclaimed picture book for ages 5 through 10, gives the history of the building of the Erie Canal from start to finish.

Also See

For more boating adventures, *see* Sailing; Snorkeling and Diving; *and* Wildlife Encounters. You'll find a mix of small and large boats, slow and fast boats, and waters around the world to explore.

KAYAKING

Families have taken to kayaking like, well, ducks to water. That's not surprising. Kayaks can take you anywhere from the ocean to the pristine wilderness lakes and rivers of America's heartland. You can glide through still waters or challenge yourself on rapids in almost every corner of the continent. In a kayak there's an unmistakable feeling of being not just on the water but of it, which gives an added thrill to the already fantastic opportunities to experience wildlife and nature.

Older children, in particular, have embraced the sport in record numbers, at least partly because kayaking allows a measure of independence other types of boating do not. As manufacturers begin to design kayaks especially for a child's size, weight, and strength, more and more youngsters can paddle their own. These child-size kayaks are easier to learn on and to handle, creating a great sense of accomplishment in young paddlers.

Kayaking promotes family togetherness, too. Two- and three-person kayaks make it possible for parents to take even young or inexperienced children with them on flat-water trips. Some kayaks are made with an extra-large cockpit opening that can accommodate up to two adults and a child. This sport also has special appeal for families with teenagers, who rarely think that family outings are cool. Kayaking is definitely cool, and it's a vacation idea that most preteens and teens will greet with an enthusiastic thumbs-up. Although kayaking is not the best choice for families with infants, toddlers, or preschoolers, almost any other family can find a boat, class, or trip that's right for them.

Questions to Ask

Do you work regularly with children the age(s) of mine? Kayaking requires special skills in both paddling technique and safety practices, and it's important that instructors convey this information in an age-appropriate manner. Although instructors in children's classes probably have the requisite experience, many kayak schools say they welcome older children in adult classes. However, that doesn't mean the teacher will know how to work with this age group. Adults and children learn differently, and even preteens and teens often learn best through games. So before you put your 12-year-old in an adult class with you, make certain he or she will be taught appropriately and be welcomed.

Are child-size life vests and clothing provided? Any time you're in a boat, you need a Coast Guard–approved life jacket in the correct size. If the company you choose doesn't have the right-size vests, purchase them ahead of time from a marine or sporting goods store.

Are wet suits needed, and do you have them in my child's size? Some kayaking courses and trips take place in cold water. A child—or an adult, for that matter—who's cold will have a miserable time. Ask the company if it provides or rents suits in the sizes you need. If not, either borrow them from someone you know, or check with local dive or other marine supply stores about buying or renting suits.

Do we need helmets? On a lake or pond you probably won't need a white-water helmet, but on any river water, even the slow-moving variety, a helmet is a good idea. Ask about a helmet for yourself and for your children.

Is the guide/instructor trained in child CPR, lifesaving, and first aid? What type of emergency equipment do you carry? Child CPR requires different steps than adult CPR. If you'll be far from a hospital or medical help, someone should be completely familiar with the procedures for reviving and rescuing children. Many parents take these courses themselves—a good idea even if the outfitter is trained. Also find out whether an outfitter is equipped with a radio for emergency contact with a home base or local medical personnel and whether there is emergency equipment on hand appropriate for both children and adults.

Are instructors certified by a reputable organization, such as the American Canoe Association or the British Canoe Union? Certification means instructors are up on techniques and safety procedures, and it's one way to compare schools and instructors.

What kind of kayaks are provided? Sea, or touring, kayaks tend to be more stable than their white-water counterparts, and easier for inexperienced boaters to handle. They're used not just in the ocean and open water but on lakes, ponds, rivers, and streams. There are double kayaks with two cockpits, which are perfect for one parent and one child, and even triples (three cockpits). Ask about the pros and cons of each type with regard to the ages and abilities of your children. Many outfitters also have sit-on-tops—kayaks without the traditional cockpit. These are wonderful for the slightly claustrophobic, and they're extremely easy to steer and keep stable. Children and beginners usually love them, though they're more for fun than for serious learning.

Are child-size kayaks available? This isn't a requirement by any means, but it can make a difference between accomplishment and frustration, for young children especially.

How strenuous is the course or trip? All the courses and trips listed are for beginner or intermediate paddlers unless otherwise noted. This means you don't need a lot of paddling experience; however, you should be in good physical condition. Ask how long your family will be paddling each day and what the conditions are likely to be. Will you be paddling against wind or tides, for example (either of which can be exhausting)?

Are there other activities on the trip? Courses may have you out from 9 to 4, with a break for lunch, so your free time is in the evening. On extended trips, however, about six hours of paddling a day is typical before pulling into camp. With this schedule, there should be time for hiking, exploring, maybe beachcombing. These activities are often as important to children as the paddling, so find out what guides are likely to offer before you book.

What's included in the cost of the course or trip? Courses that take place at a school or an area near the school, whether they last one or two days, generally provide equipment, instruction, transportation from the school to a local river (if necessary), and lunch. Lodging is usually not part of the package, but schools can often help arrange it. On multiday trips the fee includes tents and most meals—plenty of hearty, excellent food—in addition to what courses cover. The vast majority of kayaking trips are camping trips. Prices for all courses and trips include what is listed above unless otherwise noted.

Instruction

Aside from paddling technique, Eskimo rolls (in which you rotate your kayak 360° in the water, so you go from right side up to upside down and back without getting out of the cockpit), and other technical aspects of kayaking, you'll receive instruction on basic safety, water rescue and survival, and wilderness emergency information. This is especially important for parents taking children out into the wilderness and around water.

If your child is too young for regular courses or for the special children's courses, be sure to ask about private instruction. These sessions often accommodate younger children, and they allow families to learn and play together.

Finding the Fun

Northeast: Maine Island Kayak Company, Wilderness Expeditions & The Birches, Zoar Outdoor. **South:** Nantahala Outdoor Center. **Midwest:** Kayak & Canoe Institute, Trek & Trail, Wilderness Inquiry. **Southwest:** Wilderness Inquiry. **Rockies:** Boulder Outdoor Center. **West Coast:** REI Adventures, Wilderness Inquiry. **Alaska:** Nantahala Outdoor Center, REI Adventures. **Canada:** Kayak & Canoe Institute, Northern Lights Expeditions, Outside Expeditions, Wilderness Inquiry. **Mexico:** Maine Island Kayak Company.

Favorite Schools and Outfitters

Boulder Outdoor Center

8+

Nearly 20 years ago the center opened as the Boulder Kayak School. Today, as the Boulder Outdoor Center (BOC), it continues to focus on kayaking, with classes for every level and in every season. If winter doldrums get you down, you can head to Colorado and learn how to paddle and roll in one of Boulder's warm indoor pools. When you've had enough of the water, you can ski on some of the best terrain in the Rocky Mountains, only a couple of hours away. In summer Boulder and the Rockies offer hiking, rock climbing, friendly people, and good restaurants.

FOR FAMILIES. Children ages 8 and up are welcome in novice lake clinics, which are offered in Boulder. Lake clinics are either all day or 3½ hours on each of two days. If you have children under the age of 12, go for the one-day lake clinics and ask about private lessons. For those with paddlers at least 12 years old, a good choice is the novice three-day clinic, which combines a day of lake learning in Boulder with two days on a nearby river, generally the Colorado through Glenwood Canyon. You can expect to paddle from 5 to 10 mi (8 to 16 km) each day on the river, and swimming skills are a requirement. All children under 16 must take classes with a parent.

Although BOC specializes in getting paddlers ready for white water, it also offers sea kayak and touring clinics, similar to its lake clinics. In addition, there are classes for intermediate and advanced paddlers in which you'll learn rolling, surfing, and play-paddling. You can challenge yourselves on class II to class IV rapids on almost any of Colorado's rivers, including the Cache La Poudre, Arkansas, Roaring Fork, and Colorado.

Boulder Outdoor Center, 2510 N. 47th St., Boulder, CO 80301, tel. 303/444–8420 or 800/364–9376, www.boc123.com. Year-round: 2 hrs–3 days, $34–$359 adults; 50% discount on lake clinics, novice river clinic, and roll classes for children under 16. Private instruction $125–$275 per person per day, depending on day and number of people; half-day instruction also available.

Kayak & Canoe Institute

7+

The institute is part of the University of Minnesota at Duluth's Outdoor Program, which aims to "create an environment where participants can develop skills, learn about themselves, relax, enjoy, and share their gifts with others." Duluth, tucked into the western tip of Lake Superior and surrounded by protecting bluffs, is an ideal location for inner harbor expeditions. It's also near one of the country's great kayaking destinations, Wisconsin's Apostle Islands.

FOR FAMILIES. In general, best for families with young children is private instruction; just call to go over your interests and goals and the staff will schedule a program for your family. Ages 15 and up are welcome to join all courses and multiday trips. White-water and sea kayaking fundamentals classes and tours run in length from four hours to four days, ranging from basic instruction to rolling, kayak "rodeo" moves, and slalom training and racing. Intermediates who choose a three-day trip to the Apostle Islands, Lake Superior's magnificent archipelago, will see sea caves, sandy beaches, rocky inlets, lighthouses, and sunken ships. The institute also schedules multiday summer kayaking and hiking trips for all skill levels to explore such places as Voyageurs National Park and the northwest tip of Vancouver Island. Trips change from year to year, so call to see what's new.

Families in the Duluth area who want to test-drive a kayak before signing on for more intensive courses can try a couple of tours, which are manageable even for young children. Spend an afternoon kayaking in the shelter of Duluth Harbor, watching the aerial lift bridge go up and down and big freighters coming and going from the docks. While you're on the four-hour Duluth Waterfront Tour, be sure to paddle right up to the docked *William A. Irvin*, a former flagship of the U.S. Steel Great Lakes Fleet and a look-alike of the famed *Edmund Fitzgerald*, the last big ship to sink in Lake Superior. It's an awesome view looking up from a kayak. Another tour takes in the Split Rock Lighthouse by land and sea and, if weather permits, you'll paddle over a shipwreck.

Kayak & Canoe Institute, University of Minnesota at Duluth, Outdoor Program, 121 Sports and Health Center, 10 University Dr., Duluth, MN 55812, tel. 218/726–6533, www.umdoutdoorprogram.org. May–Aug.: 4 hrs–17 days, $40–$1,350, discounts for family groups on some courses. Price does not include lunch for single-day classes.

Maine Island Kayak Company

10+

Maine Island Kayak Company is oriented as much to environmental concerns and the wilderness as it is to kayaking. What the staff likes best is taking people on multiday tours in and around Maine's wild islands. Children must be at least 10 years old, be able to swim, and have some athletic ability and enough muscle strength to paddle a kayak. The company is based about 20 minutes by ferry from Portland, Maine.

FOR FAMILIES. Families have lots of choices. Scheduled three-day Family Fun trips explore Maine's islands and inlets, but if the dates don't work for you, MIKCO will design courses and expeditions for particular family groups. You can also sign up for a scheduled class or expedition. Regular course offerings include half- to three-day instruction classes, along with half- to five-day expeditions. Some expeditions are camping trips, while on others you stay in bed-and-breakfasts. For advanced paddlers, there are guide and instructor training clinics. All boats are sea kayaks—either singles or doubles (family trips usually use doubles).

MIKCO's tours take paddlers in and around Casco Bay, Jewell Island, and Penobscot Bay. One of the most popular trips goes from Stonington to Acadia National Park's Isle au Haut, with its rugged cliffs and rocky ledges. On easy trips you can expect to paddle about 5 mi (8 km) per day; on moderate trips, 10 mi (16 km). For those with children ages 12 and up, there are also winter kayaking tours in international waters, but multiday paddling experience is necessary.

Call the company to discuss the ages and abilities of your family—they'll find or design a trip for you. Wet suits are provided; a small should fit a good-size 10-year-old.

Maine Island Kayak Company, 70 Luther St., Peaks Island, ME 04108, tel. 207/766–2373 or 800/796–2373, www.maineislandkayak.com. May–Oct.: ½–5 days, $55–$975 adults, family trips, $375 adults, $350 children in double kayak. Children's pricing available on some trips. Ask about winter tours.

Nantahala Outdoor Center

8+

Nantahala, in the majestic Great Smoky Mountains of western North Carolina, is one of the premier paddling schools in the country. The company is employee-owned, which may help account for the enthusiasm and high quality of its instructors. Courses begin on flat water (a lake) and move on to cover between one and four rivers, depending on the class you choose. Plan to stay in the area either before or after your trip; Nantahala is only about 30 minutes from the southern entrance to Great Smoky Mountains National Park and 1½ hours from Asheville, rich in history and opportunities for family sightseeing.

FOR FAMILIES. NOC's two- or four-day family courses in kayaking are for parents with kids age 12 and older. You can take either novice level or level 1 intermediate courses, which are offered during several weeks throughout spring and summer. The regular two- to six-day standard courses, for ages 16 and up, include novice, intermediate, and advanced levels, as well as special rolling classes. Clinics include packed lunches, breakfast and dinner at NOC's restaurant, and lodging in shared cabins. Optional slide shows, vidoes, and gear info sessions are offered nightly, and these activities are designed to strengthen family bonds through camaraderie and fun. For a quick dip into boating, try the Family Paddling Sampler, which is aimed at families with kids as young as 8 and starts with a practice session on the lake before heading to the river. Another option for families is private instruction. Note that you should always discuss your child's weight, size, athletic ability, and interest with the school before signing up for a trip.

In addition to regular classes, Nantahala also has special children's courses at all skill levels throughout the summer. Divided by age (9–11, 12–15, or 14–18), these emphasize learning in a fun, high-energy atmosphere. Parents can take adult-oriented classes at the same time.

Base facilities at Nantahala include several restaurants and three types of lodging: a base camp bunk house (co-ed, shared facilities), a standard motel, and cabins featuring two to 10 bedrooms (the majority with equipped kitchens, decks, grills, and other amenities). Day care is available for small children while parents are kayaking. Wet suits can be rented, although there's a limited number of children's sizes.

Nantahala's travel department schedules 7- to 11-day instructional and international adventure tours throughout for kayakers of various ages and abilities. A parent who's a strong paddler might be able to bring a preteen on a trip by using a double kayak. Call and discuss your skills and the ages of your children.

Nantahala Outdoor Center, 13077 U.S. 19W, Bryson City, NC 28713, tel. 800/232-7238, www.noc.com. Courses, Mar.–Oct.: 1–6 days, $95–$1,150 adults, $95–$950 children (ask about discounts for kids on sampler courses and about pricing on kids' camps). Trips, year-round: 7–11 days, $895–$2,560.

Northern Lights Expeditions

ALL

Since 1983 this company has taken people into the wilds of British Columbia, focusing on providing a high-quality experience that introduces visitors to the region's vast natural resources. Committed to protecting BC's wildlife and pristine wilderness, Northern Lights strives to be a leader in creating ethical guidelines for wilderness travel. The company takes its mission seriously, but don't get the wrong idea. The staff also knows that a vacation is supposed to be fun, with just the right amount of challenge thrown in for an optimum experience. What could be better?

FOR FAMILIES. All ages are welcomed on the 40-ft Spirit Bear, a salmon trawler remodeled into an elegant vacation vessel. Meticulously retrofitted for modern travel, the Spirit Bear now accommodates families and other groups of up to four (five if two are small children) who want a fine floating base from which to explore the BC coast. Hot showers, gourmet meals, kayaks, and an inflatable power boat are all part of the package—as is your naturalist guide, who will take you through the Inside Passage, the Great Bear Rainforest, and the Great

Bear coastline just south of the border between Alaska and Canada. This is a charter-only boat where you plan the journey, and it's an excellent base from which to see orcas, humpback whales, dolphins, and other wildlife. The minimum age for kayak trips is 15.

One of the best trips for families with teens is through the spectacular Inside Passage, a glacier-carved waterway between the Canadian mainland and thousands of coastal islands, including Vancouver. It's one of the finest sea kayaking destinations in the world, particularly in summer, when sunny days, 70°F (21°C) temperatures, calm waters, and thriving wildlife set ideal conditions for a journey. Here, orcas and dolphins leap, eagles sweep the skies, and kayakers are the privileged few who can see it. Guides tote underwater microphones so you hear the marine mammals as well as see them.

The Inside Passage trips are camping journeys, while inn-based adventures include the Farewell Harbour outing, based at a remote, four-star island lodge in the heart of the Inside Passage. For something even more rustic, head to the Lost Islands, what the folks at Northern Lights Expeditions call the northern Canada's remote offshore wilderness. The meeting point is in Prince Rupert, the most northerly town on the BC coast, from where you'll take a spectacular seaplane flight to the first wilderness camp. Here, according to the brochure, "you're more likely to hear a wolf howling than to see another human." It's the quintessential way to get away from it all, into pristine wilderness, wildlife, and placid waters.

Northern Lights Expeditions, Box 4289, Bellingham, WA 98227, tel. 360/734–6334 or 800/754–7402, www.seakayaking.com. May–Oct.: 6–7 days, $1,295–$1,795 per person. Spirit Bear, $6,995–$7,995 per week, including food, fuel, equipment, and guide.

Outside Expeditions

ALL

Based on Canada's Prince Edward Island (PEI), Outside Expeditions offers guests an insider's view of one of the east's great kayaking destinations and a locale renowned for its beaches, inns, travel-poster scenery, and exceptional food.

FOR FAMILIES. PEI's shallow, sheltered shoreline makes it ideal for both families and beginning paddlers. The Gulf of St. Lawrence is as warm as the waters along the Carolinas, so swimming and wading are musts. On Families Only overnights you'll study seaweed (and soon know the difference between green blade kelp and Irish Moss) and learn about such winged residents as the Great Blue Heron. Tidal estuaries provide plenty of opportunities for hands-on learning, to say nothing of fun, and guides are trained to work with children and families. Typically, these trips depart from either North Rustico Harbour on PEI's north shore, or from Murray River or Brudenell River Provincial Park on the eastern shore. Most are camping outings, but inn-to-inn options are also available. The company may soon be setting up new, north island base camps for five-day family trips, so ask if that sounds appealing. Custom itineraries are available, too.

In summer, the company runs several two-day WOW (Wonderful Outside World) programs for kids 10–14, as well as a Teenager's Kayak Kamp. While kids participate in these, parents can join Outside Expeditions' more adult-oriented hiking, biking, or paddling offerings on and around PEI.

Outside Expeditions' regular trips are suitable for ages 16 and older. There are many on PEI, but others are in Nova Scotia, Newfoundland, and the Magdalene Islands.

Outside Expeditions, Box 337, North Rustico, Prince Edward Island, CA C0A 1X0, tel. 902/963–3366 or 800/207–3899, www.getoutside.com. Feb.–Oct.: 2–19 days, $149–$2,495 adults, $31–$1,996 children up to age 10.

REI Adventures

15+

REI, the nationwide outdoor store from which many adventurers buy their gear and apparel, doubles as an excellent outfitter, with trips incorporating a number of sports, including kayaking. The best for families are around the islands off the coast of Washington state and Vancouver Island and in the dramatic waters and scenery of Alaska's Glacier Bay. Neither requires previous kayaking experience.

FOR FAMILIES. Among the best choices for families with younger kayakers is the Alaska Adventure Cruise, suitable for ages 8 and up. It's based on a 34-passenger ship that cruises through the Alaskan wilderness, including Glacier Bay National Park. Paddlers glide through waters that offer views of glacial landscapes and teem with such wildlife as eagles, sea otters, sea lions and puffins, and humpback whales. Plan on five to six hours of kayaking and nature excursions daily. The tour includes a pre-cruise overnight at Glacier Bay Lodge, one of our country's premier wilderness retreats.

Families with kids age 12 and older can choose from a Kayak Kauai adventure in Hawaii (which also has hiking and snorkeling on the itinerary) and a Greek Multisport adventure. Depending on the season, kayaking in Kauai takes place below the cliffs of the Na Pali coast or along the South Shore (where snorkeling is awesome). This is a mixed camping and cabins trip for 4 to 12 participants. In Greece, a country that has long celebrated athletic endeavors, you can mix city hotels, island guest houses, and beach camping as you explore the islands of Lefkada and Karpensi, and paddle along the coast of Scorpios, once the residence of Aristotle Onassis. When you're not discovering unspoiled beaches and sea caves, you can trek, swim, snorkel, visit museums in Delphi, and spend an evening in the Plaka, Athens' old quarter. Three of the 11 days will be spent sea kayaking four to six hours daily, while on other days you'll hike 6 to 10 mi (10 to 16 km). In between, you'll enjoy picnics and dinners featuring Greek delicacies.

Most other REI trips have minimum ages of 14 or 16, and there are plenty to choose from. A good one for teens would be the six-day, naturalist-led Islands Kayaking sea kayaking trip, which has departures from June through September and focuses on learning about the environment in addition to paddling. The San Juan Islands, off the coast of Washington, are home to harbor seals, river otters, and bald eagles. Orcas also inhabit the area, and as you paddle a safe distance away guides will tell you about their complex social structure and place in this marine environment. Nights are spent in campsites on island beaches.

REI Adventures, Box 1938, Sumner, WA 98390, tel. 253/437–1100 or 800/622–2236, www.rei.com. Mar.–Dec. (not all trips all months): 6–11 days, $895–$2,090. Price does not include $15 REI membership per family; nonmembers add $100 per person.

Trek & Trail

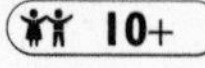

Based in Bayfield, Wisconsin, on a peninsula at the west end of Lake Superior, Trek & Trail has been running outdoor learning adventures in the Apostle Islands National Lakeshore and on Lake Superior since 1978. The company has a strong commitment to bringing families into the wilderness and is enthusiastic about working with children.

FOR FAMILIES. T & T's paddling school offers courses from a basic safety class (required for all renters) to a three-day expedition preparation course. The two-hour introduction to sea kayaking is a good way to get down the basics and to try out the sheltered waters of the Bayfield harbors. There are several trips that are especially good for families. The Basswood Island Paddle is a one-day adventure with an open-water crossing from Bayfield to Basswood Island. An ideal weekend adventure is the Sand Island Overnight, which begins with a safety clinic and includes exploring sea caves and an old lighthouse and hiking to the abandoned fishing village of Shaw. One of the most popular scheduled outings is the three-day Paddle Through Time, on which you discover the mystery and richness of Lake Superior's environment, with stops at five islands and overnights on two (Oak and Sand islands).

T & T's custom-designed, four-day Island Base Camp adventure is also perfect for families of at least four paddlers. You stay in an established base camp, so there's no setting up and taking down campsites, which allows for more time to paddle. You'll also hike, learn about Ojibwa history, and fish, in addition to taking advantage of excellent paddling instruction. Sand, Oak, or Stockton Island serves well as a base camp. The specific routes and itinerary are based on your family's abilities and interests. Trips depart every Monday, Memorial Day through Labor Day.

Families and children (usually ages 10 and up, but check with the company) are welcome on all other Trek & Trail trips, too. Most courses run between Memorial Day and Labor Day. Wet suits can be rented. *Trek & Trail, Box 906, Bayfield, WI 54814, tel. 715/779–3320 or 800/354–8735, www.trek-trail.com. May–Sept.: 2 hrs–6 days, $30–$649; Island Base Camp, 4 days, $389 per person. Basic courses generally offer 30% discount for children under 12.*

Wilderness Expeditions & The Birches

8+

The Birches is a rustic resort on the shores of 40-mi (64-km) Moosehead Lake in north-central Maine. Set in a grove of birches in an 11,000-acre wilderness preserve, the resort and its outfitting service, Wilderness Expeditions, offer adventure opportunities based at a comfortable cabin tent or rustic log cabin. Although kayaking is available, it's by no means the only activity, which makes this an ideal getaway for the family that loves to stay together, but doesn't always play together.

FOR FAMILIES. Family Camp is a four-day adventure vacation with something for everyone, as part of your time is spent at a wilderness campsite and part at the resort. It starts with a 5-mi (8-km) "ducky" float to the campsite on the Kennebec River, where a deluxe cabin tent awaits. The next day you can choose white-water rafting or hiking, then head back to the Birches Resort on day three for a kayak eco-tour on the lake. The morning Moose Cruise on day four is a must, as you'll search out moose, deer, bear, bald eagles, osprey, and falcons via pontoon boat on Moosehead Lake. In the afternoon, you can opt for more kayaking, canoeing, swimming, biking, or windsurfing. Resort facilities include a restaurant, pool, hot tub, sauna, and such evening family activities as campfires, storytelling, and sing-alongs. *Wilderness Expeditions & The Birches, Box 41-N, Rockwood, ME 04478, tel. 207/534–7305 or 800/825–9453, www.birches.com. June–Aug.: 4 days, $349 per person.*

Wilderness Inquiry

5+

A leader in wilderness adventure for two decades, this company places a special emphasis on making trips available to people with and without disabilities. On these trips children have the opportunity to learn new skills and appreciation for nature, along with respect for the differences among people. The company is based in Minneapolis but leads trips around the United States and Canada.

FOR FAMILIES. Because these trips are in 21-ft touring kayaks, which hold two to three people, children as young as age 5 can go on most of them, although shorter trips may be best for younger children. There are three- and five-day Apostle Island tours in northern Wisconsin, and a seven-day Isle Royale tour in Michigan, all of which include time for hiking and exploring on land. Families with teenagers might consider the six-day San Juan Islands or Lake Powell tours, or the nine-day trip in the British Columbia's Queen Charlotte Islands in British Columbia, the latter of which are known as the Galápagos Islands of the North due to their abundant animal and ecological diversity. On all of these trips you camp along the way.

For longer trips such as the one to the Queen Charlotte Islands, some experience and good physical condition are important. Wet suits may be required on some trips, and Wilderness Inquiry provides both adult and child sizes at no additional cost.
Wilderness Inquiry, 1313 5th St. SE, Box 84, Minneapolis, MN 55414-1546, tel. 612/379–3858 or 800/728–0719, www.wildernessinquiry.org. May–Sept.: 3–9 days, $350–$1,850.

Zoar Outdoor

10+

Zoar's 80-acre campus in the Deerfield River valley in northwestern Massachusetts combines everything a family needs in order to try out the sport of kayaking, including a campground, a bathhouse with hot showers, and an outfitters store. Zoar Outdoor has been teaching kayaking and other outdoor sports since 1989, and it continues to grow and get better each year. Co-owners Bruce Lessels and Karen Blom are also the authors of an excellent book on introducing kids to paddling (*see* Resources, *below*), so pick up a copy before taking a class.

FOR FAMILIES. Zoar has a two-day parent–child beginner clinic on its extensive list of instructional courses. Offered in July and August, it's for children 10 to 16 with one or both parents. Families with children ages 14 and up can take part in any of the clinics scheduled from April through October. There are beginner, intermediate, and advanced instructional clinics that run two or five days, as well as special one-day rolling and playboating (instruction in cool moves like "surfing" and "squirting") clinics. Families may opt for customized classes, too. You may also choose to sign up children (ages 10 through 15) for Kids Kayak Craze, a one-day course offered during July or August, while you take a course of your own.
Zoar Outdoor, Box 245, Charlemont, MA 01339, tel. 800/532–7483, www.zoaroutdoor.com. Apr.–Oct.: 1–5 days, $130–$525 adults, $85–$525 children 10–15. Price does not include lodging for some clinics.

Resources

Organizations

America Outdoors (Box 10847, Knoxville, TN 37939, tel. 865/558–3597, www.americaoutdoors.org), a national association for outfitters and river guides, has a magazine listing outfitters and guides. The **American Canoe Association** (7432 Alban Station Blvd., Suite B232, Springfield, VA 22150, tel. 703/451–0140, www.acanet.org) publishes a newsletter and certifies guides and instructors.

Books

Paddling with Kids: AMC Essential Handbook, by Bruce Lessels and Karen Blom (Appalachian Mountain Club Books), comes from the directors of Zoar Outdoor and is an excellent primer on introducing kids to the sport. AMC also publishes a series, Quiet Water Canoe & Kayak Guides, which though not aimed specifically at families is a good choice for parents interested in paddling family-friendly waters. Globe Pequot Press publishes the largest number of sea kayaking books in the nation. Among its excellent instructional and touring guides are *Complete Book of Sea Kayaking, Expedition Kayaking, Eskimo Rolling,* and *Basic Book of Sea Kayaking,* all by kayaker Derek Hutchinson. Another well-known name in the sport, Nigel Foster, has *Nigel Foster's Sea Kayaking* and *Nigel Foster's Surf Kayaking.* More Globe Pequot titles include *Fundamentals of Kayak Navigation,* by David Burch, and *Basic Essentials: Sea Kayaking,* by J. Michael Wyatt. They also have a regional sea kayaking series, which includes guides for southern Florida; central and northern California; Lakes Superior and Michigan; Lakes Huron, Erie, and Ontario; and southeast Alaska.

Periodicals

Canoe & Kayak (Box 3146, Kirkland, WA 98083, tel. 800/692–2663, www.canoekayak.com) has many family-oriented articles, and most issues carry an extensive resource listing of outfitters, schools, and guides. *Paddler* magazine (Box 775450, Steamboat Springs, CO 80477 or www.paddlermagazine.com), which is owned by the American Canoe Association, publishes lots of articles on getting kids started in paddling, family paddling adventures, and essential safety for families out on the water.

Also See

Families that love the water should see Canoeing; Sailing; Rafting; Snorkeling and Diving; *and* Wildlife Encounters.

NATIVE AMERICAN EXPERIENCES

Native American peoples have been integral to our country's cultural fabric, and today it's easier than ever for families to explore their history. The importance of these firsthand encounters became clear to me on a visit a few years ago to the Cherokee Heritage Center in Tahlequah, Oklahoma. My then 4-year-old kept peering intently at the Cherokee people working there. He seemed confused. Finally he asked, "But where do they keep their horses?" His sole experience of Native Americans, I'm embarrassed to say, had been obtained from reruns of the spectacularly awful television show *F Troop,* but he left the center with a different perspective.

Fortunately there are many ways for any child to be exposed to the richness of native life rather than the old stereotypes, and these trips are one of them. Although native people were once reluctant to share their culture with outsiders, that is no longer the case. In recent years tribal elders have agreed to meet with visitors to share their wisdom and knowledge, and native guides have begun to offer tours of their lands that focus as much on tribal history and cultural life as on the land itself. Native people across North America have devoted time and resources to preserving, or reestablishing if necessary, traditional languages, fine and performing arts, lore, spiritual practices, agricultural and hunting traditions, and crafts. The primary benefit of a renewal in traditional ways is, of course, a stronger native culture; but it also provides exciting learning opportunities for people outside the culture.

Questions to Ask

How do I know this program is legitimate? If your family has a desire to experience authentic Native American culture, the last thing you want is a hokey, "canned" experience. By talking at length to the people running the trips, you can usually tell if there's a real interest in native culture and if they have worked closely with Native Americans to organize the trips. You can also check with the tourism departments of the states you're going to visit, and you might want to ask for references from people who have traveled with the group.

What is the focus of this particular trip? Is it native culture? History? Tribal lands? Crafts and artwork are featured on some trips; on others the point is to experience the present-day lifestyle of a tribe. Some experiences with native guides focus on an activity—fishing or horse packing—and native culture is secondary. Many trips combine several elements.

Can we participate in tribal activities such as crafts or other traditional pastimes? In many cases, yes. If this appeals to your family, talk to outfitters ahead of time to be sure native hosts and leaders at the villages know you want to try some activities. And let them know your children will be interested, too, if that's the case.

Will there be opportunities for one-on-one discussions? If this is important to you, choose a trip that offers a more customized or personalized experience rather than one geared to a group.

Will there be recreational activities in addition to cultural learning? You may be able to go horseback riding or fishing or hiking as part of some trips. Others focus almost entirely on the cultural or learning aspect. Young children have a more limited capacity for lectures and grown-up talk, so make sure there's enough action and diversity to keep your children's interest.

If someone in the family has a particular interest, can you make arrangements beyond what is described in the itinerary? Outfitters and tour operators that handle custom trips are the most likely to be able to arrange special activities. If you can't find what you want on a set itinerary, call some of the customization specialists in this chapter. Quite possibly you'll be able to design your own trip and still stay within your budget.

Will my children have native children their age with whom to interact? Trip leaders don't always give thought to this, so try to arrange it in advance. Children learn a great deal from each other through play and other activities.

What kind of lodging is available? Some outfitters arrange stays with Native American host families; others give you the opportunity to stay in a traditional tepee on a reservation or other land. In some cases you stay in motels, visiting tribal areas during the day. There are combinations of all of the above, too. Choose the trip that best meets your family's expectations for immersion in Native American culture.

What kind of food will we eat? Native foods are often part of the experience, and some may be strange to you or your children. You'll want to try everything, but do bring snack foods that your children like.

What's included in the cost? For the trips in this chapter, and in most other cases as well, lodging, some meals, and local transportation are included. Sightseeing, activities at reservations and villages, and participation in powwows, dances, and meetings with tribal members are also part of the package. It's up to you to get to and from the trip's starting and ending points.

Instruction

All these trips involve learning; many include instruction in native crafts, dances, and music or in such traditional activities as fishing or tracking wildlife. Sometimes you can learn to prepare foods or make medicines. In every case tribal elders or experts will guide and teach you. Native encounters offer a rare opportunity for multicultural learning in its purest sense.

Finding the Fun

Northeast: Journeys into American Indian Territory. **Midwest:** Journeys into American Indian Territory. **Southwest:** Crow Canyon Archaeological Center, Grandtravel, Off the Beaten Path, Journeys into American Indian Territory. **Rockies:** Grandtravel, Off the Beaten Path, Journeys into American Indian Territory. **Alaska:** Athabasca Cultural Journeys. **Canada:** Arctic Odysseys, Off the Beaten Path. **Mexico:** Crow Canyon Archaeological Center.

Favorite Experiences

Arctic Odysseys

12+

As its name implies, Arctic Odysseys specializes in introducing people of all ages and backgrounds to an area once accessible only to the most daring of explorers. This trip takes place in northern Canada with the Inuit. It still requires a special kind of family to venture into this wild and remote land, but those that do find that the rewards far outweigh the hardship or expense that Arctic travel involves.

FOR FAMILIES. The Summer Wildlife and Cultural Odyssey combines wildlife viewing and exposure to the traditional Inuit lifestyle. This is a totally customized experience, so you and your Inuit guide can modify the itinerary to suit your interests. For that reason, younger children can often be accommodated, but talk to owner Robin Duberow first.

You spend some time in established communities, such as Cape Dorset and Iqaluit (still shown as Frobisher Bay on some maps), on Baffin Island. During most of the trip, however, your family is traveling by 25-ft powered utility boat; the length of the ride varies with your particular itinerary, but may average four or five hours each day. You pick your way through the icebergs and stop at Inuit summer camps to visit with friends and relatives of your guide or to watch Inuit artists at work. You can usually see caribou, seals, walrus, and snow geese. If you have a license, you can learn to fish for Arctic char. A special experience is a stop at the West Baffin Co-op in Cape Dorset, which has world-renowned galleries with carvings and other work by Inuit artists. Lodging at summer camps is typically in double-wall tents. The trip begins and ends in Ottawa, Ontario, and the cost includes the flights between Ottawa, Iqaluit, and Cape Dorset. Temperatures range between 30°F and 60°F (1°C and 16°C), so pay attention to clothing lists.

Arctic Odysseys, 2000 McGilvra Blvd. E, Seattle, WA 98112, tel. 206/325–1977, www.arcticodysseys.com. July–Aug.: 9 days, $3,999.

Athabasca Cultural Journeys

8+

The Athabascan people did not want their ancestral home in north-central Alaska destroyed by mining or logging, so they embarked on a commercial tourism enterprise to help sustain their tribe. The goal was to allow visitors to meet real families and see everyday Athabascan life while learning about the tribe's unique history and culture. Athabasca Cultural Journeys, owned and operated by the Athabascan people of Huslia, Alaska, describes the tours as "a wilderness and cultural adventure" in which guests "experience Alaska through the eyes of native peoples."

FOR FAMILIES. Huslia is remote—a 90-minute bush-plane flight from Fairbanks. You pass over native villages, the Yukon River, the Trans-Alaska Pipeline, and historical and working gold mines. The Athabascan host families traditionally are volunteer tribal elders, but if guests ask for host families with children, the company will try to accommodate that request. From Huslia most guests travel with their hosts by riverboat deep into the Koyokuk National Wildlife Refuge to a native wilderness camp. Only six people at a time are allowed, both to maintain the quality of the experience and to lessen the impact on the wilderness area.

The wildlife refuge, home to thousands of nesting migratory birds and birds of prey as well as to moose, caribou, bears, wolves, otters, and beavers, presents many opportunities to see and photograph wildlife. You can also fish, hike, and visit archaeological sites. For the trip's cultural component, tribal members teach native history, traditions, and animal lore and share traditional myths and legends. Families can try crafts and explore the use of barks and roots for eating and healing. At the primitive campsite, you stay in cabins or wall tents, and there is no running water. Food, however, is plentiful and includes native recipes using moose, caribou, bear, beaver, and fish.

Summer in Alaska means almost constant daylight, so there's plenty of time for all your activities. In fact, each itinerary is customized. You can spend more time in Huslia or opt for a traditional fishing camp—where you'd participate in drying and smoking salmon—instead of the wilderness camp. As with the wilderness camp, the fishing camp's facilities are quite bare bones.

Athabasca Cultural Journeys, Box 72, Huslia, AK 99746, tel. 907/829–2261 or 800/937–0899. June–Aug.: 3 days, $1,650. Flights between Fairbanks and Huslia are included in the cost.

Crow Canyon Archaeological Center

8+

This prestigious, nonprofit archaeological center, whose main work is preserving, protecting, and uncovering ruins in southwestern Colorado (see Archaeology Adventures), also offers cultural explorations of ancient and present-day native societies in various parts of the American Southwest and Mexico. Trips change from season to season; the ones described here are representative of what Crow Canyon is likely to offer.

FOR FAMILIES. The eight-day Family Travel Program is the only trip aimed squarely at parents and children. Its variety of activities can keep even 8-year-olds happily busy and learning. Families travel with an archaeologist (who may bring a child along) through the Four Corners area of Arizona, Colorado, and Utah, exploring the cliff dwellings at Mesa Verde, rafting to rock art sites on the San Juan River, and horseback riding in Northern Arizona. There are opportunities to meet and learn from Navajo (or Dine) and Pueblo people, including a hike to visit with a Navajo family at their sheep camp in Canyon de Chelly.

There are several other family-appropriate trips in Crow Canyon's catalog. Because they have a stronger scholarly focus, they're best for families with teens. Monument Valley on Horseback is a journey through one of the most historic and visually stunning regions of the American Southwest, in northeastern Arizona and southeastern Utah. The Navajo people had—and have—an intimate relationship with this valley, where their hogans blend almost seamlessly into the landscape. On this tour, led by a Navajo scholar, the group learns about the natural and human history of Monument Valley, as well as the significance and story of the mesas, buttes, and jutting volcanic monoliths. Another trek for horse lovers, through the White Mountains of Arizona, is led by an Apache tribe member and an archaeologist. The Apache still live in the region today and continue to influence it with their rich culture and traditions. Four Corners Country is a study of the archaeology and native peoples of the Colorado Plateau, from the ancestral Pueblo Indians to present-day Navajo and Hopi. It includes a visit to Mesa Verde National Park, Canyon de Chelly, Chaco Canyon, and sites along the San Juan River. Or, blend an interest in astronomy with a desire to learn about Native American cultures on the Navajo Skies and Star Ceilings trip. A Native American and a scientist who have worked together studying astronomical evidence in the Navajo culture will introduce you to the scientific and spiritual aspects of Canyon de Chelly and Dinetah (the Navajo sacred homeland). During group stargazing, they'll point out Navajo constellations and share traditional stories and myths related to the world above.

If the center has scheduled a trip to Mexico's Copper Canyon and the other canyons of the Sierra Tarahumara, where the Tarahumara people have lived for centuries, consider joining it. You can hike in the canyons—the deepest is more than ¼-mi deeper than the Grand Canyon—and meet Native Americans who will talk about their homeland and its recent changes. Another possibility is a journey to the state of Chiapas, where ancient Mayan and contemporary native cultures enhance a diverse landscape of forested highlands and tropical jungle lowlands. You can learn to recognize the colorful textiles worn by local Indians; each design is identified with a particular village. There's also time to explore local markets, bright with traditional weavings and embroidery.

Accommodations on Crow Canyon's trips range from tents to first-class hotels; most meals are included.

Crow Canyon Archaeological Center, 23390 Road K, Cortez, CO 81321, tel. 970/565–8975 or 800/422–8975, www.crowcanyon.org. Feb.–Nov.: 6–9 days, $875–$4,195, $1,375 for children in the family program. A required family membership costs $75; membership for other programs runs $20–$50, depending on age.

Grandtravel

7–17

A pioneer in intergenerational travel, Grandtravel makes available a wide variety of journeys for grandparents and grandchildren. These trips broaden a child's horizons by promoting the discovery of new and exciting places and, perhaps most important, new perspectives. The itineraries are geared for both age groups and include such activities as riding and rafting.

FOR FAMILIES. On the Our Native Americans trip, family members gain firsthand knowledge and understanding of Native American tribes throughout the Southwest. The trip, which starts in Albuquerque and ends in Phoenix, is run twice each summer: once for adults with grandchildren from ages 7 to 11, once for those with grandchildren from 12 to 17. The majority of travel is by motor coach and train, but the trip also has a Navajo-guided jeep tour of Arizona's Canyon de Chelly; a train ride near Durango, Colorado; and a white-water rafting trip.

In Albuquerque the group rides the Sandia Peak Tramway to Sandia Peak's 10,674-ft summit. From the top you'll have a stunning panorama view of approximately 14,000 square mi (36,260 square km) of land that has long been important to native peoples. In Santa Fe grandchildren and grandparents attend a Pueblo Ceremonial Feast Day and take a guided "storywalk" through the historic streets of the oldest capital city in the United States. Taos, New Mexico's 800-year-old pueblo is an important stop, as is the Jicarilla Apache Reservation. In Canyon de Chelly, the ancestral home of the Navajo people, there's a Navajo ranger campfire program in addition to the Jeep tour. A visit to the Hopi Reservation in Arizona gives insight into how trade affected Native Americans in the 1880s; explorations of a variety of ancestral Puebloan ruins and petroglyphs add further historical perspective. *Grandtravel, 6900 Wisconsin Ave., Suite 706, Chevy Chase, MD 20815, tel. 301/986–0790 or 800/247–7651, www.grandtrvl.com. June–Aug.: 10 days, $3,415–$3,710, depending on number in family group.*

Journeys into American Indian Territory

6+

Anthropologist Robert Vetter, along with a staff of Native Americans, is wholly dedicated to the concept of giving nonnative people a chance to experience the diversity of native cultures through one-on-one contact with Native Americans around the United States. An educational consultant when not running Journeys, he is totally enthusiastic about including children in that process.

FOR FAMILIES. The best trip for families with younger children is the three-day Catskill Mountains experience, which generally takes place in August. Vetter will consider children younger than 6 on an individual basis. This gathering of native people from the West and the East has separate activities for children and adults, but close interaction with native people is at the heart of everyone's experience. Unlike most other powwows, where nonnatives are spectators, this event is about participating; you learn traditional dances, games, and songs. Expect storytelling, lectures, and a chance to learn about native foods (one activity is an herbal plant walk) and crafts. In addition to Native American activities, there's also swimming, hiking, canoeing, and fishing on the 372-acre site in New York's lower Catskills.

Older children—12 or 13 and up—who have a real interest in Native American cultures can join the company's other journeys. Although none has activities especially designed for children, all offer firsthand learning opportunities. In Oklahoma, nine-day sessions provide interaction with people from the Kiowa, Comanche, Apache, Cheyenne, Arapahoe, Wichita, Caddo, and Delaware tribes. The focus is on a very personal experience, one on which guests meet native families in their homes and attend small local events in addition to powwows. You will learn traditional dances and attend informal lectures and discussion groups to help you get the most out of your daily experience with native people. The trip is based in Anandarko, but you'll also travel through the Wichita Mountains, a sacred site for the Kiowa and Comanche people and a place where buffalo and elk still roam.

Although we often think of Native communities thriving primarily west of the Mississippi, many eastern states have large Native populations. The ancestral home of the Mohawk is in upper New York state, about 50 mi (81 km) west of Albany. Though forced out by Europeans 200 years ago, the Mohawk have returned and created a new community dedicated to the preservation of the Mohawk language, ceremonies, philosophies, and teachings. Kanatsiohareke is named after the 12-ft limestone potholes found in a local creekbed, but it also refers to a new start by the Mohawks, a place of spiritual cleanliness in which they can reclaim their heritage. Autumn weekend programs here center around sharing that heritage. New for 2002 is a spring program in Puerto Rico, on which Taino/Arawak guides show you the beautiful, sacred, and untouristed side of this Caribbean island.

Most accommodations for these trips are in hotels and cabins, but there are also options for staying overnight in a traditional tepee. The price of the Upstate New York Experience covers all meals; some journeys include two meals daily. To allow for one-on-one contact and discussion, most trips are limited to a maximum of 20 participants.

If your schedule doesn't allow participation in these scheduled trips, ask about homestays with Native American families. Through joining daily routines and having close interaction with your host family, you'll experience native customs, traditions, and foods, and learn about native family histories. The regions in which homestays are offered vary year to year, so call for the most current information.

Journeys into American Indian Territory, Box 929, Westhampton Beach, NY 11978, tel. 516/878–8655 or 800/458–2632, www.indianjourneys.com. Feb., June–Sept., and Nov.: 3–9 days, $340–$875 adults, $190 for children participating in the Catskill Mountains program.

Off the Beaten Path

ALL

Off the Beaten Path (OBP) excels in customized adventures for people of all ages. Owner Bill Bryan has a long personal and professional history with Native American people, and he's a published authority on the tribes of Montana (*see* Resources, *below*).

The company handles planning and arrangements, working with each family to put together the right trip. There are generally two options to choose from. Custom Journeys have pre-set itineraries and pricing and are self-guided; OBP consultants match your family up with the right journey. With Personal Travel Consulting, OBP designs your intinerary from scratch specifically for your family, based on your interests, ages, abilities, and time-frame; for this you pay a consulting fee in addition to the costs of the actual adventure itself. On either type of trip you can expect private Indian guides and other authentic experiences.

FOR FAMILIES. Totally customized or predesigned encounters might include a day spent with tribal members at reservations in various parts of the West or multiday journeys with Native American guides. You might, for example, book several nights in the hogan of a Navajo outfitter, who will guide your family around Canyon de Chelly, the Navajo homeland in northern Arizona. You can stay with families who have ranches or fishing lodges or travel with guides who run horse-packing and fishing trips. OBP works with Blackfeet and Flathead tribe members in Montana; Blood and Piegan natives in Alberta, Canada; and numerous tribes throughout the Southwest. Your customized trip can concentrate on spirituality, family life, history, or any aspect of native culture you may want to explore.

Each year OBP also offers its own scheduled, fully guided 8- to 10-day tour for singles, couples, and families with relatively mature children (talk to the company first about your child's interests and abilities before signing up). The trip, with about 14 participants, focuses on the history and present-day culture of tribes in Montana, southwestern Colorado, and in Alberta, Canada. The group spends time with tribal council members and reservation school principals and visits hospitals and historic sites. Some meals are with tribal members. Participants usually learn how to raise a tepee; they have the option of staying overnight in one as well. Two examples of these trips are A Journey Through Time to the Four Corners, which includes interaction with Ute and Navajo tribe members, and Tracing the Flight of the Nez Perce, which follows the 1,200-mi (1,932-km) route through four states taken by Chief Joseph and his people in 1877. The flight of the Nez Perce is one of the most powerful and sorrowful sagas in the history of the American West, and all of it is vividly brought to life on the trail by a leading authority on the Nez Perce, who accompanies guests on this trip.

Off the Beaten Path, 27 E. Main St., Bozeman, MT 59715, tel. 406/586–1311 or 800/445–2995, www.offthebeatenpath.com. Year-round (all trips not available at all times): 7–10 days, $150–$175 per person, per day. Scheduled trip: $2,000 per person. Ask about children's discounts, offered on some trips and varying with specific circumstances. Consulting runs $200–$1,000, depending on the complexity of the trip.

Smithsonian Study Tours

7+

Smithsonian Study Tours offers several intergenerational programs, all of them aimed at expanding both adult and children's horizons and satisfying their curiosity about the world around them. Study leaders are chosen not only for their expertise—and few institutions have a more stellar group of experts from which to choose—but also for their ability to share their enthusiasm, a crucial element when it comes to touring with families.

FOR FAMILIES. They call it Canyons, Mesas, and Pueblos: A Native American Adventure for Families, and it's an excellent mix of historic and cultural sites, outdoor adventure, arts and dance activities, and time in the homes of Native American families.

Smithsonian Study Tours, Ripley Center, Suite 3077, 1100 Jefferson Dr., SW, Washington, DC 20560-0701, tel. 202/357–4700 or 877/338–8687, smithsonianstudytours.org. Aug.: 9 days, $2,595 adults, $1,995 children ages 7–17.

Temagami Anishnabai Tipi Camp

5+

Virginia McKenzie is a mother, grandmother, and a Temagami Anishnabai who has spent much of her career in the field of social work. It has long been her vision to create a place where "people can enjoy the simplicity and beauty of creation, while having an empowering experience that heals the spirit." Temagami Anishnabai Tipi Camp, on an island in Lake Temagami in northern Ontario, is the embodiment of that dream. Virginia welcomes both families and individuals to retreats that foster a sense of belonging to creation.

FOR FAMILIES. There are both five-day and weekend retreats on Bear Island, which is in Temagami First Nation territory. Groups are small, usually no more than about seven people, and each day is a mix of Native teaching and enjoyment of the impressive natural beauty of the area. Bear Island has one of the world's last old-growth pine forests; the magnificent trees here are at least 300 years old, and whether you opt for the five-day or weekend retreat, a visit to the forest is an important part of the program. Other activities include canoeing, swimming, fishing, identifying and learning about healing plants, visiting one of the tribe's best-known artists, and taking part in a traditional sharing circle. After a home-cooked meal each night there are activities around a campfire, such as hearing Anishnabai creation stories and listening to the teachings of a tribal elder. On the last night of the five-day retreat, families take part in an Anishnabai social with stories, songs, and "lots of laughter." Guests sleep in comfortable tepees, where the calls of the loons and the sound of the waves to lull you to sleep.

Bring your own sleeping bags and personal items, but everything else is provided.

Virgnia knows her guests will leave having experienced new friendships, insights, and feelings, but she believes the greatest gift one takes away from the retreat is a sense of inner peace and calm. In today's frenetic world in which families are so often on the run from one activity, one event, or one must-do chore to another, this is a great gift indeed—and very much at the heart of what is unique and meaningful about wilderness vacations.

Temagami Anishnabai Tipi Camp, Bear Island, Lake Temagami, Ontario, Canada P0H 1C0, tel. 705/237–8876, www.temagamitipi.com. June–Oct.: 2½–5 days, C$325–C$950 adults, generally a 50% discount for children 15 and under.

Resources

Organizations

For a list of reservations that allow camping or for Native American events you can attend, write to the **Bureau of Indian Affairs** (U.S. Department of the Interior, Washington, DC 20245); tell them which states you want to visit. **Northern Ontario Native Tourism Association** (Site 7, Comp 154, R.R. 4 Mission Rd., Thunder Bay, Ontario, P7C 4Z2, Canada, tel. 807/623–0497, www.nonta.net) can provide information on native cultural experiences and adventures within northern Ontario.

Books

Kids Explore the Heritage of Western Native Americans (John Muir Publications), by the Westridge Writers Workshop, was written by students, many of whom live on reservations. Profiles of six families show what it means to be Native American today. Marlene Smith-Baranzini and Howard Egger-Bovet's *The Brown Paper School US Kids History: Book of American Indians* (Little, Brown) mixes historical anecdotes with stories, drawings, and projects. Bryan and Cherry Alexander's *What Do We Know About the Inuit?* (NTC Publishing Group) has information about the ancestors of the Inuit and the Inuit people today. *They Dance in the Sky: Native American Star Myths* (Houghton Mifflin), by Jean Guard Monroe, collects stories about the constellations from tribes across North America. Travelers to the Southwest should look at *Stories on Stone* (Little, Brown), by Jennifer Owings Dewey; it's out of print but should be in libraries.

Anyone booking a trip with Off the Beaten Path should see William L. Bryan's *Montana Indians: Yesterday and Today* (Faircountry Press).

Also See

Families interested in present-day Native American peoples may find the study of ancient civilizations appealing. Archaeology Adventures lists digs that focus on native cultures.

RAFTING

My love of rafting began when I first ran the McKenzie and Rogue rivers in the early '70s as a student at the University of Oregon. My older daughter, Kira, was luckier. She had the fun of experiencing her first river—the New, in West Virginia—when she was just 8. Molly, her sister, explored Jackson Lake and the Snake River, down through Moose, Wyoming, at the age of 4, and their brother, Hutch, ran the New at the ripe old age of 6 and at 7 explored the wonders of the Salmon River canyons. In our family, it just isn't summer if we haven't gone rafting.

Rafting is simply a great family vacation. You don't need any experience or skills, and you can choose a trip on which you paddle or one on which you sit back and watch the scenery drift by as guides wield the oars. However and wherever you do it, the combination of floating downriver under blue skies and camping at night under millions of stars is unbeatable. The roomy rafts also make it possible to carry an amount and variety of food unheard of on many wilderness trips. When my children and I joined River Odysseys West on the Salmon River, steak, tortellini salad, an awesome tomato-cilantro-onion salad, and carrot cake were all on the menu. Did we see spectacular wilderness areas and view wildlife up close? You bet. Did we rough it? Hardly.

Rafting outfitters have done more to entice children and parents onto North American rivers than any other water-sports group. Family-only raft trips seem to increase in number every season, with ever-better amenities for river-running children. Storytellers, child-oriented naturalists, and off-river activities counselors accompany some trips; excursions to historical sites are part of others. Guides on family trips are chosen as much for their ability to work effectively with children as for their rafting skills.

On the other hand, most trips that welcome families do not send you through the intense white water that sets your heart pounding and adrenaline rushing. Family trips tend to tackle rapids from Class I to Class III only, which means easy to moderate white water, appropriate for children age 12 or 13 and younger. What you trade in excitement on a family river trip with younger children, however, you make up in wildlife viewing, side hikes, and the joy of introducing your children to rivers and wilderness areas. If you are among the river-loving families with teens, you have a whole world of thrilling, chilling, and exquisitely beautiful rivers from which to choose.

Dozens of rivers throughout North America are perfect for family raft trips. A number of outfitters work the same rivers, but your experience will be different depending on which you choose. Finding the right river is important; choosing the right outfitter is crucial. Each has a distinct personality and creates a particular atmosphere on the river and in camp. Make lots of calls before you make a decision.

Questions to Ask

Are Coast Guard–approved life vests available for a child the size and age of mine? Most vests are sized according to height and weight, not age, so give outfitters your child's measurements to be sure they have one that will fit. If the right size isn't available, you'll have to borrow a life vest or buy one at an outdoor or marine supply store.

Are the guides trained in wilderness and water safety, first aid, and CPR? Always ask. Wilderness rivers take you a long, long way from medical care or help. If an accident occurs, you want guides who know the right emergency procedures.

How strenuous are trips, and what do the classifications of rapids mean? The most common white-water classification system used in this country rates rapids from Class I to Class VI; Class I is barely more than a riffle, and Class VI is virtually unrunnable. Most family trips fall into Class III or below, though children 8 and up are sometimes allowed on rivers with a Class IV rapid or two. Outfitters take several things into consideration: the time of year, the speed of the water, and the height of the water. A second classification system, more common among the Grand Canyon outfitters than others, has from Class I to Class X ratings. If you're uncertain which system an outfitter is using, ask.

How many hours will we raft each day? From five to six hours a day is average, though water level, weather, and the ability of guests and guides doing the paddling or rowing affect rafting time. Still, the pace allows for unhurried breakfasts and early enough arrivals at camp each afternoon to hike, fish, or relax. Daily stops along the way are part of all river journeys. Trips designated especially for families often have more frequent stops and shorter days on the river.

Does the trip have scheduled activities other than rafting? Hiking and fishing are the two most common river-camp activities, and you must usually bring your own fishing gear and arrange for licenses for teens and adults ahead of time. Family trips almost always have camp activities, such as storytelling, crafts, games, nature walks, or berry-picking hikes.

What kinds of rafts are used on the trip? On most but not all of the trips listed, you'll be in oar-powered rafts that the guides are primarily responsible for maneuvering and rowing. Guests almost always have the option of a paddle raft if they request it, and a couple of trips use paddle rafts only. In these, all the passengers stroke according to the guide's directions. Very few of the outfitters in this chapter use motorized rafts. Typically, the rafts hold 6 to 12 people. Almost all outfitters will also bring along inflatable kayaks for additional fun.

Are the rafts self-bailing? This is by no means a requirement, but families seeking more comfort and less work may prefer self-bailers, which release water on their own. They stay drier on the bottom, so your feet and gear will be drier, too. And no one will ask you to help bail if it rains or after you go through the big splashes. A self-bailer is also more stable and easier to maneuver than a raft with water sloshing around the bottom, and when it comes to children on the river, stable is always preferable.

Are dry bags available? Most outfitters provide a dry bag for storing clothing and camping gear each day, but you generally can't get to your stuff until you camp. On-raft containers hold cameras and other items you want on board. A small dry bag or waterproof day pack of your own is a good idea because shared containers don't usually have room for rain gear and warm layers for the children.

Are snacks provided on the river? Children need to eat far more often than adults, so this is important. If the guides won't have easily accessible snacks in the rafts, bring your own on board in a day pack.

What's the average group size? Most outfitters listed here go out with from 10 to 20 participants, plus between two and four guides. Some trips may take only from six to eight people, however, and a few outfitters run trips with as many as 25.

What kind of lodging is provided? On most trips, you camp overnight—in some cases, right on a beach. In the listings below, we've noted the exceptions to this general rule.

What's included in the cost? All meals, guides, and local transportation to the put-in (launch site) and from the takeout (where the river trip ends) are included, as are life vests for all passengers, unless otherwise noted. Most rafting outfitters will bring along inflatable kayaks for a change of pace for adults and older children, but some charge extra for this. In most cases you must bring your own tent, pad, and sleeping bag, or rent from the outfitter for a small additional cost. A few outfitters provide this equipment as part of the basic cost. Outfitters almost always arrange a safe place for you to leave your car during the trip; it might be their own parking lot or the lot of a local motel.

Instruction

Guides begin every trip with safety instructions for rafting and camping. These help both adults and children understand the importance of being careful around water. They also teach those who will be paddling how to do so. You'll probably be taught a bit of river lingo, too, so you can follow the guide's paddling instructions. Beyond that, all you need to do is have fun.

Finding the Fun

Northeast: Northern Outdoors, Unicorn Rafting Expeditions. **Mid-Atlantic:** Class VI River Runners. **Southwest:** American River Touring Association, Arizona Raft Adventures, Canyonlands Field Institute, Far Flung Adventures, GORP Travel, Grand Canyon Dories/O.A.R.S. Dories, Holiday Expeditions, Outward Bound, Sheri Griffith Expeditions, Tag-A-Long Expeditions. **Rockies:** American River Touring Association, Canyonlands Field Institute, Glacier Wilderness Guides/Montana Raft Company, GORP Travel, Grand Canyon Dories/O.A.R.S. Dories, Holiday Expeditions, Hughes River Expeditions, Idaho Afloat, O.A.R.S., Outdoor Adventures, Outward Bound, Ouzel Outfitters, River Odysseys West, Salmon River Outfitters, Wilderness Aware Rafting, Wilderness River Outfitters. **West Coast:** American River Touring Association, GORP Travel, Hughes River Expeditions, O.A.R.S., Outdoor Adventures, Ouzel Outfitters, Rogue River Raft Trips. **Alaska:** Canadian River Expeditions, River Odysseys West, Wilderness River Outfitters. **Canada:** Canadian River Expeditions, Wilderness River Outfitters. **Mexico:** Far Flung Adventures. **Europe:** River Odysseys West. **South America:** River Odysseys West.

Favorite Rafting Companies

American River Touring Association

6+

The American River Touring Association—popularly known as ARTA—donates a portion of its revenues to conservation organizations each year. The philosophy of this nonprofit organization is a belief that exposure to the wilderness benefits both individuals and the environment. Yes, ARTA is earnest about nature, safety, and environmental concerns—but it's just as serious about people having fun on its trips throughout the West.

FOR FAMILIES. Trips run from spring through fall, but in summer ARTA schedules numerous family departures on five rivers. You can choose from among the South Fork of the American in California, Oregon's Rogue River, two portions of the Green in Utah, and either the Salmon or the Middle Fork of the Salmon in Idaho. Each river gives rafters something special in terms of scenery and focus. The American is a great two-day escape that uses only paddle rafts; the Rogue offers excellent wildlife-viewing possibilities; the geology and history of the Green are fascinating; and the Salmon abounds in great beaches, hot springs, and swimming opportunities.

To encourage families to explore these rivers together, ARTA has a special price for children on family departures. Guides on all family trips genuinely enjoy working with youngsters, and the many side activities provided range from hiking and storytelling to pondering nature's mysteries.

American River Touring Association, 24000 Casa Loma Rd., Groveland, CA 95321, tel. 209/962–7873 or 800/323–2782, www.arta.org. Apr.–Sept.: 2–7 days, $199–$1,230 adults, $150–$975 children.

Arizona Raft Adventures

5+

I asked a rafting outfitter whom he rafts with when the season is over in his neck of the woods. His answer, without hesitation, was AzRA. That this is a river guide's river-guiding company attests to AzRA's high level of professionalism and dedication. What sets this company apart are its guides, most of whom have been taking people down the Colorado and the San Juan—the two rivers in which AzRA specializes—for an average of at least 10 years. That adds up to a lot of experience and knowledge, both of which are crucial to a good family trip.

FOR FAMILIES. AzRA runs dedicated family trips on the San Juan, a southwestern river that was central to the ancestral Puebloan culture. Today the San Juan marks the northern border of the Navajo Nation and flows through areas of compelling geological and archaeological interest. The San Juan is also surrounded by national parks and lands important to native people: Canyonlands, Mesa Verde, Canyon de Chelly, Monument Valley, Natural Bridges, and Navajo National Monument. AzRA's San Juan voyages run from three to seven days. The shortest starts in Bluff, in southeastern Utah, and runs 27 river mi (43 km) to Mexican Hat. A longer run takes families from Bluff to Lake Powell, 83 mi (134 km) to the west; there's a 56-mi (90-km) option, too. From remote canyons to lazy swimming holes, the San Juan is a rafting family's paradise. Children ages 7 and up are welcome on any San Juan trip; ages 5 and up can join non-family-specific trips if they've had previous camping and rafting experience, and they're always welcome on designated family runs.

The Colorado River through the Grand Canyon is probably the classic river trip of this continent. Trips last from 6 to 15 days and cover from 89 to all 225 mi (143 to 362 km) of the canyon run. The company has motorized and nonmotorized expeditions. Children as young as 10 can go on motorized trips; 12 is the minimum age for "hybrid" runs—those utilizing two types of nonmotorized rafts. On all-paddle rafting adventures (ones on which guests and a guide provide paddle power), the minimum age is 16. Grand Canyon rafting adventures are also about hiking through the awesome terrain accessible from the river and about exploring side canyons, too. The shorter trips require good physical condition and a willingness to hike a challenging and steep trail either in or out. If hiking is something you love, talk to the guides, who always customize each trip according to the wishes of the group.

Arizona Raft Adventures, 4050 E. Huntington Dr., Flagstaff, AZ 86004, tel. 520/526–8200 or 800/786–7238, www.azraft.com. May–Oct: 3–15 days, $450–$2,885; fourth family member age 17 and under goes free; 15% discount for all children under 18.

Canadian River Expeditions

8+

The icy Tatshenshini River flows through the Yukon and British Columbia, empties into the Alsek, and finally spills into the sea at the Gulf of Alaska. On the way it carves through a vast wilderness landscape that humbles and awes its viewers. Canadian River Expeditions (CRE) has been guiding on the Tat and the Alsek for more than 25 years. The guides know and love the Tat, and they willingly share this river with the families that dare to come. The Tat is a personal favorite, but the company's trips through other parts of British Columbia are phenomenal, too.

FOR FAMILIES. The Tatshenshini challenges you, but the rewards are worth it—and then some. Be prepared for windy and alternately warm and chilly days, and know that fishing and swimming are not the Tat's strong suits. None of this matters, however, when you're walking on glaciers or observing wildlife such as black bears, moose, wolves, and even grizzlies. One spectacular hike with an ascent of about 3,800 ft is probably too much for anyone under age 12 or 13 (although children as young as 8 are welcome on this trip), and if you have a child who wearies of just observing nature's wonders, this 12-day expedition may not be for you. On the other hand, if your family wants to travel hundreds of miles without finding one sign of human civilization, this trip will provide memories to last a lifetime.

Company owner Johnny Mikes recommends the 11-day Best of B.C. trip as ideal for families with younger children. This adventure is remarkable for both its diversity of experience and its magnificent settings. From Vancouver the group travels by boat into the Discovery Islands and the coastal region's fjords, then by seaplane over the glaciers of the Coast Mountains and on to 40-mi (64-km) Chilko Lake. After you fish and hike among the ancient firs for two days, the rafting begins. You journey on three rivers—the Chilko, the Chilcotin, and the Fraser—passing from the mountains down through wide-open grasslands and into the arid sandstone and cactus canyons of the Fraser. With its huge volume of water, the Fraser has plenty of the big roller-coaster rapids that all rafters love. A four-hour train ride takes you back to the coast through Whistler.

Families that want to raft the great northern rivers but don't have two weeks or more to do it have two options. There's a six-day Chilcotin Fraser expedition, which basically duplicates the last six days of the 11-day Best of B.C. itinerary described above. You'll pack in fantastic landscape views—grasslands, canyons, and enormous hoodoo formations—not to mention daily runs on the best rapids. You meet in Williams Lake, spending the first two nights at Big Creek Ecological Reserve, which is a good place to hike. The second camp is opposite the Chilcotin-Fraser Junction Bighorn Sheep Reserve. Here you're likely to see impressive rams and perhaps a black bear or two. Another option is the six- or eight-day Upper Alsek adventure; on this trip, you'll experience the awesome Alsek terrain of Kluane National Park and Tatshenshini-Alsek Wilderness Park. The trip begins and ends in Whitehorse in Canada's Yukon.

Canadian River Expeditions, Box 1023, Whistler, British Columbia, Canada V0N 1B0, tel. 604/938–6651 or 800/898–7238, www.canriver.com. June–Aug.: 6–12 days, $1,250–$2,650, 20% discount for children under 18.

Canyonlands Field Institute

8+

Canyonlands focuses primarily on its youth program, in which students from Utah, Colorado, and beyond learn about the wonders of the Colorado Plateau—its geology, wildlife, night skies, waterways, and more. Naturalists and other outdoor educators make up the institute's staff. Although family courses are limited, they are exceptional. Few river trips have an educational component as extensive as these.

FOR FAMILIES. Working with Elderhostel, the nonprofit organization well known for its study programs for older adults, Canyonlands sponsors intergenerational trips that bring grandparents and grandchildren together for six days of discovery as they raft the San Juan River. Naturalists lead hands-on nature activities, teach participants low-impact camping and river-running skills, and delve into botany, geology, and a study of prehistoric rock art—all while having fun on the river. The group camps for four nights; the first night is spent at a lodge in Bluff, Utah, where the trip begins. Those who are a little more adventurous can opt for the seven-day San Juan with Duckies (inflatable kayaks) run.

The Institute also schedules designated family trips for parents with kids 12 and up on the Dolores and San Juan rivers. On the four-day Dolores trip, the run starts just above the town of Slickrock, where the river leaves the Ponderosa Pine forests around the town of Dolores, Colorado for the high desert and a narrow, winding sandstone canyon. Along the way to Bedrock, families can take canyon hikes, splash in side pools, and see ancient rock art. San Juan family trips cover the same territory as Elderhostel adventures.

With three months' notice, the institute will set up customized river trips for groups of at least eight. Families with children 12 and up can run portions of the Colorado or Dolores River. A naturalist leads and outfits each trip, providing the same learning opportunities found on scheduled trips.

You don't have to be an institute member to join any of the adventures, but members do get a discount of 10%, up to a maximum of $15 (no member discount on Elderhostel trips).

Canyonlands Field Institute, Box 68, Moab, UT 84532, tel. 435/259–7750 or 800/860–5262, www.canyonlandsfieldinst.org. Apr.–Sept.: 3–7 days, $410–$815 adults on scheduled trips, $275–$575 children age 12–17; $50–$130 per day for adults and $35– $85 per day for children 18 and under for customized trips. Family membership (optional) is $35.

Class VI River Runners

6+

If you think all the best white water is out West, you haven't run the New or Gauley River in the Appalachian Mountains of south-central West Virginia. The New—which in spite of its name may be second only to the Nile in geologic age—cuts a deep and impressive gorge, with walls 1,000 ft high in places. As for the Gauley River, each fall white-water enthusiasts arrive from all over the world to test their skills against a river that drops 650 ft in 27 mi (198 m in 43 km) and churns up more than 100 major rapids along the way. Class VI caters equally to 6-year-olds rafting for the first time and 16-year-olds looking for the ultimate adrenaline high. Parents will find in Dave Arnold and his co-owners the intelligence and spirit that characterize the very best river outfitters.

FOR FAMILIES. The upper New treats families with children 6 and up to Class I and Class II rapids, with a Class III thrill toward the end of this one- to three-day trip. Great swimming and rock jumping along the way plus wildlife and historic points of interest make this a memorable experience. For a one-day adventure, parents and teens can raft the more difficult portions of the river while family members under 12 have their own guided adventure on the upper New. You get together again in the late afternoon at Class VI's headquarters; while there, check out the excellent barbecue at Smokey's, the outfitter's restaurant.

The lower New River Gorge is for children age 12 and up after June 1; the minimum age prior to that is 14 the rest of the season. Prepare yourself for Class III–V rapids, along with the spectacular scenery of the deeply forested Appalachians. In spite of the rapids, swimming is good here, too. Special theme adventures on both the lower and upper New, for those from age 6 to adult, include River Ecology, an ecologist-led trip on which families learn about the plants and creatures living in and around the New River, and birding trips to areas where herons, falcons, egrets, eagles, hawks, and songbirds may be spotted.

The Gauley is for children at least age 15. The faint of heart, out of shape, or sit-back-and-relax types should look for another river. The Gauley is work—and worth every bit of it, with a payback of world-class white water and thrills. You can choose between one- and two-day trips.

For lodging before and after trips, you can choose from among an excellent campground minutes from Class VI and a variety of motels, cabins, and bed-and-breakfasts. The elegant Greenbrier resort, with its own outstanding children's program, is about 1½ hours away. Class VI can help arrange these accommodations.

Class VI River Runners, Box 78, Lansing, WV 25862, tel. 304/574–0704 or 800/252–7784, www.raftwv.com. Mar.–Nov.: 1–3 days, $85–$355 adults, $50–$320 children.

Far Flung Adventures

5+

For more than 20 years this company has introduced rafters to the geologically diverse regions and rivers of the Southwest and Mexico. Although Far Flung Adventures doesn't market itself as a family outfitter, many parents and children sign up for these river trips—and have a great time.

FOR FAMILIES. Far Flung guides on seven major rivers, and the minimum age for these trips varies. One of the very best for families, the Rio Chama, flows from the Colorado–New Mexico border down toward the Rio Grande. Most of the 24-mi (39-km) journey on this two-day trip is at 6,000 ft, with terrain that ranges from wide-open spaces to forests of fir and pine. It's Class II and III all the way. For an all-around great river and an excellent introduction to rafting, the Rio Grande and a series of canyons in and near Big Bend National Park in Texas provide a range of river experiences, from wide and tranquil to steep, narrow, and fast. The seven- or eight-day, 85-mi (137-km) run in the Lower Canyons, just east of the park, takes rafters through a maze of limestone cliffs and a stark landscape. Besides being a good rafting river, the Rio Grande is a good swimming river. Families with older children can also join trips on Arizona's Salt River and on the Arkansas in Colorado.

Very adventurous families with time in the fall or winter should consider trips to Mexico's Río Antigua, Río Actopan, and Filobobos, all in the Veracruz area. Lots of Class IV rapids on the Antigua keep everyone on edge, and native freshwater lobsters and tropical fruits satisfy the most demanding palate. The Filo and Actopan rivers are mostly Class II and III and lots of fun. Aside from one night on the Filo, these aren't camping adventures; instead, you'll stay in a lovely, restored hacienda. Mexican trips are for ages 10 and up, but make certain your children are interested in learning about a foreign culture and capable of 10 days on a river.

If you have a group of four or five and want an upscale version of the Big Bend experience, the company will help you as you plan every aspect of your trip, from menu to music. On these trips the food is top-notch and the service highly personal.

Far Flung Adventures, Box 377, Terlingua, TX 79852, tel. 800/359–4138, www.farflung.com. Year-round (all rivers not available all months): 1–10 days, $62–$1,075, 10% discount for children under 16.

Glacier Wilderness Guides/ Montana Raft Company

6+

Using a few of the million acres of mountains, lakes, and streams in Montana's Glacier National Park, this company guides on both land and water and has first-class combination trips. The owners have hiked, camped, rafted, fished, and explored the Glacier area for most of their lives. They love it, and they know the secret places others will love, too.

FOR FAMILIES. Rafting adventures take place on the Middle and North forks of the Flathead. Families can join two- and three-day rafting-only adventures, but the gems in the trip list are hike-and-raft and Saddle 'n Paddle combinations in and near Glacier. You can structure the hike-and-raft several ways: a half day of each activity, 2½ days of each, or between four and six days of hiking and two days of rafting (with a motel stay in between). Groups are small, usually from four to six guests. For the ride-and-raft, choose a one- or four-day combination with equal time for horseback riding and rafting. Glacier Wilderness Guides works with a horse-packing outfitter for that portion of the trip.

Glacier Wilderness Guides/Montana Raft Company, Box 535, West Glacier, MT 59936, tel. 406/387–5555 or 800/521–7238, www.glacierguides.com. May–Sept.: 1–8 days, rafting only $260–$430 adults, $200–$370 children age 12 and under. Combo trips $78–$960 adults, $68–$960 children.

GORP Travel

6+

The extensive list of rafting vacations in the company's catalog shows just how much the business has grown. This trip broker represents many of the rafting outfitters in this chapter. In addition to plain old rafting, this company offers excellent combination trips—ranch stays and rafting, or biking and rafting. If your family is debating which adventure to pursue, one of these may be the answer.

FOR FAMILIES. If you can't choose between a ranch stay and a raft trip, go for the Westwater Canyon Ranch & Raft Combo. Families with kids 8 and older fly into remote Tavaputs Ranch on Utah's Tavaputs Plateau for riding, hiking, and four-wheel-drive vehicle tours. On day three, fly to the Westwater stretch of the swift-flowing Colorado River as it races through Granite Canyon. If you'd rather combine rafting with cycling, the Westwater Bike & Raft (minimum age 14) is an option.

In terms of traditional raft adventures, you can run California's Klamath, the Green through Lodore Canyon in Utah, the Rogue in Oregon, or the Colorado as it squeezes through the Grand Canyon. Minimum ages range from 6 to 9.

GORP Travel, 10055 Westmoor Dr., Suite 215, Westminster, CO 80021, tel. 720/887–8500 or 877/440–GORP, gorptravel.gorp.com. May–Oct.: 3–6 days, $470–$1,850 adults, $390–$1,850 children; age requirements for children's pricing varies with trips.

Grand Canyon Dories/ O.A.R.S. Dories

7+

If you've never thought about running a river, let alone rafting for 19 days, call and ask for the illustrated O.A.R.S. Dories brochure. Dories, four-passenger wooden boats maneuvered by oars, have a long and celebrated heritage. They provide an experience totally unlike riding in today's big synthetic rafts. They're controlled differently than synthetic rafts, so you feel the river in a unique way. If this appeals to you and if you can take the time to immerse yourself in the natural world, this is the company for you.

FOR FAMILIES. Most families with children over age 12 can handle O.A.R.S. Dorie's longest river journey, the full length of the Colorado from Lees Ferry to Lake Mead. For 19 days you explore the Grand Canyon's rock layers—half a billion years' worth of geologic history in shades of rose, gold, and violet. The dories shoot through mile-high walls and raging rapids. Camping experience might help, but you'll soon be old hands. Good hikers who are able to handle the near-vertical portion of the 9-mi (14-km) trail between Phantom Ranch and the South Rim can join the group for either the 8- or 13-day partial trip. Whether you're going up or down, it's a strenuous hike. Those who choose to can leave or join up at Whitmore Wash, rafting for 16 or 5 days, respectively; the exchange is by helicopter. If you travel all 19 days, you start and end in Flagstaff.

Less grand, perhaps, but equally satisfying are trips on the Salmon and Snake rivers in Idaho. These rivers are great for families with younger children and perfect for dories; the Northwest was the birthplace of the river-style dory. The free-flowing Salmon River is the largest undammed river in the American West. You can run the Middle Fork, the upper portion of the Main Salmon, or the Lower Salmon on four- to six-day trips, or combine all three in the 17-day Full Salmon Experience. Along the way are fine hikes; long, clean beaches perfect for swimming; and natural hot springs for soaking.

The 400-mi (648-km) Salmon River empties into the Snake River at Hells Canyon, the deepest gorge in North America. On three- to five-day adventures, guides share the legends of the Nez Perce who lived here, including some tales about mythic spirits who shaped the rugged landscape and the Snake's roaring rapids. For all its wildness the Snake River also shows rafters a gentler side. In a dory you'll feel the rock and rhythm of the currents as you cannot in a raft.

Grand Canyon Dories/O.A.R.S. Dories, Box 1119, Angels Camp, CA 95222, tel. 209/736–0811 or 800/877–3679, www.grandcanyondories.com. Apr.–Oct.: 3–19 days, $775–$4,000 adults, $709–$4,000 children.

Holiday Expeditions

5+

Holiday has several decades' experience taking all kinds of people rafting on the great rivers of Utah, Colorado, and Idaho. Dee Holladay, the company's founder, has a passion for rivers and river history. He believes that rafting is more than the sum of its parts—scenery, wilderness, solitude, and incredible white-water rapids: it's the time of your life. The company has also discovered that when rafting is combined with mountain biking or a few days at a century-old cattle ranch, the thrills get even better.

FOR FAMILIES. Trips on the easiest rivers, the San Juan and the Desolation Canyon section of the Green River in Utah, and Idaho's Lower Salmon, take children 5 and up. Families with children who are at least age 8 can try such intermediate rivers as the Colorado (which is experts-only at certain times of year), the Lodore Canyon section of the Green, and the Yampa, all of which run along the Colorado–Utah border. Idaho's great waterways, the Snake and the Salmon rivers, are other possibilities for those 8 and up. On each trip there's a waterproof 'kid kit' with activities related to area history, geology, and nature studies: making petroglyphs, studying plants and insects under a magnifying glass, and creating crafts. The most adventurous families with teens at least age 16 can go for an adrenaline rush on the Lochsa River in Idaho and on the Colorado and lower Salmon rivers in high-water season.

A new tour is the Mother/Daughter Women's River Retreat, for moms with daughters age 14 and older. As with all of the Women's Retreats, this one is led by women guides and facilitators. Mornings often include yoga and meditation, while afternoon off-river experiences range from learning massage techniques to hiking. Mothers and daughters can learn together how to use stress reduction and other wellness techniques for combating the pressures of work, school, and day-to-day challenges. This trip is an opportunity for a parent and child to reconnect and to see each other in new ways, and to create memories that will last a lifetime (nice for both of you to have during those turbulent teen years).

Holiday also has terrific combination adventures. A seven-day Desolation Canyon trip for families with children ages 5 and up offers five days on the Green River with two days at Tavaputs Ranch, a century-old working cattle ranch in eastern Utah's Tavaputs Plateau. A four-day ranch-river adventure combines the Colorado River, starting just above Westwater Canyon, with a stay at Rock Creek Ranch. Because the Colorado is a more challenging river, this trip is for families with children at least 8 years old.

Three rafting and mountain-biking tours give families the best of two adventures. On the White Rim Trail of Canyonlands National Park in Utah, you bike 65 mi (105 km) in three days past spectacular formations. Then the group piles into rafts for a four-day run through the Colorado River's legendary Cataract Canyon. The Colorado is matched with another bike trip near the world's mountain-bike mecca—Moab, Utah. Two days of quintessential wilderness biking through 25 mi (40 km) of ponderosa pine country and red-rock desert is capped with two days on the Westwater section of the Colorado. Another trip pairs two days of biking on 46 mi (74 km) of remote dirt road with five days of rafting the Yampa. All these combination trips are for ages 14 and up (except the White Rim–Cataract trips in spring, which have a minimum age of 16) and those in good physical condition. Can you and your teen keep up with each other? Find out and forge a bond you may never have thought possible.

Holiday Expeditions, 544 E. 3900 S, Salt Lake City, UT 84107, tel. 801/266–2087 or 800/624–6323, www.bikeraft.com. May–Sept.: 2- to 5-day rafting trips, $299–$1,181 adults, $275–$1,086 children under 18. May–Sept.: 4- to 7-day combination trips, $720–$1,410 adults, $662–$1,210 children under 18 on the ranch combo only.

Hughes River Expeditions

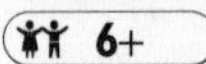

Jerry Hughes and Carole Finley, who run this company, have more than 50 years of guiding experience between them, and this alone would make them a good choice for almost any rafter. But they've also explored rivers with their own three children, so they are knowledgeable about introducing youngsters to the pleasures of rafting. Jerry and Carole grew up in Idaho and specialize in the state's white water. No outfitter knows more about rafting the Salmon and Snake rivers than these two—which is probably why they were chosen to lead trips for the National Geographic Society.

FOR FAMILIES. The huge beaches and warm, clear water of the Salmon River canyon make it one of the best trips for young rafters, who can build sand castles and play safely in the many shallow back eddies away from the main current. Along with untouched river wilderness, the Salmon has roller-coaster rapids that are both exciting and safe, whether you stay in the rafts or use the inflatable kayaks. Sites right on the sandbar make camping easy, too—no carrying gear over boulders and steep terrain.

The Snake River–Hells Canyon trip, with its pioneer and Native American sites, is another great choice for families, as is the Middle Fork of the Salmon River. Families with younger children that want to try the Middle Fork should pick a date after late July, when the water is warmer and flows are lower. This river runs through the 2.36-million-acre River of No Return Wilderness Area, the such reserve in the continental United States. If early season suits your group, join the Wallowa–Grande Ronde adventure in Oregon, preferably in June. Beautiful grassy flats slope right down to the banks for exceptional camping; older children can try an inflatable kayak on this trip.

Hughes has no special family departure dates, but you're likely to find children on any summer trip. Check with the company ahead of time, and they'll be happy to tell you the dates of trips already booked by other families. If you have a child under 6 who's comfortable around water and likes camping, call Jerry or Carole; they sometimes make exceptions to the age limit.

Hughes River Expeditions, Box 217, Cambridge, ID 83610, tel. 208/257–3477 or 800/262–1882, www.hughesriver.com. May–Sept.: 3–6 days, $800–$1,585 adults; 10% discount for children college age and under who are financial dependents of their parents.

Idaho Afloat

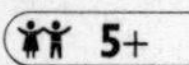

Idaho Afloat is one of a number of outfitters specializing in Idaho's great family rivers, the Lower Salmon River gorge and Main Salmon, and the Snake River through Hell's Canyon. On every trip owners Bruce and Jeanne Howard prove that rafting and pampering can coexist in a pristine wilderness area. They enjoy having families along and take more of them out each year. Bruce especially loves to help children catch their first fish, so be sure to bring the fishing gear. Because the Howards don't have minimum trip sizes, they won't cancel a trip. If just your group shows up, they'll make certain you have a vacation your whole family will remember forever.

FOR FAMILIES. Choose any trip on the Salmon or the Snake River, and your nightly campsite will be set with lawn chairs and a tablecloth on the dinner table; the guides will be ready with hors d'oeuvres and wine. The Howards supply all camping equipment, including sleeping bags and tents. Because your tent is set up for you, the whole family has plenty of time for guided hikes. You can explore petroglyphs, pit house ruins, and burial sites, as well as pioneer homesteads. When the guides aren't cooking feasts, leading hikes, or negotiating rapids, they share their love of storytelling with everyone. The rivers, of course, provide the lion's share of the entertainment and all the natural beauty a family could want.

Idaho Afloat, Box 542, Grangeville, ID 83530, tel. 208/983–2414 or 800/700–2414, www.idafloat.com. May–Sept.: 3–6 days, $750–$1,200, 15% discount for children ages 5–15.

Northern Outdoors

8+

With two resort centers in central Maine—the Forks, 18 mi (29 km) north of Bingham near the Kennebec River, and the Penobscot, 15 mi (24 km) west of Millinocket by the Penobscot River—Northern Outdoors has many options for adventurers in terms of location, river, accommodations, and experience. It's a good choice for East Coast families whose members may have differing views on how to spend time on their adventure vacation.

FOR FAMILIES. Most of this outfitter's trips are only one day long (good for first-timers), but there are a few overnight experiences and combination-adventure possibilities. Families with children as young as 8 are welcome to try the big roller-coaster waves of the Kennebec or, on selected dates, the action-packed rapids of the Dead River. Ages 15 and up can raft the Dead River anytime. Children as young as age 12 can experience the challenge of the lower Penobscot River, while those 15 and older can go for the thrills of the Penobscot's upper gorge. In addition to family dates on the Dead River, Northern Outdoors has family overnights on the Kennebec River. The East Outlet Family Overnight, scheduled every Wednesday–Thursday in July and August (or anytime for family groups of six or more), combines rafting, tubing, and motoring between Moosehead Lake and the Forks.

The Forks resort has swimming in a pool or lake, a hot tub, platform tennis, rock climbing (minimum age 12), canoeing, fishing, volleyball, basketball, a restaurant, and a choice of accommodations including lodge rooms, condos, cottages, cabins, and tent sites. The remote Penobscot resort has a hot tub, sauna, river swimming, lake kayak touring, canoeing, fishing, a restaurant, and roomy tent cabins. Families can mix rafting with rock climbing, guided fishing, or relaxing at the resorts. Do it all together, or go for the adventure that calls to you and catch up with the rest of the family at day's end.

All trips include equipment (even wet suits, when necessary), lunch, use of facilities at one resort, and a personal video of your adventure. Lodging at the resorts is extra. Overnights include tents, sleeping pads, all meals, and dry bags; you supply your own sleeping bags.

Northern Outdoors, Box 100, Rte. 201, The Forks, ME 04985, tel. 207/663–4466 or 800/765–7238, www.northernoutdoors.com. May–Oct.: 1–2 days, $85–$244 adults; $43–$159 children under 16. Lodging costs $11 per campsite–$67 per person in a 2-bedroom cabin.

O.A.R.S.

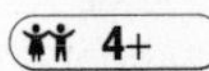

The acronym stands for Outdoor Adventure River Specialists, but everyone knows this outfitter as O.A.R.S. With more than 25 years of guiding experience and an extensive selection of family-friendly programs on a multitude of rivers, O.A.R.S. is a natural choice for families. I traveled with them on Jackson Lake and the Snake River in Wyoming. Although the trip has changed somewhat since then (you travel in kayaks instead of rafts on the lake now), the high quality of the guides remains the same.

Working with a big company such as O.A.R.S. has advantages and disadvantages. You don't talk to or meet the owners as you can with small companies. On the other hand, you can take advantage of the large staff of travel specialists, who will book not only your rafting experience but also your flight, lodging, and rental car.

FOR FAMILIES. Family trips explore the Salmon and Snake rivers in Idaho, the lower Klamath and Tuolumne rivers in California, the San Juan River in Colorado, the Colorado River through Cataract Canyon in Utah, the Rogue and Grande Ronde rivers in Oregon, and the Wyoming stretch of the Snake River and Jackson Lake. With so many family departures, you can pick the river and terrain you want and still be guaranteed playmates for your children. Minimum ages range from 4 on the lower Klamath River and Jackson Lake and the Wyoming portion of the Snake River to 12 on the Tuolumne, so check with O.A.R.S. for specifics on the river you choose. All offer something special: alpine meadows and wildflowers on the Grande Ronde, thrilling (and technical) rapids on the Tuolumne, and rafting through the heart of Canyonlands National Park on the Colorado, to name a few highlights. For the very young, though, the kayaking–rafting combination on Jackson Lake and the Snake River is a water play dream come true. Four-year-olds can sit in the front of a kayak or ride in motorized skiffs (each with at least one parent). This trip also offers plenty of exploring right around the base camp on Grassy Island.

Guides are well attuned to children's needs and really help parents out if youngsters get restless. The company designates one guide on each family trip as Fun Director, who keeps children entertained. Each child also gets a Fun Bag of games and toys for whiling away river time.

O.A.R.S., Box 67, Angels Camp, CA 95222, tel. 209/736–4677 or 800/346–6277, www.oars.com. Mar.–Sept.: 2–6 days, $355–$1,307 adults, $295–$1,181 children under 18.

Outdoor Adventures

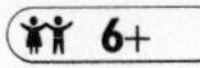

Outdoor Adventures believes there's a big difference between rafting trips that are just "okay for families" and designated family trips. This company has thought of every detail and is genuinely committed to making river adventures for parents and children both fun and affordable. The Salmon River in Idaho and the Kern River in California are their favorite rivers for families. The guides on these trips are specially trained in working and playing with children.

FOR FAMILIES. The company's Salmon River family expedition is one of the best-ever trips for families. The six-day adventure runs nine times each summer—and it fills fast, so you need to book early. The river has everything a rafting family could want, from warm, lazy eddies to rolling rapids. Off-water activities have plenty of child appeal, too: bug collecting, making musical instruments out of natural objects, panning for gold, carving sticks, weaving, hiking, or fishing (bring your own gear). Wide, sandy beaches make riverside camping exceptional. The trip price covers the flight back to Boise. Ask about Kids Float Free trips; they're a great deal, although children (under 17) still pay off-river expenses, such as the flight to Boise.

Two-day lower Kern River family trips start in June. The Kern flows through Sequoia National Forest and is a river of surprising beauty and terrific white water. (And it's warm, which makes it perfect for children.) It's also the closest rafting river to Los Angeles, which is just three hours away. Special family rates apply for this trip. These rates, good on Monday and Wednesday only, vary with the size of your family: the bigger your family, the larger the discount.

Outdoor Adventures, Box 1149, Point Reyes Station, CA 94956, tel. 415/663–8300 or 800/323–4234, www.gorafting.com. Apr.–Sept.: 2–6 days, $258–$1,295 adults, $258–$795 children under 16; ask about Kids Float Free and Kern family discounts.

Outward Bound

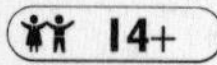

As with all Outward Bound parent–child courses, the white-water adventures are meant to help parents and teens fine-tune their cooperation, communication, and problem-solving skills. But these courses aren't just about learning and facing challenges, they're also about fun on big rivers with big rapids running through awesome country.

FOR FAMILIES. The Family Whitewater Adventure takes place on the Green and Yampa rivers as they wind through Dinosaur National Monument in western Colorado and Utah. Roaring through rapids with names like Hell's Half Mile and Disaster Falls, participants depend on their skills and new-found abilities to get them through. It's about learning to work together as a team, from scouting difficult rapids to serving as captain of the crew. In addition to time on the river, families hike up side canyons, view ancient Native ruins, and learn about low-impact camping. Of course, rock climbing and rappelling are also part of the program, as they are for almost all Outward Bound courses.

Outward Bound, National Office 100 Mystery Point Rd., Garrison, NY 10524-9757, tel. 914/424–4000 or 888/882–6863, www.outwardbound.org. June–Aug.: 6 days, $895 per person, plus $75 application fee.

Ouzel Outfitters

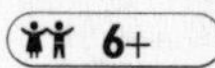

Approximately 80% of Ouzel's clients have rafted with the company before or have been referred by someone who went on an Ouzel trip—and, as the statistics tell, those who raft with Ouzel love it. Families are a large part of the company's business, but the literature doesn't steer families toward particular expeditions or rivers; instead, consultants take your family's requirements into consideration before suggesting a trip. Best of all, Ouzel runs several great family rivers in Oregon and Idaho, so you have choices as well as plenty of individual attention.

FOR FAMILIES. The Wild and Scenic River Act protects an 84-mi (135-km) stretch of Oregon's Rogue River. Three-, four-, and five-day trips run through the 34-mi (55-km) section designated as "wild" (roadless wilderness), as well as a few miles of the section called "recreational" (limited road access). The Siskiyou Range, through which the Rogue runs, has deep forests and clear creeks. Wildlife is abundant, including otters, eagles, ospreys, herons, deer, and bears. The cool nights make for excellent sleeping, but days are usually hot and dry. The Rogue has the thrills rafters seek in rapids such as Blossom Bar and Rainie Falls; sandy beaches on which to camp and play and good places to swim add to its appeal. Family Fishing was recently added to the company's September and October trips on the Rogue, a perfect option for those who want to spend the day float-fishing for salmon and steelhead while the rest of the group shoots the rapids in paddle rafts and explores the canyon. If you want a touch of culture on your adventure trip, the Oregon Shakespearean Festival in Ashland is nearby.

Other rivers have a variety of attractions for families. The Deschutes, in the high desert of Oregon's eastern Cascades, combines miles of lazy drifting with treacherous white water that demands your attention. Desert canyons and excellent fishing are additional highlights on these one- to three-day trips. Families can also join Ouzel for half- or full-day trips on the McKenzie, a river less than an hour from Eugene, Oregon, whose exhilaratingly cool waters spill from the western slope of the Cascade Range. It's practically all Class II and III, but hold on to your raft when you reach Martin's Rapid. If you want more choices, Ouzel schedules trips on the Salmon in Idaho, too.

Ouzel Outfitters, Box 827, Bend, OR 97709, tel. 541/385–5947 or 800/788–7238, www.oregonrafting.com. Apr.–Oct.: 1–5 days, $55–$775 adults, $50–$700 children age 17 and under.

River Odysseys West

5+

The Salmon River in Idaho has become the river of choice for many outfitters with family trips, including River Odysseys West (known as ROW, to rafting enthusiasts everywhere). Owners Peter Grubb and Betsy Bowen have two children of their own—in fact, Mariah and Jonah Grubb, both under 10, often come along on the summer family trips on the Salmon River. Peter and Betsy definitely know how to run an exceptional family rafting journey; their experience and approach make them one of the best family outfitters anywhere. I've never seen guides work as well with children, nor have I seen a river activities program for children better than this one. ROW states in its brochure that it aims to run all its trips "with uncommon professionalism, unsurpassed personal service, and a commitment to protect and preserve the environment." This it does, but it also runs its trips with a lot of heart.

FOR FAMILIES. ROW has five-day Family Focus trips on the Salmon River geared to parents or grandparents traveling with children ages 5 through 15. Typically, from three to five families join these specially designated expeditions, which run weekly during July and August. Led by guides with degrees in environmental education, these trips give children a chance to learn about geography, geology, native and pioneer history, nature, and wildlife through hikes, nature games, campfire readings, crafts, and just floating through the magnificent canyons of the Salmon River. There's also plain old river fun, like free-for-all water fights (trust me, the adults are more dangerous than the children) and leaping off high rocks into the water below.

ROW takes both paddle rafts and inflatable kayaks on all family trips. These are great for children who can handle independence and who want to challenge themselves physically. On family trips guides stop a bit more frequently, and swimming is excellent off the Salmon River's wide, sandy beaches (with life jackets on, of course). ROW's menu, always superior, adds more children's foods; children have an early dinner, at about 6, so adults can unwind before they eat. Tents are already set up when you arrive in camp each afternoon; all you have to do is pick a tent and put your gear in it.

In addition to its rafting expeditions on a variety of western rivers, ROW welcomes families on its rafting adventures in Ecuador, and its adventure cruising explorations off the coasts of Turkey, Croatia, Greece, and in Alaska's Inside Passage. Even if you think some of these destinations are too far afield for your children, talk to Peter before making a decision. He's taken his own young children—and the children of clients—to all of these places with great success.

River Odysseys West, Box 579FB, Coeur d'Alene, ID 83816, tel. 208/765–0841 or 800/451–6034, www.rowinc.com. May–Sept., Family Focus trips July–Aug.: 5 days, $1,165–1,265 adults, $995–1,075 children under 17.

Rogue River Raft Trips

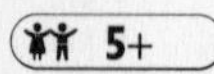

This outfitter has been running white-water excursions on Oregon's Rogue River since 1967. Its lodge-based trips set the company apart; you can run the river during the day and sleep in a remote wilderness lodge at night, complete with private bathrooms, hot showers, and fresh linens. Those who want just a little camping experience can choose a three-day lodge-camping combination trip, and camping enthusiasts can join the four-day all-camping trips. All trips begin at Morrison's Rogue River Lodge, about 16 mi (26 km) downriver from Grants Pass, Oregon.

FOR FAMILIES. The Rogue, with rolling rapids, sandy beaches, and lots of wildlife, is an ideal family river. The outfitter uses both paddleboats and oar boats, depending on whether the group wants to participate or sit back and let the guides do the work. Children have opportunities to swim, hike, and pan for gold. Guides bring along inflatable kayaks, which give older children a chance to test their paddling skills. But most important, having river lodges as an option opens up this adventure to many families that might not otherwise try it.

Families should also consider combining a rafting experience with a stay at Morrison's Rogue River Lodge. Built in the '40s as a steelhead fishing retreat, Morrison's is now a terrific family destination in its own right. Set among towering pines on a lazy bend in the river, the lodge has a 5-acre lawn that slopes down to the water, where you can wade, fish, and swim. The lodge has rooms and cottages, a heated pool, a hot tub, and two tennis courts. You can visit nearby Oregon Caves National Park, Crater Lake National Park, or the Oregon Shakespearean Festival. Lodge stays include a four-course gourmet dinner, full breakfast, and use of all facilities in summer. In fall, when families come for steelhead fishing, rates also include evening hors d'oeuvres and a packed picnic lunch each day.

Rogue River Raft Trips, 8500 Galice Rd., Merlin, OR 97532, tel. 541/476–3825 or 800/826–1963, www.rogueriverraft.com. May–Aug.: 1–4 days, $69–$560 per person. Lodge stays are $175–$360 per room or cabin, depending on season, accommodations, and the number of adults and children.

Salmon River Outfitters

5+

Steven Shephard can make rafting the Salmon River one of the best family adventures ever. He's been a guide for 30 years and has operated Salmon River Outfitters (SRO) since 1980. Steven knows everything about the Salmon and how to run it, and he believes that good service means taking care of absolutely everything—safety, well-trained guides, camp chairs, river gear, and everything you need for dining and sleeping. He even sends you a duffel bag for your personal items. You have to pack it yourself, but that's about it. When you arrive in Idaho, the SRO staff will transfer it into a waterproof bag for you. What could be easier?

FOR FAMILIES. The Salmon is an excellent intermediate river, with some Class III rapids. It has big beaches, few rocks, and virtually no mosquitoes. Any of SRO's expeditions is fine for families, but two specialty trips are worth noting. The Native American Indian Lore trip is generally run twice each summer. Idaho writer Darcy Williamson leads nature walks and shares her knowledge of regional native lore, including how plants were used for food and medicine. Families gather indigenous plants and make their own sachets, tea, and ceremonial Indian sage bundles to take home. The Storyteller & Harpist trip is usually a once-a-season event featuring Patrick Ball, who has spent years in Scotland, Ireland, and Appalachia gathering stories that are part of those areas' rich oral traditions. As an accompaniment to the epic legends and folk tales, Patrick plays the Irish harp. Few river campsites are as entertaining.

Salmon River Outfitters, Box 519, Donnelly, ID 83615, tel. 800/346–6204, www.salmonriveroutfitters.com. June–Sept.: 6 days, $1,395 adults, $1,295 children.

Sheri Griffith Expeditions

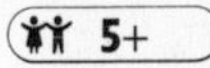

Sheri Griffith Expeditions runs only protected rivers in national parks and national landmarks or proposed Wild and Scenic rivers. She prefers these because regulations so severely limit the number of people permitted in the water that there's never a problem with wilderness gridlock. Sheri and company, whose slogan is "With a Touch of Class," run trips that beautifully combine a wilderness, conservation ethics, and experience with first-class service and professionalism.

FOR FAMILIES. Geared to families with children from ages 5 to 16, the Family Goes to Camp–Expedition Style is a five-day trip scheduled eight times each summer through Desolation and Gray canyons on Utah's Green River. In spite of its name, Desolation is remarkably beautiful. Here Butch Cassidy and his Wild Bunch hid from the law among the red sandstone formations. You explore the ranch of the McPhersons, who homesteaded the grassy river bottomland and often provided assistance to outlaws, including Cassidy. Before the cowboys arrived, ancient native tribes carved their stories into the rocks. Today the Green River runs through the Uinta and Ouray Indian reservations; the tribes farm and ranch in these canyons. Guides point out the 300 million years of rock exposed on the canyon walls, and you're almost guaranteed to see wildlife. When not riding the river, you'll be hiking, camping, and relaxing on the expansive white sand beaches. The guides lead special kids-only outings along the way, too. The trip starts at the Canyonlands Airport in Moab, Utah, where you fly to a mesa high above the river. The return to Moab is by van from the takeout site. Both shuttles are included in the trip price.

At family camp assistants lead interpretive field trips and organize games for everyone. Parents and children have time with each other and with their peers. If you're hoping to find activities that will get your family working and playing together, look no farther. These paddle raft trips require team effort and spirit. If someone really doesn't want to paddle, there's always room in the oar-powered supply boats, and there are inflatable kayaks to ride during the more than 50 rapids on this trip.

Sheri Griffith Expeditions, Box 1324, Moab, UT 84532, tel. 435/259–8229 or 800/332–2439, www.griffithexp.com. June–

Aug.: 5 days, $874 adults, $674 children age 16 and under.

Tag-A-Long Expeditions

5+

Based in Moab, Utah, Tag-A-Long has been offering river and trail experiences for several decades. The company categorizes its trips three ways: Signature Expeditions (the very best), Create Your Own (customized trips), and Special Value Trips (value pricing). You can mix and match adventures with this group by adding on jet boat rides, jeep tours, or a three- to five-day camping and hiking experience.

FOR FAMILIES. The best family trip is the five-day Green River tour by raft or inflatable kayak, a "special-value trip—family style" for ages 6 and up. The magnificent scenery and ancient Native American sites are a draw, but what children usually like best about this river is that there are rapids every day (50 in all), which you can run in the support raft or inflatable kayaks, which your children help paddle. If your family wants to concentrate more on the camping, there's a four-day trip into the isolated Maze region of Canyonlands National Park where you can see the famed Great Gallery rock art panels and such pictographs as the Harvest Scene. This adventure includes a 44 ride, hiking, and jet boating, and you can rent sleeping bags and tents if you don't have your own. There's no minimum age, but there's a lot of hiking, geology, and history, so kids should be fit and interested. You can also add a half- or full-day rafting trip on the Colorado onto a scheduled camping trip. The age limit on this, like most rafting expeditions, is really based on weight rather than age. A child for all of these rafting trips and the jet boat excursion must be at least 40 lbs (18 kg).

Tag-A-Long Expeditions, 452 N. Main St., Moab, UT 84532, tel. 800/453–3292, www.tagalong.com. Apr.–Oct. (all trips not available all months): 5–6 days, $650–$1,030 adults, $560–$1,030 children. Prices for add-on jeep, jet boat adventures, ½- or 1-day rafting trips, $33–$89 adults, $26–$79 children.

Unicorn Rafting Expeditions

6+

Unicorn's wilderness base camps in north-central Maine–Lake Parlin Resort, near the Forks, and the Penobscot River Outpost in Millinocket, serve as headquarters for its river trips and starting points for adventures on land as well. Maine's rough-and-tumble white-water rivers have a high minimum age, often 10 or 14, making them especially good for families with teens. Unicorn has a couple of trips for younger children, too.

FOR FAMILIES. Families with river lovers ages 10 and up can tackle Alleyway and Magic Falls on the upper Kennebec River; ages 14 and up test their strength and skills against Elephant Rock and Poplar Falls on the Dead River. Families with kids age 8 and up can go for the one-day Dead River adventure when the river's lower and slower during the summer months, while children age 6 and up can choose a gentler, one-day ride on the lower Kennebec. Non-rafting youngsters ages 3 to 12 can play at Unicorn's base camps, where sitters (extra charge) will take them swimming and canoeing, play games, or arrange treasure hunts. At the end of the day your family can either cook dinner in your cabin or tent or eat at the restaurants (extra charge) at Lake Parlin or Penobscot River Outpost.

If you and your children age 10 and up want to go for an overnight, the two-day camping and rafting trip on the Kennebec River uses small rafts and 'funyaks' in the Class I, II, and III rapids the first day, before you tackle the Class IV thrills on day two. A noontime steak barbecue and a Maine lobster dinner are included in the cost.

Families can book a four-day adventure package at Lake Parlin Resort, which includes a lakeside cabin and rafting, canoeing, mountain biking, hiking, and more. You can just hang out in the hot tub or pool, too.

On any stay with this outfitter, one of the most popular family pastimes is the evening Moose Hunt, in the woods around camp. Unicorn owner Jay Schurman says they find a moose to watch about 90% of the time.
Unicorn Rafting Expeditions, Rte. 201, Jackman, ME 04945, tel. 207/628–7629 or 800/864–2676, www.unicornraft.com. Apr.–Oct.: 1–2 days, $83–$229 adults, $69–$123 children 16 and under. On Kennebec weekday trips, kids are ½-price with an adult. The 4-day adventure package is $729 for a family of 4.

Wilderness Aware Rafting

6+

This company has been running multi-day trips on the Arkansas and other Colorado rivers since 1976 and has twice won the Colorado Company of the Year award. Wilderness Aware is dedicated to quality, safety, and service, as well as to preserving the wilderness while sharing it with families. The company's huge headquarters in Johnson Village on the banks of the Arkansas make it especially convenient for those who choose to raft that river.

FOR FAMILIES. Ages 8 and older can join two-, three-, or five-day adventures on the Arkansas. On the two-day trip you run through the Narrows and Browns Canyon, or through Browns Canyon and calmer waters downstream. Three- and five-day trips provide a calm break after the thrills, with views of the soaring Sangre de Cristo range. From the vantage point of the river, rafters can see some of Colorado's famous "fourteeners," peaks of 14,000 ft and above. The awesome scenery doesn't change but the river does, rolling into the big, powerful waves of Bighorn Sheep Canyon. Three-day adventures include either the two canyons or the Narrows, while the five-day serves them all up for adventurous families.

For parents with kids as young as 6, your best bet is the Upper Colorado through Little Gore Canyon. Not far downstream from Rocky Mountain National Park and the headwaters of the Colorado, the river flows gently, belying the torrent it will eventually become as it squeezes through the Grand Canyon. On this easy, upper portion of the river, Class II rapids provide just enough thrills in between sunbathing and swimming. By contrast, families with fit, adventurous kids 10 and up can opt to run Colorado's most remote wilderness river, the Gunnison. Gunnison Gorge, adjacent to Black Canyon of the Gunnison National Park (one of the country's newest), is all about classic white water. In addition to negotiating some heavy-duty rapids on the two-day run, rafters must hike, carrying their personal gear, about a mile (1½ km) down to the river. Only two groups of 12 people per day are permitted to raft the Gorge, meaning that your work getting there will be rewarded with both spectacular wilderness and remarkable solitude.
Wilderness Aware Rafting, Box 1550, Buena Vista, CO 81211, tel. 719/395–7238 or 800/462–7238, www.inaraft.com. May–Sept.: 2–5 days, $269–$589 adults, $215–$475 children 6–16.

Wilderness River Outfitters

8+

Joe and Fran Tonsmeire started running rivers while in college during the '60s. They worked together on the Colorado River and eventually founded Wilderness River Outfitters in Salmon, Idaho. Although the company continues to evolve, rafting remains its central activity. The Tonsmeires' innovative trip list also has intriguing multi-activity adventures, especially those that combine hiking and rafting with packhorse support. This company also has bike-and-raft combination trips (see Biking).

FOR FAMILIES. The nine-day Salmon River rafting-hiking combination trip takes families with children ages 12 and up into remote backcountry for four days of trekking the high ridges that divide the Sawtooth and Salmon River mountains from the Bitterroots. The adventure starts at almost 9,000 ft in the heart of the River of No Return Wilderness Area, but the pace is easy—hikes average from 4 to 8 mi (6 to 13 km) a day. There's plenty of time to fish in the alpine lakes (bring your own gear) and relax. You can do it all with nothing more than a day pack because horses carry the camping equipment. The last 4-mi (6-km) hike down a steep trail leads to the river's edge, where the group loads the rafts for a five-day journey on the Salmon River. This trip begins in Salmon and ends in Boise, and everything, including tents and sleeping bags, is provided. Another eight-day hike-and-raft trip is led in Montana, where you trek through the awesome Bob Marshall Wilderness over Holland Pass and down to the South Fork of the Flathead River. This adventure starts and ends in Kalispell, Montana. Both trips are available without horse support if you want a complete backpack experience.

Families that want more horses with their rafting can opt for the 10-day ranch and Salmon River adventure, which gives you four nights at Hayden Creek Ranch, a working cattle ranch in the Lemhi Mountains 30 mi (48 km) south of Salmon, Idaho, in addition to five nights on the river.

You can depend on Wilderness River for excellent rafting-only trips, too. The best for families are six-day adventures on the Salmon River in Idaho (minimum age 8) and the Middle Fork of the Flathead River in Montana (minimum age 11). At least one Salmon River trip each summer is a designated family adventure. The company also runs one of the great rivers of the north, the Tatshenshini, which flows down from the Yukon through British Columbia and Alaska. Rafters on this 11-day journey should be at least 12 years old, as the river is colder and the hikes are longer than on most other trips.

Wilderness River Outfitters, Box 72, Lemhi, ID 83465, tel. 208/756–3959 or 800/252–6581, www.wildernessriver.com. June–Aug.: 5–11 days, $1,140–$2,200 for rafting only; 8–9 days, $1,650–$1,800 for raft-hike trips. Families choose 1 discount option: 30% discount for children under 13 or 5% discount for families of 5 or more.

Resources

Organizations

America Outdoors (Box 10847, Knoxville, TN 37939, tel. 865/558–3597, www.americaoutdoors.org) is the national association for outfitters and river guides. Ask for the organization's magazine listing outfitters and guides; America Outdoors cannot, however, recommend one outfitter over another. The **Professional Paddlesports Association** (7432 Alban Station Blvd., Suite A-111, Springfield, VA 22150, tel. 703/451–3864, www.propaddle.com) will send information on guides and outfitters. They also have a list of books and periodicals.

Periodicals

Canoe and Kayak (Box 3146, Kirkland, WA 98083, tel. 800/692–2663, www.canoekayak.com) is a magazine devoted primarily to canoeing and kayaking but has many articles on equipment, technique, and environmental issues that will interest rafters. The resource section lists many rafting opportunities from schools and adventure outfitters. *Paddler* (Box 775450, Steamboat Springs, CO 80477, www.paddlermagazine.com) covers all paddle sports, including rafting. There are lots of articles of interest to families, from getting kids into paddling to safety on the water.

Products

Nike, Patagonia, REI outdoor stores, and **Crazy Creek Chairs** make good river wear or river accessories for children and adults. Nike has river sandals and aqua socks, and Patagonia is a good source for warm, quick-drying fleece and quick-drying pants. REI has retail outlets, a catalog, and an online site (www.rei.com) with reasonably priced fleece and other warm, fast-drying apparel; the company also sells life vests for children and adults, as well as any camping equipment you could ever want or need. For information about these companies, *see* Resources *in* Hiking and Backpacking.

RANCHES

A spirit of rugged adventure and the romance of the American West, past and present, are alive and well in guest ranches across the country. At a ranch your family can indulge its Wild West fantasies—and you can all learn a lot about riding, ranching, being a cowhand, and caring for livestock as well. Fun for everyone is almost guaranteed.

Ranch stays make perfect family vacations because they can accommodate many ages, abilities, and interests. I know this from my own family's experience. My lifelong love of riding made me a natural for a ranch guest, but my husband, Bill, was uneasy around horses. On our first visit to Paradise Guest Ranch in Wyoming, Kira was 11, Molly was 4, and Hutch was just a year old. Of the children, only Kira had ever even been on a horse, and Molly and Hutch were too young for the ranch's regular riding program. Nonetheless, Paradise was a resounding success for all of us. Bill lost his fear of riding and learned to lope, as did Kira. Molly thrived in the children's program, and Hutch made both human and animal friends. We took advantage of the riding program and the naturalist-led hikes; Bill carried Hutch in a backpack on these while I indulged in advanced rides in the afternoon. Sometimes we just retreated from the action and took time to enjoy each other.

There are ranches for every budget and taste, from very simple to spectacular. Riding is definitely the central ingredient of a ranch vacation, but some ranches have so many additional activities that their guest lists frequently include nonriders. Many ranches have an organized children's activity program, and a few provide infant care. Others simply include children in all ranch activities. You can find a place with rustic accommodations and hearty, basic fare, or one that has elegant, well-appointed cabins and serves meals accompanied by fine wines. Guest capacity ranges from six people to well over a hundred, and seasons vary from three-month to year-round operations. Some real working ranches accept guests, but most are primarily guest farms with a bit of ranch work on the side that must be done.

Although each ranch creates its own unique atmosphere, all help bring families closer together. Sing-alongs and bonfires, hayrides, and other events give you a chance to see each other in new and wonderful ways. At the end of a family ranch stay, you may well take home, as we did, not only the requisite western bandannas and hatbands but also a renewed appreciation for each other and what you've accomplished individually and together. Who could ask for more than that from any vacation?

It's important to note, though, that although every ranch listed in this chapter is terrific, not every ranch is right for every family. And unlike most of the other adventures in this book, a ranch vacation is not a single-activity vacation, so there are more things to consider when making a choice. For families the most important criteria in choosing a ranch are its size; whether there is a children's program and, if so, for what ages; the riding program; and the activities other than riding, both for families as a whole and for adults. Because these factors are important in finding a good match, each ranch listing has a general introduction and then sections on the children's program, riding program, and activities besides riding.

Questions to Ask

Are all stays at least one week, or are shorter stays possible? Almost all ranches require a minimum one-week stay during the summer high season (or winter high season for those ranches in the Southwest), but some allow briefer vacations in off-seasons. A few ranches have shorter minimum stays—or even none at all. Keep in mind, though, that ranches offering short-stay options in the off-season may not have counselors or children's programs during these times.

Are families welcome all the time? Many ranches have adults-only periods—sometimes just a week, sometimes a month or more—during times children are in school, such as September or October. Spring is always an off-season for ranches (except those in the Southwest), so although families may be welcome, there may be no children's activity program and probably only a few children present. Most formal children's programs run in the summer months only (or summers and holidays for year-round ranches), when college students are available to be counselors.

What is the riding program? These programs vary widely. Some ranches have walk-only rides; others offer slow, medium, and fast rides each day. Some have only hour-long outings; other ranches have short rides, all-day rides, and even overnight rides. Children may or may not be permitted on adult rides, although parents can sometimes join the children's rides. Some ranches provide more formal instruction than others; ask about this if it's important to your family. Rides may have as few as four participants and as many as 25. Typically, there are morning and afternoon rides each day, along with special rides—brunch, lunch, all-day, or evening cookouts—throughout the week. For safety reasons, however, guests cannot go out on trails alone but are led by a ranch's wranglers.

Does each person get the same horse for the whole week? What if you don't like the horse? Most ranches with minimum weeklong stays assign each guest a horse. That way, rider and horse get used to each other and become comfortable as a team, which can make a difference even to a seasoned rider. On the other hand, sometimes this doesn't work out. A ranch should be flexible enough and have enough horses to be able to make a change for members of your family who request it.

Are guests required to have riding boots, and if so, are loaner boots available? Most ranches prefer but do not require riding boots; they do require sturdy shoes or other boots with heels. Riding boots can be an expensive proposition if you need to get them for the whole family. Some ranches have a trunk of boots that are lent to guests, although there may be no way to guarantee your size or your child's size is available. If you decide to buy boots, break them in before your vacation.

At what age are children permitted to ride in the regular riding program and to go out on the trail? Six or 7 is often the age given, which is usually dictated by insurance. However, some ranches won't allow kids out on the trail until they're 8, 9, or even 10. A few permit parents to put younger children in the saddle with them, which can be risky even for accomplished riders. If your children are too young for the trail, you'll probably want a ranch that has options such as a supervised children's program. Parents can also take turns staying at the ranch with younger children and taking part in other ranch activities.

Is there an organized children's program? If you have young children, especially children too young to ride with you, this will be important. While you are out riding, your youngsters can participate in age-appropriate activities, such as hiking, wildlife tracking, swimming, fishing, and learning Native American lore. Some ranches have corral riding sessions for children not able to go on the trail; at others, the staff may lead small children on ponies. You can usually make use of the programs in a variety of ways: just in the mornings or afternoons, or all day. You can sign the children in one day and not another. The bottom line: a good children's program is a place that they *want* to be, a place where they can meet children from other parts of the country and the world and hang out with cool counselors. When available, children's programs are almost always part of the ranch package; care for infants and toddlers, however, sometimes costs extra.

If there isn't a supervised children's program—or if there is but my child is too young for it—is baby-sitting available on an individual basis? Families with a baby or toddler will want a ranch with something for this age group for at least part of the day so parents and older children can spend time together riding or taking advantage of other activities. Another option is to choose a ranch that allows you to bring along your own baby-sitter for free or for a nominal charge. Parents can also split up during the day, one spending time with the youngest child, the other being one on one with an older child.

Where do we stay on the ranch? Most ranches have cabins of various sizes; some ranches also have rooms in a main lodge, although not many of these accommodate families. Cabins often have kitchens, which are handy for families with babies and with young children who get hungry between the ranch's set mealtimes. Western decor is prevalent, as are porches, fireplaces, and grand views. You probably won't spend a lot of time in your cabin, but it's nice to know that most are roomy, cheerful places.

What kind of food is served, and where do we eat? Hearty, delicious, and plentiful best describe ranch food; three meals a day are usually part of the package. Breakfast and lunch are often buffet affairs—except when you eat lunch out on the trail, which is common throughout the week. Ranchers like to go all out for dinner; some even provide candles, wine, and gourmet fare. Many ranches serve meals family style: Guests sit at long tables, making it easy for families to get to know different people during the week. In general, ranches are not places to cut calories; barbecued meats and homemade pies and cobblers are often a big part of a week's menu, which also will include salads and fruit. If you do have any type of restrictive diet, however, the vast majority of ranch chefs will accommodate you.

Do parents and children eat meals together? At some ranches with supervised children's programs, youngsters eat lunch with counselors, either at a different time or at the same time but apart from parents. At others, families usually eat together after the morning ride. If there is an all-day or lunch ride scheduled for adults or children, however, families won't see each other again until late afternoon. Many family ranches also schedule an adults-only dinner at least once a week, during which counselors take their groups for a special children's cookout or other activity. At a few ranches children eat most or even all meals with counselors, usually at an earlier time, allowing parents to relax and meet other guests. Ask questions and know your family preferences before you choose a ranch.

If an adult doesn't ride, is there a reduced rate? What other activities are available? Some ranches do have a nonrider's rate; if an adult in your group doesn't want to ride at all, look for a ranch with this kind of discount. Keep in mind that ranches these days have a variety of activities besides riding. Almost all have fishing. In addition, depending on the ranch, you can also take guided nature hikes, swim, play tennis, mountain bike, picnic, go boating or rafting, or even play golf. Some ranches have hot tubs and saunas; massages are available at a few. A number of ranches are near towns with places of historical interest, museums, or fun places to shop.

What's included in the cost? Ranch vacations are primarily all-inclusive. Lodging, meals, riding, the children's program, and other activities are included in the cost, unless otherwise noted. If the program includes an overnight trip, the use of gear is generally included (ask ahead for specifics). Baby-sitting for infants and toddlers is usually extra, unless you bring your own baby-sitter. Off-property activities, such as rafting, guided fishing trips, and visits to museums and local rodeos, are often—but not always—an extra charge. If it's available, alcohol is generally extra as well. Most ranches will provide airport transportation for an extra charge.

Prices given here are for high season, except as noted; sometimes rates are reduced for large families. Many ranches use two or more age brackets for their children's rates, and the range of prices according to age can be quite substantial. Considering all that's included, ranch vacations can be a very reasonably priced family vacation. However, if you want to save, plan a trip early or late in the season, when rates are almost always lower. Not all facilities and activities are available in the off-season, though.

Instruction

Just about every ranch has instruction in horsemanship, although some ranches are more formal about it than others. Wranglers check all guests' abilities the first day, and progressive instruction helps riders move from walk-only rides to those that include trotting or even loping or cantering. Even if your family arrives with varying skill levels, it's likely you will be able to ride together at some point. (Advanced riders, of course, can always choose to ride with less advanced riders at any time.) Although riding is a skill that can take years to develop to its highest level, it's also a sport in which you can improve quickly with practice and good instruction.

In addition to horsemanship, some ranches teach you about caring for horses, roping, and other skills. There are fishing classes for children and adults at many ranches, as well as instruction in skeet- or trapshooting. A few ranches have courses in other types of activities, including photography, environmental issues, rock climbing, and wildflower or bird identification. In winter cross-country ski instruction may be available. Some classes may be part of the regular program; others are an extra charge.

Finding the Fun

Because each adventure option in this chapter is in a fixed destination, the selections listed are organized by region.

Favorite Ranches

NORTHEAST

Pinegrove Resort Ranch

ALL

A five-minute talk with Dave Ohalloran, general manager and a member of the Tarantino family that owns and operates Pinegrove, will convince you this is a place to bring your family. Although Pinegrove is in New York's Hudson Valley region, everything has been done to provide not only a family atmosphere but a genuinely western one as well. There are roping and blacksmithing demonstrations, cattle drives, and nightly cattle calls, during which guests call cattle in from the pasture to feed them. Lodging is in modern rooms with TVs and telephones, but you'll probably be too busy to make use of them. Pinegrove is a big place that can accommodate more than 300 guests, yet it's also small enough that families feel safe giving children freedom to explore on their own. One of the nice family features is that snacks are available all day and evening (until midnight) from the free Chuck Wagon Snack Bar.

CHILDREN'S PROGRAM. The nursery, for ages 6 weeks through 3 years, has one staff person for every two to three children. Activities include pony rides, time at the playground, visits to the baby animal farm, and indoor fun such as arts and crafts. In day camp, for ages 4 through 10, campers go swimming, play miniature golf, spend time at the playground, and have nature hikes, pony rides, and hayrides. Private baby-sitting at night is also available for an extra charge.

RIDING PROGRAM. Daily rides meet the needs of beginner to advanced riders; groups are large, typically from 15 to 20 people. Trail riding is generally for those ages 8 and up, although younger children will be permitted if they can control a horse. Children can ride with parents but don't have to; they can join any ride that suits their skill level and interest. The ranch also has Jr. Instructional Rides, aimed at ages 5 through 7, which give kids the skills and confidence to progress from pony rides on a lead to the daily trail rides. From Memorial Day to Columbus Day, Pinegrove also runs cattle drives (extra charge) for advanced riders. There's riding in winter, too.

BEYOND RIDING. You can choose from among the following, all on the property: fishing, boating, hiking, tennis, swimming indoors and out, miniature golf, boccie ball, and archery. Tractor rides are also a favorite activity. There's live entertainment on summer evenings, as well as campfires and marshmallow roasts at the tepees. In winter there's downhill skiing for beginners and intermediates, plus ice skating and snow-tubing at the ranch; equipment and lessons are included.

Pinegrove Resort Ranch, Box 209, Kerhonkson, NY 12446, tel. 845/626–7345 or 800/346–4626. Year-round: 7 days, $280–$850; children under 4 free. Family of 3 Summer Special $629–$1,299.

Rocking Horse Ranch

ALL

Just 75 mi (121 km) north of New York City in the historic and scenic Hudson Valley, Rocking Horse has 500 acres, its own lake, three pools (one indoors), a petting zoo, and a playground. A hot tub and two saunas give guests a break from nonstop activities. Guests stay in modern, motel-style rooms or lodge rooms with TVs, phones, air-conditioning, and carpeting. And yet the ranch has a definite western feel, as well as a focus very much on families.

CHILDREN'S PROGRAM. Counselors take children ages 4 through 6, 6 through 9, and 9 through 12 to swim, fish, and play a variety of sports every day from 9 to 5. Sometimes the group goes out on speedboat or banana-boat rides. Visits to the petting zoo and playground and pony rides are part of most days, especially for children under age 7. Children in the daily program eat lunch with counselors and get a snack of milk and cookies in the afternoon. There is a nursery available (extra charge) for children under age 4.

RIDING PROGRAM. Children ages 7 and older go on the trail with parents. Rides are about 1¼ hours long, and each guest is assigned to a minimum of one ride each day. If you want to go more often, you can stand by on a space-available basis for other rides. Occasionally in the fall, longer rides are offered, and this is one of the few ranches with winter riding.

BEYOND RIDING. The list of the ranch's family activities is so extensive you couldn't possibly get to all of them in a weeklong stay. There's everything from tennis, water skiing, miniature golf, adult and children's water slides, and hayrides in summer to skiing, tubing, skating, and sleigh rides in winter. One of the ranch's three pools is just for children.

Rocking Horse Ranch, Highland, NY 12528, tel. 845/691–2927 or 800/647–2624, www.rhranch.com. Year-round (2-day minimum): $100–$175 per day adults, $45–$65 per day children ages 4–15; children under 4 free. Ask about the many special family packages available throughout the year.

Timberlock

ALL

Part family camp, part ranch, part resort, Timberlock is a rustic, informal retreat in the Adirondack Mountains of northern New York. Only the main kitchen has electricity; guests' cabins are lighted with gas lamps. Propane creates hot water, and heat comes from woodstoves. You pay separately for riding here, and there's no structured program, no required activities—nothing, in fact, that anyone *has* to do. The Catlin family, owners since 1964, just want to give families an opportunity to spend time together in a way they can't back home. Timberlock succeeds admirably, which is why guests return year after year. Because the ranch accommodates only about 65, it's a good idea to book as early as possible.

CHILDREN'S PROGRAM. Timberlock has a supervised play area for children ages 2 through 6 so parents can pursue some activities their young children can't. There's no additional charge for the program, which runs three days each week. Parents can sign up at the beginning of the week for their chosen days and times. For the most part, though, families eat, play, and relax together.

RIDING PROGRAM. Adults and children age 6 and up can ride out on the trail, either English or western style. There are three trail rides each morning, beginner to advanced. Guests can also take lessons in the riding ring, and there's a weekly mountain picnic ride of about three hours. Timberlock has hard hats for children.

BEYOND RIDING. You can take advantage of 15-mi (24-km) Indian Lake, along which Timberlock sits, for canoeing, sailing, fishing, and swimming. Tennis and archery are other options, or you can choose nature walks and birding. Guided hikes and canoe trips for groups of guests are an important part of any weekly stay. Don't miss the wood shop, in which you can make your own canoe paddle or birdhouse.

Timberlock, Box 1052, Sabael, NY 12864, tel. 518/648–5494 (in season); 1735 Quaker St., Lincoln, VT 05443, tel. 802/453–2540 (off-season), www.timberlock.com. Late June–late Sept.: $84–$105 per day adults, $49–$80 children; children under 2 free. Rides $20–$45 each, depending on length and destination; multiday trail ride packages available.

SOUTH

Scott Valley Resort & Guest Ranch

ALL

Scott Valley's 625 acres in the Ozark Mountains are mostly lush meadows and woodlands. Guests stay in one- and two-bedroom units with air-conditioning and heating; they aren't fancy, but they're clean and comfortable. There are plenty of hiking trails to explore, as well as a playground and petting zoo. Scott Valley tries to meet the needs of a wide variety of guests: single parents, nonriders, and ecotourists among them, which is just one reason experts and guests have consistently voted this ranch, in business for more than 45 years, one of the country's great family resorts.

CHILDREN'S PROGRAM. The ranch has no formal program; families are encouraged to spend time together. With tennis, badminton, horseshoes, pool, and other family activities available, this isn't hard to do. If parents want to try a ride or hike that's not appropriate for younger children, free babysitting is available.

RIDING PROGRAM. The ranch owns and raises its own gentle horses, the majority being Missouri Fox Trotters. Age 7 is when most children start riding alone and can be assigned a horse for the week; however, if younger children show an interest and ability to follow directions, they may be given lessons and ride on the trail. Wranglers provide instruction to all guests, and there are a minimum of two rides a day for beginners to advanced riders.

BEYOND RIDING. When not feeding and interacting with the goats, pigs, geese, cats, or dogs, as well as a variety of wild creatures, you can try fishing on the White River, playing lawn games, swimming, or relaxing in the hot tub. Canoes are available for those who want to float down a nearby river. Dinner is served on a ferry on Lake Norfolk one evening during summer weeks, and favorite excursions for families with children of all ages are the nearby Ozark Folk Center, Blanchard Springs Caverns, and Branson, Missouri. Evening activities for families are scheduled in the summer months. Golf and guided fishing trips can be arranged (at an extra charge).

Scott Valley Resort & Guest Ranch, Box 1447, Mountain Home, AR 72653, tel. 870/425–5136 or 888/855–7747, www.scottvalley.com. Mar.–Nov.: $115–$145 per adult per day, $55–$125 ages 2 to 12; under 2 free.

MIDWEST

Dakota Badland Outfitters

The Husted family has been ranching in South Dakota for five generations. They are horsemen and women through and through, and a stay at their ranch is not a typical guest ranch experience. This is a working horse operation that runs 60 to 70 head of horses year-round. During spring and fall, when the ranch is open to guests, lodging is provided in authentic cowboy bunkhouses. Each cabin, decorated with the needs and tastes of the old-time horseman in mind, sleeps two and has a private bath. This is a true west adventure that's not for every family. If you want to learn about training and working with horses, however, you won't find a better family from whom to learn, or a better place at which to learn.

RIDING PROGRAM. There are no children's activities, but there is an exceptional horsemanship program, which includes riding, training, grooming, feeding, sorting, and "doctoring" ranch stock. The program is designed for beginners as well as advanced riders, but participants should be in good health and at least moderately good physical condition, whatever their riding abilities. At the core of the program is the opportunity to ride with and learn from trainers who practice Minimal Resistance Horsemanship (as seen in the movie "The Horse Whisperer"). Foals trained on the ranch go on to be roping horses, or trail and ranch horses. Guests spend time with the trainer as he works the foals, which are in various stages of training. The Husteds hope that by participating actively in the training—and they encourage hands-on participation—guests will come away with a new understanding of the American cowboy and his horse. Training includes developing an understanding of how human reactions affect horses, learning how to read your horse's expressions, and how to use this knowledge to become a better rider. The Husteds have made their ranch the ideal place to safely and effectively learn and develop new skills, so you don't have to have previous knowledge or skills to participate. And they've simplified the Natural Horsemanship techniques, making their teaching style applicable to all abilities and ages. Daily trail rides into the Black Hills are a regular part of each horse's training and exercise routine, and a highlight of each day's activities.

BEYOND RIDING. The ranch is all about horses, but the Black Hills are rich in history, heritage, and adventure. You can visit Mount Rushmore and the Crazy Horse monument, pan for gold, rock-climb, dig for fossils, explore vast national forests—and much more. Ask the Husteds for suggestions of off-ranch destinations and activities.

Dakota Badland Outfitters, Box 85, Custer, SD 57730, tel. 605/673–5363, www.ridesouthdakota.com. May, Sept.–Oct.: $170 per person per day.

SOUTHWEST

Mayan Dude Ranch

ALL

Bandera, 47 mi (76 km) northwest of San Antonio in the heart of Texas Hill Country, is home to this bighearted, hospitable ranch. Judy and Don Hicks and all 12 of their children are here to make guests feel welcome—up to 167 of them. Accommodations are in stone cottages furnished with many handmade objects. Some have fireplaces; all are air-conditioned. There are also two-story lodges with motel-like rooms. Mayan is big, but it's down-home friendly and an ideal choice for families that really want to relax, perhaps by floating in a tube on the meandering Medina River as it flows through the ranch.

CHILDREN'S PROGRAM. The children's program runs primarily in summer, although there are children's activities during holiday periods, too. Ages 3 through 6 and 7 through 12 are placed in separate groups, which meet from 10 to noon and again from 1 to 3. The younger children don't ride on the trail but keep busy with arts and crafts, treasure hunts, games, and outings. The older group joins parents on trail rides. They also swim, try roping and archery, play baseball, and make leather crafts. The program is fairly flexible, and activities can change to suit the interests of the group. Children eat dinner with their group and counselors twice a week.

RIDING PROGRAM. Daily, hour-long rides into one of the most beautiful areas of Texas take place each morning and afternoon. Typically, 25 guests go on each ride. Children age 7 and up can join parents on the trail.

BEYOND RIDING. You can swim, tube, and fish (some poles available) in the cool Medina River or use the pool and two tennis courts. For an extra charge, you have access to an 18-hole golf course. Those who wish to explore Hill Country can visit the Frontier Times Museum in Bandera, which has artifacts from pioneer days, and the late President Johnson's boyhood home, about 60 mi (97 km) away in Johnson City. Sea World of Texas and Fiesta Texas, a family-oriented theme park, are in San Antonio.

Mayan Dude Ranch, Box 577, Bandera, TX 78003, tel. 830/796–3312, www.mayanranch.com. Year-round (2-day minimum): $120–$125 per day adults, $55–$80 children up to age 17. Children under 3 are discouraged.

White Stallion Ranch

ALL

The True family, which owns and runs White Stallion, believes guests get the best of two worlds on their 3,000-acre ranch. Although mountains and rugged, picturesque high desert surround the property, it is only 10 minutes around the mountain from Tucson. Longhorns graze the ranch, where up to 75 guests stay in Spanish-style adobe bungalows that have views of the cactus garden and the Tucson Mountains.

Aside from the natural beauty of the area, White Stallion has much to offer families, not the least of which is plenty of time together.

CHILDREN'S PROGRAM. There are no formal programs; parents and children of all ages are welcome to participate in ranch activities. With enough notice, however, baby-sitting can usually be arranged (extra charge) during the day or at night.

RIDING PROGRAM. One unique aspect of the program is that many rides take you into nearby Saguaro National Park to see the 50-ft cacti and abundant wildlife. Children age 5 and up ride the trail with their parents on their own horse. At about age 8, children can be tested to see if they meet the requirements for loping or cantering rides. There are at least two fast and two slow rides a day; during the week all-day and breakfast rides are offered, as is a hayride that takes you to a lunch cookout. For those with a little riding experience, team cattle penning is very popular. Both children and adults can help groom and saddle their horses.

BEYOND RIDING. You can swim in the pool, take nature hikes, use the two tennis courts, play lawn games, or relax in a hot tub. Golf is available nearby for an extra charge. The evening programs are very creative: During the busiest season, a wildlife rehabilitator stops by with rescued animals, and a local astronomer brings telescopes to the ranch once a week so you can take a closer look at the stars. Tucson is well worth exploring for an afternoon or even a full day. The Arizona-Sonora Desert Museum, a microcosm of a desert environment, has exhibits and programs that appeal to children of all ages.

White Stallion Ranch, 9251 W. Twin Peaks Rd., Tucson, AZ 85743, tel. 602/297–0252 or 888/977–2624, www.wsranch.com. Sept.–May: 7 days, $574–$1,239; children under age 3 free. Ask about daily rates.

Y.O. Ranch

ALL

One of the biggest working ranches in Texas, the Y.O. is also the largest exotic wildlife ranch in North America. Most guests come to view the more than 12,000 animals that live here, including giraffes, wildebeests, oryx, antelope, and zebras. The ranch is also famous for its herd of well over 1,000 Texas longhorns. The Y.O. can accommodate 42 guests in century-old renovated log cabins or in rooms in a larger house on the property. The chef is a master of southwestern fare.

CHILDREN'S PROGRAM. The ranch welcomes families with children of all ages, but it has no children's programs or baby-sitting services. However, during the summer there are one- to three-week sessions of Ranch Adventure Camp, for ages 9 through 14, so a family could book a Y.O. vacation and camp experience at the same time. The camp emphasizes environmental learning, with minicourses in ornithology, herpetology, ecology, firearm safety, rappelling, canoeing, swimming, and riding.

RIDING PROGRAM. There's a separate fee for the limited horseback riding, and you must reserve times before your arrival. Rides go out for a minimum of an hour. Good riders can participate in longhorn cattle drives each spring (at an extra charge).

BEYOND RIDING. Safari-style vehicles take you out to observe the animals each day, and there are wildlife photographic safaris as well. These tours cost extra but are well worth the money. Although the safaris are the only scheduled programs, the Y.O. also has a swimming pool and 40,000 acres of land to hike and explore. Families have plenty of time to relax and to savor the delicious meals, too.

Y.O. Ranch, Mountain Home, TX 78058, tel. 830/640–3222, www.yoranch.com. Year-

round: 1 day, $125 adults, $62.50 children 12 & under; no minimum stay required. Adventure Camp, June–Aug.: 7–14 days, $695–$1,195. Riding is $28.50 per hr.

ROCKIES

Aspen Canyon Ranch

ALL

Just 70 mi (113 km) west of Denver in the Williams Fork River valley, Aspen Canyon Ranch is easy to reach even though it's tucked away at 8,400 ft among the aspen and lodgepole pines. The ranch borders Arapaho National Forest and is a short drive from Rocky Mountain National Park. From 30 to 35 guests stay in cozy log cabins with fireplaces, private baths, refrigerators, and coffeemakers. Aspen Canyon is a relatively small ranch with a wide range of activities as part of its regular program. The staff is enthusiastic about providing a western experience during which you will both relax and learn.

CHILDREN'S PROGRAM. The ranch has day care for children from infants to age 5; the activity program divides children ages 5 through 18 into two groups by age. Five-year-olds ride on lead lines in the corral; youngsters age 7 and up can go out on the trail with their group. There are also games, hiking, fishing, and crafts.

RIDING PROGRAM. The rides, on ranch property and through Arapaho National Forest, take small groups of similar ability. Outings range from easy trips in the morning and afternoon to a challenging all-day ride. Kids age 7 and up can ride with their children's group or with their parents. You can choose personal instruction, and the wranglers will teach you not only how to ride but also how to saddle up or rope like an old pro. For an extra charge the whole family can opt for an overnight pack trip. Winter activities include snowmobiling.

BEYOND RIDING. Mountain biking and skeet shooting are popular family activities here, as is soaking in the two hot tubs. Fishing, hiking with or without a guide, and wildlife viewing are also options. You can always take on a job around the ranch, such as haying. For an extra charge, families can sign up for rafting on the upper Colorado River, mountain biking (adults only), or local hot-air ballooning.

Aspen Canyon Ranch, 13206 County Rd. 3, Star Rte., Parshall, CO 80468, tel. 970/725–3600 or 800/321–1357, www.aspencanyon.com. May–Oct., mid-Dec.–Apr.: 7 days, $1,295 adults, $800 children 7 to 16, $650 children 3 to 6, under 3 free.

Brush Creek

3+

This 6,000-acre working cattle and guest ranch is located in southeastern Wyoming, near the Medicine Bow Wilderness area, about 65 mi (85 km) from Laramie and 195 mi (314 km) north of Denver. It has a long and interesting history—parts of the flower gardens were constructed and planted by German POWs stationed at nearby Ryan Park—and it continues to be a thriving ranch today, meeting the needs of both cattle and human guests. The comfortable cabins are well appointed, and some of the guests also stay in rooms at the lodge. Families are warmly welcomed everywhere, as Brush Creek aims to bring families together (though there's some separate time, too).

CHILDREN'S PROGRAM. Although children age 7 and older participate in regular ranch activities with their families, the program for ages 3 to 7 meets five half-days per week and includes activities geared to introduce kids to authentic ranch life through exploration, education, and fun. Children visit the wranglers and horses in the barn, learn about grooming and equipment, and ride specially trained "beginner" horses. On the morning of the breakfast ride, the kids head out to the cookout camp and help set up everything. After the riders leave, kids stay on the range to learn about the settlement of the Wild West. During the week children also take a wildflower safari to learn current and Native American names for what they find, search for wild critters who call the ranch home, and get down and dirty discovering what's fascinating and fun about creek ecosystems. They also create their own "brand" and learn all about cowboy life, from roping to tending cattle. Childcare is available (extra charge), and you can hire a babysitter on request.

RIDING PROGRAM. A variety of rides are available each day, from easy meanderings through gently rolling hay meadows to more challenging mountain treks. Because this is a working ranch, guests may also have the opportunity to help move cattle from one grazing area to another. There are cook-out rides several times a week, and wranglers will give you any instruction you need to feel comfortable in the saddle. Overnight pack trips are also available at a nominal extra charge.

BEYOND RIDING. Fishing is big here—this is an Orvis-endorsed ranch, meaning there's an Orvis-approved guide. Guests have access to 3 private mi (5 km) of Brush Creek, but you can also explore many rivers in the Saratoga and Encampment valleys. Most famous in the area is the highly recommended "Miracle Mile" of the North Platte River (extra charge). There's more hiking through the Medicine Bow National Forest than you could get to in a week, plus mountain bike trails, four-wheel-drive excursions (extra charge), roping demonstrations, and the dances in the loft of the big barn. Bring binoculars, as there's plenty of wildlife to spot, from Rocky Mountain marmots to antelope and moose. In winter, there's cross-country skiing, snowshoeing, dogsledding, and snowmobiling.

Brush Creek, Star Route 10, Saratoga, WY 82331, tel. 307/327–5241 or 800/726–2499, www.brushcreekranch.com. Year-round (except Nov. and 1st 2 wks Dec.: 7 days, $1,050–$1,250 adults, $650–$1,000 3 to 15, under age 3 free. Ask about daily winter rates.

Cherokee Park Dude Ranch

ALL

One of the oldest guest ranches in Colorado, Cherokee Park was a stagecoach stop between Fort Collins and Laramie before it became a dude ranch back in 1886. Its authentic Old West character shows in furnishings and historical memorabilia from the early days, but among the many modern amenities are a heated pool and spa. Up to 35 guests stay in the main lodge or in cabins with two to four bedrooms. Owners Dickey and Christine Prince are renowned for their warm hospitality; their attitude carries over to the staff, too. Attentive care and enthusiasm are especially evident in the children's program.

CHILDREN'S PROGRAM. Children from ages 3 to 5 and 6 to 12 are in separate groups. The younger ones take pony rides around the ranch; the older ones have their own horses and a daily ride out on the trail. Other activities include hiking, fishing, nature studies, crafts, riflery, and an overnight in a tepee. The ranch schedules special hikes for teens, too, when enough are visiting. Children eat with their parents unless adults are on the trail; an exception is a weekly adults-only candlelight dinner, during which the children have a pizza party. You can bring your own sitter or nanny free of charge.

RIDING PROGRAM. Personal instruction is available every day in the riding ring, and trail rides for different levels range from an hour to all day. The terrain includes open prairie as well as mountain trails. You can join one of the popular lunch rides, and no one should miss the opportunity to join an overnight pack trip (extra charge).

BEYOND RIDING. Besides swimming in the pool, from mid-May through mid-August you can take to the water for a day of rafting (extra charge); ages 7 and up can paddle. There are free fly-casting classes for novice anglers of all ages—the ranch provides equipment, and there's an Orvis-certified fishing guide to give lessons each Sunday afternoon. Guided hikes are free, and there's trapshooting, too.

You can take a complimentary sightseeing trip to nearby Rocky Mountain National Park, or for an extra charge visit Laramie's Wyoming Territorial Park, where the children get to reenact a prison break. Don't miss the evening activities, when a "mountain man" visits the ranch to talk about trapping and western life in the mid-1800s. *Cherokee Park Dude Ranch, 436 Cherokee Hills Dr., Livermore, CO 80536, tel. 970/493–6522 or 800/628–0949. May–Oct.: 7 days, $1,000–$1,250 adults, $750–$950 children ages 3–12.*

Colorado Trails Ranch

5+

The majestic San Juan Mountains in southwestern Colorado are a dramatic backdrop for Colorado Trails, which has one of the best riding programs of any ranch in the country. The ranch managers have a straightforward goal: to "see that every guest, child or adult, has the best vacation they ever had." That has been the ranch's goal for 39 years, and children's activities have always been a focus. Up to 65 guests choose from three styles of cabins; some children's rooms have two bunk beds to accommodate large families. Also on the property are an opera house that is used for evening shows and entertainment, an old-fashioned soda fountain, and a petting zoo. The managers don't feel alcohol and children mix, so ranch policy is BYOB for consumption in your own cabin only.

CHILDREN'S PROGRAM. The extensive program usually has three groups: ages 5 through 8, 9 through 12, and teens. The flexible program de-emphasizes competition but gives children a chance to participate in all ranch activities, including archery, riflery, swimming, and fishing. The 9-to-12s and teens each have their own camp-out, too. Kids ages 5 and up take trail rides daily; the counselors who accompany the groups are adept at teaching children as they ride. Although there's no specific program for children 4 and under, they're welcome at the ranch and may participate in the children's activities to their level of ability. Babysitting is available.

RIDING PROGRAM. Headed by the American Riding Instructors Association, Colorado Trails offers superb instruction—even advanced riders can learn something new. A special strength of the program is the instructors' ability to make those who have never even been near a horse feel comfortable and in control. Rides head out each day at a variety of gaits (walk, trot, canter, and instructional), with only about six riders to a group. Family rides are also set up during the week, if that's what children and parents want. Many forest trails are groomed.

BEYOND RIDING. Guests who want to learn to shoot can take instruction in archery, riflery, and trapshooting; there's an extra charge for the ammo and clay pigeons. In recent years the ranch expanded its fishing program and completed a fish habitat project on the mile of stream that runs through the property. There's fishing instruction and two stocked ponds, ideal for children and parents. Guests also have access to several lakes and streams nearby, though a guide is required for some waters (extra fee). Hiking and nature walks are popular as well. Those who want a change of scenery can visit Vallecito Lake, 12 mi (19 km) away; the ranch provides a boat, driver, floating dock, and equipment for water-skiers and power tubers. You'll probably want to see Durango, a town with great shopping and a theater offering turn-of-the-20th-century melodramas, as well as a pro rodeo. The ranch will tell you the cost of tickets for these and the popular narrow gauge railroad. Ask about guided trips to Mesa Verde National Park with its 1,000-year-old ancestral Puebloan cliff dwellings.

Colorado Trails Ranch, 12161 County Rd. 240, Durango, CO 81301-6306, tel. 970/247–5055 or 800/323–3833, www.guestranches.com/coloradotrails. Early June–Aug.: 7 days, $4,290–$5,190 for a family of 3; $5,600–$6,400 for a family of 4, depending on size of cabin; $1,310 for each additional person in your cabin.

Drowsy Water Ranch

1+

"We treat your children as we do our own—with understanding, patience, love, and respect," owners Ken and Randy Sue Fosha say, and they mean it. This ranch just south of Rocky Mountain National Park in Colorado happily caters to families with children from one year old to the teens. It has one of the few programs for children under 5 that has activities, rather than just being a baby-sitting service. Most families will stay in the rustic but bright and cheerful log cabins that sleep up to nine people; there are lodge rooms, too. Cabins overlook Drowsy Water Creek or the ranch ponds. There's a good old-fashioned feel here and plenty of warm western hospitality for about 60 guests.

CHILDREN'S PROGRAM. One- to 5-year-olds are kept busy while adults participate in scheduled ranch activities for part or all of the day. They have rides on lead lines, crafts, nature hikes, and games—lots of outdoor fun. Children ages 6 through 13, called Range Riders, get their own horse for the week and ride together on the ranch and out on the trail. Counselors also lead games and crafts and take the group for picnics and hikes. These youngsters can try archery or the obstacle course, too.

RIDING PROGRAM. Slow, moderate, and fast rides go out daily, and you can get in extra riding on all-day and cookout rides during the week. Instruction is always available. Many trails above the ranch have views of the Continental Divide and the Gore Range. Although the Range Riders can't ride with adults on the trail, parents can choose to ride with the children. For an extra charge, parents and children 6 and up can take an overnight pack trip.

BEYOND RIDING. There's fishing on the property; the ranch provides equipment for beginners. Children also love the ranch's playground. Your stay includes a rugged Jeep trip up into the mountains. You can arrange rafting, golf, and tennis nearby for an extra charge. For romantics there's an adults-only hayride at the end of the week while children have their own hayride and dinner.

Drowsy Water Ranch, Box 147FA, Granby, CO 80446, tel. 970/725–3456 or 800/845–2292, www.drowsywater.com. June–mid-Sept.: 7 days. Family rates $1,160 each first two people, $1,020 each additional, $550 ages 4 and under. Nonriders deduct $210.

Elk Mountain Ranch

3+

At 9,535 ft Elk Mountain is the highest guest ranch in Colorado, with a spectacular setting in the San Isabel National Forest. There are deer, elk, and wildflowers in abundance amid thousands of acres of unspoiled wilderness. Log cottages or a suite in the main lodge are ideal for families; the guest capacity is limited to 30. You'll always find fresh flowers and a gift basket in your room. Although the ranch has a full children's program, families spend a lot of time together.

CHILDREN'S PROGRAM. Children ages 3 through 7 have an extensive program. Aside from riding twice a day in the ring, they go on scavenger hunts, create crafts, and fish, among other pastimes. Children 8 and up are welcome in all the ranch's activities, including riding. It's especially nice that even those younger than 8 can take part in brunch rides—vehicles bring them up to meet riders so the whole family can enjoy the meal and the views. The ranch has no organized program for children under age 3, but they are welcome; parents should arrange baby-sitting (extra charge) when they book their stay.

RIDING PROGRAM. Riding is exceptional at Elk Mountain. Each day there are rides on and off the trails, as well as excellent instruction in riding, tack, and the care and feeding of horses. You ride in very small groups through rock canyons, across high plateaus, and on trails through stands of shimmering aspens. Children age 8 and up can go out with parents on the adult rides. Don't miss the weekly brunch ride or the overnight camping trip; the overnight is included in July and August (additional charge in June and September).

BEYOND RIDING. Elk Mountain has free guided hikes to a nearby ghost town and high meadows filled with wildflowers. There's also archery, riflery, and trapshooting. Bring your own fishing gear, and the ranch will cook up your catch. You can also join complimentary van trips to Aspen. Parents and children age 8 and up can spend a day rafting the Arkansas River with a local outfitter, while younger kids and their counselors hang out at the hot springs pool in town; this excursion is included in the price of your ranch stay.

Elk Mountain Ranch, Box 910, Buena Vista, CO 81211, tel. 719/539–4430 or 800/432–8812, www.elkmtn.com. June–Sept.: 7 days, $1,135–$1,335 adults, $735–$935 children age 12 and under.

Hidden Creek Ranch

ALL

Adventure and ecological awareness go hand in hand at this ranch in the mountainous lake country of Idaho's panhandle. Iris Behr and John Muir, who opened Hidden Creek in 1993, envisioned a place where people could reconnect with nature (and with themselves) as well as ride horses. All products used at the ranch are natural, biodegradable, and packaged in recycled containers; none has been tested on animals. There are cabins (built of dead standing timber) with accommodations for 40, but you shouldn't think spartan just because the philosophy is harmony with nature. Food is exceptional, the children's program is extensive, and the "chocolate fairy" turns down your bed each night.

CHILDREN'S PROGRAM. From mid-June through August the ranch has a full program for children age 3 to teens, although it's entirely optional; families can spend as much of their day together as they wish. The youngest guests ride at the ranch under the supervision of counselors, while children 6 and up can join the regular trail rides. Other activities include hiking, fishing, crafts, nature studies, and picnics, and there's an emphasis on helping children approach nature in the harmonious ways of Native American cultures. Children have their own campfire, with Native American storytelling and an overnight in a tepee. Care for children under age 3 (extra charge) must be arranged in advance.

RIDING PROGRAM. "If you want to see what men have made, you can ride in a car. If you want to see what God has made, you have to ride on a horse." That's the philosophy of the Hidden Creek riding program, called Centered Riding, which is all about fostering a balanced, skilled, and harmonious partnership between human and horse. The staff refers to it as a sort of "Tai Chi" of horseback riding. Once out on the trails, you'll ride through forests, grassy meadows, and magnificent mountain settings. There are daily rides for all abilities; groups are small. No one's left out of the weekly specials either—these include everything from a walk-only dinner ride to a challenging fast ride for advanced equestrians. Children under age 6 stay at the ranch for riding, but families with children age 6 and up can ride the trails together. Families with riders 10 and older can also sign up for a two-night pack trip (extra charge).

BEYOND RIDING. Two programs travel far beyond traditional ranch activities: Body, Mind & Spirit WellBeing, a ranch-meets-spa itinerary, which includes yoga, stretching, relaxation training, scenic and fitness hikes, and massage; and the Earth Philosophy program, which evolved out of Native American traditions and places an emphasis on exploring ancient cultures. The former program includes time at the well-equipped fitness center, while the latter features a medicine-trail hike (on which you can learn about traditional medicinal plants), sweat lodge ceremonies, and Native American Living History Weeks. In summer, the adventure challenge program tests guests on a ropes course and a 58-ft climbing tower.

Additional ranch activities include trapshooting, riflery (extra charge for targets and ammunition), archery, mountain biking (guides, equipment, and instruction available), and fishing in the stocked pond—and when you're done, you can jump in the hot tubs day or night. Winter activities include snowshoeing, cross-country skiing, sleigh rides, murder mystery games, and snowmobiling (extra charge).

Hidden Creek Ranch, 7600 E. Blue Lake Rd., Harrison, ID 83833, tel. 208/689–3209, www.hiddencreek.com. May–Oct.: 6 days, $1,629–$1,969 adults, $1,615 children 3–11; Dec.–mid-Mar.: 4 days, $987 adults, $789 children 3–11. Children age 2 and under free. Ranch guests age 18 and older only May–mid-June and Sept.–Oct.

Lake Mancos Ranch

ALL

The Sehnerts, owners of Lake Mancos Ranch, believe that a lot of American families still want an old-fashioned vacation, without video games, cable TV, or bars. At Lake Mancos Ranch you can ride and relax in the heart of southwestern Colorado's authentic cowboy country. Up to 55 guests stay in cabins of various sizes; all have porches, two baths, and refrigerators. You can bring your own liquor for use in your cabin. This ranch is a good choice if at least one person in your family doesn't ride, as nonrider rates are available.

CHILDREN'S PROGRAM. Li'l Ropers is for children ages 4 and 5; Cowpokes is the 5 through 9 group; Buckaroos is for those 9 through 12; and teens are the Mavericks. Li'l Ropers have the opportunity to learn about horses while on the lead line at no extra charge. All other age groups spend time riding with their counselors if they opt to be in the riding program. The ranch also offers hiking, fishing, scavenger hunts, lawn games, hayrides, cookouts, camp-outs, and more. Teens have plenty of action of their own, including various sports and a jeep trip.

RIDING PROGRAM. Adults and children (usually ages 5 and up) who choose to participate in the program go out on the trails in supervised groups. Parents and children generally ride separately, but there are family rides three times a week. In this rugged terrain most rides are walk-trot only, but you won't be bored; each day you explore a different area, from the ranch lands to the adjacent San Juan National Forest. Instruction takes place primarily at the beginning of your stay and in a "non-intimidating" environment, but wranglers give pointers throughout the week. Adults can sometimes help work cattle, too.

BEYOND RIDING. Some favorite activities are guided hikes, mountain biking, gold panning, time in the pool, and guided four-wheel-drive trips up into the San Juan Mountains. Guests of all ages can fish because there's equipment even for children. You could also head off-property to ride on the Durango and Silverton Narrow Gauge Railroad or visit the famed ruins at Mesa Verde National Park, just 17 mi (27 km) from the ranch; you'll even get a box lunch to take along. Rafting is another option for families with children from about age 6 and up (at an extra charge).

Lake Mancos Ranch, 42688 County Rd. N, Mancos, CO 81328, tel. 970/533–1190 or 800/325–9462, lakemancosranch.com. June–Aug.: 7 days, $1,225–$1,350 adults, $850–$1,095 children under 18. Rates include gratuities. Adults only in Sept.

Lone Mountain Ranch

ALL

The Schaap family, which owns Lone Mountain, believes the enjoyment of nature is good for both the body and the mind. The ranch's location, high in the mountains at the northern end of the Greater Yellowstone ecosystem in Montana, provides abundant opportunity for nature discovery and learning for all ages. You have a choice of many activities and programs. Up to 70 people stay in cabins with fireplaces; ranch amenities include a massage therapist, who for an extra charge is ready to soothe sore muscles during your stay.

CHILDREN'S PROGRAM. Children ages 4 through 12 and teens participate in a variety of activities; there's no program for those under age 4, but the ranch has information on quality day care in Big Sky, and special rates are available if you bring your own nanny. The 4- and 5-year-olds are given pony rides by counselors; ages 6 and up go on their own wrangler-led rides. Activities can include nature discovery hikes, animal tracking, panning for gold, orienteering, mountain biking, climbing wall challenges, and camp-outs, depending on the age group. Parents can join their children for any or all of these activities. Teens also take adventure hikes and participate in other special activities.

RIDING PROGRAM. Adults and children ages 6 and up are assigned their own horse. Children can ride in the regular adult program rather than on children's rides if space allows. Half-day, all-day, and instructional rides are available for guests of every ability. First-time riders learn in the ring, building up skills and confidence before going out on the trail.

BEYOND RIDING. Lone Mountain has many programs for nonriders, including hiking and skiing (see Cross-Country Skiing and Snowshoeing). There's some fishing equipment and instruction for children, and Orvis-certified guides and instruction for adults; birding is popular, too. The ranch's friendly llamas will carry a picnic lunch while you and the children lead them on a day hike; you can also choose to relax in the hot tub. Guided tours of Yellowstone, best for families with children age 6 and up, are part of any weeklong stay. Extra-charge activities include naturalist-led canoe trips and, in nearby Big Sky, golf, tennis, gondola rides, rafting, and rock climbing. For more information on the ranch's winter activities, see Cross-Country Skiing.

Lone Mountain Ranch, Box 160069, Big Sky, MT 59716, tel. 406/995–4644 or 800/514–4644, www.lmranch.com. Year-round (riding available June–Oct.): 7 days, $2,150–$2,465 adults, $475–$1,285 children ages 3 to 5; children under 2 free.

North Fork Guest Ranch

ALL

A mere 50 mi (80½ km) from Denver and yet surrounded by the Mt. Evans Wilderness Area, North Fork is a ranch that encourages families to spend time together and to try a variety of activities as part of its regular program. Lodging is in log cabins, an impressive stone building, or the main lodge; capacity is about 45 guests. The North Fork of the South Platte River runs through the property. If your children are looking for animals to pet and feed, this is the place. There are calves, pygmy goats, bunnies, and chickens.

CHILDREN'S PROGRAM. Counselors care for infants and children up to about age 6; depending on age, children can try pony rides, hiking, fishing, swimming, crafts, nature studies, and camp-outs in a tepee. The program's main purpose is to provide fun for children too young to accompany parents on rides or on river rafting. The ranch has no supervised evening program or baby-sitting; nighttime activities are geared to the entire family.

RIDING PROGRAM. Wranglers give instruction throughout the week for those who want or need it, and each guest is assigned a horse for the entire stay. Rides for small groups, both loping and non loping, go through high alpine meadows or stands of aspen and ponderosa pine. Children age 6 and up can accompany parents on rides. Helmets are recommended but not provided.

BEYOND RIDING. North Fork is unusual because river rafting and an overnight pack trip are included in the regular weekly rate, so almost all guests participate. Parents with children under age 8 can still bring them along; counselors will take the children on a land-based excursion on their own while parents are on the river. The eight-hour ride up to the campsite is best for ages 12 and up, but younger children and other nonriders can travel to the campsite by vehicle and join their families. There's a weekly fly-fishing class (good for ages 10 and up), as well as hiking, trapshooting, and archery. The ranch has a heated pool and spa.

North Fork Guest Ranch, Box B, Shawnee, CO 80475, tel. 303/838–9873 or 800/843–7895, www.guestranches.com/northfork. May–Sept.: 7 days, $1,295–$1,495 adults, $500–$1,295 children ages 11 & under.

Paradise Guest Ranch

ALL

The ranch brand, FUN, is the first thing you'll see when you drive into Paradise. It's a promise owner Leah Anderson attempts to fulfill for all ages over the course of the weeklong stay. Beautifully renovated but authentically rustic log cabins provide families of all sizes with comfortable lodging and views of the surrounding valley in Wyoming's Big Horn Mountains. In July and August there are often 80 guests, many of them returnees who greet each other like long-lost friends. And then there's Reba, the ranch bloodhound, who greets everybody, period.

CHILDREN'S PROGRAM. Children ages 3 through 7 and those age 8 and up are grouped separately, and there are programs with hiking, fishing, crafts, and nature studies to occupy those under 7 and any older children who don't want to join the adult rides. A ranch nanny will watch children under the age of 3 in the mornings only; private baby-sitting can also be arranged (extra charge). Children have an overnight on the hill just above the ranch, and the teens have their own overnight pack trip.

RIDING PROGRAM. Children age 6 and up join their parents out on the trail. There are long, short, slow, and fast rides. Exceptional are the Learn to Lope rides high on the mesa. Paradise wranglers seem to be able to get almost everybody loping like pros before week's end. Good riders can learn team cattle penning and receive specialized instruction for a modest extra fee.

BEYOND RIDING. Guided and self-guided hikes, fishing instruction and guided trips for both children and adults (equipment provided), swimming, and a once-weekly town trip into Buffalo all provide a change from riding. So does the hot tub. Paradise breeds and raises mules, and learning about these intelligent, hardworking animals is surprisingly interesting. Parents have a weekly adults-only candlelight dinner while the youngsters are on their overnight, and the whole family will be intrigued by the legend of Butch Cassidy on a visit to his famous "Hole-in-the-Wall" hideout, not far from Paradise. For an extra charge adults can arrange a pack fishing trip.

Paradise Guest Ranch, Box 790, Buffalo, WY 82834, tel. 307/684–7876, www.paradiseranch.com. May–Sept.: 7 days, $1,100–$1,650 adults, $300–$1,550 children ages 12 & under. Ask about family discounts June and Aug.–Sept.

Rainbow Trout Ranch

ALL

Located in southwestern Colorado in the rugged and remote Conejos River valley, Rainbow Trout is 185 mi (290 km) from Colorado Springs and just 80 (129 km) mi from Taos, New Mexico. The centerpiece of the ranch is the 13,000-square-ft main lodge, built in the 1920s without, it is said, a single nail. Cabins are a short distance from the lodge and have a variety of floor plans, though all have porches. This ranch is a family haven where 60 guests of all ages are warmly welcomed and cared for.

CHILDREN'S PROGRAM. There are three groups: ages 3 through 5, 6 through 11, and 12 and up. Children age 6 and up have a full riding program with instruction both in the arena and on the trail. Children ages 3 through 5 are led by counselors in the arena and around the ranch. When not on horses, youngsters here are hiking, fishing, swimming, and exploring the natural surroundings. The teen program is very flexible, but hikes, basketball, and fishing are all likely activities in addition to riding.

RIDING PROGRAM. Small groups, divided by ability, go on a variety of rides: slow, fast, long, short, leisurely, and scenic. Adults can join the children for games and lessons in the arena if they wish, and if families want to ride together, the ranch will arrange it.

BEYOND RIDING. Once a private fishing retreat for wealthy businessmen, Rainbow Trout has, as its name suggests, exceptional fishing. Lessons are given for beginners in fly-fishing, and supplies can be purchased at the ranch. Get your license (mandatory for ages 15 and up) before arriving. The ranch also has a heated pool and hot tub. You can take guided hikes or use trail maps to plan your own. Families can raft on the Rio Grande (extra charge), combining that adventure with a tour of Taos (about 1½ hours away); rafting is for children age 6 or so and up. One of the thrills for most families is a chance to ride the Cumbres & Toltec Scenic Railroad (extra charge), "America's longest and highest narrow gauge." Ask the ranch how to go about arranging these excursions; it may be best to make reservations before you arrive.

Rainbow Trout Ranch, Box 458, 1484 FDR 250, Antonito, CO 81120, tel. 719/376–2440 or 800/633–3397, www.rainbowtroutranch.com. Late May–late Sept.: 7 days, $1,200–$1,400 adults, $150–$1,200 children 11 and under. Ask about children's discounts and minimum 2-day stays in May and Sept.

Red Rock Ranch

6+

Here's a small horse ranch in Wyoming that loves families. "Children are an important part of Red Rock. It wouldn't be the same without them," states the brochure, and the programs and facilities for children are indeed extensive. Set in a high valley of Jackson Hole's mountain country, the ranch gets its name from the imposing red-rock formations in the area. Lodging is in authentic log cabins that accommodate no more than 30 guests in any given week.

CHILDREN'S PROGRAM. There are no activities or baby-sitting services for children younger than age 6. Children age 6 and up go on daily rides with wranglers. Along the way they might look for fossils, stop to wade in a crystal-clear mountain creek, or search for wildlife. There's also a weekly overnight. Parents can ride with their children on kids' rides, but only children age 13 and up join adult rides. Children eat dinner with their wranglers three times a week.

RIDING PROGRAM. Part of Red Rock's operation is the raising and care of fine horses. The staff know the horses well, which makes matching guests with the right mount that much easier. The ranch has morning and afternoon rides for all abilities, as well as all-day lunch rides on which you might see antelope, moose, coyotes, and other native wildlife. The high mountain trails yield views of the Teton, Wind River, and Absaroka ranges.

BEYOND RIDING. Fishing, hiking, swimming in the heated pool, and relaxing in the hot tub are ranch favorites. Slopping the pigs (when these animals are in residence) is a favorite among younger children. Almost everyone likes to visit Jackson for shopping or for the local rodeo and "shoot-out." The National Elk Refuge, just north of town, is well worth the visit, as is the Wildlife of the American West Art Museum.

Red Rock Ranch, Box 38, Kelly, WY 83011, tel. 307/733–6288, www.theredrockranch.com. June–Sept.: 6 days, $1,584.90.

Seven D Ranch

ALL

The Seven D Ranch is 50 mi (80½ km) northwest of Cody, Wyoming, in the Sunlight Basin, surrounded by the Absaroka Mountains and the Shoshone National Forest. Taking only 32 guests at a time, the ranch has log cabins set in a tranquil aspen grove with a crystal-clear creek meandering nearby. Few places are as peaceful as this, and few offer more for families. There are conveniences for parents with infants—cribs, babysitting, free laundry facilities, and microwaves—and a superb children's program that focuses on environmental education and western history as well as riding.

CHILDREN'S PROGRAM. For infants and children up to age 6, there's baby-sitting at no charge during the adult rides. Younger children will have a chance to experience lead-line rides in the corral. Children ages 6 through 12 participate in an extensive program that includes environmental education, hiking, woodsmanship, and cave exploration. This group also learns about ranch life and the natural history of the area. There are opportunities for riding and riding instruction every day except Sunday.

RIDING PROGRAM. Each guest age 6 or older is assigned a horse; children ride with counselors. Instruction is available for all ages and levels. There are morning, afternoon, and all-day rides on trails with names as lovely as the Little Sunlight Trail or as evocative as the Oh My God Trail (named by a guest). Multiday pack trips for good riders are possible with advance notice; there's an extra charge for these.

BEYOND RIDING. You can try world-class fly-fishing on Sunlight Creek (clinics provided), hiking, backpacking, and trapshooting at the ranch. Off-property excursions vary;

you could visit the Cody Rodeo and the Buffalo Bill Historical Center in Cody, which includes the Whitney Gallery of Western Art, the Plains Indian Museum, and the Cody Firearms Museum. Most guests choose to spend all their time in the relaxing atmosphere at the ranch, but day trips to Yellowstone and the Beartooths are sometimes arranged. In the evening, everyone joins in square dancing and sing-alongs, among other activities.

Seven D Ranch, Box 100, Cody, WY 82414, tel. 307/587–9885, www.7dranch.com. June–Aug.: 7 days, $1,390– $1,560, 15% discount for children 1–12, children under 1 free.

Sky Corral

ALL

At Sky Corral the emphasis is on family activities and a flexible, low-key schedule. The ranch, which accommodates 32 guests, is 23 mi (37 km) from Fort Collins, Colorado, in the Roosevelt National Forest, and a short drive from Rocky Mountain National Park. The main lodge has several rooms; families can also choose rustic cabins, some of which have woodstoves or fireplaces.

CHILDREN'S PROGRAM. Since Justin and Karen O'Connor bought the ranch a few years back, they added a full-time children's program for ages 3 to 12. Youngsters are divided into groups of ages 3 to 6 and 7 to 12. Although children always have the option of being with their parents, they can also elect to join the rides, crafts, hikes, bonfires, and assorted adventures that the counselors have going each day. Guests under age 7 can't ride on the trail, but they can join counselors on rides around the ranch.

RIDING PROGRAM. Families ride together and separately, and each guest age 7 and up is assigned a horse for the week. Groups are small, just six guests and a wrangler for trail rides that wind through the Roosevelt National Forest and high into the mountains with views of the Continental Divide. An overnight camp trip is included in your stay.

BEYOND RIDING. The ranch has hiking, fishing in its own stocked lake, volleyball, and tennis. Amenities include a heated pool, sauna, gym, and hot tub. Raft trips are part of the package from June to August for everyone ages 7 and up. And regardless of age, the petting zoo is a popular spot.

Sky Corral, 8233 Old Flowers Rd., Bellvue, CO 80512, tel. 970/484–1362, www.skycorral.com. May–Oct.: 6 days, $1,525 adults, $1,150 children 7 to 12, $900 children 3 to 5; $150 children 2 to 3. Daily rates May, Sept.–Oct., $210 adults, $150 children 7 to 12, $100 children 3 to 6; $75 children 2 to 3. Children under age 2 free.

Skyline Guest Ranch

ALL

Skyline, in the increasingly popular vacation town of Telluride in southwestern Colorado, is extraordinarily beautiful, with views of 14,000-ft snowcapped peaks. Owners Dave and Sherry Farny formerly ran the Telluride Mountaineering School, so it's not surprising that Skyline has all kinds of outdoor activities, including guided climbing and mountain biking. You stay in lodge rooms or cabins. Only 35 guests visit at a time, so there's both an intimacy and a wonderful sense of comfort at Skyline.

CHILDREN'S PROGRAM. Many activities at the ranch are designed for children and parents together. Children age 6 and up learn not only riding but horse care, tack, anatomy, and other aspects of general horsemanship. Although the ranch welcomes all ages, most activities are best for those age 6 and older. However, at the nearby all-day Summer Adventure program run by Telluride Ski & Golf Company, children ages 3 to 12 hike, bike, and explore surrounding peaks and valleys on 4x4 tours. Note that the Adventure program costs extra but is arranged by the ranch. Baby-sitting is available at the ranch for children under age 3 (extra charge), but this should be arranged well in advance.

RIDING PROGRAM. "Natural horsemanship" is the focus and philosophy of the riding program here. The idea is to help humans forge a relationship with their horse for the week—a relationship based on respect and honor—with the result that even new riders will feel comfortable and safe around horses. Guests are invited to groom, saddle, and feed their horse throughout the week. Half- or all-day rides are offered, and an overnight pack trip is part of a week's stay. All ages can participate.

BEYOND RIDING. The ranch has a midweek trip to Mesa Verde National Park, about a 1½-hour drive away. You can also take guided and self-guided hikes to a mining town, wildflower fields, and a hot springs, among other areas. You can climb a San Juan peak—including 14,017-ft Wilson Peak—with an experienced guide, but most climbs are for adults and older children who have some hiking experience. Skyline also has guided fishing trips and fishing instruction; equipment is available. Mountain bikes are available at the ranch, and guided bike rides are offered. For an extra charge, experienced riders can join spring and fall pack trips. In winter there's cross-country skiing at the ranch (equipment available for those wearing a size 5 shoe or larger) and transportation to the Telluride ski area, 5 mi (8 km) away, for downhillers. Horse-drawn sleigh rides are offered, but no horseback riding.

Skyline Guest Ranch, 7214 Hwy. 145, Telluride, CO 81435, tel. 970/728–3757 or 888/754–1126, www.guestranches.com/skyline. June–mid-Oct. and mid-Dec.–Apr.: 7 days (summer only; ask about daily rates in winter), $1,800 adults; 50% discount for children 3–5, children under 3 free.

Vista Verde Ranch

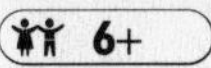

Vista Verde is about 25 mi (40 km) north of Steamboat Springs, Colorado, near the Wyoming border. The ranch's log cabins and lodge rooms can accommodate about 40 guests in summer, 24 in winter. Accommodations are furnished with antiques and western art, and each cabin has its own hot tub and wood-burning stove. There's also a spa building with workout facilities, although whether or not your horse will be impressed is another matter altogether.

CHILDREN'S PROGRAM. Ages 6 to 12 and teens have separate programs. For the younger group it's a nice mix of time away from parents and family time. Kids hang out at the Coyote Corral, and teens, who may think it not so cool to hang with parents, have their own rides, fishing trips, and overnights.

RIDING PROGRAM. There are a variety of rides and trails to choose from each day, and instruction is available for those who want or need it, whether you're a beginner or an experienced rider hoping to brush up on skills. Vista Verde also has its own "Horse Whisperer" who gives clinics in the arena one day each week. They say he's not as good looking as Robert Redford (so few are), but they guarantee he knows a whole lot more about horses and horsemanship. Some of the trails through the 1.4 million acre Routt National Forest adjacent to the ranch were used by old-time wranglers and outlaws, including Butch Cassidy. A favorite with guests is Hole in the Wall Canyon, where Butch and company eluded the law. Guides will be happy to tell you all about life back in the day.

BEYOND RIDING. Head into Steamboat to see the rodeo. Back at the ranch, there's mountain biking, hiking, fishing, rafting (the

Colorado River trip is the best bet for families), kayaking on the Yampa River, rock climbing, or just relaxing in your hot tub looking out over a stunning landscape. You won't be lacking for things to do, but this is a place that encourages relaxing and rejuvenating, too. In winter, Vista Verde is a place to ski (among the options are backcountry treks), snowshoe, and enjoy cozy sleigh rides. *Vista Verde Ranch, Box 465, Steamboat Springs, CO 80477, tel. 970/879–3858 or 800/526–7433, www.vistaverde.com. Jan.–Oct., Dec.–Mar., Sept.: 7 days (5 in winter), $1,100–$2,200 adults, $700–$1,700 children ages 11 & under.*

WEST COAST

Coffee Creek Ranch

ALL

Coffee Creek is a river-canyon ranch on the edge of the Trinity Alps Wilderness area in California. This is the perfect ranch for families with nonriders, as you only pay for the amount of riding you really want to do. Wildflowers and wildlife abound, and all cabins have porches and wood-burning or potbelly stoves. The ranch accommodates up to 50 guests.

CHILDREN'S PROGRAM. Cowboys and Cowgirls are children ages 3 to 7; Junior Wranglers ages 8 to 12; and Bronc Busters are ages 13 to 17. Although counselors don't take children riding, there's plenty to do. Depending on their age, children have pony rides, care for baby animals, pan for gold, take roping lessons, learn orienteering, and fish. Each child takes home at least two finished projects from the excellent creative arts program. There are also skits, lawn games, swimming, archery, and riflery. The youngest guests go in the wading pool; the older children swim, slide, and jump in Coffee Creek. During trail-ride hours, care is provided for children under age 3 in the Kiddie Korral.

RIDING PROGRAM. The ranch breeds its own thoroughbreds and Appaloosas, so wranglers know every horse very well. The twice-daily rides are grouped by ability, not age. Kids as young as age 6 can go on some trails, and there are all-day, breakfast, and picnic rides. Coffee Creek has separate daily and weekly ride fees; an overnight pack trip is included in the weekly cost. Private lessons are also available (extra charge); however, ages 6 to 11 get one free half-hour lesson at the beginning of each week. The international staff, part of a cultural exchange program, includes ranglers from Australia and New Zealand, who give you a feel for cowboy life in another hemisphere. For an extra charge families can arrange multiday wilderness pack trips.

BEYOND RIDING. Possibilities include visiting the health club, swimming in the heated pool or in the creek, canoeing on the pond, taking guided hikes, fishing (equipment provided for children only), mountain biking, panning for gold, lawn games, archery, and riflery or trapshooting. In winter you can try cross-country skiing, tubing, snowshoeing, sleigh riding, ice fishing, and dogsledding. *Coffee Creek Ranch, HC 2, Box 4940, Trinity Center, CA 96091, tel. 530/266–3343 or 800/624–4480, www.coffeecreekranch.com. Year-round: 7 days, $819.50–$960 adults, $300–$944 children 17 and under. Riding is $30 for regular ride, $40 for all-day outing, or $300 for wk.*

Rankin Ranch

ALL

The Rankin family has been ranching in California since 1863, and their 31,000-acre spread in the Tehachapi Mountains, northeast of Bakersfield, has an old-fashioned, down-home atmosphere, from the cozy duplex cabins to the baby calves the children love to feed. The ranch is casual and western, but there are elegant touches for its 30 to 45 guests: linen tablecloths, candles, and fresh flowers on the dining room tables. Family reunions are popular here—you can book all 14 rooms—and the Rankins are proud of the fact that their ranch is a welcoming place for single women and for grandparents.

CHILDREN'S PROGRAM. The program is for children age 4 and up, but baby-sitting for younger children can be arranged in advance for an extra charge. Children ages 4 through 11 join counselors for swim meets, picnics, games, and guided nature hikes, as well as a terrific crafts program. Children eat breakfast and lunch with their families; at dinner children sit at a special table with their counselors, or they can join their parents if they like.

RIDING PROGRAM. You can sign up for one-hour morning and afternoon rides, which are mostly at a walk because of the terrain. A few wide-open meadows provide opportunities for advanced riders to canter and gallop. Because this is a working ranch, you can sometimes help wranglers with chores, such as moving cattle. Children under age 12 do not go on adult rides, but parents are welcome to sign up for the children's rides. There are special teen rides when enough of that age group is present, and there are two rides daily (one on Sunday) for youngsters age 6 and up.

BEYOND RIDING. You use your own equipment for fishing and tennis; archery and hiking are other options. If you bring your own bikes, you'll find plenty of paved and dirt roads on which to discover some exquisite scenery. One of the most popular activities is simply relaxing around the pool. Families with young children also love the petting farm with its baby calves, sheep, pigs, and chickens. In spring, parents and children can sign up for the full-week art workshops, with classes in drawing and watercolor. These are included in the daily rate during this time period.

Rankin Ranch, Box 36, Caliente, CA 93518, tel. 661/867–2511, www.rankinranch.com. Week before Easter Sun.–Oct.: $80–$170 per day adults, $40–$170 children.

Rock Springs

ALL

Rock Springs sits just outside Bend, Oregon, in the foothills of the Cascade Range. About 50 guests visit at a time, staying in cabins with knotty-pine interiors and sundecks. "Family tradition is revered at Rock Springs," says owner John Gill, and there's no question that families are important here. Every detail has been thought of, down to the cookies, fresh fruit, and beverages that are always in the lodge so guests of all ages can help themselves between meals.

CHILDREN'S PROGRAM. Divided into groups for children ages 3 through 5 and 6 through 12, the program is available between 9 in the morning and 8:30 in the evening. Children can spend as much or as little time with counselors as they wish. In this very child-directed program, youngsters decide together what activities they would like throughout the week. Choices include riding, outdoor games, nature walks, swimming, sports, arts and crafts, an overnight, folklore, and storytelling. There are also a playground area and playhouse. Families eat breakfast together, but children generally eat lunch and dinner in their own dining room adjacent to the adult dining area.

RIDING PROGRAM. Twice-daily rides go out with no more than six people, grouped by age, ability, and interests. Children ages 6 and up can join some trail rides with parents or go in groups with their counselors; younger children are helped on a lead line around the barn area. There's an all-day lunch ride, and riding instruction is available if staffing permits.

BEYOND RIDING. The ranch has a heated swimming pool and a boot-shape hot tub. There are two lighted tennis courts; you can ask about its special tennis weeks with free clinics by well-known coaches. Fly-fishing guides can be hired for trips off ranch property. For an extra charge families with children ages 6 and up can try white-water rafting on the Deschutes River, 15 mi (24 km) from the ranch; families preferring calm water can canoe in a clear mountain lake. The ranch provides transportation for both adventures. There are also plenty of opportunities for day trips to nearby museums, including the High Desert Museum and Warm Springs Native People's Museum. The caves at Lava Lands State Park are another popular area attraction, as is the lift ride up Mt. Bachelor for views of the Cascades, Three Sisters, and Newberry Crater.

Rock Springs, 64201 Tyler Rd., Bend, OR 97701, tel. 541/382–1957 or 800/225–3833, www.guestranches.com/rocksprings. Late June–late Aug.: 7 days, $1,875–$2,200 adults, $1,350 children ages 6 to 16, $1,080 children ages 3 to 5; ask about special rates for infants and nannies.

Resources

Organizations

The **Dude Ranchers' Association** (Box 471, LaPorte, CO 80535, tel. 970/223–8440) has more than 100 members in western states. An excellent magazine with all kinds of information about ranches and ranch stays is available from this group. The **Colorado Dude and Guest Ranch Association** (Box 300, Tabernash, CO 80478, tel. 970/887–3128) and the **Wyoming Dude Rancher's Association** (Box 618, Dubois, WY 82513, tel. 307/455–2584) send out material about ranches.

Some tour operators or specialty travel advisers can make reservations for you at ranches as well as provide information that will help you choose a ranch. **American Wilderness Experience/GORP Travel** (2820A Wilderness Pl., Boulder, CO 80301, tel. 303/444–2622 or 800/444–3833) books vacations at ranches throughout the West and Southwest. **Off the Beaten Path** (27 E. Main St., Bozeman, MT 59715, tel. 406/586–1311 or 800/445–2995) specializes in custom western adventures and works with dozens of ranches. **Rascals in Paradise** (650 5th St., Suite 505, San Francisco, CA 94107, tel. 415/978–9800 or 800/872–7225) has organized a couple of different family weeks at ranches and has a stellar reputation as a family travel resource. **Pat Dickerman's Adventure Guides** (7550 E. McDonald Dr., Scottsdale, AZ 85250, tel. 602/596–0226 or 800/252–7899) can help you match your family to the right ranch.

Books

Gene Kilgore's *Ranch Vacations* (John Muir Publications; revised 1999) is an outstanding resource that covers almost every ranch in the United States and Canada. Although there is only limited information about children's programs, the guide states clearly which ranches have children's programs and whether families are welcomed at those that don't have formal programs.

Also See

Cross-Country Skiing lists a number of ranches that have facilities for skiing.

ROCK CLIMBING

Not long ago, the words "rock climbing" were not part of the vocabulary of most Americans and were certainly not related to anything families might do together on a vacation. That's all changed. Today 5-, 6-, and 7-year-olds scramble up indoor climbing walls from Connecticut to California and every place in between. Parents are stepping into harnesses, too, joining their children in a sport that is challenging, exhilarating, and a self-esteem builder of the first order.

Rock climbing has become a relatively safe sport as equipment and technique have improved over the years. Generally you climb—in a harness attached to safety ropes—from the ground up a rock face, finding hand- and footholds as you go. After reaching the top (or however far you choose to climb) you descend, using your feet against the rocks to help you down. Those passionate about the sport think of it as a kind of natural puzzle, one that stimulates the mind as well as the body. There seems to be no single profile that fits the average rock climber. Although good physical condition is a must, you and your children of all ages might be surprised to find that working your way up a hunk of granite out in beautiful country does more for your soul than you believed possible. Happily, a variety of opportunities exists to discover the rock climber in you.

Many indoor climbing schools schedule weekend or even weeklong courses in addition to their daily classes. Several of the top outdoor schools in the country have integrated rock climbing into their programs. Both types of courses are excellent choices for families just beginning the sport, as well as for those who really want to have fun with it as a recreational pastime. America's premier alpine climbing schools, on the other hand, are for people who want to be serious climbers. Guide-training and intensive mountaineering courses are the core of what these schools offer. If you and your family want to work toward self-guided trips in the backcountry, a dedicated mountaineering and climbing school would be the best choice.

Courses vary in terms of how long you spend on the ground and how long on the rocks; from four to six hours of actual climbing is typical on the first day, with six or seven possible on days two and three. Climbs of 50 ft are typical of beginner routes. You will probably be paired with a partner, and you will take turns climbing and belaying (handling the safety ropes of the other climber) throughout the course. Children 12 and over can usually learn to belay, too. Climbers younger than that are too small and not technically skilled enough to handle belaying.

Questions to Ask

Is there child-size equipment, including helmets and harnesses, that can be adjusted to fit a child properly? For safety it's imperative that helmets and harnesses fit correctly. Although climbing shoes aren't mandatory in some courses, they do provide better traction than tennis shoes and will certainly make a difference at the intermediate level. Some instructors believe these shoes make a difference for beginners, too. If rock shoes are not supplied, ask about a rental source near the school or even consider buying them.

What is your teaching accreditation or certification, and how many years' experience do you have? American Mountain Guides Association (AMGA) is the U.S. organization that accredits schools and guide services and certifies individual guides. In Europe, Canada, and a number of other countries, an international union of mountain guides grants such accreditations and certifications. Accreditation means a school has met certain educational standards and uses approved teaching methods. Instructors must keep up on the latest technology and safety issues and participate in a peer review process. Look for schools accredited by AMGA, not just members of it; an organization can pay to be a member but does not have to meet standards or be subjected to peer review. Individual guides certified by AMGA have passed rigorous exams and technical tests. These critical guidelines can indicate that someone is a good climber, but they don't tell if he or she is a good teacher. Always ask how long a guide or instructor has been climbing, then ask specifically about his or her experience with family teaching. Even on the phone you can get a feel for whether a school or a guide will be accepting and welcoming.

What is the ratio of students to instructors? Three students to one teacher is an excellent ratio, though in some beginner classes a slightly higher ratio is acceptable because only one or two students will climb at a time.

What kind of emergency training do you and your staff have? You need someone trained in basic first aid and rock rescue, at a minimum. Although rock climbing has become a safer sport, it's best to climb with someone trained to help on the spot. Moreover, if someone in your group gets halfway up the rock face and can't make it down, you want a teacher who can help that person descend.

What happens if my children or I panic halfway up a rock? The truth is, both children and adults may be certain they can complete a climb until they actually get stuck. You don't want an instructor who uses teasing or belittling ("My 5-year-old niece can do this climb" or "Crying is what babies do") to get frightened climbers to continue. Compassion, encouragement, and positive reinforcement are the skills good teachers use, and no student should be made to feel bad for making it only halfway up. There's always a next time.

If my children are too young for regular courses, is private instruction an option? Regular rock-climbing courses, like those for kayaking and some other sports, are often designated for teens and older. Most schools, however, do give private instructional trips for families with children as young as 6.

At what age can my child climb in a course without me? You may be a more advanced climber, or you may feel that your child learns better with peers; you may even think your child will have more success with instruction if you aren't there. That's okay. Some schools have courses just for children, or they'll take children in courses without parents as long as parents give permission and can be reached if necessary. You can take your own class and be with your children after your climbs. If this kind of setup seems best for your family, find a school that will accommodate you.

If lodging isn't provided, do you have a list of options or will you help with booking? Many multiday courses are in wonderful camping areas, and the prices for these sessions generally, but not always, include camping. Other courses take place near inns or motels; a number of areas even have special climbers' inns, with dorm-style lodging. Some climbing outfitters will help with lodging and book rooms for you; others may just give you a list and let you make reservations.

What's included in the cost? The prices for courses include guides, instruction, and technical climbing gear, such as harnesses and ropes, unless otherwise noted. Some outfitters supply helmets as part of the gear; others require you rent them. Rock-climbing shoes are available for rent from outfitters or from a local store recommended by the outfitter; a few outfitters, as noted, include shoes in the course price. Many, but not all, schools and guides provide local transportation to climbing sites. Most will also give clients information on local lodging, but lodging is not included, except as noted. Lunch is sometimes supplied, but more often you must bring your own, even if you are camping. With such a wide range of possibilities, it's a good idea to ask about specifics.

Instruction

Rock climbing is not a sport you can teach yourself; instruction is an absolute must. All the courses and trips are instructional, whether they take place on the grounds of the school or on some of the most famous rock faces in the country.

A Note About Ages

The minimum age listed first is for regularly scheduled outdoor courses. When two ages are given, the second is for private or indoor classes, depending on the school. Younger children are often accepted for private instruction, but few schools are willing to pinpoint a specific age. Read the complete listings for details. Most schools make the decision on a case-by-case basis, taking into consideration a child's previous climbing experience, athletic ability, familiarity with the wilderness, enthusiasm for the sport, and the parents' own attitudes and abilities.

Finding the Fun

Northeast: Adirondack Rock & River Guide Service, Appalachian Mountain Club, Eastern Mountain Sports Climbing School, Zoar Outdoor. **Mid-Atlantic:** Appalachian Mountain Club. **South:** Outward Bound. **Midwest:** Sylvan Rocks Climbing School & Guide Service. **Southwest:** Eastern Mountain Sports Climbing School. **Rockies:** Colorado Mountain School, Eastern Mountain Sports Climbing School, Exum Mountain Guides, Sylvan Rocks Climbing School & Guide Service. **West Coast:** Alpine Skills International, American Alpine Institute, Eastern Mountain Sports Climbing School, Joshua Tree Rock Climbing School, Outward Bound. **Canada:** American Alpine Institute, Yamnuska, Inc. **South America:** Eastern Mountain Sports Climbing School.

Favorite Schools and Outfitters

Adirondack Rock & River Guide Service

14+, 6+

Rock & River, whose core curriculum is climbing, has an unsurpassed setting—the 6-million-acre Adirondack Park, birthplace of the mighty Hudson River and depository of some of the oldest rocks known to humanity. The park, which encompasses nearly two-thirds of upstate New York, is a geologist's and rock climber's dreamscape.

FOR FAMILIES. Adults and teens age 14 and up can take two-day courses in beginning and novice rock climbing. The student–teacher ratio is four to one in the beginner course, two to one in the novice. Low-key and no pressure are the operative descriptions of these courses. There's a 30-ft indoor wall at the school's facility, so courses run rain or shine; the introductory courses begin here. Children age 6 and up can be accommodated in private classes, and the school highly recommends these for families. You can also combine excellent one- to five-day adventures in remote regions of Adirondack State Park, including private guiding and instruction.

This school has its own reasonably priced lodging, ranging from a streamside lean-to to lodge rooms with private baths. Lunch is included in courses.

Adirondack Rock & River Guide Service, Box 219, Keene, NY 12942, tel. 518/576–2041, www.rockandriver.com. Apr.–Oct.: 1–5 days, $165–$395 per person in basic courses, $180–$740 for parent–child teams privately guided, $40 per day each additional child. Group rates available for families of 4 or more.

Alpine Skills International

12+

Based high in California's Sierra Nevada, surrounded by Tahoe National Forest, Alpine Skills International (ASI) has been teaching mountaineering and backcountry skills for more than 20 years. The training center and headquarters is at Donner Pass, near Donner Memorial State Park, which commemorates the infamous Donner Party stranded there by blizzards in 1846. Those who survived resorted to cannibalism to do so.

FOR FAMILIES. ASI has a number of possibilities for families. Klimbing Kids Rockskills, a class for ages 12 through 17, is scheduled several times each summer. Its dates coincide with the Rockskills Seminar, a five-day course that accommodates beginning and experienced climbers, who learn or refine their techniques.

ASI will take families with children 12 and up in other courses as well. Talk with the directors about your youngsters first, however, and let them help you choose the right course and time. The most basic course offers two days of learning skills and practicing on routes that present a variety of challenges. Once you are confident about basic belaying, rappelling (a method of descending), and movement, try the Next Move, the two-day intermediate course. The student–teacher ratio ranges from two to one to eight to one, depending on the course.

Alpine Skills International, Box 8, Norden, CA 95724, tel. 530/426–9108 or 888/274–7325, www.alpineskills.com. June–Sept.: 2–5 days, $144–$578.

American Alpine Institute

17+

The American Alpine Institute in northern Washington has access to excellent climbing sites in both the United States and Canada. This very technical school is for people who have a serious interest in climbing, especially those who are learning rock climbing as a foundation for other alpine skills, such as ice climbing, climbing with crampons, and ascending world-class peaks. But the school is also appropriate for some beginners. "If a skill is learned the correct and safe way the first time, it needs to be learned only once," the institute's brochure notes, and the school aims to help students do exactly that.

FOR FAMILIES. Regular courses are for people ages 17 and up. You can take the two-day Introduction to Rock or more advanced courses at locations in the Cascades, Canada, California, or the French Alps. Camping and lodging are available in most areas; the school will give you suggestions.

The Cascades are best known for their volcanoes (Mount St. Helens is probably the most famous), but these mountains are geographically and ecologically diverse. Two favorite areas for Intro to Rock are Leavenworth, on the warm and sunny east side of the Cascades, and Index, cooler and shadier because of its west-side location; both have fine-grained granite and a range of climbs. Because the region has excellent crags for both beginners and experts, it makes a particularly good destination for families whose members have varying experience and skills.

An hour north of Vancouver, British Columbia, and 90 mi (145 km) above Bellingham, Washington, Howe Sound cuts into the Canadian coast to create a fjord almost 30 mi (48 km) long. At its head is the logging town of Squamish and its striking white-granite walls. Mountain bikers, sailboarders, and rock climbers come here, but it's still far from any crowds. Whether you're a beginner or an expert, you'll find a pitch and a climb here. Beginners can spend days on the Smoke Bluffs perfecting the one-pitch climb. Climbers who are ready for multipitch (rock faces with a variety of angles) and steep ascents can tackle the Apron, with more than 50 separate routes, or perhaps the Chief, a 2,000-ft wall of near-vertical granite.

Beginner courses have a maximum four to one student–teacher ratio, intermediates a maximum three to one. On guided climbs the ratio can range from one on one to five students per guide. The price changes accordingly. If parents and children choose private guiding, the institute will consider climbers under 17; however, previous backpacking experience and a demonstrated willingness to work well with adults are musts. Talk with the staff about your child's skills, physical ability, and experience.

American Alpine Institute, 1515 12th St., Bellingham, WA 98225, tel. 360/671–1570, www.aai.cc. Mid-Apr.–Oct.: 1–5 days, $260–$1,250, depending on length and level of course and ratio of students to teacher. Private instruction and guiding cost $145–$295 per day, depending on student–teacher guide ratio.

Appalachian Mountain Club

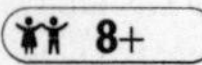

The Appalachian Mountain Club (AMC) has climbing courses at its outdoor centers in New Hampshire's White Mountains, New York's Catskills, and in the Delaware Water Gap National Recreation Area on the New Jersey–Pennsylvania border. White Mountains workshops take place in some 700,000 acres of national forest, with the Presidential Range as a backdrop. The instructor at the Catskills location is licensed by the state and teaches for Outward Bound as well. Families choosing workshops in the Delaware Water Gap Recreation Area in the Pocono Mountains use the Mohican Outdoor Center as a base. All areas have many recreational activities for all ages.

FOR FAMILIES. In July and August, families can join Introduction to Rock Climbing in the White Mountains, famous for their Cathedral Ledge and White Horse cliffs. This two-day course is designed for beginners and those with little previous experience. You'll learn the technical aspects of climbing and bouldering (moving without a harness on rocks), including rappelling, tying harness and rope knots, and belaying. The price of the class covers two nights' lodging and meals. The club's lodge at Pinkham Notch Visitor Center accommodates more than 100 overnight guests in two-, three-, or four-bunk rooms. Pillows, linens, and towels are provided; you share bathrooms and hot shower facilities. The hearty meals are served family style, and you can buy trail lunches to take to your class.

Two-day beginner courses run in June and August at AMC's Catskill center. This is a real fundamentals course with orientation to equipment, knot tying, rope handling, top rope set-up, belaying, and more. All equipment is supplied, and the course fee includes two nights' accommodations at the Full Moon Lodge, as well as most meals.

A Weekend on Rock is scheduled in June, July, August, and September at the Delaware Water Gap center. The course focuses on such basic skills as equipment inspection, belaying, and rappelling. Lodging in rustic cabins and a stick-to-your-ribs dinner on Saturday night are included in the price. Cabins have bunk rooms that sleep four to 10 people. Pillows are provided, but you have to bring other bedding and towels. Note: Regardless of the course location, however, you should notify AMC in advance that children will be taking the class.

Appalachian Mountain Club, Box 298, Gorham, NH 03581, tel. 603/466–2727 for White Mountain courses or 908/362–5670 for Delaware Water Gap course, www.outdoors.org. May–Sept.: 2 days, $328–$365.

Colorado Mountain School

14+, 4+

The only guide service licensed to operate in Rocky Mountain National Park, Colorado Mountain School (CMS) has a personal, flexible approach to teaching. CMS has partnered with REI's Outdoor School for some of its courses, primarily the half- and one-day options, and together they have a wide range of possibilities in both rock climbing and mountaineering. There are also courses in ice and lead climbing and more advanced skills.

Rocky Mountain National Park, with its high meadows and wildflowers set against Colorado's snowy peaks and deep blue skies, is an adventuring family's playground. Besides climbing here—where some of the world's great alpine climbers test themselves on such classics as Longs Peak—you can hike on more than 355 mi (539 km) of trails, attend ranger talks, ride, and fish. Camping is good, too; there are five public campgrounds in the park and numerous private ones just outside it. Your family might also take a drive on Trail Ridge Road, which at 12,183 ft is the highest continuously paved road in the United States. CMS also has summer options in Boulder and Eldorado canyons, and winter climbs in Arizona and Utah (booked at private guiding rates).

FOR FAMILIES. Children ages 14 and up can join regular classes. Your family can be your group, or you can ask to join another family with children of compatible ages (there are no guarantees, but the school will try). CMS takes a learn-by-doing approach, so plan on plenty of climbing even in beginner courses. The best bets for families are the one- or two-day intro courses, which give you information and then let you practice and reinforce what you've learned. If you know rock climbing is for you, jump right into the five-or seven-day course. At the end of it you'll be climbing rocks other people can only dream about. The six-day basic mountaineering course is for beginners and intermediates, and rock-climbing is one of several important skills taught. CMS has worked with children as young as 4 in private instruction; if you have very young children, ask what they recommend.

Colorado Mountain School, Box 1846, Estes Park, CO 80517, tel. 970/586–5758, www.cmschool.com. Year-round (not all courses all months): 1–6 days, $110–$810 per person; private guiding rates: $70–$400 per person, depending on course and size of group.

Eastern Mountain Sports Climbing School

13+

Affiliated with the outdoor stores of the same name, this school is serious about climbing and has classes in a variety of areas. It's headquartered in North Conway, New Hampshire, in the foothills of the White Mountains, where gently sloping granite cliffs—perfect for beginners and intermediates—abound.

Classes are also held in Connecticut in the Trapp Rock region, about 20 minutes west of Hartford, and in New York's Shawangunks, near New Paltz. The Gunks, as they are called, are climber-friendly even though they're steep because they have plenty of hand- and footholds. On weekends, however, they can get pretty crowded. The EMS Adirondack School in Lake Placid is now open year-round and offers all rock courses in addition to its winter programs in other sports. In Colorado you can take the entire range of rock (and ice) courses all along the Front Range, including Boulder and Eldorado canyons.

FOR FAMILIES. Standard basic and intermediate courses, for ages 13 and up, run from one to four days. These courses, which cover all of the basics from movement techniques to belaying and rappelling, are given throughout the week in all of the school's locations across the country. The student–teacher ratio is three to one.

If your family is ready for serious treks, the school also offers destination climbing in Red Rocks, Nevada; Joshua Tree National Park in California; in Canyonlands National Park in Utah (classic desert climbing); Valdez, Alaska; Mexico; the high peaks of

Bolivia and Ecuador; and Argentina. All equipment, including rock shoes, are supplied for domestic courses.

Eastern Mountain Sports Climbing School, Main St., Box 514, North Conway, NH 03860, tel. 603/356–5433 or 800/310–4504, www.emsclimb.com. Apr.–Nov.: 1–4 days, $135–$250 per person per day, depending on the location and the number of people in the group.

Exum Mountain Guides

13+

One of the top schools in the country, Exum has been teaching and guiding since 1926. The Tetons, northwestern Wyoming's spectacular, rugged peaks, provide a dramatic landscape on which to hone your skills.

When you aren't climbing, your family will find plenty to do in Grand Teton National Park, in nearby Yellowstone, and in the town of Jackson. Don't miss the nightly "shoot-out" in Jackson or the weekly rodeo, both summertime activities.

FOR FAMILIES. Adults and children age 14 and up can join one-day climbing schools at basic to advanced levels. Moms and daughters may be interested in Women That Rock, a course just for women. Exum also has one- and two-day climbs in various parts of the Tetons for ages 13 and up. The student–teacher ratio can go as high as eight to one in beginner courses, but six to one is far more common. Families with younger children should book a private guide; call the school first to discuss your child's physical ability, size, and experience.

Many students stay at the American Alpine Club Climbers' Ranch, 2 mi (3 km) south of Jenny Lake, which offers bunks and the companionship of other climbers. The school will help you find other lodging if you wish.

Exum Mountain Guides, Grand Teton National Park, Box 56, Moose, WY 83012, tel. 307/733–2297, www.exumguides.com. May–Sept.: Courses: 1–4 days, $95–$750 per person for groups of two or more. Ask for prices on more advanced multiday expeditions.

Joshua Tree Rock Climbing School

13+, 4+

Wind, weather, and time have eroded the outcroppings of California's Joshua Tree National Park into boulder gardens of arresting beauty. The rocks draw climbers and many other visitors, although the Joshua trees that gave the monument its name are striking in their own right. From September through June this American Mountain Guides Association–accredited school holds classes in Joshua Tree. During July and August lessons take place at Suicide and Tahquintz rocks, 7,000 ft up in the cool pine forests of the San Jacinto Mountains above Palm Springs. Both areas are less than 50 mi (81 km) from Palm Springs and about three hours from San Diego and Los Angeles.

FOR FAMILIES. Parents and teens age 13 and up can participate in any of the regular courses. The basic two-day rock seminar is most popular with beginners, but there are also four-day seminars for beginner, intermediate and advanced climbers. The student–teacher ratio is a maximum of six to one in the school's basic courses.

Families with children as young as 4 or 5 can arrange private guiding and instruction. A family of four can save money by signing up for private instruction during the week, when the cost is only $5 more per person than for a scheduled class. For groups of eight or more, Rock Climbing Experience (ages 4 or 5 and up welcome) gives you private instruction at a very family-friendly rate.

The school supplies rock shoes for students of all ages and will give you the names and numbers of motels and campgrounds near the climbing sites.

Joshua Tree Rock Climbing School, HCR Box 3034, Joshua Tree, CA 92252, tel. 760/366–4745 or 800/890–4745, www.rockclimbingschool.com. Year-round, courses: 1–4 days, $80–$295. Private guiding and instruction are $90–$110 per person per day, for a group of 3 or 4.

Outward Bound

Outward Bound's goal is to help students expand self-awareness individually and as members of a working team and to have them leave a course knowing they are capable of things they never believed possible. The organization's parent–child rock climbing course begins and ends in Asheville in North Carolina's Appalachian and Great Smoky mountains. Lush and green, this region has the highest peaks in the Appalachians, as well as trails, white-water rivers, and historic sites to explore before or after your course.

FOR FAMILIES. The eight-day parent–child sessions for ages 14 and up combine rock climbing and backpacking, in addition to a ropes course. You have your choice of three summer dates. Aside from the basics of rock climbing—top-rope and multipitch techniques, rappelling, and safety skills—a good portion of the course focuses on developing skills in map and compass navigation, as well as "leave no trace" camping and wilderness first aid. By the end of the course you and your teen will be able to tackle some of the great multipitch climbs in the Appalachians, including Table Rock, White Rock, or Cedar Rock mountains. Outward Bound supplies some equipment, but the organization doesn't consider rock shoes a necessity.

Outward Bound, Rte. 9D, R2 Box 280, Garrison, NY 10524, tel. 800/243–8520, www.outwardbournd.org. Parent–child course, June–Aug.: 8 days, $945 per person.

Sylvan Rocks Climbing School & Guide Service

10+

Rich in history and legend, the Black Hills of South Dakota have ghost towns, craggy peaks, lakes, and, of course, the Mount Rushmore National Monument and Crazy Horse Memorial. The Black Hills are the result of a massive geologic uplift that pushed a dome of ancient granite to the earth's surface, and the vast Black Hills National Forest spreads over more than a million acres. These features, along with many other natural and man-made attributes, make this part of western South Dakota a vacationer and climber's delight.

Sylvan Rocks provides its students with physical and mental challenges, safe climbing, fun, and teachers who have not only extensive climbing experience but the ability and attitude to teach all ages and all levels. The school is accredited by the American Mountain Guides Association.

FOR FAMILIES. The two-day beginner package is for parents and children 10 and up. It focuses on building confidence on steep rock faces, safety, proper use of equipment, tying knots, belaying, and rappelling. The second day takes you out on awesome summits to reinforce the previous day's instruction. The maximum student–teacher ratio is four to one. Climbing shoes and all gear are included in beginner packages.

There are also one- to five-day classes. Those who have completed basic courses can join trips to Devils Tower (the northeastern Wyoming formation made famous in the movie Close Encounters of the Third Kind), and there are trips to climbing meccas such as Joshua Tree, too.

Sylvan Rocks Climbing School & Guide Service, Box 600, Hill City, SD 57745, tel. 605/574–2425, www.sylvanrocks.com. Apr.–Oct.: 1–

3 days, $115–$350, depending on length and level of course and student–teacher ratio. Devils Tower: $195–$250 per day, depending on climber/guide ratio. Call for prices on other trips.

Yamnuska

14+, 6+

Canmore, on the boundary of Banff National Park in Alberta, was once a mining town supplying coal to the railroad. Now it serves as a base for many recreational activities in the nearby mountains. The majestic Canadian Rockies provide plenty of rewards for both new and experienced climbers. From the international airport at Calgary, it's an easy drive to Canmore and also to the interior ranges of British Columbia, where Yamnuska schedules some of its trips.

FOR FAMILIES. Parents and children age 14 and up are welcome on weekend courses. Basic Rock, Basic Rock Plus, and Advanced Rock are all two- to four-day courses. Complete Rock is six days of intensive instruction; talk to the school about your teen before signing him or her up for this more adult-oriented course. Group instruction ratios range from six to one to two to one, depending on the difficulty of the climbs. Yamnuska also has extensive private instruction, which it highly recommends for families. If your children are at least 6 years old, you can schedule private guiding and courses in and around Banff, Canmore, and Lake Louise, all areas with much to offer whether you're climbing or not. If you have a teen interested in mountaineering, Yamnuska also offers a week-long Intro to Mountaineering course for ages 13 to 17 in July; it's based on the Wapta Icefields just north of Lake Louise.

Banff and Canmore have reasonably priced lodging; in the mountains, Yamnuska often uses huts, which are available to its clients at nominal rates. You can rent shoes, but they are not available in very small sizes. Note that the course prices below are listed in Canadian dollars.

Yamnuska, Ste. 200 Summit Centre, 50 Lincoln Park, Canmore, Alberta, Canada T1W 1N8, tel. 403/678–4164, www.yamnuska.com. May–Sept.: 1–6 days, C$150–C$580, Intro to Mountaineering, C$790. Call for private guiding rates.

Zoar Outdoor

10+

Cool, densely forested, and green, the Berkshire Mountains of Massachusetts have several excellent climbing locations and are among the most popular vacation destinations in the eastern United States. Zoar's 80-acre complex in Charlemont, in the far northwest corner of the state, is just a short drive from Chapel and Rose ledges, two excellent places for families to learn together. Zoar's experience working with families and children is extensive, and the school truly welcomes them in classes.

FOR FAMILIES. Zoar's parent–child clinic, a two-day beginner course for climbers ages 10 to 16 and one or both parents, is designed to promote communication and trust between parents and their children while they enjoy the fun and challenge of climbing. These clinics, with a student–teacher ratio of six to one, cover basic climbing skills and are offered once each in July and August. The center's regular rock climbing clinics are one- to two-day sessions aimed at ages 14 through adult. Private instruction is also available.

You can stay at Zoar's campground in one of their cabin tents complete with four cots, a gas lantern, a grill, and a deck (bring your own bedding), or in your own tent at a site with a picnic table. If you prefer a nearby motel, inn, or bed-and-breakfast, Zoar will send you a list of area accommodations.

Zoar Outdoor, 7 Main St., Box 245, Charlemont, MA 01339, tel. 413/339–4010 *or 800/532–7483, www.zoaroutdoor.com. May–Oct.: 1–2 days, $110–$210. Private instruction runs $110–$225 per person per day, depending on the number of students.*

Resources

Books

For general books on basic climbing skills, check out *The Complete Idiot's Guide to Rock Climbing* (Alpha Books), by Joe Glickman and Stefani Ellen; *Rock Climbing Basics* (Stackpole Books), by Turlough Johnston and Madeleine Hallden; *Gym Climb* (How to Rock Climb series, Chockstone Press), by John Long; and *Climbing: A Woman's Guide* (McGraw-Hill), by Shelley Presson. These generally cover both indoor and outdoor climbing with an emphasis on basic technique and equipment. *Two for the Summit: My Daughter, The Mountains, and Me* (E.P. Dutton), by Geoffrey Norman, is an inspiring, and very personal account of how outdoor writer Norman and his 15-year-old daughter tackled mountaineering together as novices, eventually conquering both Grand Teton and the Andes' Aconcagua. *Extreme Sports: Rock Climbing* (Barrons Juveniles) is a look at the sport for ages 9 to 12. Amazon.com also has many books on climbing specific areas and states, including most of those mentioned in this chapter.

Organizations

The **American Mountain Guides Association** (AMGA; 710 10th St., Suite 101, Golden, CO 80401, tel. 303/271–0984, www.amga.com) can send you a list of accredited schools and certified guides across the country.

Periodicals

Climbing (0326 Hwy. 133, Suite 190, Carbondale, CO 81623, tel. 970/963–9449) publishes eight issues a year plus a gear guide and occasionally has articles on family climbing and on introducing children to the sport.

RV ADVENTURES

When my children were 1, 5, and 11 years old, I piled them into a 27-ft motor home and traveled from Virginia to Florida and back, stopping at campgrounds each night. Since then I've logged more than 25,000 mi (40,250 km) in various recreational vehicles (RVs) and covered most of the country, visiting national parks and monuments, national and state forests, and a variety of private and public campgrounds. My children rank these among their best vacations ever.

Recreational vehicles are ideal for family vacations, including intergenerational trips with grandparents. Young families are the fastest-growing segment of the RV population, and with good reason: RVs get you into the outdoors and the wilderness safely and easily. Very young children, who are unfamiliar with sleeping bags, latrines, and tents in the middle of the woods, may feel more at ease in an RV than at a backcountry campsite. Families with infants can take a two-week camping trip and still have a way to refrigerate and warm formula or baby food. For parents who worry that a toddler might wake up and wander away from a tent in the middle of the night, RVs have doors that lock. Many grandparents are likely to appreciate the physical comforts of an RV adventure, too.

Many campgrounds that welcome RVs have spacious wilderness surroundings and privacy; some are veritable outdoor resorts, with restaurants, hiking trails, fishing, boating, and swimming. Some have hook-ups that allow you to use the campground's water and electrical supplies; others are remote sites providing only a relatively level spot in a spectacular setting.

Because different kinds of places appeal to different people, this chapter describes a range of RV destinations: national parks, forests, and monuments; state parks; and private campgrounds. The selections are based on my family's experience and the opinions of other seasoned RV travelers. Keep in mind that there's no reason a family has to stay at the same type of campground every night. You can opt for a full-service RV resort one night; the next evening you might camp in a wilderness area with nature's own amenities—a sky full of stars and a peaceful, welcoming solitude.

Note: at press time (spring 2002) the National Park Service had a toll-free number for reservations at 23 national parks, as well as several national seashores, lakeshores, historic sites, and recreation areas. This number, 800/365–CAMP (800/365–2267), is listed for applicable parks, and you can call as early as five months in advance for most reservations. For campgrounds, you have to call on the 5th of the month—for example, if you call on Jan. 5, you can make reservations for Jan. 6–Jun. 4. You can also go to reservations.nps.gov or search www.americanparks.net to find several private reservations services. National Park Reservations doesn't mark up the basic park charges to cover the costs of their service, but they do add an additional 10% of your reservation price. For general information on all of America's parks and what's available at each one, check the National Park Service Web site, www.nps.gov.

Questions to Ask

Where can I rent or buy an RV? There are RV dealers across the country; many have both sales and rental departments. Look under "Recreation Vehicles—Renting and Leasing" in the yellow pages for the sources nearest you. For a complete listing of dealers, contact any of the RV organizations listed in Resources (*see below*), such as the Go RVing Coalition or the Recreation Vehicle Rental Association.

What kinds of RVs are best? You have many options. Some families prefer motor homes, all-in-one vehicles that range in length from 17 to 40 ft. In a motor home you can get snacks and use the bathroom without having to stop and search for a gas station or restaurant. (Children and adults should always be buckled into seat belts or car seats when the vehicle is in motion.) Another choice is a pop-up, which you tow with your car by day and literally pop up into a spacious and well-equipped camper at night; beds, bathroom, and often a refrigerator and air conditioner are included. Truck campers (those fitted onto the bed of a pickup truck) and full-size travel trailers (fully equipped trailer homes you tow) are also available. Prices vary greatly according to the size of the vehicle and, if you're renting, the season.

How far in advance is it necessary to reserve? Summer is the most popular time for RV vacations; rental companies may well be out of the vehicle you want on a particular week unless you book several months in advance.

Are RVs allowed in all campgrounds? No, but they are welcome in most. Some sites, especially publicly owned campgrounds, may have a size limit for RVs. Listings in campground directories and government campground publications often mention the maximum length allowed; read the specifications carefully.

What kind of gas mileage do RVs get? If you're driving a motor home, from 6 to 12 mi (10 to 18 km) per gallon is possible; about 8 mi (13 km) per gallon is typical. Pulling a car or boat behind your RV will decrease the mileage your vehicle ordinarily gets. Other factors affecting mileage are your vehicle's engine size and capabilities, the type of terrain, and the weight of the RV. Pulling a pop-up or trailer home with your car will affect your gas mileage, too.

What service is available in case of a breakdown? Before your trip, find out whether your RV rental company has breakdown insurance or a roadside help policy that will cover you. You might also consider joining the Good Sam Club (see Resources, *below*), which offers road service for RVs.

How is sewage disposal handled? Dumping waste is easier than it sounds. When you pick up your rental RV, you'll learn how to attach a hose to a campground's sewer hook-ups and how to flush the waste by opening and closing valves. Keep a pair of gloves handy for handling the waste hose. If you stay at a campground without sewer hook-ups, eventually you will have to stop at a campground with a dump station and pay a fee of a few dollars to empty your waste tanks. A good campground directory (*see* Resources, *below*) will tell you where to find dump stations. You will always need to return your rental with the waste tanks emptied.

What is the electrical source in an RV, and can it be tapped only when the RV is parked? Most campgrounds have electrical hook-ups—outlets into which you plug the RV's heavy-duty electrical cord. If there are no hook-ups, you switch on the generator found in most RVs. With few exceptions, the only time you'll need your generator while driving is if you use the microwave, the water pump (either to make the sink faucet run or to flush the toilet), or the VCR, or if you need additional air-conditioning or heat. When you've stopped in a campground without hook-ups, you'll use the generator for all of the above and for lights. In most modern RVs the refrigerator and stove work on propane (included in rentals), so even when you're parked and the generator is off, your refrigerator will stay cool, and you'll be able to use the stove.

If I'm renting a pop-up and towing it with my car, do I need a special hitch? Some companies can supply what you need; others require that you purchase a low-cost part. Ask before you rent.

What's included in the cost of a rental? This varies widely, so shop around. Generally speaking, you get the vehicle at a daily or weekly rate plus a mileage allowance—typically 100 mi (161 km) per day. Beyond these basics, there are many variations. Bedding packages, for example, are available from some suppliers; dishes, silverware, and pots and pans may or may not cost extra. Some suppliers have CD players, TVs, and VCRs, which give antsy children something to watch when they can't see out the window at night. Before renting an RV, consider the options and your needs, and then judge the prices accordingly. Also, ask whether you'll incur an extra charge if the gas and propane tanks aren't filled when you return the RV.

What's included in the cost of a campground? Campgrounds charge per RV site. The base rate is generally for two adults and does not include hook-ups (these are the rates quoted in the individual listings). Another $1–$3 per night is added for water and electricity, and sewage hook-ups cost an additional $2–$5. A nominal fee is usually charged for children—typically $2–$5 per night. Most campgrounds let very young children stay for free, although the age cutoff varies widely. If you're camping in a national park, a national monument, or a state park, you may be required to pay a separate park entrance fee. If your family plans to visit a number of national parks and monuments, consider buying a National Parks Pass, which costs only $50 and covers the entrance fees to all parks that you visit during one year. These passes are available at any park with an entrance fee. Golden Age ($10, for visitors who are at least 62) and Golden Access (free for people with disabilities) passes must be purchased in person. These have no expiration date.

Instruction

Most rental companies will show you how to work everything before you leave in your vehicle. RVs aren't hard to drive, but they take a little getting used to. If you've never driven an RV, ask for pointers on how to back up, how to hook up the electrical and water lines at campgrounds, and how to dump waste water. Make certain you also know how the generator works, and listen to safety instructions about which switches must be shut off when you stop for gas.

Finding the Fun

Because each adventure option in this chapter is in a fixed destination, the selections below are organized by region.

Favorite RV Destinations

NORTHEAST

Lake Placid/Whiteface Mountain KOA

ALL

Kampgrounds of America, known far and wide as KOA, is a national chain of campgrounds. KOAs are privately owned but must meet standards set by the national headquarters, so certain features and facilities remain consistent. All are family-friendly, and prices are reasonable—even more so if you get a KOA Value Kard (see Resources, *below*). Showers and rest rooms are clean and well maintained; you can generally find a playground and a well-stocked store and/or a snack bar; and there are almost always outdoor activities for families. Pools, lakes, or streams are quite common, and KOAs generally welcome pets. Many KOAs now have Kamping Kabins, too, so grandparents or other non-RVers can meet you on vacation and have a place of their own.

The Lake Placid/Whiteface Mountain KOA is an excellent choice for families visiting northern New York. Just 9 mi (14 km) northeast of the town of Lake Placid, in the heart of Adirondack Park and the ancient Adirondack Mountains, this 70-acre campground gives you access to many outdoor adventures. Although the facility is not remote, its pine and white birch forest setting at the base of Whiteface Mountain is splendid.

FOR FAMILIES. In summer you can hike or fish right at the campground along a ½-mi (¾-km) stretch of the Ausable River, famous for its trout. Other campground activities are tennis, miniature golf, and swimming in a heated pool. Full, partial, and non-hookup sites (144 in all), plus cabins and cottages, give families plenty of options.

Adirondack Park is an excellent place for hiking, rock climbing, and multiday canoeing; Whiteface Mountain has great skiing, too. Lake Placid has hosted the Winter Games twice, and the Olympic facilities are well worth touring.

Lake Placid/Whiteface Mountain KOA, Fox Farm Rd., Hc2 Box 38, Wilmington, NY 12997, tel. 518/946–7878 or 800/562–0368, www.koacampground.com. Apr.–Nov.: $20–$3 per night; cabins more.

MID-ATLANTIC

Shenandoah National Park

ALL

National parks are among the most popular RV camping destinations. All are excellent for families on adventures, but some parks have special appeal for RVers. One of these is Shenandoah, which lies along a breathtaking stretch of the Blue Ridge Mountains in northwestern Virginia. Within the park, the 105-mi (169-km) Skyline Drive follows the crest of the mountains and is one of the most scenic roads in America and a must for anyone on wheels. Also, 100 mi (161 km) of the Maine-to-Georgia Appalachian Trail runs through the park, approximately parallel to Skyline Drive.

FOR FAMILIES. Big Meadows Campground, site of one of the park's two visitor centers, is among the most popular campgrounds in the park; reservations are essential between May and October, at least on weekends. There's a restaurant at Big Meadows and access to the Appalachian Trail. Three other campgrounds—Lewis Mountain, Mathews Arm, and Loft Mountain—have sites available on a first-come, first-served basis. None of the campgrounds has hook-ups.

The park has excellent opportunities for hiking, fishing, and bird-watching. Ranger-led family programs in summer give children and parents insight into the natural and cultural stories of Shenandoah.

Shenandoah National Park, Superintendent, 3655 U.S. 211E, Luray, VA 22835, tel. 540/999–3500 or 800/365–CAMP, www.nps.gov/shen. Mar.–Oct.: $14–$17 per night plus $10 park entrance fee.

THE SOUTH

Chattahoochee National Forest

ALL

The many national forests scattered throughout the United States are another terrific camping option for RVing families. Although most have true wilderness settings, it's not unusual for a national forest campground to be close to a major city, near well-maintained roads; such is the case with Chattahoochee National Forest. This wild land of deep gorges and rushing water lies about 100 mi (161 km) north of Atlanta, close to the Tennessee and North Carolina borders. The Appalachian Mountains in northern Georgia are untamed but remarkably accessible.

FOR FAMILIES. Lake Conasauga Campground is within Chattahoochee National Forest, about 20 mi (32 km) north of Chatsworth. An extensive network of hiking trails readily accessible from local roads makes this area ideal for RV adventures. The 35 campsites (plus overflow area) have no hook-ups, but the campground has what most families love: a lake. No motors are allowed on the water, so you can fish, boat, and swim in peace. This is a primitive campground with no amenities—just gorgeous scenery to explore and enjoy.

Chattahoochee National Forest, Cohutta Ranger District, 3941 Hwy. 76, Chatsworth, GA 30705, tel. 706/695–6736, www.fs.fed.us. Apr.–Oct.: $8 per night.

Cherokee/Great Smokies KOA

ALL

This KOA is in Cherokee, North Carolina, at one of the gateways to Great Smoky Mountains National Park (*see below*). If you want to take a break from exploring wilderness or America's highways, you can spend a couple of days here taking advantage of all that's at your RV's doorstep. Between activities at the campground and excursions to the park and the town of Cherokee, your family will have plenty to do.

FOR FAMILIES. At the campground three stocked trout ponds provide a perfect outlet for the youngest anglers; you can rent fishing poles at the KOA store. Among the other facilities are a playground, tennis courts, a pool, a kiddie pool, a river for swimming, and a hot tub. Most of the 430 sites have hook-ups. For those who want to leave their RVs parked and set up, the campground has shuttle service into the national park and other local attractions.

Besides outdoor recreation, families can experience the cultural aspect of the area, which has long been inhabited by the Cherokee. A short drive from the campground are many Native American institutions and sites, including the Cherokee Heritage Museum and Gallery, with an interpretive center that focuses on tribal culture and history; the Oconaluftee Indian Village, a replica of a native village of about 250 years ago; and the Museum of the Cherokee Indian. All have valuable information about the Cherokee people's past, present, and future.

Cherokee/Great Smokies KOA, 92 KOA Kampground Rd., Cherokee, NC 28719, tel. 828/497–9711 or 800/825–8352, www.koacampground.com. Year-round: $19–$34 per night; children under 18 free.

Everglades National Park

ALL

Not all national parks are summer destinations. In fact, although Everglades National Park in southern Florida is open year-round, the best times to visit are in late fall or winter, when insects are not a problem and the heat and humidity are quite bearable. Renting an RV is also less expensive in winter, so if savings are important to your family, a winter RV trip to Everglades National Park may be rewarding in many ways.

FOR FAMILIES. Encompassing 1.5 million acres, Everglades National Park is a fragile ecosystem that supports an astonishingly diverse population of plants and animals; children of all ages will find it intriguing. Though much of the park is accessible only by boat, land activities—such as hikes, bird-watching treks, and interpretive programs—are also highlights. Rangers give talks throughout the year, but these are far more frequent in winter months.

Flamingo Campground, in the park at the southern entrance, has no hook-up facilities or hot showers, but it is the site of one of the park's visitor centers. The 340 campsites are available by reservation. Campers can explore adjacent hiking trails and rent canoes or skiffs for water-based exploration. Just 6 mi (10 km) from the park's southern entrance is the 108-site Long Pine Key campground, which has no hook-up facilities or showers, but does have a network of hiking trails through the pine forests around it.

Everglades National Park, Superintendent, 40001 State Rd. 9336, Homestead, FL 33034, tel. 305/242–7700 or 800/365–2267, www.nps.gov/ever. Year-round: $14 per night plus $10 per vehicle park entrance fee.

Great Smoky Mountains National Park

ALL

Because the Smokies are a wonderful—and popular—family destination, it pays to know more than one camping option. Families that want to concentrate on Great Smoky Mountains National Park, which straddles North Carolina and Tennessee, may find that staying inside the park is the best way to experience it fully.

FOR FAMILIES. The park's verdant deciduous forests shelter more than 1,600 types of flowering plants, as well as bears and other wildlife. If your children love flowers, and if they have even a remote interest in birds, this is the place to be. The park has nature walks and interpretive programs for all ages, mainly during the peak summer and fall seasons. Two facilities, The Great Smoky Mountains Institute at Tremont and The Smoky Mountain Field School, also offer programs for families, children, and adults. You can ride horses on well-maintained trails. Although the park merits a visit on its own, your family can combine a stay with other adventures that take place nearby; the Canoeing, Kayaking, Rock Climbing, *and* Trekking with Llamas and Burros chapters all list outfitters in the vicinity.

Three of the park's 10 campgrounds—Elkmont, Cades Cove, and Smokemont—can be reserved up to five months ahead of time, and note that reservations are required during the busiest period from mid-May to the end of October. The other campgrounds take campers on a first-come, first-served basis. None of the park's campgrounds has hook-ups or showers; fill your water tank before arriving so you can shower, cook, and use the bathroom in your RV.

Great Smoky Mountains National Park, Superintendent, 107 Park Headquarters Rd., Gatlinburg, TN 37738, tel. 865/436–1200 or 800/365–2267, www.nps.gov/grsm. Year-round: $12–$17 per night; no park entrance fees.

Mammoth Cave National Park

ALL

This national park has a single focus—the Mammoth Cave. The longest cave system in the world, Mammoth extends for more than 350 mi (564 km), and rangers suspect that there's much more to discover. Most parents don't feel experienced enough to take their children caving on their own, but at Mammoth you can combine an RV trip with a highly informative guided caving adventure.

FOR FAMILIES. If the huge vertical shafts and eerie underground rivers don't impress your children, the strange inhabitants of the caves surely will; these include eyeless fish, white spiders, and blind beetles, though you're most likely to see cave crickets and bats. Exploring the caves with park rangers is the main event here; cave walks of various lengths and varying degrees of difficulty make it possible for almost anyone to visit, and some tours are designed especially for children. On the Introduction to Caving and the Wild Cave tours, you'll be equipped with hard hats and miner's lights. There's a minimum age of 10 on some cave tours. For those adventurers who prefer to stay above ground, the park has backcountry hiking trails, guided nature walks, summer interpretive programs, and boating.

None of the three park campgrounds has hook-ups, and only two take reservations. Headquarters Campground has 109 sites with hot showers and a laundry; Maple Springs is for groups and campers with horses. Houchins Ferry has just 12 primitive sites and does not accept reservations. Also keep in mind that although the park is open year-round, its stores and services are open seasonally.

Mammoth Cave National Park, Box 7, Mammoth Cave, KY 42259, tel. 270/758–2328 or 800/967–2283, www.nps.gov/maca. Campgrounds open Mar.–Nov.: $10–$25 per *night, cave tours $3.50–$35; no entrance fee to park.*

MIDWEST

Porcupine Mountains Wilderness State Park

ALL

State parks are an excellent camping choice for families with RVs. Some are primarily back-to-nature experiences with little in the way of amenities, which suits those families looking for a great place to camp in the woods. Porcupine Mountains Wilderness State Park is just such a place—a 59,000-acre wilderness area on the northwest end of Michigan's Upper Peninsula, not far from the Wisconsin border. Make your first stop at the visitor center, where multimedia programs and exhibits highlight the beauty of the landscape and the diversity of wildlife.

FOR FAMILIES. Otters, bears, coyotes, grouse, deer, and bald eagles all make their home among the forests, streams, and mountains here. Humans, too, are in evidence, hiking more than 90 mi (145 km) of trails in spring, summer, and fall and cross-country or downhill skiing in winter. Fishing, swimming, and picnicking are other prime activities in the park, or your family can spend time simply relishing the sight of deep gorges and awesome waterfalls. Rangers offer guided hikes and programs throughout the year. Union Bay Campground has 100 sites with electrical hook-ups; Presque Isle Campground has 90 sites, none with hook-ups. Both have flush toilets and showers; however, not all facilities are open year-round. For families ready for a more back-country adventure, there are 16 hike-in wilderness cabins.

Porcupine Mountains Wilderness State Park, 412 S. Boundary, Ontonagon, MI 49953, tel. 906/885–5275 or 800/447–2757. Year-round: campgrounds, $6–$14 per night; cabins, $45 per night; vehicles, $4 per night. Children 12 and under ski free.

Ludington State Park

ALL

In addition to stunning wilderness areas, Michigan also has fabulous recreation areas next to civilization, places that are ideal for families who want camping with easy access to modern amenities and lots of children's activities. If you're targeting water sports, your best bet is to head for Ludington on the shores of Lake Michigan, where my grandmother lived and where I spent a wonderful part of my childhood playing on the shores of the great lake that seemed as big as any ocean. I never tired of walking the fine, white-sand beach with my father, or on the breakwater wall all the way out to the lighthouse. After a day of playing in the sand and water, we would get scoops of home-made ice cream from a shop near the shore while we waited for the sunset and an even bigger event: the arrival of the ferry from Wisconsin. The beach is still excellent, the ice cream shop is still there, the lighthouse still guards the harbor, and the ferry still arrives around sunset. Not far from the pier there's even a street with my name on it—Loomis Street (yes, I made my children take a zillion pictures of me standing under it). My parents never camped, but they missed out because Ludington State Park is a true gem and it's hard to imagine a family who wouldn't have a fine time camping here.

FOR FAMILIES. The park is in an enviable position between two lakes. On one side, you'll find 6 mi (10 km) of the Lake Michigan shoreline and an excellent beach within park boundaries, while on the other side is Hamlin Lake, with its calm waters, small beach, peaceful woods, and boat rentals. The latter in particular is perfect for families with younger kids or those who want to putter around in pedal boats and canoes; in fact, there's even a canoe trail to follow. Both beaches have concession stands, and there's a picnic site near Hamlin Lake as well.

Between the park's Cedar, Pines, and Beechwood campgrounds, there are nearly 350 sites, all with electricity. Campground facilities include flush toilets and showers, and there's a park store at Cedar. Beechwood has waterfront sites on Lake Hamlin. The park, encompassing 5,300 acres, has virgin conifers, ravines, shady groves, hills, and, of course, Lake Michigan's famous dunes. There are some 18 mi (29 km) of paths that wander through the woods and over the dunes, as well as 16 mi (26 km) of cross-country ski trails. At the Great Lakes Visitor Center you'll find interpretive displays and presentations on the wildlife, geology, and history of the Great Lakes region. While there's plenty to occupy families in the park, do go into town, walk out on the breakwater, and have some ice cream. If you find yourself on Loomis Street, take a picture for me.

Ludington State Park, Box 709, Ludington, MI 49431, tel. 616/843–8671 or 800/447–2757. Park open year-round, campgrounds, May–Oct.: $13–$15 per night.

Rafter J Bar Ranch Campground

ALL

The Rafter J Bar is about as family-friendly and action-packed as a campground can get. Like many other private campgrounds, it's a destination in itself, a place traveling families can stay put for a couple of days—or longer—and enjoy a campground just as they would a hotel or resort. The area has plenty to attract families: South Dakota's Black Hills, in which the Rafter J Bar is set, are filled with history, legends, and adventure opportunities (*see* Rock Climbing *and* Covered Wagon Adventures). The ranch is an easy drive from Mt. Rushmore, Crazy Horse Monument, Wind Cave National Park, Mammoth Site of Hot Springs, and Custer State Park.

FOR FAMILIES. The Rafter J Bar sits at 5,200 ft, among wooded, rolling hills. Large meadows separate five camping areas shaded by ponderosa pines; most of the 258 sites have full or partial hook-ups. The campground has a pool and a hot tub, and four lakes are a short distance from the ranch. You can rent bikes to explore 35 mi (56 km) of the George S. Mickelson Hiking/Biking Trail right from the ranch. Families can also ride horses on a trail in the Black Hills National Forest. Those too young for the trail have supervised pony rides at the campground and use of the playground. A trout stream on the property entices anglers; bring your own poles. Rental cars are available for people who want to explore while leaving their RV parked and hooked up.

If non-RVing family members or friends want to join you on vacation, this is a great place to meet. The Rafter J Bar has cabins that sleep six people.

Rafter J Bar Ranch, Box 128, Hill City, SD 57745, tel. 605/574–2527 or 888/723–8375. May–Oct.: $22.95–$32.95 per night for 2 people; cabins start at $40.95 per night.

SOUTHWEST

Lake Powell Resorts & Marinas

ALL

These campgrounds are less intriguing for their amenities than for their location on the shores of Lake Powell. This 186-mi (299 km) stretch of brilliant blue, banked by imposing red-rock formations and sandy beaches, starts just below the Arizona border and extends well into Utah. Families come to Lake Powell from all over the country to try their hands at piloting a houseboat (see Houseboating) and to explore other parts of the Glen Canyon National Recreation Area, which covers more than a million acres. At nearly every campground families can combine RVing with boating and hiking adventures.

FOR FAMILIES. Lake Powell Resorts & Marinas operates National Park Service campgrounds as well as its own private campgrounds in the same locations: Wahweap, Bullfrog, and Hall's Crossing. The park service sites are primitive, with no hook-ups, and no reservations are accepted, but the campgrounds do have interpretive programs by rangers throughout the summer. The private campgrounds accept reservations and have full services and full hook-ups.

At the south end of the lake, near Page, Arizona, are the Wahweap campgrounds. The company runs a lodge, as well as a marina that sells groceries and camping supplies, and it's a place where you can rent a houseboat and set out to explore the lake. The park service visitor center here has exhibits that appeal to all ages.

Hall's Crossing and Bullfrog, at the lake's midpoint but on opposite shores, also have marinas; Bullfrog has a visitor center. You can rent houseboats at these marinas, and the ferry between the two takes RVs.

In addition to standard services at all the marinas, good-value RV packages combine two nights at camp with boat tours or houseboat rentals. You can also make reservations for Colorado River float trips—although there's no white water—through this company.

Lake Powell Resorts & Marinas, Box 56909, Phoenix, AZ 85079, tel. 602/278–8888 or 800/528–6154, www.visitlakepowell.com. Year-round: $15–$28 per night.

Palo Duro Canyon State Park

ALL

In the middle of the horizon-to-horizon desolation of the Texas Panhandle, about 18 mi (29 km) south of Amarillo, Palo Duro Canyon is an improbable paradise of all-encompassing beauty. At 110 mi (177 km) long, the canyon is one of the largest in the country, and it will intrigue even those who thought they had no interest in geology. Its bottom layer of rock matches the top layer of the Grand Canyon; if you set Palo Duro on top of the Grand Canyon, almost every known geologic layer of the earth would be represented. The area has more than canyon walls of muted purple, red, and gold, though: Palo Duro State Park combines an extraordinary landscape with a multitude of services and amenities.

FOR FAMILIES. You can camp in a variety of places in the canyon's bottomland. Cottonwoods, grasslands, and the Prairie Dog Town Fork of the Red River create shady, pleasant spots from which to explore. Five camping areas have a total of 108 sites for RVs and tents; some sites have electricity and water. The park also has three restored cabins, originally built in the 1930s, which are the only overnight facilities up on the scenic canyon rim.

Families can try hiking and mountain biking trails. The Lighthouse Hiking Trail is a 6-mi (10-km) round-trip, but very young children can at least walk the first part. Be alert for interesting creatures along the way—you might even see tarantulas in their native habitat. For a moderate fee you can also take a trail ride on horseback.

If you have older children who can stay up late, don't miss the summer production of *Texas!* at the amphitheater. The canyon walls serve as a backdrop, and a brilliant fireworks display ends the show.

Palo Duro Canyon State Park, 11450 Park Road 5, Canyon, TX 79015, tel. 806/488–2227 or 512/389–8900, www.palodurocanyon.com. Year-round: $9–$12 per night, cabins $65, plus $3 per adult park entrance fee.

ROCKIES

Colorado National Monument

ALL

Administered by the park service, national monuments range from natural landmarks to man-made structures and sites of historical importance. The Colorado National Monument falls under the first category: vast canyons, towering monoliths, and unusual rock formations create compelling vistas at this often-overlooked site near Grand Junction. Hikers, bikers, and rock climbers find challenges in and near the monument. The area is also a favorite among dinosaur lovers, who come to participate in digging expeditions at nearby Mygatt-Moore Quarry and to visit the superb Dinosaur Journey, part of the Museum of Western Colorado (see Digging for Fossils). Families will enjoy the monument for its own sake, however, and for its campground high above the canyon floor, on the scenic rim drive.

For families. Peace and quiet abound at the 5,800-ft Saddlehorn Campground, a relatively primitive campground with 80 sites, but only a few can accommodate RVs, depending on the size of the vehicle. None have hook-ups. The campground does not accept reservations. Hikers of all abilities will find plenty of trails leading down from the canyon rim; the hardy can hike from the canyon floor up. For families with very young children, an excellent, easy nature walk of about ½ mi (¾ km) begins at the visitor center, just down the road from the campground on the rim drive. Another hike popular with families ends at Devil's Kitchen, a canyon formation that looks like a huge red-rock kitchen, complete with appliances. You can reach that trail from the lower road. There are also junior ranger and campfire programs.

Colorado National Monument, Superintendent, Fruita, CO 81521, tel. 970/858–3617, www.nps.gov/colm. Year-round: $10 per night plus $4 per vehicle entrance fee.

Great Sand Dunes National Monument and Preserve

ALL

At the base of the jagged Sangre de Cristo Mountains in south-central Colorado are the 750-ft dunes of the Great Sand Dunes National Monument and Preserve. Rising from a base of more than 8,000 ft above sea level, these are the highest dunes in North America and a unique playground for families. The monument campground provides a very different perspective from that at Colorado National Monument (*see above*), one from which you look up, not down, for the best views. In October 2000, the Senate and House passed the Great Sand Dunes National Park and Preserve Act, which authorizes the expansion of the nearly 39,000-acre monument into a national park of over 150,000 acres. However, Great Sand Dunes doesn't officially receive national park designation until the additional 100,000 acres of adjacent Baca Ranch is acquired.

FOR FAMILIES. You can hike for miles, find places to be alone, and play in Medano Creek at the monument—but you probably won't be able to get your children to do anything but jump like crazy around the dunes. Although interpretive talks and nature activities are given throughout the summer, the ideal time to visit is in late spring and early summer, because the creek dries up by August. It's best to walk on the dunes in the early morning and late afternoon, as they're often too hot in the middle of the day.

Pinyon Flats Campground, the only one in the monument, has 88 sites, but not all the spaces can accommodate vehicles of every size. Although the campground has no hook-ups and no reservations, being inside the monument makes up for it. If Pinyon Flats is full (as it is on many weekends), you can also try Great Sand Dunes Oasis, a campground and lodge just outside the monument that's nearly as nice. For more information on other activities within the monument, check out the visitor center on U.S. 150.

Great Sand Dunes National Monument, 11999 U.S. 150, Mosca, CO 81146, tel. 719/378–2312, www.nps.gov/grsa. Year-round: $10 per night plus $3 per adult entrance fee.

WEST COAST

Big Bear Shores RV Resort & Yacht Club

ALL

Big Bear Shores is an excellent example of a private RV resort and campground right in the middle of a national forest. California's huge San Bernardino National Forest stretches from the city of San Bernardino to Palm Springs and encompasses several wilderness areas, ski areas, mountains, and lakes. The facility is in Big Bear Lake, a resort town that has become a year-round community with an emphasis on outdoor activities.

FOR FAMILIES. At Big Bear Shores RV Resort, on the shoreline of Big Bear Lake and 6,700 ft up in the San Bernardino Mountains, you can indulge in lake and pool swimming, relaxing in hot tubs, boating (rentals available), tennis, and fishing. Both summer and winter are busy here, as the crowds return after snowfall for cross-country and downhill skiing and snowboarding. There are 170 sites, all with hook-ups. Families should note that this is not a campground in the strictest sense. No tent camping is allowed, and campers built on trucks are not accepted either. Reservations are mandatory.

Big Bear Shores RV Resort & Yacht Club, 40751 North Shore Dr., Box 1572, Big Bear Lake, CA 92315, tel. 909/866–4151, www.bigbearshores.com. Year-round: $54–$69 per night.

Joshua Tree National Park

ALL

Joshua Tree National Park, in California, is most appealing in what is off-season for many other areas: Because of extreme weather conditions (heat and wind), the best times to visit are from February to April and from October to December. The park, about 140 mi (225 km) east of Los Angeles, covers 1,238 square mi (3,206 square km) and preserves sections of the Mojave and Colorado deserts. Rock climbers worldwide (see Rock Climbing) test their skills on mountains that rise to heights of 1,000 to 6,000 ft, and hikers can explore many magnificent trails. Joshua Tree is a natural for an RV adventure: The only way to cover most of this vast area is by private vehicle, and there's no better means of transport for family exploration than an RV.

FOR FAMILIES. Five of the eight campgrounds are free and available on a first-come, first-served basis. The park charges a fee for Indian Cove, Cottonwood Springs, and Black Rock Canyon campgrounds, and only Indian Cove and Black Rock take reservations. All the campgrounds have access to the trees, trails, and rocks that make the monument unique. Campers must have their own water (except at Cottonwood and Black Rock, where water is available) and their own firewood, so fill your RV's water tank before arriving, and check your propane tanks if you're planning on cooking inside instead of using firewood.

You can pick up trail maps and other information at the visitor center, just north of the Twentynine Palms entrance. Guided hikes and campfire programs are scheduled in spring and fall. Families with young children should check out the Hidden Valley Nature Trail, a mile-long loop enclosed by a wall of rocks; the trail starts near Hidden Valley Campground. Other easy trails begin near the White Tank, Cottonwood Springs, and Black Rock Canyon campgrounds. Fortynine Palms Canyon (not far from the Twentynine Palms entrance) and Lost Palms Oasis (near the Cottonwood Springs campground) are reached by way of mostly moderate trails; allow several hours for these hikes.

Joshua Tree National Park, Superintendent, 74455 Park Dr., Twentynine Palms, CA, 92277, tel. 760/367–5500, www.nps.gov/jotr. Year-round: $10 per night plus $10 per vehicle park entrance fees.

Crater Lake National Park

ALL

When you stand at the caldera rim and look down into the astonishing blue of Crater Lake, it's easy to understand why this place was considered sacred to the Klamath people. The lake is misnamed, for it's not a crater but a caldera, meaning it was formed when Mount Mazama collapsed inward rather than exploding outward. The volcanic eruption, which took place about 7,700 years ago, was witnessed by early native tribes whose lore includes stories of a great battle between two chiefs: Llao of the Below World and Kell of the Above World. At battle's end, Llao's home (Mount Mazama) was destroyed.

The first white men to stumble on Crater Lake were stunned by its beauty, and it has been the same for every traveler ever since. When William Gladstone Steel looked down on Crater Lake in 1870, he was so taken with it that he made it his life's mission to protect the lake and the land around it. His dream was realized when President Theodore Roosevelt made Crater Lake a national park in 1902. This is one of our country's oldest national parks and one of its most beautiful. It is without question one of my family's favorite of all of our national parks. If you visit, you'll understand why.

FOR FAMILIES. Crater Lake's moderate size of 180,000 acres and focus on volcanoes and geology make it amazingly family-friendly. Unlike some of our larger and more famous parks, Crater Lake isn't overwhelming. Even a family with very young children can experience much of what it has to offer and leave with a real sense of place and history at the end of a weekend—not that there isn't enough to keep families here longer. It's one of the park system gems, but it's rarely crowded, with campsites available even on summer weekends (my family showed up at dusk on a Friday night in July and found a terrific site). The only facility that accommodates RVs is Mazama Campground, which doesn't take reservations. Evening ranger programs take place at the Mazama Campground Amphitheater, and there are excellent trails to hike right from Mazama, including my family's favorite, the 1.7-mi (3-km) Annie Creek Canyon loop.

There's only one trail down to the lake, Cleetwood Cove, named for the first boat explorers brought here and lowered down to the water from the rim. While it drops 700 ft in about a mile, it's not a difficult trail to negotiate, and there are places to rest on the uphill climb (which is comparable to climbing 65 flights of stairs). Take plenty of water, layer your clothes, and bring sunscreen if you're joining the highly recommended ranger-guided boat tour. On the latter journey you'll learn all about the 1,947-ft-deep (584-m-deep) lake, including why it's so blue and history behind the geological events that formed it. You'll also stop at Wizard Island (a true crater), where you can take a short hike. Once back on shore, you may wish to brave the frigid waters by leaping from rocky outcroppings on the shore.

Mazama Campground has 200 sites and a general store. Leave time to visit historic Crater Lake Lodge, where you can take in the magnificent view from the porch or dine in the restaurant. Outside, the park's extensive trail system has more than 90 mi (145 km) of trails, some (such as Castle Crest Wildflower Garden loop) easy enough for toddlers and others (such as the strenuous climb up Mount Scott) challenging enough for families with hiking experience.

Crater Lake National Park, Box 7, Crater Lake, OR 97604, tel. 541/594–2211, www.nps.gov/crla. Park open year-round, campground May–Oct.: $15.75 per night plus $10 per vehicle park entrance fee.

ALASKA

Denali National Park

ALL

For many travelers Denali is synonymous with Alaska—huge, untamed, and full of adventure. Within the park's 6 million acres is 20,320-ft Mt. McKinley, or Denali, as the native people call it; yet the moose, grizzly bears, and caribou may seem even more impressive to young visitors. If your family is ready to brave the wildness that makes Denali so awesome, camp inside the park and let its spirit seep into your soul.

FOR FAMILIES. Wildlife viewing, hiking, interpretive walks and talks, cross-country skiing, and dogsledding are all possible in Denali, though these activities are appropriate for different ages and abilities. Camping in the park, however, is an experience for children and adults alike as long as you're not looking for services and amenities. Riley Creek (100 sites), Savage River (33 sites), and Teklanika (53 sites) are the only three campgrounds accessible by private vehicle. Riley Creek has the best facilities, including a store, but none of the campgrounds have hook-ups. Reservations are strongly recommended. If you want to park your RV and leave it, park transportation is an option. Shuttle buses run between the campgrounds and visitor centers, as well as to some of the park's popular spots, such as Wonder Lake.

Denali National Park, Superintendent, Box 9, Denali Park, AK 99755, tel. 907/683–2294 or 800/622–7275, www.nps.gov/dena. Year-round (all facilities not open all year): $12 per night plus $4 one time per campground reservations fee and $10 per family entrance fee.

CANADA

Burnaby Cariboo RV Park

ALL

Many adventure-oriented families use urban campgrounds such as this one as convenient meeting places for groups preparing to travel into wilderness areas. Vancouver is particularly appealing because it has easy access to many Canadian adventures, as well as outdoor activities within the city limits. The famous Capilano Suspension Bridge, for example, stretches 450 ft across and 230 ft above the Capilano River. Lynn Canyon Park, in North Vancouver, has miles of easy and rugged hiking trails as well as a suspension bridge of its own, hanging some 20 stories above Lynn Creek. Grouse Mountain, just 15 minutes from downtown, has hiking trails, a tram that hikers can ride to alpine meadows, rivers for gold panning, and, in winter, sleigh rides and skiing. Vancouver Island, much of it unpopulated wilderness area, is popular for many outdoor activities and is easily accessible by ferry from the city of Vancouver.

FOR FAMILIES. Burnaby Cariboo RV Park, a private RV park with 217 sites, lies within greater Vancouver and yet is surrounded by the 400-acre Burnaby Lake Regional Park, where bird-watching and walking are favorite pastimes. This park has an equestrian center and a nature center with activities for families, too. A full-service, first-class facility, Burnaby Cariboo has a pool, hot tub, playground, and other amenities; it also has a tour service that will help you book guided fishing tours and other adventures. Because it's on a public transit route, you can park your RV and not have to move it to see the sights.

Burnaby Cariboo RV Park, 8765 Cariboo Pl., Burnaby, British Columbia, Canada V3N 4T2, tel. 604/420–1722, www.bcrvpark.com. Year-round: C$22–$34.75 per night.

Resources

Organizations

National Park Service (Office of Public Inquiries, National Park Service, Department of the Interior, 1849 C St. NW, Room 1013, Washington, DC 20240, tel. 202/208–6843, www.nps.gov) will send a general information kit on the parks and monuments. The **U.S. Forest Service** (Office of Communication, Box 96090, Washington, DC 20090-6090, tel. 877/444–6777) strongly recommends using two Web sites to plan your trip. The National Recreation Reservation Service site (www.reserveusa.com) has information and reservation booking services for everything from cabins to wilderness adventures. On the Recreational Opportunities on Federal Lands site (www.recreation.gov), you can pinpoint your options in each state by choosing specific activities and facilities.

Go RVing Coalition (Box 2999, Dept. P, Reston, VA 20195-0999, tel. 888/467–8464, www.gorving.com) will send you a free introduction to RVing video with rental and travel tips, plus a list of dealers and campgrounds. You can also request more detailed written information on RV campgrounds, rentals, and trip planning.

The **Good Sam Club** (Box 6888, Englewood, CO 80155-6888, www.goodsamclub.com) tel. 805/667–4100 or 800/234–3450) offers services for RVers, including road service, mail forwarding, insurance, travel information, and organized trips.

The **Recreation Vehicle Rental Association** (3930 University Dr., Fairfax, VA 22030, tel. 703/591–7130 or 800/336–0355, www.rvra.org) has a directory with more than 300 listings of American and Canadian rental outlets. For a printed version call 800/872–1074 Ext. 3. **Cruise America** (11 W. Hampton Ave., Mesa, AZ 85210, tel. 480/464–7300 or 800/327–7799, www.cruiseamerica.com) is a nationwide rental organization. It has fly-and-drive options that allow you to pick up your rental in the area where you'll be traveling. In Canada, **CanaDream** (2508 24th Ave. NE, Calgary, Alberta, Canada T1Y 6R8, tel. 403/291–1000, www.canadream.com) puts together RV vacation packages through its rental division, Canada Campers.

Each of the three major campground chains will send you a directory of its member campgrounds: **Best Holiday Trav-L-Park Association** (1310 Jarvis Ave., Elk Grove Village, IL 60007, tel. 800/323–8899, www.best-holiday.com), **Kampgrounds of America** (KOA; Box 30558, Billings, MT 59114, tel. 406/248–7444 or 800/588–2954, www.koa.com); also ask about purchasing a KOA Value Kard, which gives you a 10% discount on all registration fees, and **Leisure Systems, Inc./Yogi Bear's Jellystone Park Camp-Resorts** (6201 Kellogg Ave., Cincinnati, OH 45228-1118, tel. 513/232–6800 or 800/626–3720, www.campjellystone.com). In Canada, **Alberta Country Vacations** (Box 1206, Claresholm, Alberta, Canada T0L O2O, tel. 403/625–2295) will send you a free brochure listing its member ranches and farms, some of which have RV sites.

Periodicals

Don't leave home without a pile of campground directories in your RV. *Trailer Life Campground & RV Services Directory* (2575 Vista del Mar, Ventura, CA 93001, tel. 805/667–4100, www.trailerlife.com) comes from the Good Sam Club and includes discounts for club members. *Wheelers Recreational Vehicle Resort & Campground Guide* (1310 Jarvis Ave., Elk Grove Village, IL 60007, tel. 847/981–0100) rates the various campgrounds, giving them from one to five stars, with three being standard. *Woodall's Campground Directories* (13975 W. Polo Trail Dr., Lake Forest, IL 60045, tel. 847/362–6700 or 800/323–9076) publishes a North American edition and smaller eastern and western editions. Woodall's awards from one to five diamonds for facilities and recreation at each campground.

Books

Millbrook Press publishes two excellent books for school-age children: Michael Weber's *Our National Parks* and Eleanor Ayer's *Our National Monuments.* Both have color photographs and interesting facts.

Also See

Families that like the idea of an adventure that's a movable feast—and bed and bathroom—should look at the Houseboating *and* Sailing chapters. Keep in mind, too, that many trips *in* Archaeology Adventures, Digging for Dinosaur Bones and Other Fossils, Kayaking, *and* Rock Climbing require participants to arrange their own accommodations, often at nearby campgrounds; RVs are perfect for these.

SAILING

Sailing is about teamwork, whether you are learning the basics as a family or working together as a crew. That's a skill that will benefit both parents and children long after they've left a sailing school or vacation behind. Sailing isn't all about work, though. These adventures by their very nature are the stuff of fantasy: uninhabited islands; intriguing wildlife; turquoise waters and coral reefs teeming with exotic fish; interesting cultures—you and your family with the wind and the wide-open sea and nothing but time on your hands. How much you'll work depends on whether you choose a school or a sailing vacation. Either way you will join a long and honored heritage of seagoing families that have come to believe there is no better way to strengthen ties and explore the world than by boat.

Questions to Ask

Is the trip safe—and fun—for kids? Thousands of young children have spent time on boats, but not every boat is right for every child or family. Open railings and slippery decks, for example, are dangerous for young children who are left to play on their own; parents must ask themselves if they are prepared to be on constant watch. Some courses include the deliberate capsizing of a boat so students can learn how to handle that situation. Will your child be overly frightened by this? If so, perhaps he or she is too young to take the course, regardless of whether the school allows it. By asking questions about courses and about the layout of the boat, you'll be able to make a knowledgeable decision.

Are there life jackets on board, and will they fit my children? This is crucial: if a school or ship does not have a life jacket to fit your child, you must get one. Go to a marine supply store or reputable outdoor store, and pick a Coast Guard–approved life vest made for the type of water and area in which you will be. Read the labels carefully. A life vest intended for use in calm inland water will not protect your child on the open seas.

How many years of experience does the captain have sailing in this area? When you go on a sailing vacation, ideally you want a skipper and crew who know the area well—so you'll be safe and so they'll be able to give you interesting stories and facts about the history of the land and the waters near which you'll be sailing, about its plant and animal life, and about the local people.

Are your captains licensed? In the United States boat captains—and other sailors carrying passengers for hire—must be licensed by the Coast Guard. Other countries have corresponding licensing agencies; before you charter a boat with a captain, make sure he or she is, in fact, licensed.

Are your instructors certified, and what are their qualifications? There are organizations with certification criteria for instructors: the United States Sailing Association (US Sailing) and the American Sailing Association (ASA). These competing organizations have differing criteria, resulting in no universal standard for instructors in this country, particularly with regard to recreational sailing. Some very good instructors may not have joined or been tested by either organization. If you're looking for quality instruction, certification is just one measure. Experience is an equally valid measure, so ask how long instructors have been teaching (bad teachers don't last long with a school or company), and how long they've been sailing. This is a sport in which qualifications definitely improve with experience. If, however, you're taking bareboat cruising courses and other advanced classes for sailing boats with engines because your goal is to captain and crew your own boat, your instructor should have a Coast Guard license. When you're taking day sailing courses, Coast Guard licensing is not an issue.

Will I be certified when I finish this course? There are no universally accepted criteria for certifying students. Some schools offer their own certificate; some offer their own and one from US Sailing or ASA. A school's certificate has limited importance. On the one hand, if you were to go to the Caribbean to charter a boat, the company probably would not even ask for certification. If, however, you could not prove sailing competence based on experience, it would require you to take a licensed captain with you at your own expense—but you could still charter the boat. On the other hand, a certificate proves you've learned a certain number of things and sailed a certain number of hours, and it tells instructors you're ready to move on to the next level. And it's nice to hang on your wall.

Can we help crew? If you're joining a sailing expedition or chartering a boat, and if learning is important to your family, choose a ship on which guests are allowed and encouraged to help out and learn the fundamentals of sailing. If your children are interested in learning, make certain the captain and crew want to teach children and have some experience doing so.

Do you carry snorkeling or other recreational gear for children? Snorkeling is an ideal activity for families on boats; so is fishing. Many charters carry snorkel and fishing equipment—but not always in children's sizes. Ask ahead of time because you can't generally buy child-size gear in exotic locations.

Is any other recreational equipment available? Some boats carry kayaks or canoes; some have dinghies and inflatables. You may be able to windsurf or scuba dive from some boats. If you are interested in a particular water sport, make a request well in advance of your sailing date.

What's included in the cost? If you sign up with a sailing school, courses are usually instruction only, with no meals or accommodations included; that's the case with most of the courses listed here. If you take a course during which you live on the boat, however, accommodations and meals on board are included, unless otherwise noted. There are also resort courses, which combine sailing school with lodging and the use of facilities at the school's resort location. When you charter a boat or join a scheduled trip on a sailing vessel, accommodations, meals, activities, sailing instruction, and sightseeing are included. Airport pickup may also be part of the trip fee. Alcohol is usually extra, as is dive equipment.

Instruction

Sailing schools, of course, are mostly instruction, though they often combine learning with playing in some of the world's most popular vacation spots. Charters and sailing adventures, on the other hand, generally give live-aboard guests the option of working alongside the crew or doing nothing at all. Although relaxing is great, why not use some of the time for hands-on learning from real sailors—people who have a unique experience and perspective to share. Learning to sail this way is just too good an opportunity to miss.

Finding the Fun

Northeast: North End Shipyard Schooners, Offshore Sailing School, Outward Bound. **Mid-Atlantic:** Annapolis Sailing School, Offshore Sailing School. **South:** Annapolis Sailing School, Ocean Voyages, Offshore Sailing School, Sailing Florida Charters and Sailing School. **Midwest:** Offshore Sailing School. **West Coast:** Ocean Voyages. **Alaska:** GORP Travel, Ocean Voyages, Rascals in Paradise. **Hawaii:** Ocean Voyages. **Caribbean:** Annapolis Sailing School, Bitter End Yacht Club, Ocean Voyages, Offshore Sailing School, Sunsail, Star Clippers. **Mexico:** Ocean Voyages. **Central America, South America:** Ocean Voyages. **Europe, Africa, Asia, Australia, New Zealand:** Ocean Voyages, Rascals in Paradise, Sunsail, Star Clippers. **South Pacific:** Ocean Voyages, Rascals in Paradise.

Favorite Schools and Charters

Annapolis Sailing School

5+

Annapolis Sailing School, main campus is on Chesapeake Bay in Maryland, is the oldest and largest sailing school in the country. At more than 195 mi (314 km) long and up to 30 mi (48 km) wide—and with nine major rivers feeding into it—Chesapeake Bay is the largest estuary in North America and justly gives Annapolis its reputation as one of the country's great sailing and seafood capitals. The school has branch classrooms in St. Petersburg, Florida (at the Holiday Inn Sun Spree Resort Hotel), and Christiansted, St. Croix in the U.S. Virgin Islands. All Annapolis Sailing School courses are primarily hands-on. With the exception of about four hours of lecture time, classes take place in boats on the water.

FOR FAMILIES. Become a Sailing Family is the popular course in which parents and children work together to master the sailing of 30-ft sloops. Offered only at the Annapolis campus, the class combines the beginner weekend course with five days of cruising, and it's one of the few courses that includes lodging. Families spend three nights at hotels in Annapolis, then four nights on a boat in Chesapeake Bay. An instructor is on board each day.

If you want to vacation together but learn separately, the school suggests you combine adult courses with Kid Ship, for ages 5 and up. Scheduled only in Annapolis, Kid Ship coincides with the school's adult courses, so while parents are learning on 24-ft sloops, children are on 12-ft sailboats, which most youngsters find manageable. These are not live-aboard courses; families are out on the water from about 9 to 4, then on their own in the evenings.

Annapolis Sailing School, Box 3334, Annapolis, MD 21403, tel. 410/267–7205 or 800/638–9192, annapolissailing.com. Mar.–Oct.: 2–5 days, $295–$575 adults, $200–$375 children (Kid Ship); 7 days, $2,905–$4,520 for 2–6 students in the family course.

Bitter End Yacht Club

6+

The Bitter End Yacht Club is for both sailors and sailor wannabes. The resort is tucked into the flowering hills of Virgin Gorda in the British Virgin Islands, its beach a dazzling sweep of white against the clear turquoise waters of North Sound. The location is remote; the only way to get here is by boat. Families can stay at the resort or in live-aboard yachts moored in the harbor—or do a little of each. There's nothing pretentious about the resort; barefoot and casual is the norm. It's an incredible place for family connecting and rejuvenating. And because the resort is family-owned and operated, by the end of your trip you'll feel like part of the Bitter End family, too.

FOR FAMILIES. The Bitter End has more than 100 watercraft, with windsurfers, kayaks, and Boston Whalers in addition to the many types of sailboats—including Lasers, Rhodes 19s, Escapes, and Optimists. All guests can take the free Sailing 101 course offered by an experienced staff of instructors. The pros at the Bitter End Yacht Club Sailing and Windsurfing School also teach beginner to advanced sailing clinics (at an additional charge), as well as windsurfing, which even young children can try. Youngsters ages 7 to 12 can join the Junior Sailing Program, offered five days a week, year-round, with complimentary lessons during summer months and some school holidays. Learn to Sail and specialized regatta weeks are scheduled periodically, ideal for adults and teens who want to immerse themselves in the sport.

Although sailing is the focus here, there are plenty of other activities. Snorkel day trips leave from the resort to various reefs and coves, and there's fishing and hiking, too. Or just borrow one of the Boston Whaler skiffs and motor out to an island of your own for a family picnic away from it all.

Thanksgiving is Family Fun Week at the Bitter End. Not only are children ages 6 to 17 welcomed at significantly reduced prices, but there special activities are also scheduled. Kids can try Sail Caribbean, a traveling sailing program for ages 6 and up, or the Junior Program, which includes storytelling, beach games, sand painting, nature walks, and an introduction to sailing, windsurfing, and snorkeling. Families can also team up to race in the Turkey Day Regatta. Between April and December (called Celebration Season) the resort offers a five-night, six-day Admiral's Family Package, which includes lodging for two adults and two children in two adjoining rooms, all meals, all water sports, an introductory sailing course, daily excursions, and airport transfers (the airport is across the water on the island of Tortola).

Bitter End Yacht Club, North Sound, Virgin Gorda, British Virgin Islands. U.S. sales and reservations office, 10305 NW 41st St., Suite 219, Miami, FL 33178, tel. 305/468–0168 or 800/872–2392, www.beyc.com. Year-round: 6–11 days, Admiral's Inclusive Package $2,150–$7,700 per room; Celebration Season 5-night family package $3,400 for a family of 4.

GORP Travel

ALL

Small boats traveling along the 1,000 mi (1,610 km) of protected waterway in Alaska's Inside Passage can bring visitors closer to the real Alaska than large cruise ships ever could. Marked by deep fjords and magnificent snowy peaks, the passage has hundreds of islands, small villages, and extensive forested areas that provide food and shelter for black and brown bears and bald eagles. Along the coast you'll spot otters, seals, and sea lions, while orcas and humpbacks leap and glide in deeper waters. Sound Sailing, the local operator for this adventure, has two 50-ft sloops and a wealth of experience to share with families in America's great northern frontier. You can embark in Petersburg or Sitka.

FOR FAMILIES. Each boat has three private cabins to accommodate a family of five or six (three small children can share one double berth). No sailing experience is required, and you're welcome to help or learn to crew under the guidance of a licensed captain. The pace and itinerary are flexible: you can take the dinghy ashore for beachcombing and inland hiking, relax in a natural hot spring, or learn about natural history and Tlingit culture. There's first-rate fishing equipment on board, so plan on testing your skills against Pacific halibut or salmon.

GORP Travel, 10055 Westmoor Dr., Suite 215, Westminster, CO 80021, tel. 720/887–8500 or 877/440–4677, gorptravel.gorp.com. Apr.–Oct.: 7 days, $1,645–$1,945, depending on season.

North End Shipyard Schooners

12+

North End Shipyard Schooners consists of two owner-operated vessels working cooperatively and sailing from North End Shipyard Wharf in Rockland, Maine. The *American Eagle*, built in 1931, is a National Historic Landmark; the *Heritage* was built at the shipyard in 1983. The ships have no set itineraries but instead travel with the prevailing winds, anchoring in a different scenic harbor each night. There are hundreds of islands to sail around and explore along Maine's rocky midcoast.

FOR FAMILIES. Both the *Heritage*, a 95-ft schooner for 30 passengers, and the *American Eagle*, a 92-ft schooner for 26 passengers, welcome families with children at least 12 years old on all cruises. Families are encouraged but not required to help around the ships. Activities include whale-watching, stargazing, swimming, and exploring the small coves where the ships anchor. The captains and crew are adept at telling salty tales of the sea, and they may even teach some sailing skills such as knot tying and rowing. Every cruise includes an old-fashioned Maine lobster bake.

Only two sailors can fit in a cabin, so a family of four needs two separate cabins. If there are just three of you, your child will probably bunk with another passenger of the same sex and age unless one of the single cabins is available.

North End Shipyard Schooners, Box 482, Rockland, ME 04841, tel. 207/594–8007 or 800/648–4544, www.midcoast.com/~schooner. Late May–early Oct.: 3–6 days, $395–$805.

Ocean Voyages

ALL

For 20 years Ocean Voyages has arranged small group sailings and maritime adventures for all kinds of sea lovers, including families. Founder Mary Crowley, an accomplished sailor, introduced her daughter Colleen to sailing as a toddler. Since then they've sailed most of the world's oceans together. Whether your family is looking for a charter or a scheduled sailing, whether you want to sail in the Pacific, the Caribbean, the Mediterranean, or around the world, Ocean Voyages will find a boat and a crew to give you the oceangoing vacation of a lifetime.

FOR FAMILIES. When you call, ask for the Family Sailing information sheet, which lists dozens of yachts worldwide—all ships that Ocean Voyages knows will welcome families. Some of the boats and crews change from year to year, but here are a few typical family offerings: A 72-ft yacht crewed by a New Zealand couple that takes passengers through the Pacific islands; an eight-passenger yacht that sails around the Greek islands and along Turkey's Turquoise Coast; a 10-passenger, 71-ft yacht and its family-of-four crew, who make a nature-oriented trip around Fiji, Vanuatu, the Solomon Islands, New Guinea, and Australia; a six-passenger boat (or a 12- to 22-person schooner) that makes a sailing, snorkeling, swimming, whale-watching, and surfing trip around the Hawaiian islands; and the 87-ft, four- to eight-person *Ocean Leopard,* whose Australian crew invites you to join part of their round-the-world voyage in Indonesia, Thailand, the Indian Ocean, Africa, or beyond.

Families who want to sail in Darwin's wake can arrange six- to 30-passenger yachts to the Galápagos Islands, where you can sail for a week and then stay for another at a small, family-owned inn Isla Santa Cruz. If time allows, the company will also arrange land excursions for those who want to explore more of Ecuador.

Ships also sail off California, Florida, and the Bahamas, the Pacific Northwest, Alaska, Mexico, Tahiti, the Marquesas, Tonga, Fiji, and Vanuatu, among other places, and most vessels accommodate family groups of 3 to 16. Charters are usually for one week, but longer trips—from six weeks to the entire summer—can also be arranged. Ocean Voyages can coordinate sailing family reunions as well.

Ocean Voyages, 1709 Bridgeway, Sausalito, CA 94965, tel. 415/332–4681, www.oceanvoyages.com. Year-round (all ships not available all months): 7 days, $875–$2,850 adults, $420–$1,600 children; rates depend on location and group size; typically children under 12 receive 50% discount, some vessels take infants free of charge, and many ships offer special family rates.

Offshore Sailing School

8+

Steve Colgate, America's Cup and Olympic sailor, believes that sailing is for everyone. Since he founded Offshore Sailing School in 1964, the institution has taught more than 100,000 people of all ages and backgrounds. Offshore has schools in Jersey City, New Jersey; Chelsea Piers, New York City; Chicago, Illinois; and Stamford, Connecticut; besides branches at five first-class resort areas: South Seas Plantation on Captiva Island, Florida; Prospect Reef Resort, Tortola, British Virgin Islands; Newport Harbor Hotel & Marina, Newport, Rhode Island; Hawk's Cay Resort, Duck Key, Florida, and St. Petersburg, Florida.

FOR FAMILIES. Families with children 12 and up can join any of the school's courses. If you have at least four family members—enough to fill one boat—the school is flexible on the minimum age but feels the instruction is most appropriate for children 8 and older. A family of four participating in the same course also gets a discount. There are a variety of basic courses, which you can take at the school sites or in some cases as part of a resort package.

Learn to Sail, with three-, four-, and eight-day versions, is for beginners and intermediate sailors; it's taught on 26-ft Colgates, with no more than four students to a boat. The extensive list of topics covered includes nautical terminology, hull speed, mechanics of wind and sail, crew overboard recovery—even backward sailing. More experienced sailors can take such courses as performance sailing, bareboat cruising preparation, live-aboard cruising, and sailboat racing.

The South Seas Resort branch on Captiva offers packages that combine the sailing school with accommodations at this highly regarded family resort. Children ages 7 through 11 can also take the Offshore's Junior Captain's program; instruction is aboard Hunter 90s and daily hours coincide with parents' on-water instruction courses. For families with children not taking a sailing course, South Seas Plantation offers a supervised children's program and baby-sitting services.

Finally, families might consider Fast Track to Cruising, which combines the Learn to Sail and Live-Aboard Cruising courses at several of the school's vacation destinations. At the end of this course, you'll crew your own boat—without instructors—on a 24-hour minicharter.

Offshore Sailing School, 16731 McGregor Blvd., Fort Myers, FL 33908, tel. 941/454–1700 or 800/221–4326, www.offshore-sailing.com. Year-round (all locations not available all months): 3–10 days, $795–$1,095 for courses only, $836–$4,347 for resort packages, depending on accommodations and season; Junior Captain's course $495; ask about family packages at Captiva.

Outward Bound

14+

Well-known and highly regarded for its wilderness courses featuring climbing and solo hiking and camping, Outward Bound actually grew out of a World War II program designed to help young British recruits better survive the harsh physical challenges of wartime sailing. The school's name, in fact, comes from the nautical term for a ship leaving its home port bound for the open ocean, and it's an apt analogy for students who leave behind comfort and familiarity to challenge themselves and to grow. According to the organization's philosophy, a week-long sailing course not only develops strong nautical skills for parent and child, but it also forges bonds that will strengthen relationships on and off the water.

FOR FAMILIES. The parent–child course, generally offered a couple of times each summer, starts and ends in Rockland, Maine; participants spend about six days sailing in Penobscot Bay and two days on land activities on a few of the nearly 3,000 islands in the area. Usually from 10 to 12 people share one boat, and the weather dictates your schedule to a large extent. Your family will focus on teamwork, leadership, and seamanship skills while working on a 30-ft open ketch. The entire group rotates responsibilities throughout the course, and among the skills you master are sail handling (including tacking and jibing), navigation (chart and compass use and course plotting), and boat handling, which means helmsmanship as well as such fundamentals as anchoring and rowing. During the island stays, you try rock climbing, rappelling, and a ropes course.

At night you camp out on islands in platform tents for about half the course and sleep on the boat the rest of the time. The boat does not have berths or cover; students need to bring their own sleeping bags. In the Outward Bound tradition, you will learn how to construct a shelter over the boat if the weather demands it.

Outward Bound, 100 Mystery Point Rd., Garrison, NY 10524, tel. 914/424–4000 or 800/243–8520, www.outwardbound.org. June–Aug.: 8 days, $945 per person, plus $75 *application fee. Financial aid available for some courses.*

Rascals in Paradise

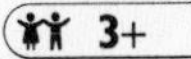

Rascals represents several yachts around the world that are ideal for one family or for two families to charter together. Like all the outfitters, hotels, and resorts with which Rascals contracts, the charter owners and captains are chosen not only for their sailing expertise and knowledge of the areas in which they work but also for their love of sharing their world with children and parents.

FOR FAMILIES. Typical of a Rascals charter is the *Discovery*, a 65-ft yacht owned and operated by Dean Rand, with help from his four young daughters. Dean tries to match his children with the children on each sailing: if older children are coming, he brings his older girls along; when families have young children, the younger daughters sail, too. The *Discovery*, which explores Alaska's Prince William Sound, has six cabins for 12 passengers; families can help out with ship chores if they wish.

Although the exact itinerary depends on the weather, the group's interests, and the location of wildlife, the boat usually sails to Barry Arm and Harriman Fjord, past the expansive Columbia Glacier with its 300-ft walls of blue ice, and through Orca Bay. Families can see where the *Exxon Valdez* ran aground and watch sea lions and puffins. There are several opportunities to go ashore via inflatable Zodiak rafts; if you like, you can hike to a waterfall. The food—freshly baked goods, seafood, steaks, salads, vegetables, and wine—will please children and parents. At night the ship anchors in protected coves. On the six- and eight-day voyages you spend two nights at a family-friendly bed-and-breakfast in the Rands' small hometown of Cordova, on Prince William Sound. There you can meet local families and explore a glacier and other sights away from the coast.

If Alaska is not for your family, consider sailing the coast of Turkey. Rascals has several ships from which to choose, some large enough to accommodate a family reunion. If you wish, you can tour Istanbul and Cappadocia in addition to cruising. Ask Rascals about charters in Fiji, Australia, Tonga, Tahiti, Papua New Guinea, Vanuatu, and the Solomon Islands, as well.

Rascals in Paradise, 2107 Van Ness, Suite 403, San Francisco, CA 94109, tel. 415/921–7000 or 800/872–7225, www.camprascal.com. Alaska, May–Sept.: 3–7 days, $2,450–$3,600, 25% discount for children 4–15. Months vary for other charters: Turkey starts at $875 per day for a family of 6, with all meals and activities.

Sailing Florida Charters and Sailing School

16+

Situated at the Renaissance Vinoy Resort in St. Petersburg, Florida, Sailing Florida offers five courses: basic sailing, bareboat chartering, basic-to-bareboat, coastal navigation, and advanced coastal cruising. Classes are available seven days a week, year-round, and the schedule is flexible so families can fit classes into their resort stay. The school uses the American Sailing Association curriculum, and all class work takes place on 29- to 34-ft Hunters. Each sailboat is fully equipped for both safety and comfort, with shade and refrigerators for snacks and lunches. Once your group is ready to leave the docks, you'll head out into the protected waters of Tampa Bay or, in the more advanced courses, the Gulf of Mexico. All successfully completed courses result in a certificate from the American Sailing Association.

FOR FAMILIES. Parents and teens can sail together in any of the courses; the school will consider children of 14 or 15 with a real interest in sailing, but talk to instructors first (a younger teen not ready for the course-work may be allowed to sail with you while you learn). The school has a minimum of four students per class. Families in the beginner classes learn all about sailing terminology, equipment, theory, points of sail, crew communication, crew overboard recovery, knots, traffic rules, and more, with an emphasis on docking and safety. No experience is required. In the more advanced courses, which have prerequisites of basic course work, the focus changes to learning troubleshooting, increasing technical (as in how cooling and electrical systems work) and safety knowledge, and accomplishing more advanced sailing techniques. The six-day basic-to-bareboat course includes one night on board the sailboat.

Originally built in 1925 as the Vinoy Park Hotel, the Renaissance Vinoy Resort has been completely renovated with careful attention to historical detail. When you're not sailing, take the hotel's history tour and luncheon. Staff members at the hotel can also help you get to all of the area's best museums and amusements. There's a supervised children's program from June through August. If you have a young child and sign up for a sailing course at another time of year, the hotel will help arrange child care.

Sailing Florida Charters and Sailing School, 1421 Bay St. SE, Suite 4, St. Petersburg, FL 33701, tel. 800/879–2244, www.sailingflorida.com. Year-round: 2–6 days, $375–$1,275, 10% discount for 2nd, 3rd, and 4th person in your group.

Star Clippers

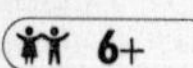

The Star Clipper line is different than most other entries in this chapter in that it offers what can be accurately described as luxury cruising. Yet to sail on the Star Clipper, Star Flyer, and Royal Clipper *is* an adventure, for these ships are authentic recreations of classic sailing clipper ships that rode the waves in the 19th century.

Both the Star Flyer and Star Clipper are four-masted, square-rigged barquentines carrying 170 passengers and 75 crewmembers. The ships measure 360 ft and require 36,000 square ft of sail. Royal Clipper, added to the line in 2000, is the first five-masted, full-rigged sailing ship to be built since 1902 when the Preussen, the classic German vessel that inspired her, was launched. She is the largest true sailing clipper ship in the world at 439 ft. It takes 56,000 square ft of sail to rig her and she carries 227 passengers and 105 crewmembers, 20 of whom are needed just to handle the sails. Traditional teak decks and mahogany rails with brass fittings hearken to a long-ago, golden age of sailing, and the ships are always under sail power when at sea unless weather or sea conditions require the addition of engines. In summer and fall the ships sail the Mediterranean along the Italian Riviera, around Spain's Catalonia and Balearic Islands, the French Riviera, and off the ports and coastal towns of Greece and Turkey. In winter, Royal Clipper and Star Clipper can be found in the Caribbean, while the Star Flyer sails through the Suez Canal and across the Indian Ocean to its popular itineraries out of Phuket, Thailand.

FOR FAMILIES. Children are wholly welcome on Star Clippers. As the brochure states, "While there is no structured program providing supervision and care for young children, they are invited to participate in shipboard activities according to their ability." There's no age restriction, and families with infants often sail. However, the layout, the experience, and the activities are really best suited for children 6 and older. Clipper ships are ideal for independent families who want to cruise but who don't want the crowds and frenetic activity of mega cruise ships. The clippers were designed to be in harmony with the environment and to go at a leisurely pace. Rather than pulling into ports overrun with tourists, the clipper ships explore smaller coves and port towns. As for adventures, there are plenty of opportunities when the ships are anchored. Hiking, biking, snorkeling and diving among reefs and wrecks, windsurfing, and other watersports are all available. But the real adventure lies in the experience of being on an ocean-going sailing vessel.

Among the most unique activities is climbing up the ratlines to lookout stations on the yardarms 60 ft above the decks. Each lookout has high safety rails and a teak settee from which to watch the onboard action or perhaps marine life in the sea far below. Before climbing, passengers don a safety vest that's tethered to a watching crewmember who keeps the lines secure while passengers make their (easy) way up. It's not for those with acrophobia, but for all others, it's an adventure long remembered.

Each double cabin can accommodate a third berth if needed. The ships also have pools, as well as such onboard activities as scavenger hunts and crab races. Other than these, though, Star Clippers don't have a lot of bells and whistles—rather, they're about recreating the experience of sailing the magnificent Tall Ships of yesteryear.

Although American parents might feel most comfortable taking a family cruise in the Caribbean, Europe also has a wonderful environment for children; Mediterranean ports are always filled with European families traveling together. Thailand, too, has an extremely child-oriented, family-friendly culture, and the resort town of Phuket is a popular international destination for European and Scandinavian families, among others. For an even greater adventure, join the ships on their ocean crossings at the beginning and end of each season.

Star Clippers, 4101 Salzedo St., Coral Gables, FL 33146, tel. 800/442–0551, www.starclippers.com. Year-round: 7 days, $1,345–$4,795 per person, children sharing with parents at third-person rate $445; ask about ocean crossing dates and prices.

Sunsail

ALL

Sunsail is well known in Europe for its 10 sailing-focused beach clubs in Greece and Turkey, and in the Caribbean for bareboat and crewed charters. In 1999 the company added Colonna Club on Antigua to its roster of beach clubs, and the name Sunsail has become increasingly familiar to North American families. Although the Caribbean is easily accessible for North Americans, it's also popular with Europeans, so Colonna Club's clientele and staff are very international. The resort is located on the northern tip of Antigua in Hodges Bay, set on a crescent of beach in a protected cove. Year-round crosswinds make the spot ideal for both sailing and windsurfing right from shore—not that that's unusual in Antigua, where clear, aqua waters and perfect breezes are the norm. Most of the resort's hotel rooms and one- to three-bedroom villas overlook either the beach or the expansive pool.

FOR FAMILIES. Sunsail's staff is excellent, possessing not only an ability to communicate the fundamentals of sailing, but a gift for working with kids of all ages, too. Sailing instruction at the resort is available in dinghys, catamarans, and day yachts, and guests can choose two- or three-day classes. For beginners, there's a daily free class as well. You can take it for just one day, or attend every day if you wish; instructors use a different vessel (a laser, optimist, topaz, sport 16, buzz, or spice) from the hotel's small-boat fleet each morning. For an extra charge, you can also use Sunsail's windsurfers, motorboats, and day yachts. An instructor generally takes two or three students per class, but larger families can learn together and include children in the class with prior arrangements. There's a minimum age of 18 for the three-day Yacht Training course, but if your family has sailing experience and you want to include your older children in that course, Sunsail will try to work with you. Talk to the instruction staff as soon as you arrive.

You can combine a stay at the resort with a bareboat or crewed charter—and get a discount by doing so. You can even sign up with one of the scheduled flotillas (groups of chartered boats) if you want company for your sailing adventure.

Sunsail isn't quite all-inclusive, but the basic price covers a lot: breakfasts, about half of your lunches and dinners, use of the small-boat fleet, daily clinics, snorkeling gear, and a trip to Shirley Heights on the south tip of the island for Antigua's famous sunset party. The club also has an exceptional year-round children's program staffed by counselors determined to help create a perfect vacation for visiting kids. It's divided by age: 4 months to 2 years, ages 2 to 4, 5 to 7, 8 to 12, and 13 to 16. The facility has its own kids' pool, playroom, nursery, and teen area, and campers can try tennis, sailing, waterskiing, and more. The program is included in the children's rates; there's a charge of $210 per week for infants younger than 4 months.

If you can't make it to Sunsail this year, you can still take advantage of its sailing classes. The Sunsail School Network Program is an affiliation of schools around the country. If you graduate from a member school, you'll get a discount on your first Sunsail charter along with other perks. Call for information or go to www.sunsail.com.

North American reservations: SunsailUSA, 980 Awald Rd., Suite 302, Annapolis, MD 21403, tel. 410/280–2553 or 800/327–2276, www.sunsail.com. Year-round: 7 days, $570–$870 per adult, $300–$420 ages 2–12 sharing with parents. Ask about daily rates. Sailing classes: $80–$220. Charters: $2,000–$3,500 per week bareboats, $8,000–$9,000 with crew.

Resources

Organizations

The **American Sailing Association** (13922 Marquesas Way, Marina del Rey, CA 90292, tel. 310/822–7171, www.american-sailing.com) and **United States Sailing Association** (Box 1260, Portsmouth, RI 02871-0907, tel. 401/683–0800 or 800/877–2451, www.ussailing.org) are the major sailing organizations in this country. Call ASA for a list of affiliate members or schools in your area that teach ASA courses. US Sailing has a "Where to Sail" pamphlet listing rentals, schools, and US Sailing programs across the country. Both organizations have books and other materials available for sale. **International Sailing Federation** (www.sailing.org) is based in Europe and is the governing authority for the sport of sailing worldwide. It works to develop sailing, represents sailors in matters concerning the sport, and is best known as providing racing rules and regulations. Contact this organization to find out about programs for disabled sailors, too.

Periodicals

Cruising World (The Sailing Company, 5 John Clark Rd., Newport, RI 02840, tel. 401/845–5100) is a monthly magazine for sailors who cruise the world in their own sailboats; it's also interesting reading for novice sailors.

Some issues include articles that discuss family sailing and educating children about cruising. An annual special section on chartering that lists and rates companies is a must for anyone considering a charter vacation. The classified ads have opportunities for crewing, too.

Also See

If you can't decide between sailing and taking an animal-encounter vacation, see Wildlife Encounters; some of these adventures include both. If you want to be on and *under* the water, see Snorkeling and Diving.

SNORKELING AND DIVING

The ocean is like a circus—a place where brilliant colors, balletic grace, and heart-in-your- mouth thrills exist in a swirling world unto itself. Or perhaps it's more like a vast, watery classroom, filled with fascinating creatures that tell us not only about life under the sea but sometimes about ourselves as well. Children, of course, know about the underwater world from myths and fairy tales as well as from science and nonfiction books. Seeing underwater life firsthand is both intriguing and educational at any age.

Families have several options for exploring underwater. Snorkelers float face down in the water and look at the sea below. Almost any child who can swim and is comfortable in the water can snorkel, though some young children don't like wearing a mask over their face or breathing through a tube. Scuba diving is more complicated. You must be certified (pass written and practical tests) or take a certification course on-site before you can dive with a licensed dive operator. The minimum age for certification is 12.

Because both snorkeling and diving are often particularly good around reef areas, many of the places listed here are ideal for both activities. Parents, however, should be aware that snorkelers and divers don't always depart together. A number of resorts with children's activity programs are included because these allow parents and teens to dive while younger children snorkel or play and explore with peers and counselors.

This chapter presents a cross section of snorkeling and diving experiences. All of these entries, like those in the chapter on Wildlife Encounters, are away from the mainland United States. Most are in other countries—places where you are not likely to encounter crowds or cloudy waters and where sea life is unusual in some way. These resorts or operators are all known for their work with children and families as well as for their expertise around the water. The selections are truly adventure vacations, which is not to say you can't don a mask and fins for half-day and day trips at many resorts in Florida, California, or even Michigan.

Of the more than 30 dive and snorkel trips here, some are based on ships, some are resort-based, and others are for adventurers who want to aid in scientific research while snorkeling or diving. The choices are for a variety of ages, abilities, and interests. Most are in places where families can learn the sports or where already certified divers can share their passion with other members of their family.

Questions to Ask

What kind of equipment is used for snorkeling and diving? Snorkelers need a mask, fins, and a snorkel. Young children will require some time to get used to this equipment. Divers use the same equipment as snorkelers; this is often referred to as personal equipment. They also use dive gear. The most important pieces of gear are regulators and BCDs (buoyancy control devices), which you inflate and deflate depending on whether you want to go up or down. Serious divers usually own their own. Divers also need weight belts to help them dive down, as well as two gauges, one to measure depth and one to measure the air in the tanks. A tank or tanks, generally carried in a backpack, provide air. Some divers wear wet suits.

Is snorkeling equipment available for rent? What about diving equipment? If you don't have snorkeling equipment and don't want to borrow or buy it, make certain rentals are available on the boat or at the resort—and in the right sizes. You'll need properly fitting masks and fins as well as snorkels small enough for your children. Also, if anyone in your family wears glasses, you may want to ask a dive shop about purchasing a prescription mask. Dive packages and dive operators generally supply the necessary diving equipment but not personal gear.

Do we have to be certified in advance to dive? At some resorts and on some boats, instruction is not an option; you must be certified and have your C-card (certification card) with you in order to dive. Be clear about this beforehand if you are not yet certified.

Do you have diving certification courses? Many resorts and resort areas have certification courses. The main certification organizations in this country are the National Association of Underwater Instructors (NAUI) and the Professional Association of Dive Instructors (PADI). Resorts and resort areas are likely to offer courses from these organizations. NAUI and PADI teach basically the same skills, although their instructional methods differ. Courses generally combine anywhere from 25 to 32 hours of instruction divided between classroom and pool work, plus checkout dives (a real dive in fairly shallow water on which your instructor tests your skills). Children ages 12 through 15 can take the same course with parents and receive junior certification; the only difference for someone with such certification is he or she must be accompanied by an adult on dives. If you want to devote more of your vacation time to actual diving, you can take the classroom and pool portion near your home and finish up in the location of your choice. If you do this, make sure the resort or operator accepts the type of certification whose process you have begun at home.

Do you have a resort course? If you don't want to commit to full certification, most resorts offer a less expensive resort course, with anywhere from 6 to 20 hours of instruction, pool work, and dive time over one to five days. Resort courses certify you to dive only at that resort and only during that stay. The minimum age is 12.

Can snorkelers go out with divers? Sometimes snorkelers and divers visit the same site together. Even operators that allow this, however, may change their minds if the weather or sea is rough or if the boat is full. If you have children who are not old enough to dive and who plan to snorkel, be aware you may not be able to go out together.

Is there snorkeling right from shore? Resorts that have snorkeling from their shores, or boats that take snorkelers to the shores of cays and islands, make life easy for parents with young children. It's much less intimidating for children to learn to snorkel in shallow water.

What happens with ear pressure? Diving creates the same kind of pressure as on airplane flights and other activities at high altitudes. If your preteen or teen is prone to ear pain in these situations, discuss ahead of time how to clear your ears by holding your nose and blowing out. Talk to your pediatrician, too.

Are shots or other health precautions necessary? Some diving trips take place in foreign countries that require inoculations and preventive medication. Check far in advance and ask a pediatrician or the local health department about health precautions in foreign countries, especially as they relate to children. Always pack basic children's medication—acetaminophen, an antihistamine, cough syrup, motion-sickness pills, and antidiarrheal pills; these can be hard to find abroad. If your child is prone to ear infections or any other ailments, you may want to ask your pediatrician for an antibiotic that doesn't need to be refrigerated.

What's included in the cost? Certification courses generally include class materials (such as a manual), instruction, gear with which to learn, transportation to dive sites, and checkout dives. Equipment for checkout dives is often an extra charge. Dive packages at resorts typically give you one or two dives daily, transportation to dive sites, and lodging. Some cover meals; this is noted in individual listings. You often get dive equipment, such as tanks, weights, and belts, as part of the deal. Personal gear—snorkels, masks, fins—is usually not included. Dedicated dive-boat vacations are pretty much all-inclusive: equipment, gear, dives, local transportation, accommodations, and meals. Diving instruction, however, is generally not provided on these boats. Any exceptions in pricing for these various experiences are noted in the individual listings.

Instruction

Depending on the resort or boat from which you're diving, you will already have had all your instruction—and a certification card to prove it—or you'll need to sign up for a resort or certification course before you can dive. Any good snorkel boat operator will give basic instruction on snorkeling if your family needs it, though practice is what will make you comfortable in the water.

A Note About Diving

When making travel plans, remember that you cannot fly within 24 hours after scuba diving.

Finding the Fun

West Coast: Jean-Michel Cousteau Family Camp. **Hawaii:** Jean-Michel Cousteau Family Camp, Ocean Voyages. **Mexico:** Rascals in Paradise. **Central America:** GORP Travel, Ocean Voyages, Rascals in Paradise. **Caribbean:** Earthwatch Institute, Hyatt Regency Grand Cayman Resort and Villas, Ocean Voyages, Rascals in Paradise. **Around the Pacific:** Earthwatch Institute, Ocean Voyages, Rascals in Paradise, World of Diving & Adventure Vacations.

Favorite Places to Snorkel and Dive

Earthwatch Institute

16+

With Earthwatch Institute, a nonprofit organization, your family can satisfy both a love of snorkeling or diving and a desire to contribute to scientific research. From the Caribbean Sea to the Indian Ocean, researchers on Earthwatch-supported projects are working to better understand marine life or to protect endangered species and threatened environments. Snorkelers and divers aid scientists by observing, photographing, and tagging fish and marine animals. If you have teenagers, pick a place or pick a species—the Earthwatch world is your oyster, so to speak.

FOR FAMILIES. You must be a certified diver to work at Earthwatch dive sites; plan on two dives a day, which means two to four hours in the water. Snorkelers average three to five hours a day in the water. Participants also do much related work on land: cataloging, marking, sketching, and sometimes working with electronic equipment. Some sites are for divers or snorkelers only; at others both groups work together. Volunteers on these projects stay in everything from campsites and field stations to houses and hotels. Lodging is generally included in the cost (though campers may need to bring their own camping equipment), and volunteers usually take turns with food preparation.

If your family loves dolphins and whales, Earthwatch probably has a research project for you. Typical is the study in Mauritius, where snorkelers (and strong swimmers) work with behavioral ecologist Delphine Legay to study how cetacean populations in the Indian Ocean are faring; research work includes underwater videotaping. Off Great Abaco in the Bahamas, families work eight-hour shifts spotting and identifying whales and dolphins, then snorkel in the turquoise waters during free time. Earthwatch also has projects involving manatees in Belize and octopuses in Costa Rica.

The health of coral reefs affects human life and health more than many of us may think, which is why the study of reefs throughout the world is of such importance to researchers. Among the many reef-related Earthwatch projects in the Caribbean is one for snorkelers on the island of San Salvador in the Bahamas, and another off Puerto Rico for certified divers only. Snorkelers and divers can aid in efforts to map coral habitats in the Grenadines, using state-of-the-art technology and a research boat. Near Barbados, volunteers study coral reef ecology by observing and tracking the reproduction and survival of damselfish.

Volunteers help marine researchers in the Pacific, too. Off Batangas, south of Quezon City in the Philippines, underwater visibility is astonishing. Here diving and snorkeling volunteers document the state of the coral, surrounding rock, rubble, sand, algae, and seagrass, and count butterfly fish and other inhabitants. Filipinos depend on fish for 60% of their animal protein, yet through current practices of dynamiting fish and careless anchoring of fishing and tourist boats, the Filipinos have been decimating the marine life they depend on. The goal of this research is to provide data to encourage the maintenance of the islands' ecosystems.

Earthwatch projects change from year to year, so check the current catalog to find the adventure that most interests your group. In addition to marine animal and reef projects for snorkelers and divers, Earthwatch sometimes sends volunteers to help with studies involving sunken ships.

Earthwatch Institute, 3 Clocktower Place, Suite 100, Box 75, Maynard, MA 01754, tel. 978/461–0081 or 800/776–0188, www.earthwatch.org. Year-round: 8–14 days, $995–$2,195.

GORP Travel

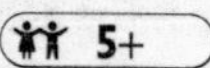

Roatán is 35 mi (56 km) off the coast of Honduras, in the Islas de la Bahía. On a palm-covered island near Roatán, the private bungalows of Anthony's Key Resort blend into a lush tropical hillside or overlook a quiet lagoon. The longest barrier reef in the Americas lies under the clear, warm Caribbean waters—a diving and snorkeling site of astonishing beauty. Several times between June and August the company has special weeks for families at Anthony's Key, with some activities beyond the usual ones.

FOR FAMILIES. Divers or anyone coming here to learn to dive will not be disappointed. Eight boats leave daily from the resort, and there is shore diving both day and night. Boats go out twice weekly for night dives, too. The waters just offshore are great for snorkeling, too; the resort organizes special guided outings.

Anthony's Key Resort has a special relationship with the Institute for Marine Sciences, which is based in the area and runs the popular Dolphin Discovery programs. Participants in the program learn about and interact with the institute's dolphins. A special Dolphin Discovery Camp for children ages 5 through 14 coincides with dive and/or snorkel weeks for parents booking through GORP Travel (see Wildlife Encounters), so whether or not the whole family dives, everyone can experience the resort's abundant marine life and natural beauty. Certified divers don't miss out on close encounters either: many wild dolphins live in these waters and frequently visit with divers.

Nondivers can sign up for a special snorkel package, ride horses on the beach, paddle in canoes, and explore nature trails. During each family week, the resort organizes children's and family activities and arranges baby-sitting, too. Meals, diving, riding, and most resort activities are included in the price of the all-inclusive package.

GORP Travel, 10055 Westmoor Dr., Suite 215, Westminster, CO 80021, tel. 720/887–8500 or 877/440–4677, gorptravel.gorp.com. Resort, year-round: 8 days, $600–$1,150 for a dive package, $600–$1,050 for a snorkel package, $600 for Dolphin Discovery Camp.

Hyatt Regency Grand Cayman Resort and Villas

3+

The Cayman Islands deserve their reputation as one of the world's top dive spots, and neither divers nor snorkelers will be disappointed in the clarity of the water or the abundance of sea life. The Caymans, however, are a popular destination, which means this adventure is in well-developed surroundings. Nevertheless, the Caymans—and particularly the Hyatt on Grand Cayman—are a good choice for families because few other places in the world offer the same quality of diving *and* a full-service, supervised activity program for very young children. Parents and older children can venture into the deep while those too young to do so can explore on land.

FOR FAMILIES. Red Sail Sports operates at the Hyatt and has both resort and full-certification courses for would-be divers. The resort course includes two hours of instruction followed by a test; pass the test, and you can dive in the afternoon with an instructor. Boats leave twice daily for a number of spots around the islands. Lodging, a sunset cruise, a round of golf, and a Red Sail T-shirt are part of Hyatt dive and learn-to-dive packages.

One of the all-time great snorkeling experiences for children (they should be comfortable with the sport in advance) and adults alike is the catamaran trip to Stingray City; the extra charge for this includes lunch. In an area of open water swim some two dozen stingrays, who are so used to human companions that you can touch them and swim among them without fear. If you want to see the rays from a deeper perspective, dive boats stop here, too. Some Stingray City "neighborhoods" are shallow enough to stand in, so if you have inexperienced swimmers in your family, ask if your boat will stop at one of these spots.

On land children can take nature walks, learn traditional Caymanian crafts and Caribbean dancing, and visit local museums with Camp Hyatt, the resort's supervised program for youngsters ages 3 through 12. The program runs daily year-round, with both day and evening programs available. All campers take snorkel lessons in the pool. Families that want a land destination to explore together can travel to the Turtle Farm in West Bay to look at turtles of all sizes and ages.

Hyatt Regency Grand Cayman Resort and Villas, Box 1588, Seven Mile Beach, Grand Cayman, tel. 345/949–1234 or 800/554–9288, www,hyatt.com. Year-round: 4–8 days, $634–$2,135 for dive and scuba school packages; a portion can be deducted for a nondiving adult in the same room. Children under 16 stay free in room with parents.

Jean-Michel Cousteau Family Camp

ALL

The Ocean Futures Society is probably best known as the group that worked to rehabilitate Keiko, Orca star of the Free Willie movies, and reintroduce him to his home waters and relatives off the coast of Iceland. The society's work, however, goes far beyond one whale. Ocean Futures is involved in many research and conservation efforts around the world, and it has a strong education branch. None of that is surprising given that world-renowned diver and conservationist Jean-Michel Cousteau is the society's president. Ocean Futures Society's mission is nothing less than to provide the global community with a forum for exploring critical issues affecting the ocean, including protecting and improving water quality, protecting and understanding marine mammals, protecting and preserving coral reefs, and protecting and restoring coastal habitats. One way it accomplishes that is through education, including family camps.

FOR FAMILIES. The Jean-Michel Cousteau Family Camp on Catalina Island off the California coast is one of the society's educational programs designed to teach children and adults about the ocean, marine life, and our oceans' critical importance to life on this planet. The five-day camp currently runs once each summer, usually in August. Campers arrive by boat on Wednesday and depart on Sunday. In between, they study and explore marine life as much or as little as they like. Activities include snorkeling (staff call it skin diving), kayaking, rock climbing, a ropes course, archery, hiking, sailing, swimming, nature studies, arts and crafts, and gardening/composting. In the evenings, Cousteau and other experts lectures on a variety of ocean-related topics, then campers might play disco bingo, sit around the campfire, or even go for a night skin dive (there's no scuba diving at camp). All ages are welcome because there are no mandatory activities, and twice each day childcare is available for ages 5 and under so parents and older children can join some of the activities not appropriate for infants and toddlers (though some intrepid 2-year-olds have snorkeled with parents and staff).

One of the highlights of the week is always the boat trip to nearby Emerald Bay, where campers snorkel with Jean-Michel Cousteau. The clear waters off Catalina are known for their emerald color, abundant marine life, and kelp forest. Accommodations are in cabins, and meals are included.

Ocean Futures Society, Catalina Island Camps, Box 94146, Pasadena, CA 91109, tel. 626/296–4040, www.oceanfutures.com. Aug: 5 days, $2,100–$2,500 per family (up to six people), depending on accommodations; if you stay on your own boat, fee is $350 per person.

Ocean Voyages

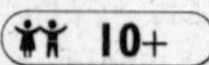

It would be difficult to find a company more dedicated to the concept of getting families onto boats and into the waters of the world. Ocean Voyages takes pride in its association with vessels and dive masters who love welcoming families on board—and they have many for snorkelers and divers to choose from. Pick an ocean or sea you want to explore, and Ocean Voyages can put together a vacation for you. The company has a range of available boats, from small, six- to 12-passenger vessels to large schooners that comfortably fit 20.

FOR FAMILIES. Look no farther than the bountiful reefs and isolated cays and islets off the coast of Belize, which has the second-longest barrier reef in the world. The waters are not only typically calm and serene, but the abundance of wildlife and world class snorkeling and diving mean children and adults will find much that is entertaining and educational. Most trips start and end in Belize City. Or you can sail down the coastline, starting in Belize and ending in the Rio Dulce area of Guatemala, or farther still into Honduras. The sleek, 55-ft sloop *Sunyata* is one of the ships that sails here, and its American captain runs excellent family voyages. The *Sunyata* sleeps six, but if you have a larger group (up to 12) the captain can arrange to have another boat sail in tandem with him.

If you want to combine sailing with land explorations, Ocean Voyages will arrange stays at a variety of eco-resorts and hotels in Belize, Guatemala, and Honduras. Typical is Hidden Valley in Belize's interior jungle, with its cottages, wildlife, and natural pools and waterfalls. The staff of an environmental institute at the resort leads nature walks and studies, and the resort's setting near Maya ruins makes it especially ideal for family learning adventures.

Ocean Voyages has numerous boats in the Caribbean. The 62-ft *Southern Comfort,* run by Captain Mike and Sandy Lampe and one of their two children, is perfect for diving families. Captain Mike is a dive master and instructor and passengers can windsurf, kayak, and waterski in addition to snorkeling and diving. In the Grenadines' excellent snorkeling waters, the 60-ft *Calliope of Arne,* captained by a Dutch couple, takes family groups of four to eight; special summer pricing is $7,500 per week for a family of eight. If the Mediterranean is more your style, there are lots of boats and itineraries to choose from. One of the best locations for families is along the Turkish coast, which offers not only great snorkeling but historic ruins to explore.

Heading west, a Gulfstar 50, sails along the Kona Coast of the Big Island—the Hawaiian island with the best snorkeling, according to some aficionados. Scuba can also be arranged. This is an intimate vessel with room for just four to six people. A larger schooner accommodates 12–22 guests and is equipped for scuba diving.

Ocean Voyages has been arranging trips in the Galápagos Islands since 1980, and the company arranges special family departures—usually during summer months—on ships like the 210-ft, 48-passenger *Eclipse.* Ships that perfectly accommodate multigeneration adventures include the 124-ft, 16-passenger *Parranda,* or the 140-ft *Alta,* which also takes 16 aboard. One of the best dive boats in this area is the 96-ft *Lammer Law,* which accommodates 16 passengers in well-appointed cabins. The 145-ft, 20-passenger Dutch schooner Modriaan, a striking, two-masted tall ship that uses both wind and motor power, features air-conditioned cabins with double or twin bunk beds and private bathrooms with showers. One cabin accommodates a family of three. The ship is equipped for diving, including a dive master or guide, but you must be certified before your trip. Bring your own snorkel gear for the family. There are two Zodiac landing craft for expeditions to investigate these remarkable islands.

Ocean Voyages also has family-friendly ships, both small and large, throughout the Pacific, and some run special snorkeling or dive trips. The custom-designed *Fai Manu,* built by a French-Italian captain, sails around the islands of Bora Bora, Tahaa, Raiatea, and Huahine. *Fai Manu* sleeps three to six passengers, and Captain Corneglia's wife and children frequently come along. Over in Fiji, the *Gallivant* has a crew especially chosen to work with family groups of three to eight, while the *Emotional Rescue* is a good choice for families who want to surf, snorkel, and dive in Fiji's waters. Snorkel and dive charters are also offered in Tonga, Australia, New Zealand, and Indonesia (considered by many to offer some of the most unique snorkeling and diving sites in the world, especially off Komodo, Flores, and Sulawesi). If you've ever wondered what it would be like for your children to live on a sailing ship, step aboard the 72-ft *Scame* in Thailand. The owner couple's 16-year-old son loves to introduce other young people to the fascinating world in which he grew up.

Ocean Voyages, 1709 Bridgeway, Sausalito, CA 94965, tel. 415/332–4681, www.oceanvoyages.com. Year-round: 8 days, $800–$2,400 adults, discounts for children and families on some ships.

Rascals in Paradise

ALL

Rascals is a tour company exclusively devoted to family vacations, whether you book custom trips or join scheduled family weeks. Rascals works with many high-end resorts around the world, but its trip list has bargains, too. On scheduled family departures, an escort arranges activities of all kinds for children and families. Because Theresa Detchemendy and Debbie Baratta, the company's owners, believe children should learn something about where they are traveling, a cultural component—such as visits with local families—is part of each trip. Although only a small portion of its family weeks qualifies as adventure, this company has many trips, and few people in the travel business know as much about traveling families as the professionals at Rascals.

FOR FAMILIES. The Divers with Kids program lists 10 resorts that are great for both divers and younger children. Most hotels offer resort and certification courses. Some allow children to snorkel at the same sites at which parents are diving, though that's never guaranteed. Still, parents and children should have plenty of time to enjoy both the marine life and each other at all these resorts. Regardless of your destination, Rascals is a full-service agency that can book your air travel (not included in prices) and anything else you need. Most trips include at least two meals a day, sometimes three, and airport transfers are almost always part of the package. Diving is often, but not always, extra, depending on the resort.

In the Caribbean you can choose from such family diving resorts as Bird Rock Beach Hotel on St. Kitts, where teens and new divers get a complimentary scuba lesson and everyone can explore the island's rain forests, and South Ocean Beach in the Bahamas, known for its reef walls, drop-offs, and caves. Tortola's Prospect Reef has its own harbor and peaceful lagoons, along with a wide variety of services for divers and nondivers alike. Families that opt for the Sand Dollar Condominiums in Bonaire can explore caves and tidal pools or sail as an alternative to viewing the marine life in the reef just offshore. Unspoiled and uncrowded, Grenada offers diversity in its diving, snorkeling, and hiking. The longest wreck in the Caribbean is here—the *Bianca C*, an Italian passenger ship that sank in 1965; it draws experienced divers from around the world. But this is a fine place to learn, too, and the resort here has a special deal for teens: a $99 certification course (teens must be accompanied by adults).

Far to the west but still in the Caribbean are resorts in Mexico, Belize, and Honduras. Mexico has one of the best and most affordable hotels for families with young snorkelers, the Club Akumal Caribe. Although Akumal is not far south of Cancún, it is everything that city is not: uncrowded, noncommercial, peaceful. You can snorkel right from the beach or take in Palancar Reef, across the water in Cozumel. There are brilliantly colored fish and exotic coral formations, along with sunken Spanish galleons. Don't miss a chance to visit nearby Tulum, the only Maya ruin on the coast. On Ambergris Cay in Belize, Journey's End Club has family snorkel and picnic trips as well as lots of water and land sports. Most important, you can explore the second-largest barrier reef in the world along with intriguing coral atolls. Rascals also has family-week departures to Anthony's Key Resort, off the island of Roatán in Honduras. Youngsters can take advantage of some of the children's and family activities at the resort, but the Rascals escort sets up special experiences and programs.

Beyond the Caribbean—way beyond in some cases—are more choices for the most adventurous families. Vatulele Island Resort on Fiji is a luxury hotel that gives equal importance to romance and family time. You dive and snorkel in shimmering aqua waters and hike through rain forests during the day. At night parents can dine together in one of the world's most beautiful spots while children visit with peers. Rascals also schedules a summer family week at Palau Pacific Resort in the Republic of Palau, a Micronesian diving paradise with world-class diving and snorkeling. A Rascals escort works with the resort to keep young ones busy with children's activities.

Rascals in Paradise, 2107 Van Ness, #403, San Francisco, CA 94109, tel. 415/921–7000 or 800/872–7225, www.camprascal.com. Year-round: 8–11 days, $1,120–$10,950 for family of 4; dive costs vary.

World of Diving & Adventure Vacations

ALL

This company began in 1993, in partnership with Continental Micronesia Airlines, as a specialist in dive and snorkel vacations in Micronesia, and was so successful that it has expanded to worldwide diving, fishing, kayaking, and live-aboard boat vacations. Its Pacific destinations, particularly Palau, remain among its most unique for families.

The Republic of Palau (also known as Belau), 550 mi (886 km) east of the Philippines and a nine-hour flight from Hawaii, comprises 343 islands spread over 100 mi (161 km) and is one of the world's top dive sites. Jacques Cousteau named Palau's Ngemelis Wall the world's best wall dive, and CEDAM International, an organization whose acronym comes from its dedication to conservation, education, diving, archaeology, and museums, nominated Palau as number one of the seven diving wonders of the world.

This is a destination for diving and snorkeling families that love to visit the hot new spots before much of the rest of the world even knows they exist. A first-rate hotel, Palau Pacific Resort, caters to families, even those with infants. With one call to World of Dive & Adventure Vacations, you can book airfare, lodging, dive and snorkel packages, museum visits, rental cars, and sightseeing.

FOR FAMILIES. A 20-minute drive from Koror, Palau's capital, Palau Pacific Resort has amenities that are unusually extensive for this part of the world. Snorkeling is excellent right from the beach—perfect for young children—and child-size equipment can be rented. Fascinating creatures, such as giant clams, can be glimpsed along the reef close to shore. The resort also has a pool, a nature trail, and lots of water-sports equipment for rent, including underwater cameras. The recreation staff can arrange a family snorkeling instructor, guided nature hikes, or kayaking lessons—all free of charge, except for equipment rental fees.

Independent tour operators have desks at the hotel for booking tours; in some cases you can even prebook through World of Adventure. One operator, Sam's Dive Tours, leads hiking tours to the Ngardmau Waterfall and to Palau's stone monoliths. You can also rent a car at the resort and drive to the Palau National Museum in Koror, where Palauan history, legends, and culture are interpreted through artifacts and traditional carved storyboards.

Palau's waters, however, with huge caverns, unspoiled reefs, and live coral formations, are what make it a world-class destination. No one should leave without taking a boat tour of the famous rock islands, which appear to float above the surface of the water. You can snorkel and dive from these boats. Among the most compelling attractions is Jellyfish Lake, filled with thousands of these eerily translucent, nonstinging creatures. Snorkelers come from all over the world to float among them; others study the jellyfish from a raft. One company, Adventure Kayaking, has kayaking tours from 1 to 10 days for those who want to see Palau from the vantage point of a hard-shell, sit-on-top kayak—boats easy enough for children to master quickly. And of course there's the diving. In order for you to dive with them, many operators require you to be age 16, certified, and in possession of your certification card. Splash, operating at Palau Pacific Resort, has both resort and certification courses.

Palauans are very family oriented, which makes the country a wonderful place to travel with children. It also helps that the main language in Palau is English and the currency is the U.S. dollar, although everyone in the family needs a passport. Packages include round-trip airfare from the U.S. West Coast, accommodations at Palau Pacific Resort, airport transfers, taxes, and five days of one of the following: Two-tank boat dives, snorkeling, or kayaking.

World of Diving & Adventure Vacations, 301 Main St., El Segundo, CA 90245, tel. 310/322–8100 or 800/945–9955, www.worldofdiving.com. Year-round: 7 days, $2,268 (snorkeling)–$2,488 (diving) per adult. Children under 18 free in room with parents; children's discounts on some meals and tours; ask about special airfares for ages 2–11. Add $200 per adult for departures from non-West Coast cities.

Resources

Organizations

Contact the following organizations for information about certification, locations of retail shops and resorts from which you can get instruction and gear, and written material on great dive destinations around the world: **National Association of Underwater Instructors** (Box 89789, Tampa, FL 33689-0413, tel. 800/553–6284, www.naui.org) and **Professional Association of Dive Instructors** (30151 Tomas St., Rancho Santa Margarita, CA 92688-2125, tel. 949/858–7234 or 800/729–7234, www.padi.com). Known as NAUI and PADI, respectively, these are *the* certification organizations in the United States. They can also tell you about snorkeling.

The **Handicapped Scuba Association International** (1104 El Prado, San Clemente, CA 92672, tel. 949/498–4540, www.hsascuba.com) is a certification agency for instructors who work with people with special needs. It also has a Dive Buddy program for family members of physically challenged individuals. If you have a special-needs teen, for example, you can learn what you need to know to dive with your child. Send $2 and a stamped, self-addressed envelope for more information.

TREKKING WITH LLAMAS AND BURROS

Children, especially young ones, require lots of gear that parents invariably end up hauling around. This system can be a problem in the world of long-distance and backcountry hiking. Parents with packs can't also carry infants and toddlers in a backpack-style child carrier, and adding another person's gear to an already heavy pack may be an impossibility. The end result: many families feel they can't trek into remote areas or hike longer, more difficult trails until their children are old enough—about 11 or 12—to walk a good distance and carry their own gear.

Fortunately, there is another way: trekking with animals. Most children are happy to help lead and care for their four-footed hiking friends, an arrangement with the added bonus of occupying them on the trail and in camp. And even though they think they're just having fun, children who hike with animals are learning responsibility and patience as well.

Perhaps best of all, trekking with animals literally takes the load off parents, freeing them up to carry preschoolers into some of North America's most beautiful terrain. Animal trekking opens backcountry areas up to school-age children, too—6- to 8-year-olds who can walk (and run and leap and dawdle) over several miles of rugged trails each day, but not with a heavy pack.

Families have several choices of animal companions. Llamas are the most popular; these smart, agile South American natives have been domesticated beasts of burden for more than 5,000 years. Although they don't like a lot of petting, llamas are gentle, good-natured souls. They're among the most environmentally friendly of pack animals because of the leathery padding on their two-toed feet; they make about the same impact on the wilderness as a deer. As for burros, they're gentle, strong, surefooted, and particularly well suited to the High Sierra in California, where they've been used as pack animals for years.

Questions to Ask

Does each hiker get to lead an animal? On some treks this is the case; on others two hikers share an animal. Sometimes the animals may be tied together in a group, with the guide leading the whole gang. Depending on the age of your children, one of these styles will probably suit you best. Find out how things work so your children won't be either disappointed or overwhelmed.

Can my children or I help care for the animals? This is a learning experience as well as a fun one, and tending to the animals can make the difference between a good and a great trip for some families. If animal care interests you, pick an outfitter that encourages you to join in.

How many miles will we walk each day? These treks average from 4 to 6 mi (6 to 10 km) in a day, though some cover as little as 1½ mi (2½ km) and others as many as 10 mi (16 km). Make sure your children can walk the distance or that you can carry them in a backpack, because riding the pack animals is never allowed.

On what kind of terrain will we hike? As important as the number of miles covered is the difficulty of the trail. One mile through a level forested area may be doable for a 5-year-old, but a mile on a steep canyon trail is not. Most outfitters rate their trips easy, moderate, or strenuous based on the difficulty of the terrain; check the classifications and ask specific questions.

Which trip is best for families? Even among the easy or moderate treks, some are better for families than others, and some are better for younger children. The outfitters listed here named their best family trips without hesitation because they've seen lots of families out in the wilderness. Listen to their advice. Even when llamas or burros are carrying the gear, children still have to be able to negotiate the trails safely and in a reasonable amount of time.

How much personal gear can we bring? Many outfitters have a limit—frequently about 20 lbs (9 kg) per person—depending on whether the animals will be carrying gear for one person or two. This is a good opportunity to teach your children how to economize on equipment and gear, weigh things, and set priorities. Of course, if they choose a second stuffed animal over a warm jacket, you'll have to convince them to choose again.

What gear must we bring? Only some outfitters supply sleeping bags. Read equipment lists carefully and ask if you are uncertain. Also, many treks are in mountainous areas, where the weather can change drastically in a matter of minutes and the temperature can fluctuate significantly from daytime to evening. Clothes that can be layered and that dry quickly are best for everyone.

Will there be other activities on the trip? A few treks include wildlife viewing, nature studies, fishing, geology lessons, and hikes without the animals as part of the itinerary. Depending on the ages and interests of your children, such activities might be almost as important to you as the main event.

Do you offer tours of your farm or ranch? Some llama outfitters, especially those specializing in day hikes, will give minitours so your family can see babies and other llamas that will not be on your trip. These tours are usually, but not always, free. This can be a very special treat for children, so don't be shy about asking. If you're staying at the outfitter's headquarters, a tour is probably part of the package.

What's included in the cost of the trip? Outfitters provide animals, guides, food, tents, and sleeping pads, unless noted otherwise. Gourmet meals are common—one outfitter even wakes you up with hot towels and coffee. Sleeping bags are not usually included, but there are some exceptions. Local transportation varies: you may meet at company headquarters and then be taken with your group to the trailhead; in other cases you must get to the trailhead on your own. Most outfitters will give you some help finding accommodations in the area before and after a trip, though they don't usually provide lodging themselves.

Instruction

Animal trekking involves minimal instruction, although before the trip you will be given information on how to lead an animal properly (if you will be doing that), how to move around them safely (for the animals' protection and your family's), and what you can expect in terms of their personality and behavior. If caring for and feeding the animals is part of the trip, you will learn as you go. Your children must listen to these instructions, too.

A Note About Ages

The age mentioned in each listing is the outfitter's suggested minimum age for children to be able to hike on their own. When two ages or ranges are given, it means the outfitter will allow children on the trip who are young enough for parents to carry in a backpack. The younger range is generally one through three; however, you know your children and your capacity for carrying them.

Finding the Fun

Northeast: Appalachian Mountain Club, Northern Vermont Llama Company, Telemark Inn. **Mid-Atlantic:** New River Llama Treks. **South:** WindDancers Lodging & Llama Treks. **Rockies:** Lander Llamas, Off the Beaten Path. **West Coast:** Hurricane Creek Llama Treks, Sierra Club, Wallowa Llamas. **Canada:** Strider Adventures. **Caribbean:** Iguana Mama.

Favorite Packers

Appalachian Mountain Club

13+

Join this venerable organization, and you'll meet other families, guides, naturalists, and a host of other people who love the wilderness and respect nature. Members get a discount on trips and courses. The Appalachian Mountain Club (AMC) has llama trekking in New York at its Catskill Mountains center in the High Peaks region.

FOR FAMILIES. The focus of this weekend trip is really to teach novices all about llamas and give them a chance to spend time around the animals. Participants arrive Friday night and stay in the Full Moon Lodge. Saturday morning everyone learns a bit about their four-footed hiking companions before the group takes off for a 6- to 8-mi (10- to 13-km) hike on mountain trails. Return to the lodge Saturday evening for dinner, videotapes, and discussions about caring for, showing, and breeding llamas. Sunday morning is spent at the lodge playing games with the llamas and finding out more about them. *Appalachian Mountain Club, Box 366, Long Lake, NY 12847, tel. 518/624–2056 or 603/466–2727. Sept.: 2 days, $225, 10% discount for members.*

Hurricane Creek Llama Treks

6+

Twelve thousand years ago glaciers carved what is now the Eagle Cap Wilderness out of northeastern Oregon's landscape. Today rugged granite and marble peaks rise from flower-filled alpine meadows and pine forests; clear streams and lakes teem with rainbow and brook trout. Elk, bighorn sheep, mountain goats, and mule deer are often seen on the ridges and in high valleys. People, however, are harder to find. Eagle Cap remains uncrowded and unspoiled, a terrific place to trek with children and llamas. You could not be in better hands than with Stanlynn Daugherty, owner of Hurricane Creek Llama Treks and the person who wrote the book on llama trekking—literally (see Resources, *below*).

FOR FAMILIES. Stanlynn recommends her base camp trips for most families. On these treks, one camp is set up and the group goes on day hikes from there, rather than moving from camp to camp each day. Among the six-day base camp treks: Early Summer Wildflowers in the Eagle Cap Wilderness, Hells Canyon Adventure on the Oregon–Idaho border above the Snake River, and Hurricane Creek Wildflowers, which follows crystal clear Hurricane Creek into the Wallowa Mountains. On all of these trips you can expect to walk a moderate 4 to 6 mi (6 to 10 km) each day, and there are other activities as well, including fishing in the many alpine lakes. There's also Wilderness Weekend Getaway in the Eagle Cap Wilderness that's shorter in length (five days) and covers only up to 4 mi (6 km) a day. Families with adolescents who are experienced and willing hikers can also join the "progressive" trips (camp to camp) in many of the same areas. Some of the trips coincide with Chief Joseph Days rodeo weekend, which is generally in late July, so plan to arrive in Joseph early to catch the action.

All Hurricane Creek trips include a night at an inn or motel in Joseph, Oregon, before and after the trip, as well as dinner and breakfast at the inn before the start of your adventure and a final dinner together after. The outfitter also supplies transportation between the inn and the trailhead. *Hurricane Creek Llama Treks, 63366 Pine Tree Rd., Enterprise, OR 97828, tel. 541/432–4455 or 800/528–9609. July–Aug.: 5–7 days, $590–$875 adults, 20% discount for children 6–18.*

Iguana Mama

3+

Introducing visitors to the lush landscapes, rich culture, and friendly people of the Dominican Republic is Iguana Mama's specialty. No outfitter serves up the mix of Caribbean Island hospitality and adventure in quite the same way. The owners live in the Dominican Republic for one thing, which gives them a knowledge and intimacy with the country and its people that outside tour operators simply can't offer.

FOR FAMILIES. The weeklong Mule Trek is one of the company's adventures designed specifically for families, and it's led by the owners' friend and local guide, Francisco Martinez. Francisco has been leading trips into the mountains since his childhood, as did his father before him. This trek explores the natural beauty and ecological wonders of Bermudez National Park, but Francisco will also share the myths and folk legends of these mountains around the campfire at night.

It all begins with a chance for your kids to play baseball with local children in La Cienega de Manabao, where Francisco lives with his wife, Ciele, and their nine children. On day two, the mules are packed up and you hike and ride through a bamboo forest and along a river (with time for a swim) on your way to Valle Tetero. It's hard to pick highlights, but certainly seeing Taino Indian pictographs and trekking across the two highest mountains in the Caribbean, La Pelona and Pico Duarte, are among them. And you may be surprised to find out that even in the Caribbean, marshmallows are a must when camping. Yet the chance to meet and stay with a local family (to say nothing of their mules), and to experience island culture in a close up, intimate way is what really sets this trip apart. You'll all be ready for a hot shower and a friendly hotel on the last night, however.

Iguana Mama, U.S. Payment Office: 38 Lake Lacoma Drive, Pittsford, NY 14534. Local address: Plaza Criolla, Cabarete, Dominican Republic, tel. 809/571–0908 or 800/849–4720, www.iguanamama.com. 7 days, $950 adults, $750 children 17 and younger.

Lander Llama Company

6+

Founded in 1985 by Scott and Therese Woodruff, this company has grown into one of the top llama outfitters in the country, yet it's still a small, family-run enterprise. Guides are thoroughly versed not only in pack llamas, but also in geography, flora and fauna, and wilderness preservation. This means that your family will learn a few things while having fun with your two- and four-footed traveling companions.

FOR FAMILIES. Scott recommends three-day adventures for beginners and five-day treks for families who have done some camping. If you're really experienced, you can opt for the "do-it-yourself-llama-rental." Multiday, guided treks wind among the peaks, meadows, and valleys of the Wind River and Absoroka ranges, or into Sweetwater Canyon or the Red Desert, east of the mountains. This part of central and western Wyoming is notable for its rugged wilderness areas and for its history. Ruts made by the wagon wheels of the thousands who followed the Oregon Trail can still be seen here. Long before that, dinosaurs and other prehistoric creatures roamed this land, and if you choose Lander's Red Desert tour, you may well see fossils of the marine animals that once lived in this basin. Today, it's more known for the rare desert elk and pronghorn antelope, and for being the only place in the United States where water flows neither east nor west but stays put for it sits directly on the Great Divide. If it rained a lot here, the land wouldn't be desert but lake.

On Wind River and Absoroka trips you'll be on the trail at about 9 AM, hiking until lunch with plenty of short breaks. You hike again until reaching camp at about mid-afternoon. While guides unpack the llamas and set up camp, you and the kids can explore, fish, or just relax. Those who choose the Red Desert or Sweetwater Canyon treks stay in one base camp, heading out on hikes and exploratory adventures each day. Before or after your wilderness trek, stay in the company's Bunk House, a ranch B&B with room for up to five and close-up views of the mama llamas and their babies.

Lander Llama Company, 2024 Mortimore La., Lander, WY 82520, tel. 307/332–5624 or 800/582–5262, www.landerllama.com. May–Sept.: 3–5 days, $495–$825 adults, $465–$775 children 12 and younger. Bunk House rates: $75 per night, plus $10 per night for each person over the five-person limit.

New River Llama Treks

7+

New River Llama Treks opened in 1997 as West Virginia's first commercial llama trekking company. Laura Davis and Gary Reynolds, the owner–guides, are committed to responsible use of the wilderness. One of the things they like best about having families on treks is "the opportunity to influence a child's appreciation of nature and to impart, subtly, an awareness of our collective role in preserving our wild places." They also have a sense of humor about their work. When asked whether llamas spit, they note that not only have their llamas never spit on a guest, no guest has ever spit on their llamas; high praise, indeed. (On the other hand, llamas do spit at other llamas occasionally, in case you were wondering.) Gary and Laura, who both play music, started the company because Laura fell in love with llamas—and because hiking with llamas is fun.

FOR FAMILIES. If you're traveling or rafting near the New River Gorge (see Rafting), these folks suggest that you also try "taking a llama to lunch"—on a hike, that is. The company's shortest one-day hike is about 7 mi (11 km) over fairly easy terrain in Cranberry Glades, which is part of Cranberry Back Country.

Cranberry Wilderness and adjacent Cranberry Back Country spread out over more than 61,000 acres of the Monongahela National Forest, the setting for two- and three-day llama adventures. Typical of the Allegheny Plateau, this is heavily forested country with broad mountains and deep, narrow valleys. Trails typically take hikers from 2,400 to 4,600 ft above sea level among hardwoods, spruce, and countless clear streams. Before you arrive, guides will ask you about your family's abilities and goals for the adventure, then set an itinerary accordingly. Although everyone starts out together, on the second day you typically have the option of moving at your own speed. One guide will lead a group that wants to cover a lot of ground, while another will head out at a more leisurely pace. At night, guides are likely to bring out a fiddle and guitar and treat guests to authentic Appalachian string music.

One of the best treks for families with young children is the Gauley Canyon Overnighter, but it's only for groups of eight or more. This is a great choice for a family reunion or for a couple of families traveling together. It can be either a two- or three-day trip and the hike into the campsite is under 3 mi (5 km). The company has a support vehicle on this trek, which can provide a little peace of mind and a break from the trail.

Don't worry about having to lug your own camping gear; all tents, sleeping bags, and pads are provided. Bring your own day pack, though, and keep in mind that each person may bring only 10 to 12 lbs (4½ to 5½ kg) of personal belongings (above and beyond the weight of the camping gear).

New River Llama Treks, Box 697, Edmond, WV 25837, tel. 304/574–2524, www.newriverllama.com. Apr.–Nov.: 1–3 days, $60–$390, children's prices or 20% discount for ages 11 and under on some treks.

Northern Vermont Llama Company

1–3, 4+

Your family can trek with llamas through the Green Mountains of Vermont near the resort areas of Smugglers' Notch and Stowe. Although this company offers day trips only, Vermont and the Green Mountains are the settings for so many family adventures—kayaking, canoeing, and rock climbing, to name a few—you could easily spend a week here and not try the same activity twice.

FOR FAMILIES. The cross-country ski trails of Smugglers' Notch, a year-round family resort, make ideal llama trekking trails in spring, summer, and fall. All treks meet at Smugglers', but you don't have to be a guest there to join up with Lindsay and Geoff Chandler of Northern Vermont Llama Company. Half-day and sunset treks are good choices for families with babies and toddlers in backpacks, or for parents with preschoolers. Walks are leisurely, with ample break time to meet the needs of the littlest explorers. Treks include fresh fruit, Lindsay's baked goods, and Vermont's own Ben & Jerry's ice cream.

If you have time at the end of your hike, follow Lindsay 10 mi (16 km) back to the farm in your car. Most of the 10 to 15 babies born each year at the 35-acre llama and Christmas tree farm arrive in summer, so there's a good chance you'll get to see a few.

Northern Vermont Llama Company, 766 Lapland Rd., Waterville, VT 05492, tel. 802/644–2257. May–Oct.: ½ day, $40 adults, $20 children age 5–12, under 5, free.

Off the Beaten Path

1+

Off the Beaten Path (OBP) specializes in custom and guided journeys in the Rockies, Southwest, Alaska, and Patagonia and works only with experienced outfitters that provide the highest-quality service. Once you arrange a trip, OBP takes care of every detail. Although custom can mean expensive, OBP is also dedicated to helping families plan the trip of a lifetime—even when budget is a consideration.

FOR FAMILIES. OBP works with llama packers in the Rockies. There are trips in the towering Tetons of Wyoming, in Colorado, and around West Yellowstone in southern Montana, among other spectacular places. Treks vary in terms of length and difficulty. When you ask about a family llama trek, OBP takes down extensive information about your family: ages, experience, budget, vacation needs and dreams, where you most want to go and what you most want to see, and how much time you have. OBP then makes suggestions about the outfitter and trip it believes will give you the best experience.

Off the Beaten Path, 27 E. Main St., Bozeman, MT 59715, tel. 406/586–1311 or 800/445–2995, www.offthebeatenpath.com. June–Sept.: $175–$275 per person per day; some trips offer children's discounts.

Sierra Club

8+

Gentle, strong, friendly, and occasionally confounding, burros make ideal trekking companions for families hiking the High Sierra in California. The Sierra Club's burro-assisted hikes are extremely popular, so if you want to go along, sign up early. These trips are lots of fun, yet good physical condition is a must.

FOR FAMILIES. Traditionally, two or three of the weeklong burro trips each summer are designated as family departures, each one accommodating about 12 people. You camp overnight on all trips, and will need to bring your own sleeping bags and tents (though you can rent tents on some trips). Family Fun in the Eastern Sierra takes families into the Sierra Nevada range and around its many lakes and high meadows. It's a 7-mi (11-km) hike to camp, and once you're there you'll spend your time climbing peaks, fishing, exploring the surrounding country on day hikes, and singing around the campfire. Mules carry all the gear and offer young adventurers a chance to get to know these highly intelligent animals. The Miter Basin and Sequoia National Park trip follows a moderate route across ridges and glaciated Sierra landscape. Fishing, day hikes, and just lounging around are all part of the agenda.

Sierra Club offers burro treks every year, but not always to the same area. Call for full trip details and a current catalog.

Sierra Club, 85 2nd St., 2nd floor, San Francisco, CA 94105, tel. 415/977–5522, www.sierra club.org. July–Aug.: 7 days, $700 adults, $600 children age 16 and under. Participants 18 and up must be Sierra Club members; application and fees ($39 per person, $47 per couple) can be sent in with the trip reservation form.

Strider Adventures

6+

If llama trekking with a small group in British Columbia's backcountry sounds like a good adventure for your family, contact Dan Hunter at Strider. You can choose treks through the alpine meadows, lakes, and high country of the majestic Canadian Rockies or the Cariboo Mountains. The company also has trips along the glaciers and rivers of Kakwa Recreation Area. If you're lucky, you'll see the magical northern lights in addition to vast star-filled skies, wildlife, waterfalls, and unforgettable panoramic views.

FOR FAMILIES. Families are welcomed on all Strider llama treks. There are two-, three-, five-, and seven-day scheduled adventures, or you can opt for a custom trip of any length. Treks vary in distance. Typical for families is the two- or three-day Fang Mountain trek, good for children age 6 and older, with its round-trip hike of 6 to 9 mi (10 to 14 km) and walks along alpine lakes and meadows, ridges, and bluffs. The Kakwa Park Adventure is a five- or seven-day, 50-mi (81-km) trek into the Canadian Rockies and up a long, gentle grade over the Continental Divide. It's best for hikers at least 10 years old. All treks are suitable not only for children but also for senior citizens, which makes Strider a good outfitter for multigenerational adventures. With llamas carrying the load, hikers of all ages have a chance to access Canada's superb mountain backcountry.

You have to bring your own high-quality, warm sleeping bag, but Strider supplies all other camping and trekking equipment in addition to transportation to and from the trailhead in Prince George. The trip price also includes traveler's insurance and Canada's goods and services tax.

Strider Adventures, 17075 Perry Rd. E, Prince George, British Columbia, Canada V2K 5E3, tel. 250/963–9542 or 800/665–7752, www.pgweb.com/strider. July–Sept.: 2–7 days, C$350.96–C$1,130.99 adults; 25–50% discount for children (depending on trip) under 16, additional 10% discount for family groups of 4 or more and seniors.

Telemark Inn

3½+

This Maine inn at the base of Caribou Mountain, on the edge of White Mountain National Forest, was built in 1900 as a private wilderness retreat. Today Telemark Inn accommodates from 12 to 14 people, who come for the serenity of the wilderness and to trek with llamas, among other activities (see Cross-Country Skiing and Snowshoeing). An appreciation for nature is at the heart of what Telemark offers; llama trekkers learn not only about the animals but also about alpine ecology, local geology, and the area's wildlife. On these treks all those who want to can lead their own llama.

FOR FAMILIES. One- to four-day llama treks take you into the surrounding White Mountain National Forest, where you'll find rushing rivers, placid beaver ponds where moose and raptors congregate, and magnificent mountain settings. These are Himalayan-style treks, meaning guides walk ahead and set up everything before your party arrives at camp each afternoon. You're awakened with hot towels and coffee brought to your roomy dome tent. Yes, it's luxurious, but the high quality of service doesn't detract from the emphasis on nature. Inn owner Steve Crone is an alpine ecologist, and his guides are geologists, botanists, and outdoor educators. And they don't forget that a trek should be fun—

there's also time to swim, hike without the llamas, and relax. You'll also spot plenty of wildlife in this region, including moose, coyotes, and black bears.

Not a camper? You can have your adventure and your cozy New England inn, too. Telemark offers three-, five-, and seven-day adventure activity packages during which you stay in rooms at the inn and go out each day for a variety of activities, including sighting bald eagles and visiting a peregrine falcon nesting site. The three-day package includes a day each of llama trekking, canoeing, and guided hiking. On the five-day package families can add a day of mountain biking or a splashing in the swimming-hole. The five-day option includes one free day, while the seven-day option has two free days when families can enjoy the inn's setting and amenities. If your family can't decide between a canoe adventure and a llama trek, ask about the six-day combo trip: three days each of llama trekking and Maine lakes canoeing, including four nights of camping and two nights at the lodge. Steve will take children as young as 3½ on any llama trek, but talk to him first about the trip and your child's personality and abilities.

Not all llama-trekking guests stay at the inn before or after a trip, but if you have the time, it's well worth a visit.

Telemark Inn, R.F.D. 2, Box 800, Bethel, ME 04217, tel. 207/836–2703, www.telemarkinn.com. June–mid-Sept.: 1–7 days, $85–$975 adults, $65–$725 children 13 and younger.

Wallowa Llamas

1–3, 6+

Although most people who have never been to Oregon think it has only fir forests and green valleys, the state also has cliff-lined coasts, high volcanic mountain ranges, red-rock desert, and areas where wheat fields sweep all the way to the horizon. Oregon's northeast corner is primarily high desert, mountains, and wilderness—the perfect setting for llama trekking.

Wallowa Llamas usually takes 10 trekkers and eight llamas, equally divided into two strings. Hikers don't usually lead their own llama; however, the guides might let you lead a string of four as you get accustomed to working with the animals during the trip. You are always welcome to help feed and water the llamas in camp and to help bring them in when it's time to break camp.

FOR FAMILIES. Like Hurricane Creek Llama Treks (*see above*), Wallowa Llamas has easy treks for families into the Eagle Cap Wilderness in the Wallowa Mountains, not far from the Idaho border. Infants and toddlers have made this four-day trip in backpacks, and most 6-year-olds are capable of walking it.

Beyond that, Wallowa Llamas offers a whole range of treks and destinations, from the easy three-day, 16-mi (26-km) round-trip Imnaha Falls adventure to the moderately difficult, 23-mi (37-km) hike in the high Sugarloaf Mountain meadows with views of the ridges of Red Mountain. There are also moderate three- to seven-day treks into the Wallowas near Pine and Crater lakes. Expect to cover about 7 mi (11 km) on five- and seven-day treks; the three-day adventure covers a little less ground. You can swim in the lakes, but the water is definitely cool. Teens and their parents who are ready for a seven-day mountain adventure can choose Across the Rugged Wallowas, the company's fairly strenuous 32-mi (52-km) trek. U.S. Forest Service regulations allow only four guests and two guides on this trip, so sign up early if this one is for you.

Wallowa Llamas, 36678 Allstead La., Halfway, OR 97834, tel. 541/742–2961, www.neoregon.com/wallowallamas.html. Apr.–Oct.: 3–7 days, $395–$1,195; discounts if you carry some of your own gear.

WindDancers Lodging & Llama Treks

ALL

Set on 270 acres of wilderness in the Smoky Mountains, WindDancers is a working llama ranch and bed-and-breakfast. Though the establishment is relatively new, the folks at WindDancers are experienced, having put hikers and llamas together for 10 years, formerly under the name Windsong Llama Treks. Their current wilderness retreat has three log lodges with nine guest rooms or suites. Each lodge room is decorated in the style of a country, state, or region: Peru, Kenya, and New Mexico among them. All have decks and fireplaces, and some are tucked high into the hills while others sit beside a stream. Organized llama treks explore the woodland trails snaking across the ranch's land.

FOR FAMILIES. If your family is taking a Far Camp Overnight, the llamas and guides will pick you up at the door of your lodge. The forest trail leads you to a tent campsite with a 60-mi (97-km) view of Great Smoky Mountain National Park, where you'll have dinner around a campfire. In the morning, you'll head back to the lodge, then perhaps on to other adventures in the Smoky Mountain region. Four full meals are included.

It's precisely because the region offers so much—RV adventures, canoeing, kayaking, rock climbing, mountain biking, and more—that families may wish to take only a short llama trek. A good option is one of WindDancers' day trips: lunch treks that combine a scenic hike with a fresh lunch, and dinner treks where dinner is served at a table by a brook up on the mountain. And because WindDancers combines adventure with a luxury B&B, this is the ideal place to come to after you've gotten an adrenaline rush on some of North Carolina's other adventures. The inn is open year-round.

All ages are welcome on any of the llama treks; however, parents should be willing and able to carry very young adventurers in a child backpack. Ask ahead of time about the length and difficulty of the trail to the overnight site to determine if your child can do it alone or would need to be carried. The company provides all equipment, including sleeping bags.

WindDancers Lodging & Llama Treks, 1966 Martins Creek Rd., Clyde, NC 28721, tel. 828/627–6986, www.winddancersnc.com. Mar.–Oct.: Overnights $150 per person; lunch and dinner treks $40 adults, $30 children under 8.

Resources

Organizations

Contact the **International Llama Association** (Box 1891, Kalispell, MT 59903, tel. 406/257–0282, www.internationalllama.org) for a catalog with information about llamas, a list of reference materials, and a list of packers and breeders across the nation.

Books

Stanlynn Daugherty, owner of Hurricane Creek Llama Treks, is the author of the informative *Packing with Llamas* (Juniper Ridge Press). Yellow Wood Llamas, Inc. has an online bookstore with this and many other titles at www.ywl.com/bookstore/llamas.htm.

Also See

If your family loves traveling with four-footed friends, *see* Horse Packing, Covered Wagon Adventures, *and* Cattle Drives. The chapter on Ranches also describes vacations in which you can get to know horses and other animals. For up-close meetings with more exotic creatures, turn to Wildlife Encounters.

WILDLIFE ENCOUNTERS

Almost from birth children show immense joy in sharing this planet with finned, winged, and four-footed creatures. Although the benefits of teaching children about animals and giving them a chance to meet the creatures of the world up close and personal are clear, there is another reason for seeking out this type of trip: wildlife encounters are also good for adults. They bring out the child in us, taking us back to a time when we saw the world as full of wonder. I have seen this transformation take place among adults on all the animal-encounter trips I've taken. In the Galápagos, adults and children vied for the sea lions' attention and made faces at the somber-eyed iguanas. When the captain of our boat announced that a troop of dolphins was leaping off our bow, the adults were the first ones to the railing.

Whether you choose a vacation on which you actually hug a wild creature (as is possible in Baja California and on the ice floes in the Gulf of St. Lawrence) or one on which you only observe them at close range, the rewards are immediate and long-lasting. Some animal encounters benefit the animals, too, because tourist dollars provide important funding or because tourists themselves provide research assistance.

It's worth noting that some outfitters and tour operators—not, of course, those described here—may be more interested in the bottom line than in the protection of animals. By choosing a trip carefully, you're ensuring that future generations will be able to experience the magic of these encounters, too. However, it's important to point out that scientists have different opinions about how close humans should come to animals in their native habitat. Some scientists feel direct contact with wildlife is not a good idea, while others believe long-term benefits outweigh potential negatives, as long as the animals engage in contact of their own volition and are not cornered, teased, or fed. If you're concerned about this, talk to outfitters to be sure that the animals' welfare is always top priority.

Unlike other family adventures, all but a few of the wildlife encounters in this chapter take place outside the United States. Of course, many adventures, such as kayaking and hiking, in various parts of this country afford you the opportunity to see wildlife, and individual trip descriptions will highlight that aspect. The encounters in this chapter, however, were chosen because they focus on the animals, many unique to the habitat you will be exploring. A family's contact with these creatures great and small can be the experience of a lifetime, with the power to change a child's perceptions not only of the world's animals but of our place in the universe.

Questions to Ask

How long will we be watching for animals each day, and is there an option to cut it short if my children get fidgety? As much as children love animals, few enjoy the long trips and dragged-out waits that many animal encounters require. That's why trips planned just for families are designed to move quickly, without unnecessarily long waiting periods and delays. Still, even on nonfamily trips, outfitters do their best to accommodate everyone, so you may be able to make special arrangements. Some trips, however, cannot be altered; when you're flying to ice floes by helicopter, for example, you're bound to a strict schedule. Study your itinerary carefully. If there are morning and afternoon encounters, you will probably have the option of going on just one. Ask about the possibility of child care while you're away from camp. Find a trip that's right for your child's age, temperament, and capacity for sitting.

Are shots or other health precautions necessary? Many animal encounter trips take place in foreign countries that require inoculations and other kinds of preventive medication. Check far in advance and ask a pediatrician or the local health department about health precautions in foreign countries, especially as they relate to children. Always pack basic children's medication—acetaminophen, an antihistamine, cough syrup, motion-sickness pills, and antidiarrhea pills; these are often hard to find in foreign countries. If your child is prone to ear infections or any other ailments, you may want to ask your pediatrician for an antibiotic that doesn't need to be refrigerated.

Is any special clothing required? On some trips, such as those to the Arctic, special cold-weather apparel is crucial. Although outfitters often provide outerwear that will fit children, they may not have all that's necessary. Finding extreme-weather clothing for youngsters can be difficult in the United States, let alone in foreign destinations, so plan ahead.

What kind of luggage and gear should we pack? Almost all flights on small planes in the Arctic or Africa have limited capacity for luggage. Because many of these adventures have lodging in small quarters anyway—tents and ship cabins, for example—it's a good idea to pack lightly. Attire for adventure is always casual; keep in mind that you'll be getting dirty. Some African safari camps offer laundry service.

What's the primary language where we're going? If you're lucky enough to travel to a foreign land, take advantage of the opportunity to expose your children—and yourself—to a new language. Buy a phrase book before you leave so your family can learn to say basic phrases and the names of animals in the local language. Audiotapes for adults and children can also help you make language part of the travel experience.

Should we tip our guides? Your guide or naturalist is your window onto a world you've paid a great deal to see. A good guide can make the difference between a mediocre trip and an incredible one. When it comes to children, good guides work extra hard to bring the world to life for them, too—not always an easy task. Parents may show appreciation for guides' efforts in the form of tips. On trips of this sort, $10 per adult per day is appropriate; an extra few dollars for the children is a good way to encourage your guides to keep up the good work. In addition, I like to have my children give their favorite guides a note, a picture, a Polaroid shot, or any other small token of their appreciation.

What's included in the cost? Lodging, most meals, transportation throughout the expedition, entrance fees to sites included in the itinerary, all group equipment, and the services of qualified guides and naturalists are part of the package, unless otherwise noted. On some camping trips you must bring your own sleeping bags. In some cases, as with those tour operators running African safaris, airfare to and from certain cities in the United States is also included. When airfare is not part of the trip cost, outfitters and operators can usually arrange it for you, often at a better rate than you could get on your own. Hotel stays may be required before and after trips because of flight schedules; these are generally an additional expense.

Instruction

Much of the instruction in preparation for these trips is about safety—both yours and the animals'—and about teaching visitors how to minimize human impact on the Earth's fragile environments. In areas where the weather and conditions are extreme, you must follow instructions about proper clothing and emergency procedures. To make this process fun for children, rather than a chore, enlist their help. They can help ensure that your family follows all the guidelines.

Finding the Fun

West Coast: Sea Quest Expeditions, World Discovery Tours. **Alaska:** Abercrombie & Kent, Alaska Wildland Adventures, Thomson Family Adventures. **Canada:** Arctic Odysseys, Blue Loon Adventures, Mountain Travel Sobek, Natural Habitat Adventures, World Discovery Tours. **Mexico:** Baja Discovery, Baja Expeditions, Mountain Travel Sobek. **Central America:** Abercrombie & Kent, Costa Rica Expeditions, Cross Country International, GORP Travel, Lindblad Expeditions, Mountain Travel Sobek, Natural Habitat Adventures, Thomson Family Adventures, World Discovery Tours. **South America:** Abercrombie & Kent, Ecoventura, Lindblad Special Expeditions, Metropolitan Touring, Mountain Travel Sobek,Thomson Family Adventures. **Europe:** Thomson Family Adventures. **Africa:** Abercrombie & Kent, Big Five Tours & Expeditions, Mountain Travel Sobek, Natural Habitat Adventures, Rascals in Paradise, Thomson Family Adventures, World Discovery Tours. **Asia, Australia, New Zealand:** Abercrombie & Kent, Mountain Travel Sobek, Thomson Family Adventures, World Discovery Tours.

Favorite Outfitters

Abercrombie & Kent

6+

A&K is all about comfort and style. In addition, they'll take care of every trip planning detail—so you don't have to think about anything but having a good time with your children. Small groups and luxury facilities are the hallmarks of this quality tour operator. Family trips give parents and children time both together and apart, and every tour includes a professional escort experienced not only in travel to the particular destination but also in taking both children and adults to that destination. A&K recognizes that it's hard for families to move to different hotels each night, so family itineraries offer stays of two- or three-nights at the various lodges throughout a trip. It's this kind of thought and attention to detail that has given A&K the excellent reputation it deserves.

FOR FAMILIES. On A&K's extensive list of family trips are many that include wildlife: Kenya, Tanzania, and Botswana in Africa; Costa Rica in Central America; the Galapagos and Ecuador in South America; Alaska in North America; and Australia and New Zealand down under. Most trips are for parents with children 6 years old and older, although the Costa Rica adventure is for all ages, the Galapagos for kids at least 7, and Botswana for families with children age 9 and older.

Australia and New Zealand give families a chance to learn about those countries' well-known—and lesser-known—wild inhabitants. Hayman Island sits right on the Great Barrier Reef, which stretches for 1,200 mi (1,932 km) off of Australia's northern coast. This natural coral landscape is filled with exotic and unique wildlife, easily seen from Hayman Resort's own reef-exploring vessel. Families will also see koalas, platypus, kangaroos, crocodiles, snakes, and tropical birds at Wild World Wildlife Sanctuary near Cairns in the tropical north. The group stays at a wilderness lodge overlooking Daintree Rainforest, and if you don't see plenty of animals at your hotel, you'll catch them on the four-wheel safari through the world's oldest rainforest, or on the Daintree River cruise. Meanwhile, for those families that choose New Zealand, a highlight is swimming with a pod of friendly Hector dolphins near the seaside town of Akaroa, near Christchurch and the trip's end.

All of the African trips are wonderful, but Botswana is a little different, offering a part of Africa perhaps less traveled by Western families than Kenya or Tanzania. The trip starts and ends in Johannesburg, South Africa, and includes a visit to and flight over Victoria Falls on the Zimbabwe–Botswana border. In Botswana, the group travels to northern Chobe National Park, where as many as 600 elephants can sometimes be seen in a single day. The park is also home to hippos and crocs, best viewed by river cruise. The Moremi Game Reserve is home to large concentrations of plains game and predators, such as lion, leopard, buffalo, cheetah, and wild dog. Some of the viewing here is done at night. On the "Jewel of the Kalahari" tour in the Okavango Delta you'll also have a chance to ride mokoros, traditional dugout canoes used for game viewing. You can't go wrong with A&K, whichever trip you choose, so pick the one with the terrain and wildlife that most appeals to your family (and save the others for another year). *Abercrombie & Kent International, 1520 Kensington Rd., Oak Brook, IL 60523-2141, tel. 630/954–2944, 800/323–7308, or 800/757–5884 (brochures only), www.abercrombiekent.com. Mar.–Dec.: 10–16 days, $2,995–$6,350 adults, $3,370–$4,805 children age 12–17, $1,925–$3,935 children 11 and under (children's prices for lodging shared with parents); airfare extra, children's pricing available on some flights.*

Alaska Wildland Adventures

6+

Alaska Wildland Adventures believes that Alaska should be experienced personally, "not passively viewed through the windows of a tour bus or via the endless buffet of a luxury cruise liner." The company, however, also understands the needs of families, from children to grandparents, as trips for multigenerations explore the real Alaska at a comfortable, easy pace.

FOR FAMILIES. Every summer special Family Safari departures cater to parents with children ages 6 to 12. On these trips you might see moose, bald eagles, and spawning salmon in the Kenai Mountains; sea otters, puffins, seals, sea lions, and maybe even whales during a wildlife cruise in Kenai Fjords National Park. There are hikes, nature walks, drives, and a train ride back to Anchorage at the end of the nine-day adventure. Accommodations are in hotels and wilderness lodges. This is the perfect action adventure for parents, children, and grandparents to share together.

If you'd rather stay put in one place for your whole vacation or even just a part of it, consider booking a few nights at Denali Backcountry Lodge, which is managed by Alaska Wildland Adventures. Because of the level of hikes typically offered at the lodge, as well as the long bus ride required to get there, this place is best for families with children age 8 and up. The lodge lies deep within Denali National Park, in Kantinsha, along spectacular Denali Park Road. Grizzlies, moose, caribou, wolves, fox, Dall sheep, and golden eagles are commonly seen on the park road and on adventures that depart from the lodge each day. Transportation to and from the park entrance is included in the cost of a lodge stay.

Alaska Wildland Adventures, Box 389, Girdwood, AK 99587, tel. 907/783–2928 or 800/334–8730, www.alaskawildland.com. June–Sept.: 1–9 days, $399–$3,795 adults, $388–$3,495 children 12 and under; discounts for groups of 3 or 4 sharing accommodations.

Arctic Odysseys

12+

Arctic Odysseys has been taking adventurers to the North Pole and the area around it for more than 25 years. The Polar Bear Odyssey may be the star in this outfitter's trip list, but families have other treks from which to choose (see Native American Experiences), all of which provide unsurpassed access to the north country.

FOR FAMILIES. One trip goes to Wager Bay, which is some 30 mi (48 km) south of the Arctic Circle in Canada and has one of the world's greatest concentrations of polar bears. Because the bay can be reached only by chartered aircraft, you view these white giants unhindered by crowds of other wildlife watchers. Boats take you amazingly close for a look at the paddling bears (if they didn't paddle, they would sink). Although polar bears are the reason most people come here, they are by no means the only wildlife in the area. On the way to and from Winnipeg, Manitoba, where the trip begins and ends, and on hikes around Wager Bay, you may see beluga whales, caribou, arctic wolves and hares, seals, gyrfalcons, peregrine falcons, and a host of other north-country birds. Accommodations at the bay are in an Inuit-owned and -operated lodge; Inuit guides lead the boat trips and hikes as well. Because of the group dynamics of this trip, participants should be at least 12 years old—but owner Robin Duberow will consider slightly younger children.

The Discover the Worlds of the High Arctic itinerary gives families insight into the fascinating history of the Arctic and a glimpse into the local cultures of the region. Caribou, snow geese, beluga whales, narwhals, polar bears, and bowhead whales are all likely to be seen from the low-flying planes that provide most of your transportation.

From boats off Cape Dorset on Baffin Island in Canada, seals are a common sight, and if you hike around the Eureka Weather Station on Ellesmere Island, you're likely to see arctic wolves, foxes, and musk oxen. Most nights are spent in hotels, and you'll stay at the Eureka Weather Station as well. The trips starts and ends in Ottawa.

Families considering either of these trips should keep two things in mind. First, the unpredictable arctic weather and tides often cause delays or force leaders to change itineraries altogether. If your family doesn't want to be flexible, look for a different adventure. Second, Arctic Odysseys uses local guides and stops at small out-of-the-way towns and villages. You have wonderful opportunities to meet regional people and learn about their unique culture.

Arctic Odysseys, 2000 McGilvra Blvd., Seattle, WA 98112, tel. 206/325–1977 or 800/574–3021, www.arcticodysseys.com. July–Aug.: 8–10 days, $3,850–$7,500.

Baja Discovery

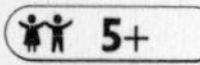

With red rock and gold sand set against deep blue seas, Mexico's Baja California is as incomparably beautiful as it is remote. Moreover, Baja is an extremely child-friendly place; local boatmen and crews on the Baja Discovery tours will make your children feel welcome and loved. The two trips specifically for families begin and end in San Diego.

FOR FAMILIES. The Gray Whale Discovery at San Ignacio Lagoon takes families to a rare place where whales regularly swim up to boats and seek human contact. Known as friendlies, these whales stick their heads up next to skiffs half their size and look whale-watchers directly in the eye. Wild and under no obligation or enticement to stay (Mexican law forbids humans from chasing, feeding, or harassing the whales in any way), friendlies love having their heads patted and their backs rubbed. They also have an incredible sense of humor; it's not unusual for one to push the skiff around and splash the humans on board for as much as an hour. Much of this trip is a waiting game—whale lovers may spend hours circling the waters in vain—so patience and the ability to sit for long periods of time are a must; 8 is the age minimum.

Accommodations for this five-day trip are at the company's tented campsite on a point overlooking the lagoon. Families can choose a departure date from January through March, when the grays come to San Ignacio to mate and give birth to their young. The price includes everything except one breakfast from the time you leave San Diego until you return.

The Sea of Cortez Islands trip is the best way to see the heart of Baja—wind-sculpted boulders, cactus "forests," wine-producing and agricultural regions, and the rich and varied flora and fauna of the central desert. You travel in a van for two days, stopping to look at things that will be engaging to even very young travelers (minimum age is 5) and spending the night at hotels. On the way down to the Sea of Cortez (also known as the Gulf of California), you visit a park, towns, a museum, a turtle research station, and more.

At the coast participants board 28-ft *pangas*, or Mexican fishing skiffs, which travel to a secluded cove and campsite. Days three to five are spent exploring the remote desert islands and emerald waters of the Sea of Cortez, home to whales, dolphins, sea lions, and countless marine birds. There's snorkeling, fishing, hiking, and relaxing by day; at night families sleep in cabins, each with cots and personal bath and shower facilities. On day six you have time for a final swim, followed by a drive up through Baja to San Diego. This trip runs in May and October and includes everything but meals at the two hotels during the van trip.

Baja Discovery, Box 152527, San Diego, CA 92195, tel. 619/262–0700 or 800/829–2252, www.bajadiscovery.com. Jan.–Mar., May, late Sept.–Oct.: 5–8 days, $1,595–$1,825; family discounts may be available.

Baja Expeditions

In business for 28 years, this company has been taking adventurers to Mexico's Baja California longer than any other. Baja Expeditions' trips are learning-oriented, with a special emphasis on the fragile and unique environment of the Baja land and seas. Lectures and slide shows are daily events.

FOR FAMILIES. On the San Ignacio Lagoon Gray Whale Adventure, the outfitter sends boats out twice daily in search of friendlies. When the whales choose to come up to your boat and look you in the eye, it's an experience like no other. Participants sleep at a desert campsite on the lagoon, with roomy cabin tents, comfortable cots, and fluffy sleeping bags. There's a shower with solar-heated water, and the food cooked by the Mexican staff is hearty and delicious.

Children are treated with extra love and care by the crew, but adults outnumber children by far on these trips; try to book a departure on which another family has signed up. Parents are responsible for their children at all times. When you sign up for the trip, you will be asked whether your child can swim and how you feel your child will function in a primarily adult environment. Also, remember that you may have to wait patiently for hours before the whales appear. This five-day trip starts and ends in San Diego and includes charter flights between San Diego and San Ignacio.

Baja Expeditions has other whale-encounter trips, such as an eight-day voyage to see blue whales, the largest creatures on earth. The trip takes place aboard an 80-ft motor vessel, and you may spot dolphins and six kinds of whales in addition to blues. About two-thirds of each day is spent cruising, but the trip allows time for hiking, snorkeling, and exploring—a combination that's ideal for children and teens. Overnights are spent on the boat. Families can also choose an eight-day adventure that brings you close to the whales, dolphins, mantas, and whale sharks of the Sea of Cortez, or a seven-day trip on Magdalena Bay—calmer than San Ignacio—to encounter Baja's magnificent gray whales. Most trips start and end in the Baja California city of La Paz.

Baja Expeditions, 2625 Garnet Ave., San Diego, CA 92100, tel. 858/581–3311 or 800/843–6967, www.bajaex.com. Jan.–Nov.: 5–10 days, $1,200–$2,195; some family discounts available.

Big Five Tours & Expeditions

ALL

Africa remains the ultimate destination for those seeking an exotic animal encounter and a cultural experience that most people can only dream about. The animals of this huge continent fill children's books, making them recognizable and, in some ways, surprisingly accessible to children. Not too long ago only hard-core adventurers traveled to Africa. Now it attracts all kinds of people, including families. Big Five Tours & Expeditions is one of the tour operators that have made it possible for children, even very young ones, to discover this amazing land.

FOR FAMILIES. Big Five has special 12-day family safaris to Kenya throughout the year. There is no minimum age, but children older than 4 are likely to appreciate and retain the experience in a way younger children cannot. Besides wildlife viewing, the rich itinerary includes visits to museums and a crafts and cultural center. All children receive daily lessons in Swahili, participate in sing-along sessions, and join the Mt. Kenya Safari

Club, an adventure organization with such special activities as nature walks, tribal games, village visits, and other programs designed to give kids a real sense of the land through which they're traveling. Stops include the famous Masai Mara Game Reserve (where much of *Out of Africa* was filmed), Sweetwaters Game Reserve, Samburu National Reserve, the Aberdare Mountains, and Lake Nakuru National Park. You'll see giraffes, zebras, elands, oryx, flamingos and eagles, and, of course, lions, leopards, elephants, and rhinos. In Nairobi, families can also have up-close wildlife encounters at the Giraffe Center, Butterfly Farm, and Mamba Village Crocodile & Ostrich Farm.

Big Five makes a point of getting off the beaten path, even in this wild land, to spend time at private ranches, wildlife sanctuaries, and wild game viewing areas. Accommodations are at deluxe hotels and luxury camps; prices include airfare via Swissair between several U.S. cities and Nairobi. Note that some trips to Kenya, Tanzania, and the Galapagos offer a companion discount of 50%. Although these trips don't include special children's activities, the reduced rates make them great for families.

The company also has a 10-day "Family Fun in the Tropics" tour to Costa Rica, designed for parents or grandparents with children. Among the highlights are a dolphin boat tour at Manuel Antonio National Park on the Pacific Coast and explorations of the colorful artisan town of Sarchi, not far from San Jose. Accommodations range from volcano-facing lodge rooms at Arenal to Pacific Ocean bungalows on a private strip of white beach. You'll see the sights for which Costa Rica is famous, as well as have a chance to raft, fish, and ride horses.

Big Five Tours & Expeditions, 1551 SE Palm Court, Stuart, FL 34994, tel. 561/287–7995 or 800/244–3483, www.bigfive.com. Year-round: 10–12 days, $2,345–$4,995 adults, from New York (Africa) or Miami (Costa Rica) depending on season; $995–$4,795 children, depending on age and season. Moderate add-on fares from other U.S. cities.

Blue Loon Adventures

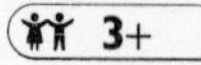

Tanya Wheeler and Laura McLennan are two biologists whose work has focused on the birds of northwest Ontario. While their research keeps them busy, they also wanted to share their expertise with families. Blue Loon Adventures was born, and come summer they make it possible for families to work side by side with researchers, banding and monitoring birds on the northern shore of Lake Superior.

FOR FAMILIES. At Blue Loon Bird Camp, families can help biologists and naturalists study song birds, raptors, water fowl, and a variety of migratory species. The camp is based at Thunder Cape Bird Observatory, on a peninsula connected to Sleeping Giant Provincial Park, not far from the city of Thunder Bay. The peninsula itself is a sort of travel marker for migratory birds, and is one of the great flyways of North America. Families participate in much of the biologists' work. Birds are captured in mist nets (fine, almost invisible nets that don't harm the birds). They're then removed from the nets and banded if they haven't been banded before. After research data is recorded, they're sent on their way. Best of all, you have the rare and thrilling opportunity to hold wild birds in your hands. Blue Loon is an experience that stays with you for a long time. More than a year after our trip, my family still talks about the purple finch Hutch held and the black capped chickadee Molly banded.

Accommodations are in cabins and large army surplus tents outfitted with cots, pillows, and all you need for comfortable camping. On request, Blue Loon can take families out to its own wilderness base camp, about 30 mi (48 km) from Thunder

Bay. The focus there is on song birds only. Blue Loon can also help arrange other adventures in the area, such as kayaking, canoeing, or visiting an amethyst mine. If you don't have your own camping gear, you can rent it in town. Fly into Thunder Bay; Blue Loon will arrange transportation to camp. Longer and shorter stays can be arranged. *Blue Loon Adventures, Box 4398, Hwy. 61, R.R. 7, Blake Township, Thunder Bay, Ontario, Canada P7C 5V5, tel. 888/846–0066, www.foxnet.net/~blueloon. Late June–Aug.: 3 days, C$720 per family of 3 or 4.*

Costa Rica Expeditions

ALL

After fighting unsuccessfully to prevent the damming of California's Stanislau River, where he was a guide, Michael Kaye went in search of rivers that still ran wild. He found them in 1978 on a visit to Costa Rica, and he's lived there ever since. His passion for the country and its vibrant ecosystem is understandable: Costa Rica is a nature-lover and activist's paradise where 25% of the land is protected in parks and reserves. Kaye founded Costa Rica Expeditions (CRE) the year he arrived, focusing on small groups interested in natural history, rafting, and wildlife.

CRE's credentials as a leader in ecotourism are impeccable. The company has developed trips for the Audubon Society, the Nature Conservancy, the American Museum of Natural History, and the New York Zoological Society among others, and the trips it runs for individuals and families have the same commitment to sharing Costa Rica's natural beauty while preserving and protecting it. Michael Kaye is an adventurer, environmentalist, and experienced travel industry professional working and living in his adopted land—and he has long believed in the importance of bringing families to experience this place he loves.

FOR FAMILIES. Several of CRE's trips are perfect for families. First and foremost is the nine-day Family Adventure for all ages. Get a good night's sleep when you arrive in San Jose, because the next morning you'll be up at 5 a.m. to wander through the traditional Farmer's Market. Later, at the National Institute of Biodiversity's INBioparque, you can learn all about Costa Rica's amazing biological diversity with interactive exhibits, multimedia displays, and interpretive trails where frogs, tarantulas, orchids, and butterflies are living examples of the country's abundance. Much of this trip is spent exploring Tortuguero National Park on the northern Caribbean coast, where 51,870 acres of rain forest are home to a huge variety of species. One of the nice things about this trip, and what makes it especially good for families with young children, is that you stay for five nights at the Tortuga Lodge (yes, there is a pool), which is owned and operated by CRE. If school is in session your kids can sit in at a local classroom, where some of the children arrive by dugout canoe, or play a soccer match with local kids. There are early morning bird walks, crafts lessons, and canal trips via canoe, kayak, or hydro-bike. The trip ends with a day of whitewater rafting on the mild Rio Pejibaye in the Orosi Valley, about two hours from San Jose.

Costa Rica Explorer is a 10-day adventure with special family departures on which children of all ages are welcome (ages 12 and up only on regular departures). This traditional itinerary takes in many parts of the country, including the Monteverde Cloud Forest Reserve, Poas Volcano National Park, and Arenal Volcano in the highlands and Tortuguero National Park on the sea. Monteverde alone encompasses six different ecological life zones and protects more than 100 species of mammals, 400 species of birds, and 1,500 species of plants. If you visit between January and July, you may be lucky enough to spot the Resplendent Quetzel. There are family departures over President's

Day, Easter, summer, Thanksgiving, and Christmas. The nine-day Costa Rica River & Rain Forest adventure also has holiday and summer family departures; because of the two-day rafting portion of the trip (camping overnight on the Pacuare River), this is for families with kids age 12 and older. In addition to rafting, you'll spend several days at Corcovado National Park on the southern Pacific Coast, and Corcovado Lodge, famous for its 115-ft Tree Canopy Platform, which gives you the rare privilege of a monkey's eye-view of the reserve.

Finally, for families that want to combine volcanoes and rainforests with mountain biking, canoeing, kayaking, and rafting, the seven-day Multisport Adventure, for ages 12 and older, is a trip of a lifetime. From biking 20 to 30 mi (32 to 48 km) a day on the flanks of Arenal Volcano to plying the remote waterways and lagoons of Tortuguero National Park, this trip is a family workout and an introduction to Costa Rica's diverse habitats and wildlife. The trip ends after a run through the steep canyons and Class III and IV rapids of the Pacuare River. No previous experience is required, but good physical condition is a must.

Costa Rica Expeditions, Box 025216 Miami, FL 33102-5216 (mail forwarding service), tel. (011) 506/257–0766 or www.costaricaexpeditions.com. Year-round (not all trips available all months): 7–10 days, $1,298–$1,998 adults, $598–$1,098 children, depending on age and trip.

Cross Country International

8+

Cross Country International (CCI) has wonderful walking adventures (see Hiking and Backpacking), but it's also one of the few companies to specialize in equestrian vacations as well. Though domesticated horses certainly don't count as wildlife, equestrian vacations do provide a close-up animal experience, and CCI has one horseback trip that brings you face to face with some of Costa Rica's most colorful wildlife.

FOR FAMILIES. The Costa Rica Trail is a five-day, six-night trek along Costa Rica's west coast in the sparsely populated province of Guanacaste. Formed by volcanic eruptions more than 60 million years ago, this is an area where mountains meet the sea, where pirates once hid treasure, and where iguanas, macaws, and sea turtles are found in abundance. You'll ride along magnificent white beaches and on country trails lined with exotic trees (keep an eye out for howler monkeys and parrots). You'll pass mango and teak plantations by day and sleep in beachfront hotels and guesthouses by night. One of the best experiences of the trip is a swim in the rolling Pacific with your horse. Trip leaders Christina Rahm and David Clark are long-time residents of Costa Rica; Christina is Swedish and David is American.

The most important prerequisite is that riders of all ages must be able to walk, trot, canter, and feel comfortable on a horse, as you'll be riding four to five hours a day. CCI will consider younger children who are good riders, but talk to them before booking. Nonriders are welcome to come along; there are several nature/wildlife tours to take from hotels while the rest of the group is out riding. Cars or vans shuttle nonriders between hotels. You can also pre-arrange a local sitter to care for younger children; the going rate is about $20 for a full day.

Cross Country International, Box 1170 Millbrook, NY 12545, tel. 845/677–6000 or 800/828–8768, www.walkingvacations.com. Nov.–May: 5 days, $1,545 adults, 25% discount for children under 12.

Ecoventura

7+

Nature, history, and science come together on the Galápagos Islands as they do nowhere else on earth. Scattered across

17,000 square mi of the Pacific Ocean about 600 mi (966 km) off the coast of Ecuador, this archipelago is home to the only marine iguanas in the world, as well as to sea lions, giant tortoises, penguins, and seals. The 13 major islands and 17 islets have more birds than most people see in a lifetime: blue-footed boobies, pink flamingos, hawks, doves, pelicans, warblers, mockingbirds, herons, ducks, cormorants, flycatchers, and, of course, Darwin's finches, the little birds that helped inspire Darwin's theory of evolution. A visit to the Galápagos, now a national park of Ecuador, will help families understand just how fragile our world is.

FOR FAMILIES. Children ages 7 and up are welcome on Ecoventura's ships. The 48-passenger, 195-ft *Corinthian* is a luxury expedition ship and the largest of the Network ships, with a 1,000-square-ft observation lounge, Jacuzzi, and solarium. The *Letty, Eric,* and *Flamingo* are identical 20-passenger, 83-ft motor yachts. The ships depart from San Cristóbal island; guests fly in from Quito or Guayaquil. All accommodations are in outside cabins; most sleep only two, though two cabins have room for three. Polished wood and superb service allow passengers to feel pampered. Rates vary by ship, cabin, and itinerary. Your choice of four- to eight-day excursions determines the number of islands you visit. Most trips give you a chance to snorkel with sea lions, and national park regulations require a stop at Darwin Station on the island of Santa Cruz (one of the islands where you can purchase souvenirs, T-shirts, and supplies).

All cruises have two naturalist-guides on board to lead hikes and provide information about the natural and cultural history of the archipelago. Each guide takes no more than 10 people at a time, and they work well with children, interspersing lectures with other activities so that even young ones remain intrigued. Everyone can use the snorkeling gear and sea kayaks on board and swim at expansive white-sand beaches on various islands. (Some snorkeling gear is available in children's sizes, but parents should ask ahead.)

In addition to the four ships, Ecoventura also has a liveaboard dive vessel with a divemaster and instructors, so if your family (teens or older children only) wants to see more of the Galápagos wildlife under the sea, ask about dive-oriented trips.

A trip to the Galápagos Islands will not be a solitary wilderness experience; several groups often visit the same islands at once. Fortunately, permits to sail the islands are severely limited by national park administrators, and guides are good at leading groups on different paths. Not included in the price of the cruise is the national park tax of about $100 per adult ($50 per child), payable in U.S. dollars on arrival in the Galápagos Islands.

Ecoventura, 7200 Corporate Center Dr., Suite 510, Miami, FL 33126, tel. 305/262–6264 or 800/633–7972, www.ecoventura.com. Year-round: 4–8 days, $750–$2,850; 50% discount for children 7–11 on the cruise; on some summer family departures ages 12–14 receive a 25 % discount. Ecoventura will help you book your airfare as well.

GORP Travel

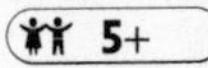

Although some dolphin-encounter programs have been accused of disregarding the dolphins' health and well-being, not all such programs are problematic. When reputable marine scientists are able to care for the dolphins and to teach humans about these remarkable animals, the programs have long-term beneficial effects for both groups. The experts at the Roatán Institute for Marine Sciences on the Bay Islands off the coast of Honduras have developed a program at nearby Anthony's Key Resort that practically guarantees a transcendent experience for all involved. GORP Travel, a specialist in environmentally friendly vacations with tour operators that are ecologically responsible, is the U.S. agent through which you can book such encounters.

FOR FAMILIES. Dolphin Discovery Camp, for children ages 5 through 14, centers on the world of the Atlantic bottle-nosed dolphin. Under the supervision of the Roatán Institute for Marine Sciences staff, children have outdoor sessions on snorkeling, dolphin feeding and training, swimming, and marine experiments, as well as short classroom slide shows and discussions. When not working with the scientists, campers go horseback riding, take nature hikes, view the awesomely clear waters and coral reefs by glass-bottom boat, and otherwise play in what can only be described as paradise. Parents are welcome to join their children for some activities, and families take all meals together. The program is designed, however, to give parents (and older teens) time to do what most adults come here to do—scuba diving or snorkeling (see Snorkeling and Diving) in water with visibility that ranges from 75 to 100 ft. Accommodations are in private bungalows set around the lush island. *GORP Travel, 10055Westmoor Dr., Suite 215, Westminster, CO 80021, tel. 720/887–8500 or 877/440–4677, gorptravel.gorp.com. June–Aug. and Christmas week: 8 days, $600–$1,150 adults, $600 children's camp.*

Lindblad Special Expeditions

6+

Founded in 1979, Lindblad Special Expeditions is a leader not only in expedition travel but in environmentally responsible travel. It's got quite a pedigree; Lars-Eric Lindblad organized one of the first tourist expeditions to the Galápagos Islands back in 1967. The staff included the vice president of the National Audubon Society, a director of the World Wildlife Fund, and one of the world's best-known ornithologists. Today the Lindblad name is still associated with such pioneering partnerships, and it continues its altruistic efforts. For instance, in the Galápagos, under the direction of Sven-Olaf (Lars-Eric's son), Lindblad and its guests have raised nearly $400,000, which has been channeled directly into island conservation projects.

FOR FAMILIES. There are special family departures to the Galápagos throughout the summer months. In addition to the expedition leader and naturalist staff, these trips include a Family Coordinator who organizes activities for families and children. Educational activities are planned throughout the seven-day voyage, both on land and on the ship. They cover the origin of species, island formation, plant and animal identification, and stargazing, among other topics.

Polaris, the 80-passenger ship that's home for this adventure, is big enough to be stable and comfortable, yet small enough to enter ports and inlets inaccessible to larger ships. While the itinerary can vary, the ship generally makes stops at eight islands, each one with its own unique environment. Isabela is home to the Galápagos penguin, northernmost of the world's penguins, while Florean is famous for its flamingos. Sea lions and blue-footed boobies are found on several of the islands, and on Santa Cruz you stop at the Darwin Research Station, home to Lonesome George the tortoise, the last of his particular kind. *Polaris* carries Zodiac landing craft for easy access to coastlines and a glass-bottom boat for remarkable, close-up underwater views. On board, families will find a specially developed activity kit with material for children and parents to use throughout the trip. There are also talks and nightly recaps geared to the entire family; children are encouraged to ask questions. Meals include child-friendly food, and all young passengers receive a pre-voyage reading list to help them prepare for this incredible journey.

If the idea of a shipboard adventure in Central America has appeal, consider the eight-day Family Adventure in Costa Rica. Aboard the 175-ft, 64-passenger *Sea Voyager*, you'll start in the port of Herradura and sail as far north as San Juan del Sur in Nicaragua and as far south as Manuel Antonio National Park, about halfway down Costa Rica's Pacific Coast. The ship has a fleet of zodiacs used for landing in places where big ships can't go, and for exploring islands off Costa Rica. Trip activities include snorkeling, kayaking, horseback riding, beach parties, and a barbecue at a working cattle ranch in addition to learning about and seeing firsthand the remarkably diverse terrain and wildlife of Costa Rica's west coast.

Lindblad Special Expeditions, 720 Fifth Ave., New York, NY 10019, tel. 212/765–7740 or 800/397–3348, www.expeditions.com. June–Aug.: 8–10 days, $2,490–$5,140 adults; ask about the $750 discount for children on some trips.

Metropolitan Touring

7+

Metropolitan Touring is one of Ecuador's largest tour companies, and one with a long record of bringing people to that living, breathing biology, zoology, and botany classroom, the Galápagos. While Metropolitan's trips don't have any special facilities or activities just for children, the company says "daily programs are flexible and can be adapted to children's preferences." Metropolitan gets lots of families on its Galápagos tours, so guides are used to working with kids and like doing so.

FOR FAMILIES. There are two options to choose from: a cruise on the 90-passenger *Santa Cruz* (with six triple and quad cabins to accommodate families) or a hotel-based stay at the Delfin on Santa Cruz Island, with daily cruises to various islands on a 120-ft motor yacht. When not touring, families can relax at the hotel's beach and pool. Both tours can be booked with a "Great Value Package" that adds on a four-night stay in Quito, a city tour, and day trip to the famous Otavalo Indian market. While the market is educational and engaging, Quito is not a great city for younger children and not, in my opinion, worth a four-day stay.

Metropolitan Touring, c/o Adventure Associates, 13150 Coit Rd., Suite 110, Dallas TX 75240, tel. 972/907–0414 or 800/527–2500, www.metropolitan-touring.com. Year-round: 3–11 days, $984 to $2,492 adults for the cruise depending on dates and cabin, $698 to $1,735 for the Delfin; 50% discount for kids under 12 sharing accommodations with parents, 25% when kids have their own room.

Mountain Travel Sobek

5+

Back in 1991 two of the world's great adventure companies, Mountain Travel and Sobek Expeditions, merged. The result was Mountain Travel Sobek (MTS), a new company with the resources, experience, and expertise to take adventurous travelers to the far-flung corners of the world. What many people don't know, however, is that Mountain Travel Sobek is not just about hardcore, on-the-edge adventures—it's also about bringing families to explore wilderness and wildlife. If you doubt this, you have only to look at the company's extensive list of family-accessible trips, where more than 17 are designated "fun for all ages" and nearly half are wildlife adventures.

FOR FAMILIES. One of the most exotic trips is also the one for the youngest travelers. Trekking & Tigers is what MTS calls "Nepal 101" and it's aimed at families with kids as young as 5. Although this itinerary doesn't take in the rarified heights for which Nepal is known—the highest elevation is only 6,700 ft—it does include nature walks, elephant rides, and a dugout canoe paddle in search of rhinos, sloth bears, exotic birds, and the elusive and endangered Bengal tiger.

The Kenya Wilderness Safari and Wilds of the Serengeti adventures are for ages 8 and older. These trips offer all the wildlife of Africa you would expect, along with a few special adventures, such as a stay at a private reserve. MTS's safari camps are deluxe, very private, and away from the major tourist routes. Both the Galapagos and Whales of Baja tours are for ages 6 and older, while Wild Costa Rica, which includes wildlife viewing on both the Caribbean and Pacific coasts, is for families with kids at least 10 years old. One of MTS's more unusual wildlife trips is Island of the Eagles, which takes families to the Broken Group Islands off the west coast of Vancouver Island in British Columbia. These islands have one of the largest concentrations of bald eagles in the Pacific Northwest, as well as colonies of sea lions and gray whales in the surrounding waters. This is an adventure on which you kayak, hike, and go on a whale-watching tour by Zodiac. Because there are no strong sea currents to speak of, this area is ideal for kayaking, even for beginners. The minimum age is 8, perfect for enjoying all the beachcombing and tidepool exploration on the itinerary.

Mountain Travel Sobek, 6420 Fairmount Ave., El Cerrito, CA 94530, tel. 888/MTSOBEK (687-6235), www.mtsobek.com. Year-round (all trips not available all months): 6–14 days, $1,345–$4,590 adults; $1,650 age 12 and under.

Natural Habitat Adventures

2+

Letting you get close to animals in their natural habitat is what this outfitter is all about. Starting with a profound respect for nature and a belief that people don't have to sacrifice every comfort to take part in the world's greatest nature vacations, Natural Habitat Adventures has become one of the premier companies of its kind. Whether you are on a pure vacation or on a trip in which you help researchers and scientists, the result is the same: an unforgettable encounter with some of the world's most intriguing inhabitants. Besides its scheduled tours, the company will customize a trip for a single family or even several families together.

FOR FAMILIES. The top family trip is indisputably the five- or six-day Seal Watch in Canada, with four departure dates in March. During that month, 250,000 doe-eyed harp seals give birth to their fuzzy white offspring on the massive floating ice fields west of the Magdalen Islands in the Gulf of St. Lawrence. Adorable and unafraid, some of the babies even allow visitors to pet them. These treks were begun as part of a plan to provide tourist dollars to the local community so selling seal skins would no longer be the only way to make a living there. As a result, participation in this trip may ultimately help save future seals from death. The trip begins and ends in Halifax, Nova Scotia, and includes family activities such as tubing, sledding, and cross-country skiing. Accommodations are in a cozy hotel. Natural Habitat Adventures will take children as young as age 6 on the seal watch, but consider carefully whether your child can handle the elements, the helicopter flights out on the ice floes, the proximity of the animals, and the travel.

You can also ask about joining any of their other regularly scheduled trips. These range from riding Tundra Buggies out to visit the polar bears in Churchill, Manitoba, to tracking lions, leopards, and cheetahs on a Wildcat Workshop in Kenya or a specially designed family program in Costa Rica. Different trips are appropriate for different ages, so talk to the staff to determine the best adventure for your family.

Natural Habitat Adventures, 2945 Center Green Ct., Boulder, CO 80301, tel. 303/449–3711 or 800/543–8917, www.nathab.com. Year-round (all trips not available all months): 5–21 days, $1,895–$6,895.

Rascals in Paradise

7+

Rascals in Paradise, a tour company just for families, works with outfitters and hotels worldwide that are especially accommodating to children. Trips with Rascals are cultural adventures in which all participants not only see new places but truly experience the people and heritage of that country. A special escort educates and entertains the children and provides support for parents. Storytelling, activities, and face-to-face contact with interesting people help families learn about the destination.

FOR FAMILIES. The 13-day Family Safari begins and ends in Nairobi, Kenya, home of the famous Giraffe Centre, where you study these elegant animals from a treetop aerie. Leaving the city, you stay in a mix of game lodges and deluxe tented camps. The itinerary includes watching the water hole at Ark Lodge in the Aberdare Forest and visiting Solio Game Ranch and Samburu Lodge, where crocodiles come up on the lawn for dinner. The Masai Mara Game Reserve with its vast herds of African wildlife perhaps best defines the animal viewing on this trek. It's not all four-footed beasts, though. One trip highlight is an immense flock of coral-color flamingos on Lake Elmenteita. You can also opt for a hot-air balloon ride and a fishing excursion on Lake Victoria. Once back in Nairobi, families can visit the home and museum of writer Karen Blixen (whose life story was portrayed in *Out of Africa*) before heading home.

Besides the standard inclusions (see Questions to Ask *in* Getting Started on the Road to Adventure), the fee for this trip covers airport transfers and $3,300 trip-cancellation insurance per family booking. Airfare is extra.

Rascals in Paradise, 2107 Van Ness, #403, San Francisco, CA 94109, tel. 415/921–7000 or 800/872–7225. Year-round: 13 days, $10,890–$13,792 for family of 4 with 2 adults and 2 children 7–11.

Sea Quest Expeditions

5+

Kayaking is the mode of travel for Sea Quest's San Juan Archipelago adventure in Washington, but the trip's focus is whale-watching. These islands, straddling the border with British Columbia, provide opportunities for families to observe orcas—sometimes up close—especially in summer. Besides orcas, visitors to the wildlife-rich San Juans can also spot eagles, minke whales, Dall's porpoises and harbor porpoises, and seals. There is no better way to approach these creatures than in a sea kayak. You can skirt the islands and camp in areas inaccessible to land-based travelers.

FOR FAMILIES. Children age 5 and up are welcome on one-day trips, provided they travel in a three-person kayak with two adults. For the multiday adventures children must be at least 8 years old. Youngsters who weigh a minimum of 100 lbs (45 kg) and are in good health can participate in paddling a two-person kayak. Sea Quest's San Juan trips begin and end in Friday Harbor on San Juan Island (accessible via Seattle, Washington, or Vancouver and Victoria in British Columbia).

Families concerned about kayaking near orcas should be aware that these intelligent animals have never injured a human in the wild. Moreover, the orcas living within the San Juan Islands are used to boaters and are among the most studied and well-known whales in the world. On these expeditions learning and adventure go hand in hand. A biologist accompanies all Sea Quest's San Juan groups, so your family's questions about the whales and other aspects of life in these islands can be answered. The trip involves kayaking between four and five hours daily, mostly with prevailing currents. No previous paddling experience is necessary, though you must be in good physical condition. No Eskimo rolls—upside-down flips—are performed in the state-of-the-art sea kayaks; the boats are extremely stable. The group receives instruction in basic paddling techniques.

Sea Quest Expeditions, Box 2424, Friday Harbor, WA 98250, tel. 360/378–5767 or 888/589–4253. May–Oct.: 1–5 days, $59–$549.

Thomson Family Adventures

6+

Rick Thomson and Judi Wineland have been in the adventure travel business for more than 20 years. They're also seasoned family travelers; their two daughters have accompanied them on trips since they were infants. They know from personal experience how to tailor a trip to a family's needs and expectations. Thomson runs family trips throughout the world, visiting Tanzania, Turkey, Costa Rica, Nepal, the Galápagos and Peru, Egypt, and Alaska, as well as the fascinating islands of Indonesia. Parents should use the age of 6 as a guideline only; Thomson doesn't have rigid rules about minimum ages, believing parents are the best judges of a child's readiness for this kind of travel. Call the company and Thomson staff will help you make an informed decision by providing you with any information you need.

FOR FAMILIES. Bali, Borneo, and the islands of Nusa Tenggara—including Komodo—are all part of the exotic Indonesian archipelago, and each piece of land has its own unique character and culture. These islands draw families because they offer discovery of both ancient civilizations and some of the Earth's wildest places. On this 18-day adventure, you'll have a chance to see wild orangutans and shy proboscis monkeys on Borneo, and (from a safe distance) fierce Komodo dragons on the island bearing this ancient lizard's name.

From Bali's and its terraced rice fields, ancient temples, and lush botanic gardens you'll travel to the island of Sumbawa to embark on a six-day cruise that includes Flores, Komodo, and Rinca islands. Wildlife abounds—not just dragons but also barking deer, wild boar, monkeys, and water buffalo. The cruise also gives families time to snorkel, swim, and sunbathe at the hidden beaches of pristine, rarely visited islands and to experience life in small villages. After the cruise the group returns to Bali for cultural celebrations, then flies on to Java and the city of Yogyakarta. This is your chance to visit the vast 1,200-year-old Buddhist temple before continuing on to Borneo and Tanjung Puting National Park, home of wild orangutans and the Orangutan Rehabilitation Center. Here kids get to interact with baby orangutans, take hikes, visit local school children and artists, and take a jungle boat cruise to a research center specializing in proboscis monkeys.

Thomson makes a point of finding lodging that melds adventure with style. Typical is the ecofriendly Kalpataru Lodge on Borneo, deep in orangutan country, which is built in the island's traditional longhouse style with a large communal dining room in the middle and a covered porch for eating al fresco. Each of the rooms has a private bath and fans, and the cuisine ranges from Indonesian specialties to Western treats. Tour prices include airfare from select U.S. cities, but land-only prices are also available.

Thomson Family Adventures, 14 Mount Auburn St., Watertown, MA 02472, tel. 617/923–0940 or 800/262–6255, www.familyadventures.com. Year-round (all trips not available all months): 18 days, $5,890 adults, $800 discount for children 11 and under, $200 discount for children 12–17. Other trips 9–16 days, $2,890–$5,290 adults, $400- $1,000 dis-

count for children 11 and under, $100–$200 discount for children 12–17.

World Discovery Tours

5+

Jackie Cohen is a parent and a travel expert who has made her company one of the most family-friendly in the business. She's included in her creative itineraries a focus on the kinds of things that she wants her own family to see and learn while traveling: history, archaeology, geology, ecology, and close encounters with local people and wildlife. World Discovery Tours may not be the biggest in the business, but it gives its guests larger-than-life experiences in North America and in some of the most exotic destinations in the world.

FOR FAMILIES. This is the company of choice for families that want to learn about and interact with that most intelligent of creatures, the dolphin. Among the most overtly wildlife-oriented trips are those to Australia and Belize for ages 7 and older, the Azores for ages 8 and up, New Zealand for families with kids at least 9 years old, and Niue in the Pacific for families traveling with children 12 and older. In Nova Scotia, ages 5 and up explore the remarkable Bay of Fundy ecosystem with a marine biologist, and in Iceland travelers at least 7 years old can get up close and personal with the Atlantic puffin. In North America, the company's home base of the San Juan Islands off the coast of Washington also provides plenty of opportunities for observing orcas, otters, and bald eagles. This trip, which mixes boat-based excursions and kayaking with hiking on the island of Orcas and fossil-finding on unpopulated Sucia, starts at the Seattle airport where the group is picked up for transfer to the ferry out to the San Juans.

World Discovery Tours' Australia trip probably offers more dolphin encounters than any other. From the Western city of Perth you'll travel to Bunbury Bay and the Dolphin Discovery Centre, where hundreds of bottlenose dolphins have been interacting with humans for years. Some of them visit the beach so often they've been given names—you might meet Cookie, Stumpy, or Sharkey, among others. From Perth you'll fly north to Monkey Mia, considered by some to be the "dolphin capital of the world." Since the early 1960s wild bottlenose dolphins have been swimming into shallow waters within wading distance from shore to seek out human companionship. From there you'll also go out by boat to search for the endangered Dugong. When not hanging with the dolphins, you'll take in the culture and diverse geology of Australia, from Aboriginal cave dwellings to sophisticated Sydney.

New Zealand is also for dolphin lovers. That itinerary includes visiting Hector's Dolphins at their home in Akaroa on the south coast of the Banks Peninsula, in addition to exploring areas of wild sea bird colonies up near Kaikoura, and swimming with fur seals near Nelson in the remote reaches of Marlborough Sounds. Want still more dolphins? How about a family adventure in the Azores, located 800 mi (1,288 km) off the coast of Portugal? Wild and remote, this archipelago is home to more than 20 different species of dolphins and whales—the greatest variety and concentration of cetaceans found anywhere in the world. This is an unforgettable adventure in learning about, observing, and, when conditions permit, swimming with these animals in their natural habitat. As if the dolphins weren't enough, the Azorean people make visitors feel warmly welcomed and set an amazing example of how to live in harmony with one another and nature.

Other trips will have you in search of bottlenose dolphins and West Indian manatee around the cayes and atolls of Belize. Parrots, toucans, Howler monkeys, red-eyed tree frogs, anteaters, iguanas, and pacas are among the other species of wildlife that call Belize home. In the South Pacific, on the little-known and remarkably pristine island of

Niue, you can interact with wild pods of Spinner dolphins and see Humpback whales on their return from Antartica. Niue, located 1,300 mi (2,093 km) northeast of New Zealand—in the center of a triangle made up of Tonga, Western Samoa, and the Cook Islands—has warm, clear waters, mammoth subterranean caves to explore with one of the island's foremost spulunking experts, and a rich diversity of plant and animal life in its rainforest. Because of its isolation, Niue's people have retained a strong cultural heritage.

Most World Discovery Tours trips include air from select U.S. cities; many trips have a land-only price as well.

World Discovery Tours, 484 Hawkins Rd. Eastsound, WA 98245, tel. 360/376–3129 or 800/262–6255 (in the U.S.). Year-round (all trips not available all months): 7–12 days, $1,975–$3,295 adults, $1,110–$2,395 children, depending on age and trip.

Resources

Organizations

Many organizations protect animals and encourage membership and participation by families and children. These groups don't sponsor trips, but they can help foster an interest in the world's wildlife. The **International Fund for Animal Welfare** (IFAW; 411 Main St., Yarmouth Port, MA 02675, tel. 508/744-2000 or 800/932-4329, www.ifaw.org) has worked particularly hard to stop both Canadian seal hunts and whaling by Japanese and Norwegian hunters. It sends out literature to schoolchildren and others, tries to answer questions, and accepts monetary support for its efforts. You can adopt an orca through **Save the Whales** (Box 2397, Venice, CA 90291, tel. 831/899–9957 or 800/942–5365, www.savethewhales.com), which also has an excellent educational program that goes to schools. If you'd rather adopt a finback whale, contact **Allied Whale** (College of the Atlantic, 105 Eden St., Bar Harbor, ME 04609, tel. 207/288–5644, www.coa.edu/alliedwhale); the adoption program funds research. **Friends of the Sea Otter** (2150 Garden Rd., Suite A3, Monterey, CA 93940, tel. 831/373–2747, www.seaotters.org) has information about otters, a map of where to spot them on the Monterey Peninsula, and a catalog of otter-related items you can buy. Ask for the Educational Packet for Children (or first check the packet out online at www.seaotters.org); money goes to support educational programs and research. **Wolf Haven International** (3111 Offut Lake Rd., Tenino, WA 98589, tel. 360/264–4695 or 800/448–9653, www.wolfhaven.org) is the organization through which you can adopt a wolf. Adoption and membership include a subscription to its quarterly magazine, *WolfTracks*. You can visit Wolf Haven's facility near Olympia, WA, and take a tour to see the wolves the organization has rescued.

Books

Swimming with Sea Lions and Other Adventures in the Galápagos Islands (Scholastic), by Ann McGovern, describes a young traveler's 15-day boat trip around the islands. There are also numerous children's books about Darwin and his discoveries; many of the best are now out of print but still available in libraries. Look for *A Visit to Galápagos* (Abrams), by Katie Lee, an excellent picture book with paintings and drawings of many of the islands' most famous inhabitants, as well as informative text. Another good choice is Piero Ventura's 70-page *Darwin: Nature Reinterpreted* (Houghton Mifflin), which tracks Darwin's entire *Beagle* voyage and takes a look at his theories and writings.

Patricia Arrigoni's *Harpo, the Baby Harp Seal* (Travel Publishers International, tel. 415/456–2697 or 800/942–7760) is a beautifully photographed story about a baby seal on the ice floes off the Magdalen Islands (where Natural Habitat Adventures' trip takes place). The book is aimed at children ages 7–10 but has appeal for all ages.

Also See

There are many other ways and places to meet animals up close. Snorkeling and Diving lists adventures with amazing marine-life encounters. Horse Packing, Cattle Drives, and Covered Wagon Adventures have trips that involve horses, and Ranches includes encounters with horses, mules, farm animals, and, in one case (the Y.O. Ranch in Texas), exotic wildlife.

INDEX

Notes

Notes

Notes

Notes